On Course

Strategies for Creating Success in College and in Life

STUDY SKILLS PLUS

On Course

Strategies for Creating Success in College and in Life

Third Edition

STUDY SKILLS PLUS

Skip Downing

CENGAGE
Learning®

Australia • Brazil • Mexico • Singapore • United Kingdom • United States

CENGAGE
Learning®

On Course: Strategies for Creating
Success in College and in Life, Third Edition
Study Skills Plus Edition
Skip Downing

VP, GM Developmental Studies: Liz Covello

Product Manager: Neha Taleja

Senior Content Developer: Amy Gibbons

Content Developer: Jason Ronstadt

Associate Content Developer:
Courtney Triola

Senior Marketing Manager:
Erica Messenger

Senior Content Project Manager:
Aimee C. Bear

Senior Designer: Diana Graham

Manufacturing Planner: Bev Breslin

IP Analyst: Ann Hoffman

IP Project Manager: Kathryn Kucharek

Design and Production Service:
MPS Limited

Compositor: MPS Limited

Cover Designer: Diana Graham

Cover Image: © Makhnach |
Dreamstime.com

For product information and technology assistance, contact us at
Cengage Learning Customer & Sales Support, 1-800-354-9706
For permission to use material from this text or product,
submit all requests online at **www.cengage.com/permissions**
Further permissions questions can be emailed to
permissionrequest@cengage.com

Library of Congress Control Number: 2015938981

Student Edition:

ISBN: 978-1-305-39748-4

Loose-leaf Edition:

ISBN: 978-1-305-64711-4

Cengage Learning
20 Channel Center Street
Boston, MA 02210
USA

Cengage Learning is a leading provider of customized learning solutions with employees residing in nearly 40 different countries and sales in more than 125 countries around the world. Find your local representative at **www.cengage.com**

Cengage Learning products are represented in Canada by Nelson Education, Ltd.

To learn more about Cengage Learning Solutions, visit **www.cengage.com**

Purchase any of our products at your local college store or at our preferred online store **www.cengagebrain.com**

Printed in the United States of America
Print Number: 01   Print Year: 2015

To Carol, my compass

Contents

3 Discovering Self-Motivation   71

4 Mastering Self-Management   101

9 Staying On Course to Your Success 247

Study Skills A Toolbox for Active Learners 257

On Course is intended for college students of any age who want to create success in college and in life. Whether students are taking a student success or first-year seminar course, a writing course, or an "inward-looking" course in psychology, self-exploration, or personal growth, *On Course* is an instruction manual for dramatically improving the quality of their outcomes and experiences. In each chapter, students learn essential study skills; however, that's just the beginning. Through self-assessments, articles, guided journals, case studies in critical thinking, and inspiring stories from fellow students, *On Course* empowers students with time-proven strategies for creating a great life—academic, personal, and professional. Students learn the techniques that have helped many thousands of students create extraordinary success!

I am grateful that in the years since its first publication in 1996, *On Course* has become a market leader in the crowded field of student success texts. Increasingly, educators are finding (as I have) that empowering students to become active, responsible learners produces significant increases in both student academic success and retention. In addition, the process empowers them to create great things in their personal and professional lives. My goal is to make this new edition of *On Course* even more helpful to the success of students and educators alike.

> [*On Course*] is the absolute best approach for a first-year seminar/college success class that there is. The philosophy and textbook are exactly what students need.
>
> Catherine Eloranto, Clinton Community College

What's New in This Edition of *On Course*: Highlights

- **College Smart-Start Guide.** Too many students get off course in their very first week of college. Author Skip Downing polled nearly 2,000 college and university educators, asking them, "What do you recommend that your students do in the first week of college to get off to a good start?" The resulting "Smart-Start Guide" provides students with essential first-week actions recommended by the collective wisdom of this large group of educators. A new activity in the *On Course* Facilitator's Manual engages students in figuring out which of the actions these instructors thought were the most important. When students follow through on these actions, they will lay an early foundation for their academic success.

- **Understanding the Expectations of College and University Educators.** This essay and related journal entry help students better understand how to succeed in the culture of higher education. In this section, they learn "Eight Key Expectations" and "A Dozen Differences

> We wanted a curriculum that went beyond study skills to address the foundational needs of first-year college students. *On Course* causes students to examine and reflect on the causes of their successes and setbacks. It challenges students to go beyond the obvious and really delves into their motivations and mindsets. Oh, yeah, and it does a great job addressing study skills too.
>
> Ann Heiny, Armstrong State University

between High School and College Culture." This information helps students quickly understand which behaviors they can continue doing and which they will need to modify, change or abandon.

- **Tech Tips.** Many websites and apps are available to help students achieve greater success. Most chapters now feature a Tech Tips section that provides suggestions for free websites and apps that can help students employ the soft skills of personal responsibility, self-motivation, self-management, interdependence, self-awareness, lifelong learning, emotional intelligence, and believing in oneself, as well as hard skills related to effective studying.

- **Discussion about Avoiding Procrastination.** Procrastination is the bane of many students' success. This discussion helps students understand why procrastination is so tempting and offers specific methods for not putting off until tomorrow what they would benefit from doing today. Included in the discussion is research from Dr. Dan Ariely, Professor of Psychology and Behavioral Economics at Duke University.

- **A Sign of Maturity.** This discussion offers an explanation about the various kinds of relationships in which people engage: dependent, co-dependent, independent, and interdependent. Advantages and disadvantages of each are explained, and students are urged to use college to develop independence but also to recognize that there are many occasions when choosing interdependence is a true sign of maturity (not to mention improving one's chances of achieving a goal or dream).

- **Increasing Happiness.** This new article and accompanying journal entry explore the emotional intelligence skill of maximizing happiness. Drawn from the scientific research of positive psychologists, students learn a number of choices they can make to increase their happiness. This topic has recently gained much interest on college campuses. For example, when a course in Positive Psychology was first offered at Harvard University, it immediately became the university's most popular course.

- **Toolbox for Active Learners.** Many *On Course* instructors asked that study skills be presented in one section (rather than distributed throughout the book). This edition honors that request. Unlike texts that present a long menu of study options, *On Course* organizes study skills based on the logical learning steps as identified by research on the brain and effective methods for learning. This section begins with a presentation of the CORE Learning Process, the four principles that—consciously or unconsciously—all good learners employ to create deep and lasting learning. Students discover how to use these four principles to learn any subject or skill. Each section of the Toolbox presents effective techniques for one of the study skills covered (reading, taking notes, organizing study materials, rehearsing and memorizing study materials, taking tests, and writing college-level assignments) and ends with an exercise to reinforce the study strategies presented therein. Compared with the regular eighth edition of

On Course, this Study Skills Plus edition contains an additional 80 pages of study strategies, along with more examples of their use. Each section ends with an activity in which students are asked to "Do One Different Thing This Week." In this activity, they experiment with one new learning skill for a week and report on their outcomes, experiences, and lessons learned. Users of the previous edition will note that no longer in the text is the Wise Choice Process employed to create an Academic Skills Plan for each study skill. This activity is now available in the Facilitator's Manual.

- **Study Skills Self-Assessment.** In addition to placing all of the study skills in one section, this edition also offers a new Study Skills Self-Assessment. Students can take this self-assessment before learning about study skills and discover areas in which they are weak. At the end of the course, they can retake the assessment to see where they have grown as learners and where they may still need to improve. Students have the option of completing the assessment in either the text or MindTap®.

- **SEVEN NEW "One Student's Stories."** A popular feature in earlier editions, these short essays—now numbering 29 in all—are authored by students who used what they learned from *On Course* to improve the quality of their outcomes and experiences in college and in life. Videos of many of the student-authors reading their essays may be viewed in MindTap.

- **Conversation with the Author.** Since the first edition of *On Course* was published more than two decades ago, many students have contacted the author with thoughtful questions. This section includes some of those questions and Skip Downing's answers.

What's New in This Edition of *On Course*: Chapter by Chapter

Chapter 1

- New "College Smart-Start Guide" provides students with 13 actions that are important to getting off to a good start in college; recommendations are the result of a poll of 2,000 college educators.

- At the request of a number of *On Course* instructors, "Money Matters" has been moved to Chapter 1, thus helping students early in the semester to reduce struggles caused by financial difficulties.

- New Journal Entry #2.

- New cartoon in "Understanding the Culture of Higher Education."

- New "Tech Tips: Money."

- New article "Understanding the Expectations of College and University Educators," including a discussion of Eight Key Expectations and A Dozen Differences between High School and College Culture.

I think these are very powerful [student] stories. . . . It's good for students to hear that other students have faced the same struggles that they are going through and they have achieved success.

Kathryn Burk,
Jackson College

On Course is life-changing for my students. I have seen students evolve in ways they never imagined in a matter of a semester thanks to *On Course*. I cannot imagine using another book. No other book encompasses the reflective, introspective, and success attributes that *On Course* does. *On Course* walks students through their journey of self-discovery and allows them to grow into the student they have always wanted to become.

Joselyn Gonzalez,
El Centro College

- New article "Understanding Yourself," including a section on Ingredients of Success.
- Revised #7 of the Self-Assessment: "Whether I'm happy or not depends mostly on me."
- Moved article "Develop Self-Acceptance" and Journal 4 to Chapter 8.

Chapter 2

- New *One Student's Story* by Taryn Rossmiller, Boise State University, ID.
- New cartoon in "Making Wise Decisions" section.
- New "Tech Tips: Personal Responsibility."

Chapter 3

- New *One Student's Story* by Brandon Beavers, Highland Community College, KS.
- New "Tech Tips: Self-Motivation."
- New *One Student's Story* by Tina Steen, Chaffey College, CA.

Chapter 4

- Added Weekly Calendar to "Creating a Leak-Proof Self-Management System."
- Repositioned "Time and Culture" section discussing how cultures differ in their beliefs and attitudes about time and what college culture's expectations are about time.
- New information on avoiding procrastination in the "Developing Self-Discipline" article.
- New "Tech Tips: Self-Management."

Chapter 5

- Added information to "Creating a Support System" on the importance of choosing wisely among various kinds of relationships: dependent, co-dependent, independent, and interdependent.
- Added parable "The Difference between Heaven and Hell," in the "Creating a Support System" article.
- New *One Student's Story* by Mitch Mull, Asheville-Buncombe Technical and Community College, NC.
- New *One Student's Story* by Teroa Paselio, Windward Community College, HI.
- New "Tech Tips: Interdependence."

Chapter 6

- New "Tech Tips: Self-Awareness."

Chapter 7

- New "Tech Tips: Lifelong Learning."

Chapter 8

- New article, "Increasing Happiness," presents research from scientific studies within the new field of positive psychology, including both the limits on increasing happiness as well as ways to become more happy.
- New Journal Entry 30 regarding "Increasing Happiness."
- New "Tech Tips: Emotional Awareness."
- Moved article "Develop Self-Acceptance" and Journal Entry 4 (now Journal Entry 31) here from Chapter 1.

Chapter 9

- Revised #7 of the Self-Assessment: "Whether I'm happy or not depends mostly on me."

Study Skills: A Toolbox for Active Learners

- Repositioned study skills materials into one comprehensive section, offering many strategies for Becoming an Active Learner, Reading, Taking Notes, Organizing Study Materials, Rehearsing and Memorizing Study Materials, Taking Tests, and Writing.
- New Self-Assessment of Study Skills, which students can take both before and after they explore the many strategies presented in the Toolbox for Active Learners. When the self-assessment is taken as a pre-test, students learn their strengths and weaknesses when it comes to learning. When the self-assessment is taken as a post-test, students learn which areas they have strengthened and which areas still need improvement.
- New *One Student's Story* by Michael Chapasko, Blinn College, TX.
- New *One Student's Story* by Ashley E. Bennet, Heartland Community College, IL.

Proven Features of *On Course*

The Eighth Edition includes all of the best features of *On Course*, updated and revised from the previous edition.

- **Self-Assessment.** *On Course* begins and ends with a self-assessment questionnaire of important non-cognitive skills ("soft skills"). Scores are provided for self-responsibility, self-motivation, self-management, interdependence, self-awareness, lifelong learning, emotional intelligence, and belief in oneself. Imagine working with students who develop strengths in all of these inner qualities! Imagine how these qualities will affect the

[*On Course*] is directed at students who live complicated lives; the One Student's Story feature is always relevant to somebody in the class. The case studies are a great way to start conversations that focus on the most urgent needs of students who are often the first in their family to navigate college.

Michelle Cochran, Rochester Community and Technical College

The Study Skills Plus edition does a good job of giving students lots of different options for techniques/tools/ approaches to the academic skills they need. It does so without getting too bogged down in lengthy explanations.

Lisa Marks, Ozarks Technical Community College

The [*On Course*] curriculum is written in a way so as to assess study skills and soft skills without intimidation and provides information and exercises to develop them. Most importantly, [it] places emphasis on mastery through reflection and practice and offers a post self-assessment in order for the student and faculty to measure accomplishment and celebrate success!

Jill Beauchamp, Washtenaw Community College

The *On Course* book and class have changed my students' lives; it gives them strategies to make wise choices and decisions that affect their college success, as well as life success. Students who had little hope begin to have hope for their lives and their futures.

Dorothy Collins, Eastern Gateway Community College

Journaling is the heart and soul of *On Course*. It helps me check the pulse of my students on a regular basis. I have countless testimonies from students who describe the journaling process as "life-changing." The most reluctant students who ultimately "give in" to journaling often become the most avid supporters of *On Course*.

Gail Janecka, Victoria College

I absolutely love these [*Case Studies for Critical Thinking*] and spend a lot of time with each of them. My favorite is "A Fish Story," and [I] start my semester with this one. I get students thinking about professors' expectations, their own expectations, motivation, taking the initiative, being prepared for class, and being organized.

Cindy Thorp, SUNY Alfred, College of Technology

choices the students make and the outcomes and experiences they create. By completing the initial questionnaire, students immediately see areas of weakness that need attention. By completing the concluding questionnaire, students see their semester's growth. Students have the option of completing the self-assessment either in the text or online in MindTap.

- **Articles on Proven Success Strategies.** Thirty-two short articles explain powerful strategies for creating success in college and in life. Each article presents a success strategy from influential figures in psychology, philosophy, business, sports, politics, and personal and professional growth. In these articles, students learn the "secrets" of extraordinarily successful individuals.

- **Guided Journal Entries.** A guided journal entry immediately follows each article about a success strategy, giving students an opportunity to apply the strategy they have just learned to enhance their results in college and in life. Many instructors of the course say the guided journal writings are extremely powerful in helping students make new and more effective choices, thus improving their academic success and persistence.

- **CORE Learning System.** All good learners employ four principles that lead to deep and lasting learning. Students learn how to use these four principles to create their own system for learning any subject or skill.

- **Case Studies in Critical Thinking.** Case studies help students apply the strategies they are learning to real-life situations. As such, they help prepare students to make wise choices in the kinds of challenging situations they will likely face in college. Because case studies don't have "right" answers, they promote critical and creative thinking.

- **Focus on Diversity.** The challenges and opportunities of interacting with new cultures is introduced in the first chapter ("Understanding the Culture of Higher Education), is explored within many articles (e.g., Responsibility and Culture), and is more extensively examined in the article "Respecting Cultural Differences."

- *On Course* **Principles at Work.** These sections in each chapter show how important the *On Course* success strategies (soft skills) are for choosing the right career, getting hired, and succeeding in the work world.

Support Materials for Students and Instructors

For additional information or for help with accessing support materials related to *On Course*, contact your Cengage Learning Consultant. If you need help finding your learning consultant, visit *www.cengage.com*, select "College Faculty" from the "Information For…" menu, and then click "Rep/Learning Consultant" at the top right of the page.

SUPPORT FOR STUDENTS

- **MindTap® College Success for *On Course*.** MindTap® College Success for *On Course*, Study Skills Plus, Third Edition, is the digital learning solution that helps instructors engage and transform today's students into critical thinkers. Through dynamic assignments and applications that you can personalize, real-time course analytics and an accessible reader, MindTap® helps you turn cookie-cutter into cutting-edge, apathy into engagement, and memorizers into higher-level thinkers. Features include digital versions of the self-assessments and journal entries, videos, and chapter quizzes and homework. MindTap® College Success for *On Course*, Study Skills Plus, Third Edition, includes access to the College Success Factors Index (CSFI) 2.0, an online resource that assesses students' patterns of behavior and attitudes in ten areas that have been proven to affect student outcomes for success in college. It allows you to identify at-risk students with early-alert reporting, validate your college success program with a post-course assessment of students' progress, and improve your institution's retention rates. Textbook-specific remediation helps your students strengthen the areas where the survey indicates they need improvement in order to achieve greater success in college. Ask your Cengage Learning Consultant for more details.

- **College Success Planner.** Instructors can package the *On Course* textbook with this 12-month, week-at-a-glance academic planner. The College Success Planner assists students in making the best use of their time both on and off campus and includes additional reading about key learning strategies and life skills for success in college.

SUPPORT FOR INSTRUCTORS

- **Annotated Instructor's Edition.** To help guide instructors to the many instructional resources found within the Facilitator's Manual, the Annotated Instructor's Edition (ISBN: 9781305584334) provides in the margins specific cross-references directly to ideas and activities available in the Facilitator's Manual. The cross-references are provided by Amy Munson, Director of Instructional Design, United States Air Force Academy, CO.

- **Revised Facilitator's Manual.** The Facilitator's Manual, now offered both in a printed version (ISBN: 9781305647671) and online at the Instructor Companion Site (see below for more information), offers educators specific classroom activities and suggestions from author Skip Downing for using *On Course* in various kinds of courses, and it endeavors to answer questions that educators might have about using the text. Additionally, the Facilitator's Manual includes "best practices" provided by *On Course* instructors; additional study skills activities written by Melanie Marine of the University of Wisconsin–Oshkosh; diversity

The information about diversity and culture that is integrated throughout the text is a much more authentic way to discuss diversity and ethnicity rather than with a one-chapter focus.

Linda McMeen,
North Hennepin
Community College

The At Work sections give students a specific venue to see how the soft skills they acquire will transfer to career success. Semester after semester students will share how their work situation improved as a result of what they learned and tried from the At Work sections. These sections are a natural fit in the *On Course* chapters, and they are packed with pertinent information.

Gail Janecka,
The Victoria College

activities provided by LuAnn Wood and Christina Davis, both of Century College; suggestions for teaching in an online environment written by Pratima Sampat-Mar of Pima Medical Institute and for using MindTap® in an *On Course* program written by Angela C. Thering of Buffalo State College; and a guide for how to successfully integrate the College Success Factors Index (CSFI) with *On Course* written by Gary Williams of Crafton Hills College. One of the most popular elements of the *On Course Facilitator's Manual* is the numerous in-class exercises that encourage students' active exploration of the success strategies presented in the text. These learner-centered exercises include role-playing, learning games, dialogues, demonstrations, metaphors, mind-mappings, brainstorms, questionnaires, drawings, skits, scavenger hunts, and many other activities.

- **Updated Instructor Companion Site.** This free protected website provides educators with many resources to offer a course that empowers students to become active, responsible, and successful learners. Read the Facilitator's Manual (which is also offered in a printed version, as explained above), download PowerPoint slides, view content from the DVD *On Course: A Comprehensive Program for Promoting Student Academic Success and Retention*, and find a useful transition guide for educators who used previous editions of *On Course*. To access the site, follow these steps:

  1. Visit *login.cengage.com.*
  2. If you have not previously created a faculty account, choose "Create a New Faculty Account" and follow the prompts.
  3. If you have created a faculty account previously, log in with your email address or user name and password.
  4. Search for *On Course* to add the available additional digital resources to your bookshelf.

  You will always need to return to *login.cengage.com* and enter your email address and password to sign in to access these resources. Use this space to write down your email address or user name and password below:

  Email Address: _____

  Password: _____

- **On Course Workshops and National Conference.** Skip Downing, author of *On Course*, offers faculty development workshops for all educators who want to learn innovative strategies for empowering students to become active, responsible, and successful learners. These highly regarded professional development workshops are offered at conference centers across North America, or you can host a one- to four-day event on your own campus. Online graduate courses (3 credits) are available as a follow-up to two of the workshops. Additionally, you are invited to attend the annual *On Course* National Conference, where hundreds of learner-centered educators gather to share their best practices. For information about these workshops, graduate courses, and the national conference (including testimonials galore), go to *www.oncourseworkshop.com*. Questions? Email *workshop@oncourseworkhop.com* or call 650-365-7623.

- *On Course* **Newsletter.** All college educators are invited to subscribe to the free *On Course e-Newsletter*. More than 200,000 educators worldwide receive these emails with innovative, learner-centered strategies for engaging students in deep and lasting learning. To subscribe, simply go to *www.oncourseworkshop.com* and follow the easy, one-click directions. Or you can email a request to *workshop@oncourseworkshop.com*.

Since first attending one of the summer retreats in 1997, I've held nine full On Course staff development trainings for our college, and I plan to offer more. They are invaluable! I strongly recommend this workshop for all faculty, counselors, advisors, administrators, and support staff.

Philip Rodriquez,
Director, Student Affairs,
Cerritos College

Acknowledgments

This book would not exist without the assistance of an extraordinary group of people. I can only hope that I have returned (or will return) their wonderful support in kind.

At Cengage Learning, I would like to thank Amy Gibbons, Marita Sermolins, Erica Messenger, Aimee Bear, and Courtney Triola for their unflagging attention to details and encouraging guidance. At Baltimore City Community College, my thanks go to my former colleagues, the dedicated teachers of the College Success Seminar. At *On Course* Workshops, thanks to the extraordinary support and wisdom of my colleagues and friends Jonathan Brennan, Robin Middleton, Deb Poese, Eileen Zamora, Mark McBride, Teresa Ward and LuAnn Wood. Thanks also to the 2000+ *On Course* Ambassadors, some of the greatest educators in the world, who work tirelessly to introduce their students and colleagues to *On Course*. And especially Carol—your unwavering love and support keep me on course. You are my compass.

Numerous wise and caring reviewers have made valuable contributions to this book, and many contributed exercises to the Facilitator's Manual, and I thank them for their contributions:

Susie P. Aceron, College of the Sequoias
Dawn Bartlett, SUNY Jefferson Community College
Jill Beauchamp, Washtenaw Community College
Susan Cain, Southwestern Community College
Rebecca Campbell, Northern Arizona University
Essie Childers, Blinn College – Bryan Campus
Michelle Cochran, Rochester Community and Technical College
Dorothy Collins, Eastern Gateway Community College
Kathleen Conway, College of the Sequoias
Audra Cooke, Rock Valley College
George Daniel, University of Tennessee at Martin
Christina Devlin, Montgomery College
Catherine Eloranto, Clinton Community College
Lalanya Ennis, College of the Mainland
Annette Fields, University of Arkansas at Pine Bluff
Debra Ford, Davidson County Community College
Janeth Franklin, Glendale Community College
Erin Frock, Truckee Meadows Community College
Joselyn Gonzalez, El Centro College
Maria E. Gonzalez, Broward College
Pat Grissom, San Jacinto College
Tuesday Hambric, Eastfield College

Dan Hayes, Chemeketa Community College

Gerald Headd, Cuyahoga Community College

Ann Heiny, Armstrong State University

Mark Hendrix, Palm Beach State College

David Hoffman, Southern State Community College

Gail Janecka, Victoria College

Dana Kermanian, Grayson County Junior College

Stephanie Kroon, State University of New York – Ulster

Sandra Lancaster, Grand Rapids Community College

Charlene Latimer, Daytona State College

Kristina Leonard, Daytona State College

Joy Lester, Forsyth Technical Community College

Lea Beth Lewis, California State University – Fullerton

Charlie Liebert, Davidson County Community College

Jacquelyn Loghry, Northwest Missouri State University

Kimberly Manner, West Los Angeles College

Lisa Marks, Ozarks Technical Community College

Kim Martin, Chemeketa Community College

Claire Maxson, Ivy Tech Community College

Rebecca McElroy, Wharton County Junior College

Linda McMeen, North Hennepin Community College

Amy Munson, United States Air Force Academy, CO

Aletia Norwood, Western Nebraska CC

Eva O'Brian, Midlands Technical College

Jennifer Palcich, University of North Texas

Taunya Paul, York Technical College

Adrienne Peek, Modesto Junior College

June Pomann, Union County College

Carrie Roberson, Butte College

Steve Schommer, San Diego City College

Jo Allison Scott, Northeast Wisconsin Tech College

Peter Shull, Pennsylvania State University

Thomas Skouras, Community College of Rhode Island

M. Somerville-Reeves, Delaware County Community College

Tanya Stanley, San Jacinto College

Jennifer Swartout, Heartland Community College

Angela C. Thering, Buffalo State College

Debbie Unsold, Washington State Community College

Judy Weaver, Goshen College

Judith Willner, Coppin State University

Katie Woolsey, Cabrillo College/UC Santa Cruz

Finally, my deep gratitude goes out to the students who over the years have had the courage to explore and change their thoughts, actions, feelings, and beliefs. I hope, as a result, you have all lived richer, more personally fulfilling lives. I know I have.

On Course is the result of my own quest to live a rich, personally fulfilling life and my strong desire to pass on what I've learned to my students. As such, *On Course* is a very personal book, for me and for you. I invite you to explore in depth what success means to you. I suggest that if you want to achieve your greatest potential in college and in life, dig deep inside yourself, where you already possess everything you need to make your dreams come true.

During my first two decades of teaching college courses, I consistently observed a sad and perplexing puzzle. Each semester I watched students sort themselves into two groups. One group achieved varying degrees of academic success, from those who excelled to those who just squeaked by. The other group struggled mightily; then they withdrew, disappeared, or failed. But, here's the puzzling part. The struggling students often displayed as much academic potential as their more successful classmates, and in some cases more. What, I wondered, causes the vastly different outcomes of these two groups? And what could I do to help my struggling students achieve greater success?

Somewhere around my 20th year of teaching, I experienced a series of crises in both my personal and professional lives. In a word, I was struggling. After a period of feeling sorry for myself, I embarked on a quest to improve the quality of my life. I read, I took seminars and workshops, I talked with wise friends and acquaintances, I kept an in-depth journal, I saw a counselor, I even returned to graduate school to add a master's degree in applied psychology to my doctoral degree in English. I was seriously motivated to change my life for the better.

If I were to condense all that I learned into one sentence, it would be this: **People who are successful (by their own definition) consistently make wiser choices than people who struggle.** I came to see that the quality of my life was essentially the result of all of my previous choices. I saw how the wisdom (or lack of wisdom) of my choices influenced, and often determined, the outcomes and experiences of my life. The same, of course, was true for my struggling students.

For two and a half decades, I have continued my quest to identify the inner qualities that empower a person to make consistently wise choices, the very choices that lead to success both in college and in life. As a result of what I learned (and continue to learn), I created a course at my college called the College Success Seminar. This course was a departure from traditional student success courses because instead of focusing primarily on study skills and campus resources, it focused on empowering students from the inside out. I had come to believe that most students who struggle in college are perfectly capable of earning a degree and that their struggles go far deeper than not knowing study skills or failing to use campus resources. As a result, I envisioned a course that would empower students to develop their natural inner strengths, the qualities that would help them make the wise choices that would create the very outcomes and experiences they wanted in college . . . and in life. When I couldn't find a book that did this, I wrote *On Course*. A few years later, I created a series of professional development workshops to share what I had learned with other educators who want to see their students soar. Then, to provide an opportunity for workshop graduates to continue to exchange their experiences and wisdom, I started a listserv, and this growing group of educators soon named themselves the *On Course* Ambassadors, sharing *On Course* strategies with their students and colleagues alike. Later, I created two online graduate courses that further help college educators learn cutting-edge strategies for empowering their students to be more successful in college and in life. To launch the second decade of *On Course*, the *On Course* Ambassadors hosted the first of many *On Course* National Conferences, bringing together an overflow crowd of educators hungry for new ways to help their students achieve more of their potential in college and in life. Every one of these efforts appeals to a deep place in me because they all have the power to change people's lives for the better. But that's not the only appeal. These activities also help *me* stay conscious of the wise choices I must consistently make to live a richer, more personally fulfilling life.

Now that much of my life is back on course, I don't want to forget how I got here!

Getting On Course to Your Success

Successful Students . . .

► **accept personal responsibility,** seeing themselves as the primary cause of their outcomes and experiences.

► **discover self-motivation,** finding purpose in their lives by pursuing personally meaningful goals and dreams.

► **master self-management,** consistently planning and taking purposeful actions in pursuit of their goals and dreams.

► **employ interdependence,** building mutually supportive relationships that help them achieve their goals and dreams (while helping others do the same).

Struggling Students . . .

► **see themselves as victims,** believing that what happens to them is determined primarily by external forces such as fate, luck, and powerful others.

► **have difficulty sustaining motivation,** often feeling depressed, frustrated, and/ or resentful about a lack of direction in their lives.

► **seldom identify specific actions needed to accomplish a desired outcome** and, when they do, tend to procrastinate.

► **are solitary,** seldom requesting, even rejecting, offers of assistance from those who could help.

College Smart-Start Guide

If you've ever bought a new computer, you'll recall that it came with a user's manual. The user's manual—whether in print or online—was many pages long and contained all you needed to know to get the most from your computer.

Think of *On Course* as your user's manual for higher education. It explains how to get the most out of college. In these pages, you'll discover how to learn effectively, how to get high grades, and how to earn the degree you want. As a bonus, many of the strategies you'll learn will help you achieve success in other key areas of your life, including your career.

Most computers also come with a brief guide that's only a few pages long. This guide describes the essential steps for getting your computer up and running quickly and successfully.

This Smart-Start Guide has that same intention for college. Complete the following actions before the end of your first week in college, and you'll be off to a great start. Some of these actions can be done in a few minutes. Others take longer. You can do them in any order you choose.

So, read and do the lucky 13 actions below. Be smart—complete one of them right now. Do a couple more every day, and you'll have them all done by the end of your first week. By then, you'll be on course to great success in higher education.

WHAT TO DO DURING YOUR FIRST WEEK IN COLLEGE

GET FAMILIAR

1. **Learn your campus.** Find out where things are so you begin to feel comfortable. What's in the various buildings? Where will you find the many services designed to help you succeed? To orient yourself, get a campus map. There's probably one on your college's website.

If your campus offers tours, take one. If not, ask a college employee or an experienced student to show you around. Or ask another first-year student to join you on a self-guided tour. As a last resort, explore on your own. See if you can fill in the location and hours for all of the services listed in Figure 1.1.

Service	Location	Hours
College Bookstore		
Advising Office		
Counseling Office		
Student Activities Office		
Financial Aid Office		
Career Center		
Registrar's Office		
Library		
Tutoring or Academic Support		

© 2017 Cengage Learning

FIGURE 1.1

▶

Service	Location	Hours
Computer Center or Lab		
Dining Facilities		
Fitness Center		
Athletic Facilities		
Student Center		
Copy Center		
Public Safety		
Health Services		
Other?		
Other?		

© 2017 Cengage Learning

FIGURE 1.1 (*Continued*)

2. **Locate your classrooms.** Find and visit every room in which you have a class. Nothing ruins your first week like missing classes because you can't find the rooms. You'll likely find a list of your courses and classrooms on the document you received when you registered. Use this information to fill in the first two columns in Figure 1.2.

3. **Learn your instructors' names, office locations, and office hours.** Instructors' names are usually listed on your registration document next to each course. If an instructor is listed as "TBA"—or something other than a name—an instructor has not yet been assigned to the class. (TBA stands for "To Be Announced.") In that case, you'll need to get your instructor's name at the department office or the first class meeting. On

Figure 1.2, record your instructors' names, office locations, and office hours. Office hours are times when instructors are in their office and available for appointments . . . and you'll want to make an appointment soon. This additional information will likely be on the first-day handout for each class. (A first-day handout is often called a "syllabus.")

4. **Study—don't just skim—the first-day handout (syllabus) for each course.** The syllabus is a contract between you and your instructor. In it, he or she presents essential information about the course. Typically, a syllabus contains . . .

   a) a course description (often the same description as in the college catalogue)

   b) learning objectives (what you are expected to learn in the course)

Course	Classroom	Instructor	Office	Office Hours

© 2017 Cengage Learning

FIGURE 1.2

▶

c) homework assignments (probably every assignment for the entire course)

d) exam schedule (when you'll be tested)

e) how your final grade will be determined (how much each assignment is worth)

f) course rules (what to do and not do, along with consequences)

g) Internet address (if course materials are posted online)

h) information about the instructor (name, office location, and office hours)

The syllabus may be the single most important document your instructors provide, so read it carefully. Now is the time to ask questions about the syllabus. Your instructor will assume that if you stay in the course, you understand the syllabus and agree to abide by it.

GET ORGANIZED

5. **Get all of your learning supplies.** Every job has both a purpose and essential tools. Job #1 in college is deep learning. So, make a list of all of the supplies you'll need to learn, such as textbooks, a computer/laptop/tablet, calculator, notebooks, three-ring binders, notepaper, pens, monthly calendars, weekly calendars, folders, and flash drives. Of these supplies, arguably the most essential are your textbooks. Required texts are listed in each syllabus (first-day handout). They can be purchased in your campus bookstore and perhaps online as well. Ideally, you'll have your textbooks in hand before your first class meeting. At the latest, get them before the end of Week 1, because any later can sabotage your success. College instructors move quickly and expect you to come to class prepared. If it's Week 3 and you're just starting to read your assignments, your chances of success plunge.

6. **Create a schedule.** Adding college assignments and activities to your life can be overwhelming. A schedule is essential for getting everything important done on time. Whether your schedule is on paper, on your smartphone, online, or you use some other method, tracking your commitments is essential. Make a weekly schedule showing recurring events such as classes, study times, or work. Make a monthly calendar showing due dates for occasional events such as a test, term paper, or meeting with an instructor. You'll find weekly and monthly calendars in the section called "Creating a Leak-Proof Self-Management System" in Chapter 4.

7. **Get comfortable with campus technology.** The use of technology is common on college campuses. Check each course syllabus to see what technology your instructors expect you to use. They may send you course updates using campus email. Or expect you to access online resources for their classes. You may be taking a class that is offered partly or entirely online via a course management system (CMS). Some of the more common course management systems are Blackboard (BB), Desire to Learn (D2L) and Moodle. It's possible your instructor will arrange some technology help for your class. Nevertheless, be proactive. Go to your campus computer lab and see if an orientation is offered. If not, ask someone in the computer lab to help you learn what you need to know (as defined in each course syllabus). Or find a classmate with good technology skills and ask for help.

8. **Manage your money.** Money problems have sabotaged many students' success in college. Some have had to drop out of college to work. Others have tried working full-time while attending college, but they

▶

became overwhelmed. An important step toward understanding your financial situation is creating a budget. That will tell you (in case you don't already know) if money is going to be an obstacle to your success in college. If you're serious about your education, there are many options to help you overcome the money obstacle. You'll find many suggestions about money management in the next section of this chapter, "Money Matters."

GET SERIOUS

9. **Set goals for each course.** Make a list of your courses. Next to each one, write your target grade for the course. Then write a goal for the most important thing or things you want to learn in the course.

10. **Attend all classes and arrive on time.** Class attendance is essential to success in college. Remember, Job #1 as a student is deep learning, and learning starts in the classroom. Many college instructors do not take attendance, but don't mistakenly think that means you don't need to be there.

11. **Participate in every class.** Active engagement is the key to deep learning. Attend each class having done all assignments beforehand. Ask questions about your homework. Answer questions your instructor asks. When an instructor facilitates an activity, she's intending that you learn something important through the experience. Participate at a high level and look for the learning.

12. **Complete and hand in all assignments on time.** Make a list of all assignments due in week one (and beyond). Record them, along with test dates, on your monthly calendar so you can see them coming. Check them off as you finish each one. Here's the double benefit. First, you'll learn more when you attend classes having completed all assigned homework. As a bonus, you'll reduce the stress that many first-year college students experience when they fall behind.

13. **Commit to your success.** At the end of your first week, think back over your experiences with each course. Be honest with yourself. Will you make the time necessary to do all of the work? Are you prepared to give the course your best effort? If not, discuss your concerns with your advisor or a counselor. If your concerns continue, now may be the time to drop the course (and perhaps pick up another course in its place). But if your answer is "yes" to doing all of the course work and giving it your very best effort, then write out this solemn commitment and post it where you will see it every day: *I promise myself to give a 100 percent effort every day to every course. Nothing will keep me from achieving success!*

Money Matters

If lack of money could be an obstacle to your college success, get your finances in order now . . . not after it's too late. There's no point heading off on a journey knowing you'll run out of fuel before reaching your destination.

The good news is that the efforts (even sacrifices) you make now will likely pay off in the future. Check out Figure 1.3 to see how level of education affects earnings and unemployment. Clearly, earning a degree increases the likelihood of greater abundance. Sadly, however, many students' money problems keep

Level of Education	Median Earnings	Unemployment Rate
Less than a high school diploma	$24,544	11.0%
High school diploma, no college	$33,852	7.5%
Some college, no degree	$37,804	7.0%
Associate degree	$40,404	5.4%
Bachelor's degree	$57,616	4.0%
Master's degree	$69,108	3.4%
Doctoral degree	$84,396	2.2%
Professional degree	$89,128	2.3%

FIGURE 1.3 Yearly Salaries and Unemployment Rates by Levels of Education (25 and older)

Source: U.S. Bureau of Labor Statistics, Current Population Survey, 2013.

them from completing the very degree that would help them achieve that abundance. They work so many hours that their learning and grades suffer. Still others drop out of college because of lack of money. If money problems threaten your college degree, read on.

In this section, you'll learn some of the basics of money management. There is, of course, much more to know. But if you effectively apply these strategies, you can look forward to building the financial resources that will see you though to graduation.

MANAGING MONEY: THE BIG PICTURE

When I was a new college instructor, a colleague and I were complaining one day about how little money we were making. Both of us had young families, and our salaries barely got us from paycheck to paycheck. One day we decided to stop complaining and do something about it. Boldly, we decided to award ourselves a raise.

To do so, we brainstormed how we could save or earn more money. Our first discovery was that we were both paying about $6 a month for our checking accounts. We switched to free checking and gave ourselves an instant raise of $72 a year. By itself, that was no big thing. But we also thought of 21 other ways to make or save money. All told, our new choices amounted to an increase of nearly $2,000 a year for each of us. That was the beginning of our realization that we had more control over our money than we had thought.

As you examine the following strategies, keep in mind the big picture of managing money. **Do everything legal to increase the flow of money *into* your personal treasury and decrease the flow of money *out*. The better you become at these complementary skills, the more money you will have to enhance your life and the lives of the people you love.** There is great abundance on our planet, and there is no reason why you shouldn't enjoy your share of it.

INCREASE MONEY FLOWING IN

1. **Create a budget.** A budget helps you define and achieve your goals. It helps you make important decisions about the dollars flowing in and out of your life. Beginning your budget is as simple as filling out the My Financial Plan worksheet on the next page. As a guideline, some financial experts suggest that expenditures in a healthy budget should be close to the following percentages of your net income (i.e., the money remaining after deducting federal, state, and local taxes):

31% Housing	7% Entertainment
20% Transportation	7% Savings
16% Food	6% Clothing
8% Miscellaneous	5% Health

   Obviously, after subtracting all of your expenses from your income, your goal is to have a positive and growing balance. If you have a negative balance, with each passing month you'll slide deeper into debt. To avoid debt, you need to increase your income, decrease your expenses, or both.

2. **Find a bank or credit union.** A bank or credit union helps you manage your money with services such as checking accounts, savings accounts, and easy access to cash through automated teller machines (ATMs). Your ideal financial institution offers a free checking account that requires no minimum balance and pays interest. Further, it offers a savings account with competitive interest rates. And, finally, your ideal financial institution offers free use of its ATMs and those belonging to other banks or credit unions as well. If you need to pay for any of these services, seek to minimize the yearly cost. Credit unions typically offer lower rates on these services than do banks. To find credit unions near you, use the search feature at creditunion.coop. Whether your checking account is with a bank or a credit union, be sure to balance your account regularly. This will save you the expense of bounced (rejected) checks because of insufficient funds.

3. **Apply for grants and scholarships.** These are financial awards that do not have to be repaid. For United States residents, a great place to get an overview of financial aid sources online is at ed.gov/fund/grants-college .html. The process of applying for financial aid dollars begins with the FAFSA, which stands for Free Application for Federal Student Aid. Using

My Financial Plan

Step A: Monthly Income	Amount	Balance
Support from parents or others		
Scholarships		
Loans		
Investments		
Earned income		
Total Monthly Income (A)		
Step B: Necessary Fixed Monthly Expenses		
Housing (mortgage or rent)		
Transportation (car payment, insurance, bus pass, car pool)		
Taxes (federal and state income, Social Security, Medicare)		
Insurance (house, health, and life)		
Child care		
Tuition		
Bank fees		
Debt payment		
Savings and investments		
Necessary Fixed Monthly Expenses (B)		
Step C: Necessary Variable Monthly Expenses		
Food and personal care items		
Clothing		
Telephone		
Gas and electric		
Water		
Transportation (car repairs, maintenance, gasoline)		
Laundry and dry cleaning		
Doctor and medicine		
Books and software		
Computer/Internet access		
Total Necessary Variable Monthly Expenses (C)		
Step D: Optional Fixed and Variable Monthly Expenses		
Eating out (including coffee, snacks, lunches)		
Entertainment (movies, theater, night life, babysitting)		
Travel		
Hobbies		
Gifts		
Charitable contributions		
Miscellaneous (music, magazines, newspapers, etc.)		
Total Optional Variable Monthly Expenses (D)		
Money Remaining or Owed at End of Month (A − B − C − D = ?)		

information you report on this form, the government decides what you or your family can afford to pay toward your education and what you may need in the way of financial assistance. Get copies of the form from your college's financial aid office or online at fafsa.ed.gov. You'll find a "forecaster" at this site that will help you estimate the amount of financial aid you can expect to receive. The deadline for completing the FAFSA form is early July. However, some colleges use the information from the FAFSA form to determine their own financial aid, so be sure to check your school's deadline or you could be out of luck (and money) for that year.

The benefit of qualifying for grants and scholarships is that, unlike loans, you don't need to pay them back. Federal Pell Grants provide financial support to students with family incomes up to $50,000; however, most Pell awards go to students with family incomes below $20,000. With a maximum award in 2014–15 of $5,730, the amount of each Pell Grant depends on four factors: 1) financial need, 2) cost of the college, 3) full- or part-time enrollment, and 4) attendance for a full academic year or less. Effective July 2012, you can receive a Pell Grant for only 12 semesters, or approximately six years. You can get comprehensive information from the Federal Student Aid Information Center in Washington at studentaid.ed.gov.

You can also search without cost for scholarships at Internet sites such as bigfuture.collegeboard.org/scholarship-search, collegeanswer.com, and fastweb.com. Perhaps most important, spend time with a counselor in your college's financial aid office and let him or her help you get your share of the financial support available for a college education. With all of these resources, there's no need to pay a private service to find you scholarships. Ron Smith, former head of financial aid at Baltimore City Community College, offers this advice: "Students should apply early, provide accurate information, and follow up until an award has been received."

4. **Apply for low-cost loans.** These are financial awards that *do* need to be repaid. Stafford Loans (staffordloan.com) are guaranteed by the federal government, so they generally offer the lowest interest rates. Depending on financial need, Stafford Loans may be up to $3,500 per year for first-year students, $4,500 for sophomores, and $5,500 for juniors and seniors. As of this writing, the maximum total loan is $23,000. The U.S. government pays interest costs until repayment begins, which is usually after graduation. Unsubsidized Stafford Loans do not depend on financial need, but the interest accumulates while you are in college.

Other federally guaranteed student loans include PLUS loans (made to students' parents) and Perkins Loans (for lower-income students). You may be approved for more loan money than you actually need and be tempted to borrow it all; just remember that what you take now, you'll need to repay later. You don't want to finish your education with the burden of an unnecessarily large debt. The standard repayment plan for student loans is equal monthly payments for 10 years. That's a long time to pay for an earlier bad choice.

Here's one last caution about loans: A report by the Brown Center on Education Policy at the Brookings Institution found that many students didn't realize that money they received was a loan that needed to be repaid. In fact, 28 percent of students who *did* have federal loans reported they did *not* have federal loans and 14 percent reported that they had no loans at all. Confusion about what they've borrowed, the report concludes, is "almost certainly leading some students into decisions that they later come to regret." The lesson? Make sure you know how much money you get for college is a loan and will need to be paid back.

5. **Work.** Even with grants, scholarships, and low-cost loans, many college students need employment to make ends meet. If this is your situation, use your financial plan to figure out how much money you need each month beyond any financial aid. Then set a goal to earn that amount while also getting work experience in your future field of employment. In other words, your purpose for working is both to make money *and* to get valuable employment experience and recommendations. In this way, you make it easier to find employment after college and perhaps even negotiate a higher starting salary. One place that may help you achieve this double goal is your campus job center. Additionally, on some campuses, instructors are able to hire student assistants to help them with their research.

   If you try but can't find employment that provides valuable work experience (or you're not sure what your future employment plans are), seek work that allows you to earn your needed income in the fewest hours—saving you time to excel in your studies. You may do well by creating a high-paying job for yourself by using skills you already possess (or could easily learn). For example, one student I know noticed that each autumn the rain gutters of houses near his college became clogged with falling leaves. With a leaf blower and ladder in hand, he knocked on doors and offered to clean gutters for only $20. Few homeowners could resist such a bargain. Averaging two houses per hour, he earned nearly $700 each fall weekend.

6. **Save and invest.** If you haven't done so already, open a savings account and begin making regular deposits. You can probably save $20 per month just by giving up a pizza and a movie. Set a goal to accumulate a financial reserve for emergencies equal to three months' living expenses. After that, consider making regular deposits in higher-income investments such as stocks, bonds, and mutual funds. These are topics beyond the scope of this book but well worth your effort to research. To gain practical experience and guidance, you may want to join (or start) an investment club on your campus. By investing money regularly, you'll benefit from compound interest (earning interest on interest). In this way, even people with modest incomes can accumulate significant wealth. A way to make your savings grow even faster is to invest in a tax-deferred retirement account.

The money you deposit isn't taxed until you withdraw it many years later, increasing the amount you can potentially save by thousands of dollars. You can open such an account through your employer (who may even make additional contributions) or by opening an IRA (Individual Retirement Account) on your own.

DECREASE MONEY FLOWING OUT

7. **Lower transportation expenses.** Cars are expensive. Beyond car payments, there are costs for insurance, registration, regular maintenance, gasoline, repairs, tolls, and parking. And if you're under 25, you'll pay more for insurance than someone over 25 (especially young men, whose rates are double or triple those of older men). So, if money is tight, consider getting along without a car for now. If you live on campus, this option should be fairly easy. If you commute, you could use public transportation or offer gas money to a classmate for rides to school.

8. **Use credit cards wisely.** You'll probably be swamped with invitations to open credit card accounts. You're not alone. "These credit card issuers circle the campus like sharks circling a fish," says Elizabeth Warren, senior senator from Massachusetts and former Harvard Law School professor. So, first, consider whether you should even *have* a credit card. Visa, MasterCard, and other credit cards provide you with short-term loans to purchase anything you want up to your credit limit. These companies are counting on you to postpone paying off the loan past the due date. That's when you start paying interest at their high rates. The consequences to your finances can be staggering. Suppose you're 20 years old, owe $3,500 on a credit card that charges 17 percent interest and you regularly pay the minimum charge. You won't pay off that debt until you're 53 years old, and the amount you will ultimately pay is nearly $11,000! And if you ever miss a payment, you'll incur a triple penalty. First, you'll be charged a late fee that can be as much as $35 for being even one day overdue. Next, some banks punish late payers by raising their interest rates to "penalty rates" of 20 percent or more. Finally, late payments can show up on your credit report, making it difficult for you to get loans for a car, house or other big-ticket items. How serious is the problem of credit card misuse by college students? One widely quoted statement attributed to an administrator at the University of Indiana noted, "We lose more students to credit card debt than to academic failure." So, use a credit card only if you can discipline yourself to pay off most, and preferably all, of your balance every month. If you can't, a wiser choice would be to cut up your credit cards—or not even apply for one in the first place.

9. **Choose credit cards wisely.** If you decide that you do have the discipline to use a credit card wisely, realize that all credit cards are not created equal.

Compare your options and choose the one with the lowest interest rates, the longest grace period (time you get to use the money before paying interest), and the lowest annual fee (preferably free). Some cards offer a reward for using them, such as cash back or frequent flyer miles. To find the best deals on credit cards, visit Internet sites such as bankrate.com or cardratings.com.

10. **Use debit cards wisely.** A debit card is similar to a credit card. The difference? The money comes not as a loan from the credit card company but as a withdrawal from your own checking account. Here's the danger. You may forget to record every purchase made on your debit card, as you more likely would if you wrote a check. Consequently, you can easily overdraw your checking account and incur financial penalties for bounced checks. Use a debit card only if you have the discipline to track every use and keep your checking account balance current.

11. **Use ATM cards wisely.** An ATM card, like a debit card, draws from your personal account, but here the withdrawal is in cash. ATM cards are so easy to use that some financial experts refer to them as "death cards." Say you withdraw $100 in cash on Monday, and by Thursday the money has dribbled away. So you take out another $100, and that disappears by the weekend. After a couple of weeks like this, your money runs out before the month does, and you're slipping ever deeper into debt. Use an ATM card only if you have the self-discipline to check your remaining balance after every withdrawal.

12. **Pay off high-rate debt.** Suppose you pay off a loan (such as a credit card balance) that charges 17 percent. That's the same as investing your money at a guaranteed 17 percent rate of return. Better yet, the 17 percent return is tax free, so you're actually earning a much greater return! Compare that to the puny interest rate you'd be earning in a savings account. Don't have extra money in savings to pay off money you owe? A variation is to transfer debt from high-interest-rate loans to lower-interest-rate loans (but watch carefully for hidden transfer costs on some accounts).

13. **Avoid credit blunders.** There are serious consequences for being financially irresponsible. Every time you create a debt, national credit agencies keep a record. When you later apply for credit, potential lenders can view your credit history for at least the past seven years. This data tells lenders whether you are a good or bad risk. If you're seen as a bad risk, your application for a car or house loan may be turned down. Or you may be offered a loan with extremely high interest rates. Your credit report might even wind up in the hands of a potential landlord or employer. This information could affect your ability to rent an apartment or even get your dream job. Bottom line, unwise financial choices in the present will follow you for years. To view your present credit report and verify its accuracy, order a copy from Equifax at 800-685-1111 (equifax.com), Experian at 888-397-3742 (experian.com), or TransUnion at 800-888-4213 (transunion.com). Depending on where you

live, the report will range in cost from free to about $8. At annualcreditreport
.com you can get a free credit report for all three agencies once a year. If you
make a credit blunder, immediately contact the company you owe and work
out a payment schedule. The sooner you clean up your credit report, the
sooner your past mistakes will stop sabotaging your future. If you need help
with debt, contact the National Foundation for Credit Counseling (NFCC)
for low- or no-cost credit assistance at 800-388-2227 (nfcc.org).

14. **Use tax credits.** Tax credits are expenses you can subtract directly from
your federal income tax. If you're paying for college yourself, you may
be eligible for an American Opportunity Tax Credit of up to $2,500 in
your first four years. For details on this tax credit (as well as the Lifetime
Learning Credit), go to irs.gov/uac/Tax-Benefits-for-Education:
-Information-Center

15. **Avoid the "Let's Go Out" trap.** Someone calls and says, "Let's go out."
You meet for food or drinks and spend $20 . . . or more. Do this a couple
times a week and you'll wind up dropping hundreds of dollars a month
into a deep, dark hole. One student reported that even after she ran out of
money for the month, friends would say, "Oh, c'mon out with us. I'll loan
you the money." That meant she was already spending next month's money.
By all means, put entertainment money into your monthly financial plan,
but, when it's gone, have the self-discipline to stop going out. Instead, invite
friends over and make it BYO—Bring Your Own. Or you could make a
great choice by staying home and studying. Studying costs you nothing now
and makes a great investment in your future income.

16. **Track your spending.** To plug a leak, you have to know where it is. So,
carry a notepad with you for at least a week and record every penny you
spend. (I know, doing this is a pain, but the benefit is worth it!) Examine your recorded expenses and look for financial leaks that don't show
up in your financial plan. One student was shocked to discover that he
was spending an average of $24 per week ($1,248 per year!) on fast-food
lunches; he started packing his lunch and saved a bundle.

17. **Examine each expense line in your financial plan for possible
reductions.** Here are some of the money-saving options my students
have come up with: Find a roommate to reduce housing costs. Car pool to
share commuting costs. Cut up credit cards. Pack lunches instead of eating
out. Change banks to lower or eliminate monthly checking fees. Exchange
babysitting with fellow students to minimize child-care expenses. Shop at
discount clubs and buy non-perishables (such as toilet paper and laundry
detergent) in bulk. Join family/friends discounts for cell phones. Read magazines and newspapers at the library, instead of buying them. Pay creditors
on time to avoid penalty charges. Delay purchases until the item goes on
sale (such as right after Christmas). Find other money-saving ideas on the
Internet at lowermybills.com.

MONEY MANAGEMENT EXERCISE

To help *increase* your flow of money in, make a list of skills you have that you could possibly turn into a high-hourly-wage self-employment opportunity. To help *decrease* your flow of money out, make a list of choices you could make that would each save you $25 or more per year. If you need help, try an Internet search for "saving money" or "budget tips." Compare your two lists with those of classmates to see if you can find additional choices you didn't think of. Add up all of the items on your list (income and outflow) and see how much you could improve your financial picture in one year by making these choices. You'll find more wise advice about managing your money at bettermoneyhabits.com.

TECH TIPS: Money

Mint is the top money management tool (5 out of 5 stars) recommended by *Personal Computing* magazine. The software connects to all of your online financial institutions, such as banks and credit unions, which means you must provide your login information. The program tracks your personal finances and helps you budget your money. (*Web, Android, and iOS*)

LearnVest, which provides paid financial planning services, also offers the option to sign up for free email newsletters filled with extensive tips for budgeting, saving money and other financial topics. (*Web; iOS*)

BudgetSimple.com offers an easy-to-use online budget that (unlike Mint) does not need to be linked to your financial institutions. It promises to help you understand where your money is leaking out and ways to cut off the flow. The free plan offers options for creating a budget and reports. (*Web*)

Bettermoneyhabits.com is a website offered by a partnership between Khan Academy and Bank of America. It offers valuable tips on how to create and stick to a budget, repay a student loan, finance a car, boost your credit score, save for buying a house, and understand your paycheck. (*Web*)

Spreadsheet programs—such as Google's free Google Sheets program and Excel, a program included in the Microsoft Office software suite—can also be used to create effective budgets.

Student loan calculators may be found online by doing an Internet search. These programs figure your student loan repayments so you can see how easy or challenging it will be for you to pay back your loan(s).

Note: All of the above are free (except for Excel), but some may offer upgraded features for a fee.

Understanding the Culture of Higher Education

FOCUS QUESTIONS   What is unique about the culture of higher education? How does understanding that culture increase your chances of success in college?

In some ways, enrolling in college is like moving to a foreign country. That's because the culture of higher education is different from other cultures you have known, even that of high school.

Geert Hofstede, a Dutch psychologist and anthropologist, has studied cultures all over the world. According to Hofstede, culture is "the collective programming of the mind that distinguishes the members of one human group from another." Every culture on Earth is programmed to operate by its own unique software. And this is true of higher education as well. The sooner you understand the culture of higher education, the sooner you will be on course to success.

"Be prepared to encounter cultural references that we're just not going to get."

Some aspects of a culture are obvious and visible, whereas others are subtle and invisible. To understand the distinction between visible and invisible culture, Brooks Peterson, author of *Cultural Intelligence*, suggests picturing an iceberg (see Figure 1.4). Above the waterline are the elements of culture we can perceive with our five senses. "Surface" culture includes such things as food, fashions, language, gestures, games, art, music, holidays, and some customs. For example, when someone speaks with a strong accent (compared to yours), you know immediately he is from a different culture.

Below the waterline you'll find the more stable and significant features of "deep culture." Most of these features are invisible to tourists and recent immigrants. Deep culture consists of the shared beliefs, attitudes, norms, rules, opinions, expectations, and taboos of a group of people. For natives, these deep-culture features are usually taken for granted until someone disobeys them. Here's a simple example. When you arrive at a ticket line, what do you do? If you're from mainstream North American culture, you automatically go to the end of the line. No sign is needed because everyone knows that's what you're supposed to do. You probably don't even think about it unless someone cuts in front of you. When someone defies a cultural rule, others get upset. Cultural programs help a group or society run smoothly by keeping people in line (literally and figuratively).

Toto, I have a feeling we're not in Kansas anymore.

Dorothy, in The Wizard of Oz

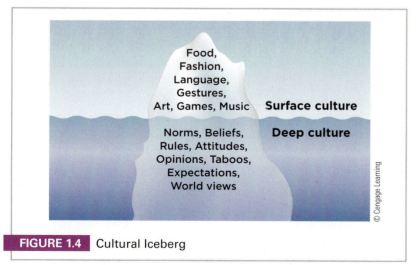

FIGURE 1.4   Cultural Iceberg

Culture, then, is the collection of surface- and deep-level customs and beliefs that get passed on from generation to generation. Each culture provides "approved" choices at significant, and even insignificant, forks in the road. Culture tells us, "This choice is normal and that one is strange." Or, "This choice is right and that one is wrong." Or, "This choice is good and that choice is bad." At each fork in the road, our inner programs give us a nudge in the culturally approved direction.

To put it succinctly, "Culture is the way we do things around here."

THE SURFACE CULTURE OF HIGHER EDUCATION

Because college is a unique culture, expect some challenges as you adapt. But fear not . . . you will adapt and very soon feel comfortable. Most differences in surface culture will be pretty obvious. They include factors such as class sizes; appropriate dress; amount of homework assigned; students' races, ages, religions; use of drugs and alcohol; holidays observed; courses offered; and methods of teaching. Like all cultures, higher education has its own language, so you'll probably hear words that sound foreign to you. Suppose your instructor announces, "The directions for the assignment are posted in the course syllabus on Moodle." These directions make little sense if you don't know the lingo. But it's not really that complicated. Here's what the natives of college culture know:

Schools, like ethnic groups, have their own cultures: languages, ways of doing things, values, attitudes toward time, standards of appropriate behavior, and so on. As participants in schools, students are expected to adopt, share, and exhibit these cultural patterns. If they do not or cannot, they are likely to be censured and made to feel uncomfortable in a variety of ways.

Jean Moule, *Cultural Competence*

- A **syllabus** is a document that most instructors provide at the first class session. It contains essential information about the course such as learning objectives, homework assignments, course rules, and how the course grade is determined. If you recognized the term "syllabus" from the Smart-Start Guide, congratulations. You're already learning to speak "college."

- **Moodle** is a computer software program that allows colleges to offer class content on the Internet. (Similar programs are Blackboard and Desire2Learn.) If your instructor doesn't provide directions for accessing course information posted on the Internet, contact the folks in your campus computer lab for help.

Keep reminding yourself that entering college is like entering another country. If you hear words and terms you don't understand, be sure to ask what they mean. It won't be long before you'll be talking like a native. Now let's take a look at a feature of cultures that is less obvious than unfamiliar words.

ONE DOZEN COLLEGE CUSTOMS

Higher education, like all cultures, has customs. These are the things the natives of higher education expect you to know and do. A dozen of these customs are explained below. Heeding them will smooth your path through college, keep you out of dead ends, and speed you on to graduation.

1. **Read your college catalogue.** Catalogues are usually available in the registrar's or counseling office. Many colleges also post a copy on their website. A catalogue contains most of the factual information you'll need to plot a successful journey through higher education. It explains how your college applies many of the customs discussed in this section. So, keep a college catalogue

on hand and refer to it often. By the way, if a requirement in the catalogue changes after you enroll at a college, usually you are bound by only the rules that existed when you first entered. So hold on to your past catalogues.

2. **Create a long-term educational plan.** This plan lists all of the courses you'll take from now until graduation. It assures that you *do* take all required courses and *don't* take any unrequired courses (unless you want to). Colleges provide someone to help you create an educational plan. This person could be an advisor, a counselor, or even an instructor (especially if you have chosen a major—see 5. below). Find out who this person is and make an appointment. It's never too early to map out your straightest route to graduation. Like most plans, it can always be revised.

3. **Complete general education requirements.** Look in your college cata- logue for a list of general education courses. Almost all colleges and universi- ties require students to complete a minimum number of credits in general education. Your institution may call them something else, such as *core require- ments, core curriculum,* or *general curriculum.* Regardless of their name, the purpose of general education requirements is to expose you to a number of broad areas of study—for example, natural sciences, communication, technol- ogy, math, languages, humanities, and social and behavioral science. Typically, you'll need to complete a certain number of credits in each area. Regardless of how many credits you earn, you can't earn a degree until you've completed all general education requirements. That's why your long-term educational plan (2. above) will always include the general education courses you intend to take.

4. **Complete prerequisites.** A prerequisite is a course that must be success- fully completed before taking a more advanced course. For example, colleges usually require passing algebra before taking calculus. Before you register for courses each semester, check each course description in your college cata- logue. Any prerequisites will be included in the course description. Confirm you have completed all prerequisites before registering for a course.

5. **Choose a major.** You'll usually choose a major area of study in your first or second year. Examples of majors include nursing, English, mechanical engineering, economics and commercial art. You'll take many courses in your major, supplemented by general education and elective courses. (An elective is a course you don't have to take but want to.) Having a career goal makes choosing your major easier. If undecided about a career, visit your campus career center. There you'll get help identifying careers that fit your interests, talents, and personality. All majors and their required courses are listed in your college catalogue. Until you've entered a major, you're wise to concentrate on completing your general education requirements.

6. **Meet with your instructors during their office hours.** Most college instructors have regular office hours. These times are usually included in the course syllabus and may also be posted on the instructor's office door. You can make an appointment before or after class, or you can call the instructor's office. Be sure to show up on time (or call beforehand to

> What we call customs rest on top and are most apparent. Deepest and least apparent are the cultural values that give meaning and direction to life. Values influence people's perceptions of needs and their choice between perceived alternative courses of action.
>
> Benjamin Paul, anthropologist

reschedule). Arrive with a goal. Maybe you'd like your instructor to clarify a comment she wrote on your English composition. Or you'd like suggestions for how to better prepare for your next math test. Another important reason to meet with your instructors is to establish a friendly relationship and make yourself more than just a name on a course roster. Building such relationships will go a long way to help if you ever need special assistance.

7. **Know the importance of your grade point average (GPA).** Your GPA is the average grade for all of the courses you have taken in college. At most colleges, GPAs range from 0.0 ("F") to 4.0 ("A"). Your GPA affects your future in many ways. At most colleges a minimum GPA (often 2.0, a "C") is required to graduate, regardless of how many credits you have accumulated. Students who fall below the minimum GPA may be placed on probation and are usually ineligible for financial aid and cannot play intercollegiate sports. Students with very low GPAs are in danger of academic dismissal. Academic honors (such as the Dean's List) and some scholarships are based on your GPA. Finally, potential employers may look at GPAs to determine if prospective employees have achieved success in college.

8. **Know how to compute your grade point average (GPA).** At most colleges, GPAs are printed on a student's transcript, which is a list of courses completed (with the grades earned). You can get a copy of your transcript from the registrar's office. Transcripts are usually free or available for a nominal charge. You can compute your own grade point average by using the formula in the following box. Or you can do it online at back2college.com/gpa.htm.

Formula for Computing Your Grade Point Average (GPA)

$$\frac{(G1 \times C1) + (G2 \times C2) + (G3 \times C3) + (G4 \times C4) + \cdots (Gn + Cn)}{\text{Total \# of Credits Attempted}}$$

In this formula, G is the grade in a course and C is number of credits for a course. For example, suppose you had the following grades:

"A" in Math 110 (4 Credits)	G1 ("A") = 4.0
"B" in English 101 (3 Credits)	G2 ("B") = 3.0
"C" in Sociology 101 (3 Credits)	G3 ("C") = 2.0
"D" in Music 104 (2 Credits)	G4 ("D") = 1.0
"F" in Physical Education 109 (1 Credit)	G5 ("F") = 0.0

Here's how to figure the GPA from the grades above:

$$\frac{(4.0 \times 4) + (3.0 \times 3) + (2.0 \times 3) + (1.0 \times 2) + (0.0 \times 1)}{4 + 3 + 3 + 2 + 1} = \frac{16 + 9 + 6 + 2 + 0}{13} = 2.54$$

At most colleges, credits in developmental (basic skills) courses do not count toward graduation, so they may or may not be used by your college for calculating a GPA. For example, if you were taking three courses and one was developmental, your GPA would be determined by the grades you received in just the two non-developmental courses. To check your school's policy about this issue, read your college catalog or ask a counselor or advisor.

9. **If you stop attending a class, withdraw officially.** Students are enrolled in a course until they're *officially* withdrawn. Do not assume that someone else will withdraw you from a course if you stop attending. A student who stops attending is still on the class roster at semester's end when grades are assigned, and the instructor will very likely give the non-attending student an "F." That failing grade is now a permanent part of the student's record, lowering his or her GPA. If you decide—for whatever reason—to stop attending a class, go directly to the registrar's office and officially withdraw. Make certain that you withdraw before your college's deadline. This date is often about halfway through a course.

10. **Talk to your instructor before withdrawing.** If sure you're going to fail a course, withdraw to protect your GPA. But don't withdraw without speaking to your instructor first. Sometimes students think they are doing far worse than they really are. Discuss with your instructor what you need to do to pass the course and make a step-by-step plan. Be sure to discuss your plans with your advisor as well. He or she might have insights about what will be best for your general education or major requirements. If you discover that failing is inevitable, withdraw officially.

11. **Know your lifetime eligibility for financial aid.** Financial aid sources often restrict the total amount of money you can receive. Pell Grants, for example, limit students to a lifetime maximum of six times their yearly award. If your yearly award is $3,000, then the maximum Pell money you can receive in your lifetime is $18,000 (6 × $3,000). This means, be careful about failing and/or dropping too many classes. Doing so eats up your award but doesn't move you toward completing your degree. After your financial aid runs out, you're on your own to pay for college—even if you have many more courses to pass in order to graduate. Check on your lifetime eligibility at your college's financial aid office.

12. **Keep a file of important documents.** Forms get lost in large organizations such as colleges and universities. Save everything that may affect your future. These include each course syllabus, completed tests and assignments, approved registration forms, scholarship applications, scholarship award notices, transcripts, and paid bills. If you're exempted from a college requirement or course prerequisite, get it in writing and add the document to your files. A year later when a college official says to you, "Sorry, but you can't do that," it's a great feeling to reach into your file, pull out a signed approval letter, and—ta da!—plop it on his desk.

WRITE A GREAT LIFE

One of the best things about the culture of higher education is that it offers the perfect opportunity to design a life worth living. A time-tested tool for this purpose is a journal, a written record of your thoughts and feelings, hopes and dreams, life lessons and next steps. Journal writing is a way to explore your life in depth and discover your best "self." This self-awareness will enable you to develop the skills needed for success in college and beyond.

Many people who keep journals do what is called "free writing." They simply write whatever thoughts come to mind. This approach can be extremely valuable for exploring issues present in one's mind at any given moment.

In *On Course*, however, you'll write a guided journal. This approach is like going on a journey with an experienced guide. Your guide takes you places and shows you sights you might never have discovered on your own.

Before writing each journal entry, you'll read an article about proven success strategies. Then you'll apply the strategies to your own life by completing the guided journal entry that follows the article. Here are five guidelines for creating a meaningful journal:

- **Copy the directions for each step into your journal (just the bold print):** When you find your journal in a drawer or computer file 20 years from now, having the directions in your journal will help you make sense of what you've written. Underline or bold the directions to distinguish them from your answers.

- **Be spontaneous:** Write whatever comes to mind in response to the directions. Imagine pouring liquid thoughts into your journal without pausing to edit or rewrite. Unlike public writings, such as an English composition or a history research paper, your journal is a private document written primarily for your own benefit.

- **Be honest:** As you write, tell yourself the absolute truth; honesty leads to your most significant discoveries about yourself and your success.

- **Be creative:** Add favorite quotations, sayings, and poems. Use color, drawings, clip art, and photographs. Express your best creative "self."

- **Dive deep:** When you think you have exhausted a topic, write more. Your most valuable thoughts will often take the longest to surface. So, most of all—DIVE DEEP!

Whether you hand-write your journal or compose it on a computer, I urge you to keep all of your journal entries together in one book or file. If you do, one day many years from now, you'll have the extraordinary pleasure of reading this autobiography of your growing wisdom about creating success in college and in life.

Let me explain why the guided journals are worth your best effort. There is a huge gulf between knowledge and achievement. Reading about the success strategies will give you the knowledge to be successful. But applying the strategies to your life—as you will do in your journal—will *make* you successful. Sure, it would be easier to simply read about the strategies. But that would be like reading about exercising and wondering why you aren't getting in shape. If

> Journal work is an excellent approach to uncovering hidden truths about ourselves.
>
> Marsha Sinetar

> I write because I don't know what I think until I read what I say.
>
> Flannery O'Connor

you're serious about creating success in college, I urge you to dive deep in every journal you write. In the very near future, you'll be very glad you did.

JOURNAL ENTRY / **1**

In this activity, you'll explore various aspects of surface culture and customs you have experienced in school.

Remember: The five suggestions for creating a meaningful journal appear earlier in this section. Please review these suggestions before writing. Especially remember to copy the directions for each step (just the bold print) into your journal before writing.... and then DIVE DEEP!

① **Contrast the surface culture of your most recent educational experience (e.g., high school, another college or university, a trade school) with that of your current school.** From the following list, choose *two* or more surface-level features where they differ. Then, in a separate paragraph for each feature, explain how the two are different. Explain the advantages and/or disadvantages you see in your present higher education culture as compared with your previous educational culture(s).

Number of students in a class	Age of students
Race or ethnicity of students	Economic class of students
Courses offered	Amount of homework
Popular out-of-school activities	Teachers' treatment of students
Alcohol	Academic preparation of educators
In-groups	Religions
Clothes	Food
Languages spoken	Dialects spoken
Sports	Amount of writing assigned
Amount of reading assigned	Drugs
Architecture of buildings	Favorite music
Holidays observed	Out-groups
Attendance policy	Methods of teaching
Involvement of parents	Classrooms

Here's how your journal entry might begin if you chose "Age of students" and "Teachers' treatment of students":

I graduated from high school last year and the ages of students there ranged from about 14 to 18 years old. Here in college the ages of students range from about 17 or 18 to 50 or even older. In my math class this semester, I have a mother and daughter who are taking the class together. Overall, students here in college seem to average about 10 years older than students in high school. A couple of the older ▶

M y journal from this course is the most valuable possession I own. I will cherish it always.

Joseph Haskins, student

students that I've talked with went to college before and dropped out. These returning students seem to be more highly motivated and they take their schoolwork more seriously than the younger students. For example, they hardly ever miss a class and they always turn in their homework. Maybe what I should do is. . . .

2 **Explore the one college custom described in the article above with which you feel most uncomfortable.** Address some or all of all of the following questions: What is the cause of your discomfort? How big a problem do you think this custom will be for you? What additional information do you want to learn about this custom? Where can you find that information? Who could help you feel more comfortable? How do you think other students in your class feel about this custom? For example, if you chose to examine "Choose a major," your journal entry might begin like this:

> I'm a little uncomfortable about choosing a major. The truth is I have no idea what career I want to pursue. I just know I have to make a change. I've been out of high school for 10 years and I've been working construction. I sure don't want to do that for the rest of my life. The work is physically demanding, and it's hard on some of the older guys. I don't want to be 60 years old and having to go up and down a ladder all day. So I know what I don't want, but not what I do want. I didn't really have any favorite subjects when I was in high school. I did okay academically, but mostly I enjoyed playing sports. A guy in one of my classes says he wants to be a doctor. His father is a doctor, so he has a really good idea what a doctor's life is like. My father sells real estate, but I don't want to do that. He's never home in the evenings or on weekends, so I didn't see him much when I was growing up. When I have a family, I want to be around to see my kids grow up. I hope I don't have to choose a major too soon. If I do, I'll probably wind up changing it a couple of times. I guess that wouldn't be so bad except I heard that by switching I could lose some credits and that could make me take longer to graduate. To pick a good major for me, what I need to find out is . . . .

The heart and soul of school culture is what people believe, the assumptions they make about how school works.

Thomas Sergiovanni

Understanding the Expectations of College and University Educators

FOCUS QUESTIONS / What is the deep culture of higher education? How can this knowledge help you get the most value from your college or university experience?

Having explored elements of the *surface* culture of higher education, you may now be now wondering, "What should I know about the *deep* culture of colleges and universities?" Great question! To get authoritative answers, I put that question to nearly 2,000 educators in an online survey.

Well, not exactly *that* question. What I actually asked was, "What are your pet peeves about student behaviors and/or attitudes?" That's because—while we may not be fully aware of our deep cultural beliefs—we're well aware of what annoys us (such as people butting in line in front of us). And what annoys us is often a window into our cultural beliefs, into our expectations of how others should think and behave.

What follows are some—but certainly not all—of the important cultural beliefs in higher education. Said another way, these are the expectations of many of the educators you will encounter on your campus. These expectations reveal what they value and, therefore, what they want you to do. Following each of the eight cultural beliefs below are related taboos—what educators said annoys them and, therefore, what they *don't* want you to do. Let these insights guide your choices in college and you'll increase your chances of success many fold. With these insights as a foundation, the rest of *On Course* will show you how.

EIGHT KEY EXPECTATIONS

1. **Educators expect students to be responsible for their education.**
   As such, they expect students to be mature and accountable for the choices they make. Here are some pet peeves that educators expressed about students who lack personal responsibility:

   - Blaming poor performance on instructors, or the book, or the time a class meets…or any number of other reasons other than themselves.

   - Slacking off, not doing all of the assigned work, and then expecting the instructor to give them second/third/fourth chances.

   - Returning to class after an absence and thinking "I wasn't here last class" is a perfectly valid excuse for being unprepared.

   - Emailing to explain an absence, then asking what they missed, when there is a syllabus and a website they can refer to in case they are absent.

   - Believing whatever is going wrong is not their fault, and they have nothing to do with it.

   - Whining rather than addressing the concern they are whining about.

2. **Educators expect students to be highly motivated to succeed.** As such, they expect students to make college an important priority in their lives, and, when necessary, to sacrifice other pursuits to complete their

Students are often shocked by the need to take on personal responsibility for so many things: time management, decision-making, problem solving, completing assignments, etc. It's time to grow up a bit and learn some adult responsibilities. Some are ready for it and embrace it, others are not.

Steve Schommer
San Diego City College, CA

academic work. Here are some pet peeves that educators expressed about students who lack self-motivation:

- Expecting instructors to motivate them.
- Having an apathetic, what-does-it-matter attitude in their courses.
- Not caring that they are failing, or, seeming to think that they will always be able to make up work, rewrite things, or re-submit things to get better grades. In other words, if they're failing, they still think they can pass the class. This is known as "magical thinking."
- Expressing that everything is boring; nothing interests them.
- Lacking any interest in making improvements, even when provided extensive feedback and support.
- Assuming that it's the professor's job to make class "interesting." Instructors SHOULD take responsibility for creating engaging classroom experiences and rich content. I work on that every day, every semester. But at the end of the day, we can't do your homework for you. We can't make the class meaningful *for* you.
- Not completing reading assignments because "it's not interesting."

3. **Educators expect students to attend classes regularly and complete all assignments to the best of their ability.** As such, they expect students to apply effective organizational skills so they can complete their work without supervision or handholding. Here are some pet peeves that educators expressed about students with poor self-management skills:

- Falling way behind in their assignments, coming to class unprepared, and expecting to get good grades with little effort.
- Thinking they can do whatever they want because they paid for the class.
- Believing things like, "If this reading is too difficult, then I shouldn't be required to read it," or "If I have something else to do during class time and I don't show up, then the teacher should catch me up on what I missed."
- Constantly being late, not coming to class, or not doing assignments.
- Acting as if they are entitled to pass a course regardless of how little work they do or how poorly it is done.
- Missing class and then coming to my office and asking me to tell them everything they missed.
- Thinking that if they just show up and sit there (and maybe stay awake), they will get credit for seat time, but they don't have to participate or do any work.

4. **Educators expect students to collaborate with peers and make use of available help to achieve academic success.** As such, they expect students to work well with other students and seek assistance from

---

My successful students are self-motivated and driven to earn a college degree.

Gerald Headd
Cuyahoga Community College, OH

The amount of reading and number of assignments a student needs to do in college is much greater than in high school. Students need to study 2-3 hours for each class session. Instructors expect students to read, save and consult the course syllabus for deadlines and tests! The first tests are often wake-up calls because they usually cover large amounts of material.

Lea Beth Lewis
California State University—Fullerton

instructors and campus support services such as tutoring, counseling, and advising. Here are some pet peeves that educators expressed about students who lack interdependence:

- Saying, "I need to do this all on my own." I tell them, no one got through school "on their own." Everyone needs help to get through the day!
- Not utilizing the college resources that are all but handed to them on a silver platter.
- Struggling with something, either subject matter or technology, and not asking for help as soon as the struggle begins.
- Not connecting with other students to study.
- Failing to ask questions when they are confused about an assignment, and not saying anything until it's too late.
- Claiming they can't learn anything by working in groups and that I need to tell them what it is they need to know. In other words, if I'm not lecturing, nothing worth learning is happening.
- Waiting until right before a course ends, panicking, and then descending on tutors in the learning center, expecting that someone there will do their work for them.

5. **Educators expect students to change when what they are doing is not working.** As such, they expect students to realize when they are off course, figure out how they got there, and try something new and more effective to get back on course. Here are some pet peeves that educators expressed about students who lack self-awareness:

- Thinking that what worked in high school will automatically work in college.
- Developing bad new habits like partying, drinking, skipping classes, doing sloppy work and making other mistakes that come with the newfound freedom of college. They are often unaware of how these habits are hurting them until it's too late.
- Being unable to see different choices that would be more effective or unwilling to make changes when they do see that something is not working.
- Not realizing that negative thoughts about their academic abilities act as anchors holding them back.
- Focusing on their weaknesses rather than developing new strengths.
- Ignoring low test scores or feedback on assignments and then asking, "How am I doing?"
- Repeating behaviors over and over even though they are not working.

6. **Educators expect students to demonstrate a passion for learning.** As such, educators expect students to be intellectually curious, thus

If students come to me voluntarily and ask for support, usually they succeed. These students might struggle a bit but they accept the fact that we all need help from time to time.

Stephanie Kroon
State University of New York – Ulster

Struggling students don't recognize when they are behind or not doing well until it is too late to change.

Peter Shull
Pennsylvania State University

pursuing knowledge rather than grades. Here are some pet peeves that educators expressed about students who aren't enthusiastic lifelong learners:

- Being unaware of what "learning" is and how to go about doing it on purpose. Students expect to walk into the classroom, flip open the top of their heads, and have the teacher pour in the necessary knowledge.
- Believing that everyone is entitled to their own opinion and everyone's opinion is different, so there is no reason/basis to form an opinion or care about having one.
- Not appreciating the advantages of getting an education. They take their financial aid for granted, waste money, and abuse the system!
- Cheating.
- Making grades their primary reason for attending a class rather than a genuine interest in learning, sometimes even in their major field. This attitude is often revealed by the famous and annoying question, "What do I need to do to pass this class?"
- Expecting to be spoon fed and thinking they have no role in their own learning.
- Not buying and/or reading their textbooks, thinking the instructors will tell them everything they need to know.

7. **Educators expect students to manage their emotions, as well as the emotions of others, in the service of their goals.** As such, educators expect students to experience normal human emotions but resist impulsive or disrespectful choices that will sabotage their success or the success of others. Here are some pet peeves that educators expressed about students who lack emotional intelligence:

- Letting fear guide their decisions; not attempting the work because they are afraid of failing.
- Being judgmental and hurtful to other students on purpose, especially those who are different from them.
- Communicating inappropriately with instructors. For example, I hate when a message from a student begins "Hey . . . ." Or they get bad-tempered when I don't reply to a phone message or email immediately.
- Lacking perseverance and grit when the going gets tough.
- Choosing short-term gratification, causing them to wait until the last moment to do homework or study for a test.
- Never speaking during a class discussion for fear of being criticized or judged.

When my successful students are in class, they are fully engaged in the classroom activities. They expect to learn new things, they don't expect learning to be easy or fast, and they are eager to learn.

Adrienne Peek
Modesto Junior College

Some of my students don't attempt the work simply because they are afraid of failing. Successful students who are afraid do the work anyway.

Kimberly Manner
West Los Angeles College

- Being openly rude and indifferent to college staff, teachers, administrators and fellow students; acting as if they are still on the streets in their home neighborhood; in short, behaving like middle-school kids.

8. **Educators expect students to have realistic self-confidence about themselves and their ability to succeed in college.** As such, educators expect students to be self-assured without being arrogant. Here are some pet peeves that educators expressed about students who believe in themselves too little or too much.

- Pretending they "know it all." They don't, but are afraid to let others know their personal insecurities.

A Dozen Differences Between High School and College Culture

High School Culture Assumes Immaturity	College Culture Assumes Maturity
Students attend high school because they are required to by their parents or by law.	Students usually attend college because of a personal choice.
Teachers offer students many reminders to complete assignments.	Instructors give assignments and expect students to hand them in on time, done well, and without reminders.
Teachers spend time disciplining students who create disruptions.	Instructors do not tolerate disruptive students and may bar them from the class.
Students typically spend 30 or more hours in class each week, and teachers cover the majority of course content during class.	Students typically spend 15 or fewer hours in class each week, and instructors expect students to learn the majority of course content outside of class. This is why doing all homework is so important.
Teachers and parents manage much of the students' time.	Students manage their own time.
Teachers are often pressured to "teach to the test" so that students can pass standardized assessments.	Instructors have more "academic freedom" in what and how they teach.
Academic standards are not always high, and savvy students often get good grades with little effort.	Academic standards are usually high, and all students need to figure out how to meet these challenging standards.
Family and friends provide students with advice or solutions for academic, social, and other problems.	Students solve their own problems or seek help at one of many support services provided by the college.
Students' choice of courses is relatively limited by graduation requirements.	Students have greater freedom to choose the courses they take and drop those they don't want to complete.
Teachers and parents minimize distractions that might otherwise hinder students' success.	Students must deal with distractions on their own, including parties, television, video games, Internet surfing, dating, sports, Facebook, drinking, drugs, road trips, and hanging out.
Educational costs are paid for by taxpayers, including textbooks.	Educational costs, including textbooks, are paid for by the student, the student's family, and/or by financial aid for which the student applies and, in some cases, must pay back.
Students have few choices.	Students have many choices.

- Quitting when they encounter the slightest hint that college may be more than they can handle. Some students are too brittle, taking every setback as a reason to give up.

- Being unwilling to struggle with learning, as if it means they are stupid. Many students "got it" so easily in high school that they don't understand what it's like to have to work to learn something.

- Having little belief in themselves, so any disappointment becomes a self-fulfilling prophesy and a cause for dropping out of school.

- Thinking that because they did well in high school, their college instructors must be wrong to offer any criticisms.

- Continuously talking about how they will never succeed in college.

- Talking big, but giving up easily.

Successful students have the ability to overcome challenge and change by seeking out strategies to help them stay on the learning path and reach their own goals. This involves the willingness to fail and make mistakes and get back up and try something else.

Janeth Franklin
Glendale Community
College

When you entered higher education, you entered into a partnership with college educators. It may be that your only goal in this partnership is to get passing grades and earn a degree. I must admit, that was my only goal when I went to college. Years later I realized that I set my sights woefully low. The educators you have partnered with—because of their culture—want much more for you than just passing grades and a degree (though they certainly want that, too).

The hope of most educators is that you become an effective learner. They want you to develop intellectual skills such as critical thinking, analytical reasoning, and communication skills. And many—including, most likely, your instructor in this course—want you to develop personal skills mentioned in their expectations above: skills such as personal responsibility, self-motivation, self-management, self-awareness, lifelong learning, emotional intelligence, and realistic confidence in yourself. Why? Because personal skills like these shape your choices and empower you to create a rich, personally fulfilling life.

So, once again, welcome to the culture of higher education. If you are open to all it has to offer, you're going to learn more on this journey than you ever thought possible.

JOURNAL ENTRY / 2

In this activity, you will explore aspects of the deep culture of higher education.

1. Which of the eight expectations of college educators (explained above) is most different from the culture of your most recent educational experience (e.g., high school, another college or university, a trade school)? Explain the differences, using personal examples wherever possible.

2. Which of the eight expectations of college educators do you think is the most important one for you to fulfill, and why? Explore how difficult you think it will be for you to fulfill this expectation, and why. Throughout your response, use personal examples wherever possible.

Understanding Yourself

FOCUS QUESTIONS What does "success" mean to you? What are the essential skills for creating that success? In which essential skills are you strong? In which would you benefit from improvement?

Have you given much thought to your future? Do you have a clear idea about what you want to have in five years, 10 years, 20 years? How about what you want to be doing? And what about the kind of person you will be? In other words, how will you know if you are a success?

WHAT DOES SUCCESS MEAN TO YOU?

I've asked many college graduates, "What did success mean to you when you were an undergraduate?" Here are some typical answers:

> When I was in college, success to me was . . .

> . . . getting all As and Bs.
> . . . making two free throws to win the conference basketball tournament.
> . . . having a great social life.
> . . . parenting two great kids and still making the Dean's List.
> . . . being the first person in my family to earn a college degree.

Notice that each response emphasizes *outer success:* high grades, sports victories, popularity, and college degrees. These successes are public, visible achievements that allow the world to assess one's abilities and worth.

I've also asked college graduates, "If you could repeat your college years, what would you do differently?" Here are some typical answers:

> If I had a chance to do college over, I would . . .

> . . . focus on learning instead of just getting good grades.
> . . . major in engineering, the career I had a passion for.
> . . . constantly ask myself how I could use what I was learning to enhance my life and the lives of the people I love.
> . . . discover my personal values.
> . . . learn more about the world I live in and more about myself . . . especially more about myself!

Notice that the focus some years after graduation often centers on *inner success:* enjoying learning, following personal interests, focusing on personal values, and creating more fulfilling lives. These successes are private, invisible victories that offer a deep sense of personal contentment.

Only with hindsight do most college graduates realize that, to be completely satisfying, success must occur both in the visible world and in the invisible spaces within our minds and hearts. This book, then, is about how to achieve both outer and inner success in college and in life.

To that end, I suggest the following simple definition of success for your consideration: **Success is staying on course to your desired outcomes and**

> Start with the end in mind.
>
> Stephen R. Covey

> College is a place where a student ought to learn not so much how to make a living, but how to live.
>
> Dr. William A. Nolen

experiences. Maybe you'd like to earn a college degree or start your own business or marry and have six kids. Maybe you'd like to experience joy or confidence or love. Maybe you'd like to be seen by others as a "self-made" person who achieved success by your efforts alone. Maybe you'd prefer to experience being a valued member of a group that is loyal and committed to one another. Regardless of what your desired outcomes and experiences may be, following the time-tested strategies presented in *On Course* will help you achieve them.

As a college instructor, I've seen thousands of students arrive on campus with dreams, then struggle, fail, and fade away. I've seen thousands more come to college with dreams, pass their courses, and graduate, having done little more than cram their brains with information that's promptly forgotten after the final exam. They've earned degrees, but in more important ways they have remained unchanged.

Our primary responsibility in life, I suggest, is to realize the incredible potential with which each of us is born. All of our experiences, especially those during college, can contribute to the creation of our best selves.

On Course shows how to use your college experience as a laboratory experiment. In this laboratory, you'll learn and apply proven strategies that help you create success—academically, personally, and professionally. I'm not saying it'll be easy, but you're about to learn strategies that have made a difference in the lives of many thousands of students before you. So get ready to change the outcomes of your life and the quality of your experiences along the way! Get ready to create success as *you* define it.

To begin, consider a curious puzzle: Two students enter a college class on the first day of the semester. Both appear to have similar intelligence, backgrounds, talents, interests and abilities. The weeks slide by, and the semester ends. Surprisingly, one student soars and the other sinks. One fulfills his potential; the other falls short. Why do students with similar aptitudes perform so differently? More important, which of these students is you?

Teachers observe this puzzle in every class. I bet you've seen it, too, not only in school, but wherever people gather. Some people have a knack for achievement. Others wander about confused and disappointed, unable to create the success they claim they want. Clearly, having potential does not guarantee success.

What, then, are the essential ingredients of success?

INGREDIENTS OF SUCCESS

For answers, let's revisit those two students mentioned above and observe them more closely. For example, let's see what happens when they receive the same low grade on an essay in their English class. The first student goes immediately to the registrar's office and drops the class. The second student goes immediately to the tutoring center and asks for help. The first student's choice eliminates any chance of learning the skills needed to succeed in the course. The second student's choice keeps the possibility of success alive. By seeking tutoring, she improves her chances of learning the writing skills she needs to pass the course and succeed in college.

So, one important ingredient of success is developing the skills necessary to accomplish a particular task. To be successful in a writing class, you need

There is only one success—to be able to spend your life in your own way.

Christopher Morely

The deepest personal defeat suffered by human beings is constituted by the difference between what one was capable of becoming and what one has in fact become.

Ashley Montagu

good writing skills. To be successful in a math class, you need good math skills. To be successful in every college class, you need good learning skills. Skills like these are often called "hard" skills. There are thousands of hard skills you might learn. Accountants need the hard skill of doing taxes. Nurses need the hard skill of taking people's blood pressure. Filmmakers need the hard skill of using editing software. Hard skills are observable, measurable, and learnable. Much of what you go to college for is to learn hard skills.

Hold on, though. There's something else going on with our two students. Remember, we said they both appear to have similar intelligence, backgrounds, talents, interests and abilities. So why did they make such different choices when confronted by a low grade? Why did one student quit and the other go for tutoring? To find an answer, we need to ponder their inner strengths.

What inner strengths would someone need to seek help rather than drop a course? Inner strengths that come to my mind include *persistence, self-confidence*, and *motivation* (among others). Like writing and math, these three inner qualities are skills, too, but of a different kind. They are often called "soft" skills. Unlike hard skills, soft skills are invisible and difficult to measure. Like hard skills, though, soft skills are learnable.

Both of these skill sets—hard and soft—influence the hundreds, perhaps thousands, of choices we make every day. Since even a few bad choices can get us far off course, it's wise to improve our choice-making ability. In *On Course*, you'll learn how to strengthen your hard skills and your soft skills. Both skill sets, as you will see, are essential for making wise choices and achieving great success in higher education . . . and beyond.

In everyday life, we usually learn soft and hard skills together. For example, learning a hard skill (such as touch typing on a computer keyboard) can simultaneously teach us a soft skill (such as patience). These two skill sets are woven into the fabric of our lives. However, for ease of learning, in this course we'll look at them separately. That way, you can focus on and develop one skill at a time. The first nine chapters in *On Course* will help you develop *soft* skills. The next section—"A Toolbox for Active Learners"—will help you develop *hard* skills, especially study skills that will make you a more effective learner. Applying them together will empower you to thrive in the culture of higher education.

ASSESS YOUR SOFT SKILLS FOR COLLEGE SUCCESS

In preparation for exploring the choices of successful students, take a few minutes to complete the self-assessment questionnaire on the next two pages. Your scores will identify soft skills that support your success. They'll also point out soft skills you may want to strengthen to achieve more of your potential in college and in life. Later on, you'll have an opportunity to repeat this self-assessment and compare your two scores. I think you're going to be pleasantly surprised!

This self-assessment is not a test. There are no right or wrong answers. The questions simply give you an opportunity to create an accurate and current self-portrait. Be absolutely honest and have fun with this activity, for it's an important step on a journey to a richer, more personally fulfilling life.

On average, about a third of a person's strengths are innate, built into his or her genetically based temperament, talents, mood, and personality. The other two-thirds are developed over time. You get them by growing them . . . . finding out how to grow these strengths inside you could be the most important thing you ever learn.

Rick Hanson, neuropsychologist

To live is to choose. But to choose well, you must know who you are and what you stand for, where you want to go and why you want to get there.

Kofi Annan, former Secretary-General of the United Nations

Self-Assessment

Read the following statements and score each one according to how true or false you believe it is about you. To get an accurate picture of yourself, consider what IS true about you (not what you want to be true). Remember, there are no right or wrong answers. Assign each statement a number from 0 to 10, as follows:

Totally False ◄ ⓪ ① ② ③ ④ ⑤ ⑥ ⑦ ⑧ ⑨ ⑩ ► Totally True

1. _____ I control how successful I will be.
2. _____ I'm not sure why I'm in college.
3. _____ I spend most of my time doing important things.
4. _____ When I encounter a challenging problem, I try to solve it by myself.
5. _____ When I get off course from my goals and dreams, I realize it right away.
6. _____ I'm not sure how I prefer to learn.
7. _____ I know ways to increase my happiness.
8. _____ I'll truly accept myself only after I eliminate my faults and weaknesses.
9. _____ Forces out of my control (such as poor teaching) are the cause of low grades I receive in school.
10. _____ I place great value on getting my college degree.
11. _____ I don't need to write things down because I can remember what I need to do.
12. _____ I have a network of people in my life that I can count on for help.
13. _____ If I have habits that hinder my success, I'm not sure what they are.
14. _____ When I don't like the way an instructor teaches, I know how to learn the subject anyway.
15. _____ When I get very angry, sad, or afraid, I do or say things that create a problem for me.
16. _____ When I think about performing an upcoming challenge (such as taking a test), I usually see myself doing well.
17. _____ When I have a problem, I take positive actions to find a solution.
18. _____ I don't know how to set effective short-term and long-term goals.
19. _____ I am organized.
20. _____ When I take a difficult course in school, I study alone.
21. _____ I'm aware of beliefs I have that hinder my success.
22. _____ I'm not sure how to think critically and analytically about complex topics.
23. _____ When choosing between doing an important school assignment or something really fun, I do the school assignment.
24. _____ I break promises that I make to myself or to others.
25. _____ I make poor choices that keep me from getting what I really want in life.
26. _____ I expect to do well in my college classes.
27. _____ I lack self-discipline.
28. _____ I listen carefully when other people are talking.
29. _____ I'm stuck with any habits of mine that hinder my success.
30. _____ My intelligence is something about myself that I can improve.

31. _____ I often feel bored, anxious, or depressed.
32. _____ I feel just as worthwhile as any other person.
33. _____ Forces outside of me (such as luck or other people) control how successful I will be.
34. _____ College is an important step on the way to accomplishing my goals and dreams.
35. _____ I spend most of my time doing unimportant things.
36. _____ I am aware of how to show respect to people who are different from me (race, religion, sexual orientation, age, etc.).
37. _____ I can be off course from my goals and dreams for quite a while without realizing it.
38. _____ I know how I prefer to learn.
39. _____ My happiness depends mostly on my circumstances.
40. _____ I accept myself just as I am, even with my faults and weaknesses.
41. _____ I am the cause of low grades I receive in school.
42. _____ If I lose my motivation in college, I don't know how I'll get it back.
43. _____ I have a written self-management system that helps me get important things done on time.
44. _____ I seldom interact with people who are different from me.
45. _____ I'm aware of the habits I have that hinder my success.
46. _____ If I don't like the way an instructor teaches, I'll probably do poorly in the course.
47. _____ When I'm very angry, sad, or afraid, I know how to manage my emotions so I don't do anything I'll regret later.
48. _____ When I think about performing an upcoming challenge (such as taking a test), I usually see myself doing poorly.
49. _____ When I have a problem, I complain, blame others, or make excuses.
50. _____ I know how to set effective short-term and long-term goals.
51. _____ I am disorganized.
52. _____ When I take a difficult course in school, I find a study partner or join a study group.
53. _____ I'm unaware of beliefs I have that hinder my success.
54. _____ I know how to think critically and analytically about complex topics.
55. _____ I often feel happy and fully alive.
56. _____ I keep promises that I make to myself or to others.
57. _____ When I have an important choice to make, I use a decision-making process that analyzes possible options and their likely outcomes.
58. _____ I don't expect to do well in my college classes.
59. _____ I am a self-disciplined person.
60. _____ I get distracted easily when other people are talking.
61. _____ I know how to change habits of mine that hinder my success.
62. _____ Everyone is born with a certain amount of intelligence, and there's not really much I can do to change that.
63. _____ When choosing between doing an important school assignment or something really fun, I usually do something fun.
64. _____ I feel less worthy than other people.

Transfer your scores to the scoring sheets on the next page. For each of the eight areas, total your scores in columns A and B. Then total your final scores as shown in the sample on the next page.

Self-Assessment Scoring Sheet

SAMPLE

A		B	
6. _8_		29. _3_	
14. _5_		35. _3_	
21. _6_		50. _6_	
73. _9_		56. _2_	

_28_ + 40 − _14_ = 54

SCORE #1: Accepting Personal Responsibility

A		B	
1. ___		9. ___	
17. ___		25. ___	
41. ___		33. ___	
57. ___		49. ___	

___ + 40 − ___ = ___

SCORE #2: Discovering Self-Motivation

A		B	
10. ___		2. ___	
26. ___		18. ___	
34. ___		42. ___	
50. ___		58. ___	

___ + 40 − ___ = ___

SCORE #3: Mastering Self-Management

A		B	
3. ___		11. ___	
19. ___		27. ___	
43. ___		35. ___	
59. ___		51. ___	

___ + 40 − ___ = ___

SCORE #4: Employing Interdependence

A		B	
12. ___		4. ___	
28. ___		20. ___	
36. ___		44. ___	
52. ___		60. ___	

___ + 40 − ___ = ___

SCORE #5: Gaining Self-Awareness

A		B	
5. ___		13. ___	
21. ___		29. ___	
45. ___		37. ___	
61. ___		53. ___	

___ + 40 − ___ = ___

SCORE #6: Adopting Lifelong Learning

A		B	
14. ___		6. ___	
30. ___		22. ___	
38. ___		46. ___	
54. ___		62. ___	

___ + 40 − ___ = ___

SCORE #7: Developing Emotional Intelligence

A		B	
7. ___		15. ___	
23. ___		31. ___	
47. ___		39. ___	
55. ___		63. ___	

___ + 40 − ___ = ___

SCORE #8: Believing in Myself

A		B	
16. ___		8. ___	
32. ___		24. ___	
40. ___		48. ___	
56. ___		64. ___	

___ + 40 − ___ = ___

Interpreting Your Scores

A score of . . .

0–39   Indicates an area where your choices will **seldom** keep you on course.

40–63   Indicates an area where your choices will **sometimes** keep you on course.

64–80   Indicates an area where your choices will **usually** keep you on course.

Choices of Successful Students

Successful Students . . .

▶ **accept personal responsibility,** seeing themselves as the primary cause of their outcomes and experiences.

▶ **discover self-motivation,** finding purpose in their lives by pursuing personally meaningful goals and dreams.

▶ **master self-management,** consistently planning and taking purposeful actions in pursuit of their goals and dreams.

▶ **employ interdependence,** building mutually supportive relationships that help them achieve their goals and dreams (while helping others do the same).

▶ **gain self-awareness,** consciously employing behaviors, beliefs, and attitudes that keep them on course.

▶ **adopt lifelong learning,** finding valuable lessons and wisdom in nearly every experience they have.

▶ **develop emotional intelligence,** effectively managing their emotions and the emotions of others in support of their goals and dreams.

▶ **believe in themselves,** seeing themselves as capable, lovable, and unconditionally worthy human beings.

Struggling Students . . .

▶ **see themselves as victims,** believing that what happens to them is determined primarily by external forces such as fate, luck, and powerful others.

▶ **have difficulty sustaining motivation,** often feeling depressed, frustrated, and/ or resentful about a lack of direction in their lives.

▶ **seldom identify specific actions needed to accomplish a desired outcome,** and when they do, they tend to procrastinate.

▶ **are solitary,** seldom requesting, even rejecting, offers of assistance from those who could help.

▶ **make important choices unconsciously,** being directed by self-sabotaging habits and outdated life scripts.

▶ **resist learning new ideas and skills,** viewing learning as fearful or boring rather than as mental play.

▶ **live at the mercy of strong emotions,** such as anger, sadness, anxiety, or a need for instant gratification.

▶ **doubt their competence and personal value,** feeling inadequate to create their desired outcomes and experiences.

FORKS IN THE ROAD

Why are these eight inner strengths so important? Because they shape many of the important choices we make. The road of life forks many times each day, and at every one we need to make a choice. Some of those choices are so significant they will literally change the outcomes and experiences of our lives. In college, students encounter opportunities such as work-study programs, lunch with an instructor, study groups, social events, sports teams, new friends, study-abroad programs, romantic relationships, academic majors, all-night conversations, diverse cultures, challenging viewpoints, and field trips, among many others.

Other choices involve dealing with disappointing grades, homesickness, the death of a loved one, conflicts with friends, loneliness, health problems, endless homework, anxiety, broken romances, self-doubt, lousy class schedules, lost motivation, difficult instructors, academic probation, confusing tests, excessive drinking, frustrating rules, mystifying textbooks, conflicting work and school schedules, jealous friends, drugs, test anxiety, learning disabilities, and financial difficulties, to name a few.

In other words, college is just like life. There are always opportunities and obstacles, and the choices we make at each of these forks in the road determine whether we achieve our desired outcomes and experiences. It takes a lot more than potential to excel in college or in life. And you're about to find out how to succeed in both ... despite inevitable challenges. You see, while life is generating a dizzying array of options, successful people are making one wise choice after another.

> I believe that choice—though it can be finicky, unwieldy, and demanding—is ultimately the most powerful determinant of where we go and how we get there.
>
> Sheena Iyengar

A FEW WORDS OF ENCOURAGEMENT

In this course, you'll be taking a personal journey designed to help you develop the empowering beliefs and behaviors that will help you maximize your potential and achieve the outcomes and experiences you desire. However, before we depart, let's see how you're feeling about this upcoming trip. Please choose the statement below that best describes how you feel right now:

1. I'm excited about developing the inner qualities, outer behaviors, and academic skills that have helped others achieve success in college and in life.

2. I'm feeling okay about this journey because I'll probably learn a few helpful things along the way.

3. I can't say I'm excited, but I'm willing to give it a try.

4. I'm unhappy, and I don't want to go!

In nearly every *On Course* group I've worked with, there have been some reluctant travelers. If that's you, I want to offer some personal words of encouragement. First, I can certainly understand why you might be hesitant. Frankly, I would have been a reluctant traveler on this journey when I was a first-year college student. I can tell you, though, I sure wish I'd known then what you're about to learn. Many students after completing the course have asked, "Why didn't they teach us this stuff in high school? It sure would have helped!" Even some of the most reluctant travelers have later said, "Every student should be required to take this course!"

I can't promise that you'll feel this way after finishing the course. But I can promise that if you do only the bare minimum or, worse yet, drop out, you'll never know if this course could have helped you improve your life. So, quite frankly, my goal here is to persuade you to give this course a fair chance.

Maybe you're thinking, *"I don't need this success stuff. Just give me the information and skills I need to get a good job."* If so, you're going to be pleased to discover that the soft skills you'll learn in this course are highly prized in the work world. In fact many companies pay corporate trainers huge fees to teach these same skills to their employees. Think of the advantage you'll have when you bring these skills with you to the job.

Or, perhaps you're thinking, *"I already know how to be successful. This is just a waste of my time."* I thought this, too, at one time. And I had three academic degrees from prestigious universities and a good job to back up my claim. Hadn't I already proven I could be a success? But when I opened myself to learning the skills that you'll discover in these pages, the quality of both my professional and personal life improved dramatically. I've also taught these skills to successful college educators (perhaps even your own instructor), and many of them have had the same experience I did. You see, there is success . . . and then there is SUCCESS!

Or, maybe you're thinking, *"I don't want to examine and write about myself. That's not what college should be about."* I understand this objection! When I was in college, self-examination was about the last thing on my to-do list (right after walking backwards to the North Pole in bare feet). Of course I had a "good" reason: Athletes like me didn't look inward. I labeled it "touchy feely" and dismissed self-exploration. I'm sure you have reasons for your reluctance: shyness, your cultural upbringing, or a host of other explanations that make you uncomfortable when looking within for the keys to your success. I urge you to lower your resistance and give this approach a try. You can learn now what it took me too many years to discover: **Success occurs from inside out, not outside in.** *You* are the key to your success. So, I hope you'll give this course your best effort. Most likely, it's the only college course you'll ever take where the subject matter is YOU. And, believe me, if you don't master the content of this course, every other course you take (both in college and in the University of Life) will suffer. I wish you a great journey. Let the adventure continue!

Intelligence plus character—that is the goal of true education.

Martin Luther King

The battles that count aren't the ones for gold medals. The struggles within yourself—the invisible battles inside all of us— that's where it's at.

Jesse Owens, winner of four gold medals at the 1936 Olympics

JOURNAL ENTRY   3

In this activity, you will take an inventory of your personal strengths and weaknesses as revealed by your self-assessment questionnaire.

❶ In your journal, write the eight areas of the self-assessment and record your scores for each, as follows:

_____   1. Accepting personal responsibility

_____   2. Discovering self-motivation

_____   3. Mastering self-management

_____   4. Employing interdependence

_____   5. Gaining self-awareness

_____   6. Adopting lifelong learning

_____   7. Developing emotional intelligence

_____   8. Believing in myself

Transfer your scores from the self-assessment to the appropriate lines above.

❷ Write about the areas on the self-assessment in which you had your highest scores. Explain why you think you scored higher in these areas than in others. Were there any surprises? Were there any high scores you disagreed with? If so, why? How do you feel about your higher scores? Your entry might begin, "By doing the self-assessment, I learned that I . . . ."

❸ Write about the areas on the self-assessment in which you had your lowest scores. Explain why you think you scored lower in these areas than in others. Were there any surprises? Were there any low scores you disagreed with? If so, why? How do you feel about your lower scores? Remember the saying, "If you keep doing what you've been doing, you'll keep getting what you've been getting." With this thought in mind, write about any specific changes you'd like to make in yourself during this course. Your entry might begin, "By doing the self-assessment, I also learned that I . . . ."

All glory comes from daring to begin.

Eugene F. Ware

ONE STUDENT'S STORY

JALAYNA ONAGA, *University of Hawaii-Hilo, Hawaii*

It's amazing how fast someone can go from being excited about college to flunking out. A year and a half ago, I received a letter from the University of Hawaii at Hilo informing me that I was being dismissed due to my inability to maintain a GPA of at least 2.0. I wasn't surprised because I had spent the whole semester making one bad choice after another. I hardly ever attended classes. I didn't do much homework. I didn't study for tests. And I never asked anyone for help. Mostly I just hung out with friends who told me I didn't need to go to college. But, fast-forward to today and you'll see a woman who has clear goals for her future, the motivation to reach those goals, and a plan to carry her to her dreams. However, it

▶

took a lot of learning in order for me to make such a huge change in my life.

After taking courses for a while at a community college, I got permission to re-enroll at the university. I was so nervous! I worried that I'd get dismissed again and I'd never do anything with my life. A counselor suggested that I take the University 101 course, and I'm so thankful I did. While writing the *On Course* journals, I learned so much about myself and how I can succeed. I realized that when I first enrolled at the university, I was taking nursing courses because my parents wanted me to and I couldn't get motivated. This

time I got inspired because my journals helped me look inside myself to figure out my own dreams for the future and to create a plan to reach them. For the first time, the plans I made were coming from my heart, not from someone telling me what I should do. I realized that I really love kids and *my* dream is to teach second- or third-graders. That's when I made a personal commitment to attend every class and learn as much as I could. In later journals I learned that making a schedule and writing everything down helped me get the important things done. I even learned to ask for help, and when I was absent

because my car broke down, I met with the teacher to find out what I had missed. Before tests, I found it inspiring to read over my journal because my own words reminded me of my dreams and why I should study hard to get them.

Best of all, my new choices really paid off. When the semester ended, I had three As and a B+ and I made the Dean's List. My University 101 course and the *On Course* textbook really changed me as a student and as a person. Not long ago, I was a student without a direction. Now I can envision myself in the near future teaching a class full of eager students, watching them learn and grow, just like I was able to do.

SOFT SKILLS   at Work

I think we have to appreciate that we're alive for only a limited period of time, and we'll spend most of our lives working.

Victor Kiam, Chairman, Remington Products

Applying the strategies you're going to learn in *On Course* will not only improve your results in college, it will also boost your success at work. You're about to explore dozens of proven strategies that will help you achieve your goals both in college and in your career.

This is no small matter. Career success (or lack of it) affects nearly every part of your life: family, income, self-esteem, people with whom you associate, where you live, your level of happiness,

what you learn, your energy level, your health, and maybe even the length of your life.

Some students think, "All I need for success at work is the special knowledge of my chosen career." All that nurses need, they believe, are good nursing skills. All that accountants need are good accounting skills. All that lawyers need are good legal skills. These are the hard skills we discussed earlier, the knowledge needed to perform a particular job. Hard skills include knowing where to insert a needle for an intravenous feeding drip, how to write an effective business plan, and what the current inheritance laws are. These are the skills you'll be taught in courses in your major field of study. They are essential to qualify for a job. Without them you won't even get an interview.

▶

continued **SOFT SKILLS** / **at Work**

But, most people who've been in the work world a while will tell you this: Hard skills are essential to get a job but they are often insufficient to keep it or advance. That's because nearly all employees have the hard skills necessary to do the job for which they're hired. True, some may perform these skills a little better or a little worse than others. However, one estimate suggests that only 15 percent of workers lose their jobs because they can't do the work. That's why career success is often determined by soft skills, the same strategies you'll be learning in this book. As one career specialist put it, "Having hard skills gets you hired; lacking soft skills gets you fired."

A U.S. government report confirms that soft skills are essential to job success. The Secretary of Labor asked a blue-ribbon panel of employers to identify what it takes to be successful in the employment world. This panel published a report in 1992 called the Secretary's Commission on Achieving Necessary Skills (SCANS). The report presents a set of foundation skills and workplace competencies that employers consider essential for work-world success. The report's timeless recommendations continue to be a valuable source of information for employers and employees alike. No one familiar with today's work world will find many surprises in the report, especially in the foundation skills. The report calls for employees to develop the same soft skills that employers include in job descriptions, look for in reference letters, probe for in job interviews, and assess in evaluations of their workforce.

The SCANS report identifies the following soft skills as necessary for work and career success: taking responsibility, making effective decisions, setting goals, managing time, prioritizing tasks, persevering, giving strong efforts, working well in teams, communicating effectively, having empathy, knowing how to learn, exhibiting self-control, and believing in one's own self-worth. The Conference Board of Canada published a similar report called the *Employability Skills Profile: The Critical Skills Required of the Canadian Work Force*. Both reports identify the necessity of having soft skills but don't suggest a method for developing them. *On Course* will show you how.

Learning these soft skills will help you succeed in your first career after college. And, because soft skills are portable (unlike many hard skills), you can take them with you in the likely event that you later change careers. Most career specialists say the average worker today can expect to change careers at least once during his or her lifetime. In fact, some 25 percent of workers in the United States today are in occupations that did not even exist a few decades ago. If a physical therapist decides to change careers and work for an Internet company, he needs to master a whole new set of hard skills. But the soft skills he's mastered are the same ones that will help him shine in his new career.

So, as you're learning these soft skills, keep asking yourself, "How can I use these skills to stay on course to achieving my greatest potential at work as well as in college?" Be assured that what you're about to explore can make all the difference between success and failure in your career.

Accepting Personal Responsibility

Successful Students . . .

▶ **adopt a Creator mindset,** believing that their choices create the outcomes and experiences of their lives.

▶ **master Creator language,** accepting personal responsibility for their results.

▶ **make wise decisions,** consciously designing the future they want.

Struggling Students . . .

▶ **accept a Victim mindset,** believing that external forces determine the outcomes and experiences of their lives.

▶ **use Victim language,** rejecting personal responsibility by blaming, complaining, and excusing.

▶ **make decisions carelessly,** letting the future happen by chance rather than by choice.

I accept responsibility for creating my life as I want it.

CASE STUDY IN CRITICAL THINKING   The Late Paper

Professor Freud announced in her syllabus for Psychology 101 that final term papers had to be in her hands by noon on December 18. No student, she emphasized, would pass the course without a completed term paper turned in on time. As the semester drew to a close, Kim had an "A" average in Professor Freud's psychology class, and she began researching her term paper with excitement.

Arnold, Kim's husband, felt threatened that he had only a high school diploma while his wife was getting close to her college degree. Arnold worked the evening shift at a bakery, and his coworker **Philip** began teasing that Kim would soon dump Arnold for a college guy. That's when Arnold started accusing Kim of having an affair and demanding she drop out of college. She told Arnold he was being ridiculous. In fact, she said, a young man in her history class had asked her out, but she had refused. Instead of feeling better, Arnold became even angrier. With Philip continuing to provoke him, Arnold became sure Kim was having an affair, and he began telling her every day that she was stupid and would never get a degree.

Despite the tension at home, Kim finished her psychology term paper the day before it was due. Because Arnold had hidden the car keys and Professor Freud refused to accept assignments sent by email, Kim decided to take the bus to the college and turn in her psychology paper a day early. While she was waiting for the bus, **Cindy**, one of Kim's psychology classmates, drove up and invited Kim to join her and some other students for an end-of-semester celebration. Kim told Cindy she was on her way to turn in her term paper, and Cindy promised she'd make sure Kim got it in on time. "I deserve some fun," Kim decided, and hopped into the car. The celebration went long into the night. Kim kept asking Cindy to take her home, but Cindy always replied, "Don't be such a bore. Have another drink." When Cindy finally took Kim home, it was 4:30 a.m. She sighed with relief when she found that Arnold had already fallen asleep.

When Kim woke up, it was 11:30 a.m., just 30 minutes before her term paper was due. She could make it to the college in time by car, so she shook Arnold and begged him to drive her. He just snapped, "Oh sure, you stay out all night with your college friends. Then, I'm supposed to get up on my day off and drive you all over town. Forget it." "At least give me the keys," she said, but Arnold merely rolled over and went back to sleep. Panicked, Kim called Professor Freud's office and told **Mary**, the administrative assistant, that she was having car trouble. "Don't worry," Mary assured Kim, "I'm sure Professor Freud won't care if your paper's a little late. Just be sure to have it here before she leaves at 1:00." Relieved, Kim decided not to wake Arnold again; instead, she took the bus.

At 12:15, Kim walked into Professor Freud's office with her term paper. Professor Freud said, "Sorry, Kim, you're 15 minutes late." She refused to accept Kim's term paper and gave Kim an "F" for the course.

Listed below are the characters in this story. Rank them in order of their *responsibility for Kim's failing grade in Psychology 101*. Give a different score to each character. Be prepared to explain your choices.

| Most responsible ▶ ① ② ③ ④ ⑤ ⑥ ◀ Least responsible |

____ **Professor Freud**, the instructor

____ **Kim**, the psychology student

____ **Arnold**, Kim's husband

____ **Philip**, Arnold's coworker

____ **Cindy**, Kim's classmate

____ **Mary**, the administrative assistant

DIVING DEEPER

Is there someone not mentioned in the story who may also bear responsibility for Kim's failing grade?

Adopting a Creator Mindset

FOCUS QUESTIONS What is self-responsibility? Why is it the key to creating the life you want?

When psychologist Richard Logan studied people who survived ordeals such as being imprisoned in concentration camps or lost in the frozen Arctic, he found they shared a common belief. They all saw themselves as personally responsible for creating the outcomes and experiences of their lives.

Ironically, responsibility has gotten a bad reputation. Some see it as a heavy burden they have to lug through life. Quite the contrary, personal responsibility is the foundation for creating success. Personal *response-ability* is the ability to respond wisely at each fork in the road, your choices moving you ever closer to your desired outcomes and experiences. The opposite is waiting passively for your fate to be determined by luck or powerful others. Whether your challenge is surviving an Arctic blizzard or excelling in college, accepting personal responsibility empowers you to make the most out of any situation.

I first met Deborah when she was a student in my English 101 class. Deborah wanted to be a nurse, but before she could qualify for the nursing program, she had to pass English 101. She was taking the course for the fourth time.

"Your writing shows fine potential," I told Deborah after I had read her first essay. "You'll pass English 101 as soon as you eliminate your grammar problems."

"I know," she said. "That's what my other three instructors said."

"Well, let's make this your last semester in English 101, then. After each essay, make an appointment with me to go over your grammar problems."

"Okay."

"And go to the Writing Lab as often as possible. Start by studying verb tense. Let's eliminate one problem at a time."

"I'll go this afternoon!"

But Deborah never found time: *No, really. . . . I'll go to the lab just as soon as I. . . .*

Deborah scheduled two appointments with me during the semester and missed them both: *I'm so sorry. . . . I'll come to see you just as soon as I. . . .*

To pass English 101 at our college, students had to pass one of two essays written at the end of the semester in an exam setting. Each essay, identified by social security number only, was graded by two other instructors. At semester's end, Deborah once again failed English 101. "It isn't fair!" Deborah protested. "Those exam graders expect us to be professional writers. They're keeping me from becoming a nurse!"

I suggested another possibility: "What if *you* are the one keeping you from becoming a nurse?"

Deborah didn't like that idea. She wanted to believe that her problem was "out there." Her only obstacle was *those* exam graders. All her disappointments

The best years of your life are the ones in which you decide your problems are your own. You do not blame them on your mother, the ecology, or the president. You realize that you control your own destiny.

Albert Ellis

The more we practice the habit of acting from a position of responsibility, the more effective we become as human beings, and the more successful we become as managers of our lives.

Joyce Chapman

were *their* fault. *They* weren't fair. The *test* wasn't fair. *Life* wasn't fair! In the face of this injustice, she was helpless.

I reminded Deborah that it was *she* who had not studied her grammar. It was *she* who had not come to conferences. It was *she* who had not accepted personal responsibility for creating her life the way she wanted it.

"Yes, but …," she said.

VICTIM AND CREATOR MINDSETS

Deborah had a problem that was going to keep her from ever passing English 101. But the problem wasn't the exam graders. The problem was her mindset.

A mindset is a collection of beliefs and attitudes. Like a lens, it affects the way you see a situation and influences your resulting choices. A **Victim mindset** keeps people from seeing and acting on choices that could help them achieve the life they want. A **Creator mindset** causes people to see multiple options, choose wisely among them, and take effective actions to achieve the life they want.

When you accept personal responsibility, you believe that you create *everything* in your life. This idea doesn't sit well with some people. "Accidents and natural disasters happen," they say. "There are muggings, murders, and wars. People are marginalized, oppressed, and brutalized simply because they are different. Blaming the victims is unfair. To say these people created the terrible things that happened to them is outrageous."

These observations are, as far as they go, true. At times, we *are* all affected by forces beyond our control. If a hurricane destroys my house, I am a victim (with a small "v"). In this case I am victimized by a force *outside* of me. But if I allow that event to ruin my life, I am a Victim (with a capital "V"). In this case I am victimized by a force *inside* of me. Whether I am victimized from the outside or from the inside is a crucial distinction. When I have a Victim mindset, I become my own oppressor. When I have a Creator mindset, I refuse to be oppressed.

Civil rights activist Rosa Parks is a perfect example of this distinction. On the evening of December 1, 1955, Parks was returning home on a Montgomery, Alabama, bus. She had just completed a long day as a seamstress in a department store. When the driver ordered her to give up her seat to a white passenger, Parks refused and was arrested. A few days later, outraged at her arrest, African Americans began a boycott of Montgomery buses that ended 381 days later when the law requiring segregation on public buses was finally lifted. As a result of choosing defiance, Parks has been called the "mother of the modern day civil rights movement." In an interview years later, Parks was asked why she chose to defy the bus driver's order to move. "People always say that I didn't give up my seat because I was tired," she said, "but that isn't true. I was not tired physically, or no more tired than I usually was at the end of a working day. I was not old, although some people have an image of me as being old then. I was forty-two. No, the only tired I was, was tired of giving in." In the face of an external oppression, Rosa Parks became an inspiring example of what one person with a Creator mindset can achieve.

Every time your back is against the wall, there is only one person that can help. And that's you. It has to come from inside.

Pat Riley, professional basketball coach

I believe that we are solely responsible for our choices, and we have to accept the consequences of every deed, word, and thought throughout our lifetime.

Elisabeth Kübler-Ross

So, is it outrageous to believe that you create everything in your life? Of course it is. But here's a better question: Would it improve your life to act *as if* you create all of the outcomes and experiences in your life? Answer "YES!" and watch a Creator mindset improve your life. After all, if you believe that someone or something out there causes all of your problems, then it's up to "them" to change. What a wait that can be! How long, for example, will Deborah have to wait for "those exam graders" to change?

The benefits to students of accepting personal responsibility have been demonstrated in various studies. Researchers Robert Vallerand and Robert Bissonette, for example, asked 1,000 first-year college students to complete a questionnaire about why they were attending school. They used the students' answers to assess whether the students were "Origin-like" or "Pawn-like." The researchers defined *Origin-like* students as seeing themselves as the originators of their own behaviors, in other words, Creators. By contrast, *Pawn-like* students see themselves as mere puppets controlled by others, in other words, Victims. A year later, the researchers returned to find out what had happened to the 1,000 students. They found that significantly more of the Creator-like students were still enrolled in college than the Victim-like students. If you want to succeed in college (and in life), having a Creator mindset gives you a big edge.

RESPONSIBILITY AND CULTURE

In the 1950s, American psychologist Julian Rotter set out to study people's beliefs about who or what was responsible for the outcomes and experiences of their lives. He called it a study of "locus of control." *Locus* in Latin means "place" or "location." So, locus of control defines where people believe the power over their lives is located. Since Rotter's study, locus of control has been one of the most examined aspects of human nature. What researchers discovered is that different cultures see locus of control differently.

People of some cultures believe they control most, if not all, of their own destiny. Researchers call this mindset an *internal* locus of control. People with this

Which mistake do you think would be better to make . . . a) to believe you are in control of your life when you really might not be [or] b) to believe you are not in control of your life when you really might be?

Brooks Peterson

mindset believe their outcomes and experiences depend on their own behaviors. This mindset is part of North American culture, where maturity is often defined as taking responsibility for one's own life. Not surprisingly, a strong part of the deep culture of North American higher education is a belief that college students are adults. As such, students are expected to make adult choices and be willing to accept responsibility for the consequences of those choices.

However, researchers found that people from some cultures assign responsibility for their fate to factors beyond their control. If you find that you are uncomfortable with the idea of personal responsibility, the cause may be found in your deep culture. For example, members of Latino culture, with roots in Catholicism, are likely to believe that a higher power is guiding their lives. The saying *Si Dios Quiere* ("If God Wants") reflects this belief. Muslims have a similar phrase in Arabic: *Insha'Allah* means "God willing" or "if God allows." Traditional Native Americans also value fate over self-determination. And members of working-class cultures—regardless of their ethnicity—may experience economic frustrations and doubt their ability to create the life of their dreams.

These differences in cultural mindsets highlight both the challenge and importance of deciding where our responsibilities begin and end. On the one hand, accepting too little responsibility is disempowering. We become little more than a feather floating on the breeze. On the other hand, accepting too much responsibility is disempowering as well. In some cases, we become like a pack mule crushed under the weight of problems not of our creation or in our control. The reality is that some choices truly are futile because of personal limitations or limitations imposed by fate or the will of others with more power. Like some kind of cosmic joke, one of our greatest responsibilities, then, is deciding what we are and are not responsible for, what we do and do not have control over. Worse, those decisions may change at the very next fork in the road. As a guideline to help you choose, in North American culture you'll usually be wise to adopt the philosophy of English poet William E. Henley, who in 1875 wrote: "I am the master of my fate; I am the captain of my soul." In fact, had Henley been a college student at the time, he might have added, "And I am the Creator of my GPA."

> G enerally, European-American teachers believe in internal control and internal responsibility—that individuals are in control of their own fate, their actions affect outcomes, and success or failure in life is related to personal characteristics and abilities.
>
> Jean Moule

> B y imposing too great a responsibility, or rather, all responsibility, on yourself, you crush yourself.
>
> Franz Kafka

RESPONSIBILITY AND CHOICE

The key ingredient of personal responsibility is **choice.** Animals respond to a stimulus because of instinct or habit. For humans, however, there is a brief, critical moment of decision available between the stimulus and the response. In this moment, we make the choices—consciously or unconsciously—that influence the outcomes of our lives.

Numerous times each day, you come to a fork in the road and must make a choice. There is no escape. Even *not* making a choice is a choice. Some choices have a small impact: Shall I get my hair cut today or tomorrow? Some have a huge impact: Shall I stay in college or drop out? The sum of the choices you make from this day forward will create the eventual outcome of your life. The Responsibility Model in **Figure 2.1** shows what the moment of choice looks like.

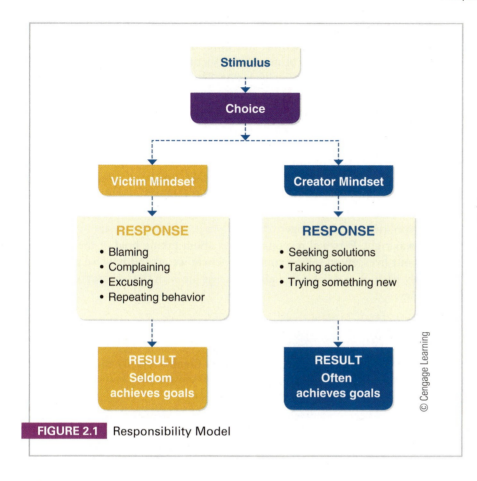

FIGURE 2.1 Responsibility Model

I do think that the greatest lesson of life is that you are responsible for your own life.

Oprah Winfrey

In that brief moment between stimulus and response, we can choose a Victim mindset or a Creator mindset. When we respond as a Victim, we typically complain, blame, make excuses, and then repeat ineffective behaviors. When we respond as a Creator, we pause at each decision point and ask, "What are my options, and which option will best help me create my desired outcomes and experiences?"

The difference between responding to life as a Victim or Creator is how we choose to use our energy. When I'm blaming, complaining, and excusing, my efforts cause little or no improvement. Sure, it may feel good in that moment to claim that I'm a poor Victim and "they" are evil persecutors, but my good feelings are fleeting because afterward my problem still exists. By contrast, when I'm seeking solutions and taking actions, my efforts often (though not always) lead to improvements. At critical forks in the road, Victims waste their energy and remain stuck, whereas Creators use their energy for improving their lives. There is only one situation I can think of where blaming and complaining can be helpful. That's when you use them to generate energy that motivates you to take positive actions. My personal guideline: Up to 10 minutes for griping . . . then on to being a Creator and finding a solution.

When you make the shift to being the predominant creative force in your life, you move from reacting and responding to the external circumstances of your life to creating directly the life you truly want.

Robert Fritz

But, let's be honest. No one makes Creator choices all of the time. I've never met anyone who did, least of all me. Our inner lives feature a perpetual tug of war between the Creator part of us and the Victim part of us. My own experiences have taught me the following life lesson: The more choices I make as a Creator, the more I improve the quality of my life. That's why I urge you to join me in an effort to choose more often as a Creator. It won't be easy, but it's worth it. You may have to take my word for it right now, but if you experiment with the strategies in this book and continue using the ones that work for you, in a few months you'll see powerful proof in your own life of the value of making Creator choices.

"Oh, I get what you mean!" one of my students once exclaimed as we were exploring this complex issue of personal responsibility, "You're saying that living my life is like traveling in my car. If I want to get where I want to go, I better be the driver and not a passenger."

She was right. Personal responsibility is about taking hold of the steering wheel of our lives, about taking control of where we go and how we get there. Ultimately, each of us creates the quality of our life with the wisdom or folly of our choices.

> I am a Shawnee. My forefathers were warriors. Their son is a warrior. . . . From my tribe I take nothing. I am the maker of my own fortune.
>
> Tecumseh

JOURNAL ENTRY | 4

In this activity, you will experiment with the Creator role. By choosing to take responsibility for your life, you will immediately gain an increased power to achieve your greatest potential.

1 **Write and complete each of the five sentence stems below.** For example, someone might complete the first sentence stem as follows: If I take personal responsibility for my education, *I will focus on really learning and not just getting good grades.*

1. If I take personal responsibility for my education . . .
2. If I take personal responsibility for my career . . .
3. If I take personal responsibility for my relationships . . .
4. If I take personal responsibility for my health . . .
5. If I take personal responsibility for all that happens to me . . .

2 **Make a choice—write about one of the following:**

A. What have you learned or relearned in this journal about personal responsibility, and how you will use this knowledge to improve your outcomes and experiences in college . . . and beyond? If you are aware that accepting personal responsibility conflicts with your own cultural or personal beliefs, explore how you will deal with that difference. You might begin, *By reading and writing about personal responsibility, I have learned . . .*

B. Share the details of a personal experience in which you did or did not take personal responsibility and explain the effects of this choice on your life.

> Life is like a game of cards. The hand you are dealt is determinism; the way you play it is free will.
>
> Jawaharlal Nehru

ONE STUDENT'S STORY

TARYN ROSSMILLER, *Boise State University, Idaho*

I was an honor student in high school, earned a 3.95 GPA, and graduated with scholarships and varsity letters in tennis and marching band. I loved high school, and I knew college was in my future. I entered Boise State University as a music education major with an emphasis in drums and percussion. I had a will to become a music teacher, and my goal was to succeed and excel.

However, in the music department, I was torn apart daily for what seemed like insignificant details. "You're rushing through the music. Your thumb is incorrectly placed. Your technique is all wrong. Have you even practiced?" Although I worked hard to improve, I returned every week to more criticism. The feedback was brutal and deflating. My instructors were commenting on me as a musician, but I took everything personally. After a year of enduring my professors' scrutiny, I stopped attending all of my music courses mid-semester. No matter how hard I worked, I thought my music career was hopeless. So, I felt my only option was to leave my courses and take the Fs. As a result, my semester GPA fell to an all-time low of 0.98. I lost my financial aid, got placed on academic probation, and had to improve my academic standing to stay in school. The whole experience was a huge blow to my confidence and self-esteem. I felt I did not belong on "probation." I went from being passionate to becoming petrified about being in college.

Over the summer, I received an email from a professor at my university. She encouraged me to take a special course that was designed for students on academic probation. Although I felt I did not need the class, I enrolled in the Student Success Seminar anyway in hopes of getting right with the university. Still, surely it wasn't my fault that I had come to this academic fate—it was my professors'; it was the music department that was too demanding; it was everyone but me. However, I soon found out in my Student-Success-Seminar-That-I-Didn't-Need that my fate had EVERYTHING to do with me. In fact, I discovered my choices are made by me, my successes depend on me, and my life is my responsibility!

For the first time, I discovered the reality about my future—I am responsible for it, and only I can get myself where I want to go. I came away with many realizations while taking this course, and one of the most important was developing a Creator mindset. This class helped me realize that I demonstrated every aspect of a Victim mindset. I put myself down, I blamed others for my failures, and worst of all—I made excuses when I didn't accomplish a goal that I wanted. I made decisions carelessly, as if it wasn't my fault when things went badly, and my inner conversation didn't help me achieve my goals either.

Thanks to *On Course*, I began seeing my life with fresh eyes. I adopted the following three

steps as my own, and I knew that I could be on my way to achieving academic and personal successes:

1. I will believe that everything I do, whether or not I like my outcomes, is my responsibility,

2. I will believe that everything I do shapes the rest of my life and the experiences I will have, and

3. I will make positive decisions to guide me to what I want out of my life.

The semester after I completed the Student Success Seminar, I finished with a 3.5 GPA and my name on the Dean's List. I was no longer on academic probation. With my grades back up, I appealed the loss of my financial aid and got it back. Since then, I changed my major to psychology, time has sped by, and now I will be graduating this May. I plan to pursue a master's degree in counseling and social work.

In the Student Success Seminar, I became empowered. Among other aspects, I learned the importance of developing a Creator mindset, how to build a sense of confidence, and how to stop my Inner Critic and Inner Defender. I no longer blame my professors, the university, or circumstances for my failures. I learned personal responsibility, and I realized that I was not a bad student; I just had a bad start. Overall, I learned I had the power to change my future, and how to take actions to improve my life. I am thrilled to maintain my Creator mindset and leave my Victim side behind. Goodbye old me. Hello, success!

Photo: Courtesy of Taryn Rossmiller.

Mastering Creator Language

How can you create greater success by changing your vocabulary?

Have you ever noticed that there is almost always a conversation going on in your mind? Inner voices chatter away, offering commentary about you, other people, and the world. This self-talk is important because what you say to yourself determines the choices you make at each fork in the road. People with a Victim mindset typically listen to the voice of their Inner Critic or their Inner Defender.

SELF-TALK

The Inner Critic

This is the internal voice that judges us as inadequate: *I'm so uncoordinated. I can't do math. I'm not someone she would want to date. I never say the right thing. My ears are too big. I'm a lousy writer.* The Inner Critic accepts too much responsibility and blames us for whatever goes wrong in our lives: *It's all my fault. I always screw up. I knew I couldn't pass biology. I ruined the project. I ought to be ashamed. I blew it again.* This judgmental inner voice can find fault with anything about us: our appearance, our intelligence, our performance, our personality, our abilities, how others see us, and, in severe cases, even our value as a human being: *I'm not good enough. I'm worthless. I don't deserve to live.* (Although nearly everyone has a critical inner voice at times, if you often think toxic self-judgments like these last three, don't mess around. Get to your college's counseling office immediately and get help revising these noxious messages so you don't make self-destructive choices.)

Ironically, self-judgments have a positive intention. By criticizing ourselves, we hope to eliminate our flaws and win the approval of others, thus feeling more worthy. Occasionally when we bully ourselves to be perfect, we *do* create a positive outcome, though we make ourselves miserable in the effort. Often, though, self-judgments cause us to give up, as when I tell myself, *I can't pass math,* so I drop the course. What's positive about this? Well, at least I've escaped my problem. Freed from the pressures of passing math, my anxieties float away and I feel better than I have since the semester started. Of course, I still have to pass math to get my degree, so my relief is temporary. The Inner Critic is quite content to trade success in the future for comfort in the present.

Where does an Inner Critic come from? Here's one clue: Have you noticed that its self-criticisms often sound like judgmental adults we have known? It's as if our younger self recorded their judgments and, years later, our Inner Critic replays them over and over. Sometimes you can even trace a self-judgment back to a specific comment that someone made about you years ago. Regardless of its accuracy now, that judgment can affect the choices you make every day.

During discussions about Inner Critic voices, I have had students say that in their culture, parents routinely criticize their children. The parents say they do it to help. A Japanese-American student said that if he brought home a test with

---

The world of self-criticism on the one side and judgment toward others on the other side represents a major part of the dance of life.

Hal Stone & Sidra Stone

A loud, voluble critic is enormously toxic. He is more poisonous to your psychological health than almost any trauma or loss. That's because grief and pain wash away with time. But the critic is always with you—judging, blaming, finding fault.

Matthew McKay & Patrick Fanning

a grade of 98 his parents would tell him that wasn't good enough. A Chinese-American woman said if she gained a pound her mother would tell her she was fat and no man would ever want to marry her. A Jewish-American student made a vase in her ceramics class and gave it to her mother as a present. Her mother proudly displayed the vase on the dining table. The next day, she asked, "What grade did you get for the vase?" My student replied that she had gotten a "C." Soon after, the vase disappeared, never to be seen again. I'm inclined to give these parents the benefit of the doubt. I'm willing to believe they thought they were helping their children, even showing love. Whatever their intentions, though, it was clear these parents had given great power to their children's Inner Critics.

The Inner Defender

The flip side of the Inner Critic is the Inner Defender. Instead of judging ourselves, the Inner Defender judges others: *What a boring teacher. My advisor screwed up my financial aid. Those people [referring to a minority group] are not as good as we are. My roommate made me late to class. No one knows what they're doing around here. It's all their fault!* Inner Defenders accept too little responsibility and, thus, their thoughts and conversations are full of blaming, complaining, accusing, judging, criticizing, and condemning others.

Like Inner Critics, Inner Defenders have a positive intention. They, too, want to protect us from discomfort and anxiety. They, too, want us to feel more worthy. One way they do so is by judging others as wrong or bad or "less than." By tearing others down, the Inner Defender tries to make us feel better about ourselves. In this light, you can perhaps see that prejudice and bias are important tools of the Inner Defender.

Another way Inner Defenders try to help us is by blaming our problems on forces that seem beyond our control, such as other people, bad luck, the government, lack of money, uncaring parents, not enough time, or even too much time. The Inner Defender of a college student might say, *I can't pass math because my instructor is terrible. She couldn't teach math to Einstein. Besides that, the textbook stinks and the tutors in the math lab are rude and unhelpful. It's obvious this college doesn't really care what happens to its students.* If I'm that student,

W hat you're supposed to do when you don't like a thing is change it. If you can't change it, change the way you think about it. Don't complain.

Advice to Maya Angelou
from her grandmother

I breathe a sigh of relief because now I'm covered. If I drop the course, hey, it's not my fault. If I stay in the course and fail, it's not my fault either. And, if I stay in the course and somehow get a passing grade (despite my terrible instructor, lousy textbook, worthless tutors, and uncaring college), well, then I have performed no less than a miracle! Regardless of how bad things may get, I can find comfort knowing that at least it's not my fault. It's *their* fault!

And where did this voice come from? Perhaps you've noticed that the Inner Defender's voice sounds like judgmental adults we have known: *You can't trust those people. They're not as good as we are. They're lazy. All they want is a handout. They are the reason for our problem!* At other times, the Inner Defender sounds like our own voice when we were scared little kids trying to defend ourselves from criticism or punishment by powerful adults. Remember how we'd excuse ourselves from responsibility, shifting the blame for our poor choices onto someone or something else: *It's not my fault. He keeps poking me. My dog ate my homework. What else could I do? I didn't have any choice. My sister broke it. He made me do it. Why does everyone always pick on me? It's all their fault!*

Notice what the Inner Critic and Inner Defender have in common. They are both voices of *judgment*. With the Inner Critic, we point the finger of judgment inward at ourselves. With the Inner Defender, we point the finger of judgment outward at someone or something outside of us. We pay a high price for listening to either our Inner Critic or Inner Defender. By focusing on who's to blame, we waste our energy on judgments instead of positive actions. We spin in place instead of moving purposely toward our desired outcomes and experiences. To feel better in the moment, we sabotage creating a better future.

Fortunately, another voice exists within us all.

The Inner Guide

This is the wise inner voice that seeks to make the best of any situation. The Inner Guide knows that judgment doesn't improve difficult situations. So

The object of teaching personal responsibility is to have the student substitute for the question "Who's to blame?" the question "What needs to be done?"

Nathaniel Branden

I used to want the words "She tried" on my tombstone. Now I want, "She did it."

Katherine Dunham

instead, the Inner Guide objectively observes each situation and asks, *Am I on course or off course? If I'm off course, what can I do to get back on course?* Inner Guides tell us the impartial truth (as best they know it at that time), allowing us to be more fully aware of the world around us, other people, and especially ourselves. With this knowledge, we can take actions that will get us back on course.

Some people say, "But my Inner Critic (or Inner Defender) is *right*!" Yes, it's true that the Inner Critic or Inner Defender can be just as "right" as the Inner Guide. Maybe you really *are* a lousy writer and the tutors in the math lab actually *are* rude and unhelpful. The difference is that Victims expend all their energy in judging themselves or others, whereas Creators use their energy to solve the problem. The voice we allow to occupy our thoughts determines our choices, and our choices determine the outcomes and experiences of our lives. So choose your thoughts carefully. As mentioned earlier, I allow myself up to 10 minutes to complain, blame, and make excuses. Then I redirect that energy and look for what I can do about the situation.

THE LANGUAGE OF RESPONSIBILITY

Translating Victim statements into the responsible language of Creators moves you from stagnant judgments to dynamic actions. In the following chart, the left-hand column presents the Victim thoughts of a student who is taking a challenging college course. Thinking this way, the student's future in this course is easy to predict . . . and it isn't pretty.

But, if she changes her inner conversation, as shown in the right-hand column, she'll also change her behaviors. She can learn more in the course and increase her likelihood of passing. More important, she can learn to reclaim control of her life from the judgmental, self-sabotaging thoughts of her Inner Critic and Inner Defender.

As you read these translations, notice two qualities that characterize Creator language. First, Creators accept ownership of their situation. Second, they plan and take actions to improve their situation. So, when you hear **ownership** and a **plan**, you know you're talking to a Creator. At any moment, you can choose either mindset . . . and that choice will shape your destiny.

> You must change the way you talk to yourself about your life situations so that you no longer imply that anything outside of you is the immediate cause of your unhappiness. Instead of saying, "Joe makes me mad," say, "I make myself mad when I'm around Joe."
>
> Ken Keyes

> Excuses rob you of power and induce apathy.
>
> Agnes Whistling Elk

Victims Focus on Their Weaknesses	**Creators Focus on How to Improve**
I'm terrible in this subject.	I find this course challenging, so I'll start a study group and ask more questions in class.
Victims Make Excuses	**Creators Seek Solutions**
The instructor is so boring he puts me to sleep.	I find it difficult to pay attention in this class, so I'll challenge myself to stay focused and take at least one page of notes each class period.
Victims Complain	**Creators Turn Complaints into Requests**
This course is a stupid requirement.	I don't understand why this course is required, so I'm going to ask my instructor to help me see how it will benefit me in the future.

Victims Compare Themselves Unfavorably to Others	Creators Seek Help from Those More Skilled
I'll never do as well as John; he's a genius.	I need help in this course, so I'm going to ask John if he'll help me study for the exams.

Victims Blame	Creators Accept Responsibility
The tests are ridiculous. The professor gave me an "F" on the first one.	I got an "F" on the first test because I didn't read the assignments thoroughly. From now on I'll take detailed notes on everything I read.

Victims See Problems as Permanent	Creators Treat Problems as Temporary
Posting comments on our class's Internet discussion board is impossible. I'll never understand how to do it.	I've been trying to post comments on our class's Internet discussion board without carefully reading the instructor's directions. I'll read the directions again and follow them one step at a time.

Victims Repeat Ineffective Behaviors	Creators Do Something New
Going to the tutoring center is no help. There aren't enough tutors.	I've been going to the tutoring center right after lunch when it's really busy. I'll start going in the morning to see if more tutors are available then.

Victims Try	Creators Do
I'll try to do better.	To do better, I'll do the following: Attend class regularly, take good notes, ask questions in class, start a study group, and make an appointment with the teacher. If all that doesn't work, I'll think of something else.

Victims Predict Defeat and Give Up	Creators Think Positively and Look for a Better Choice
I'll probably fail. There's nothing I can do. I can't . . . I have to . . . I should . . . I quit . . .	I'll find a way. There's always something I can do. I can . . . I choose to . . . I will . . . I'll keep going . . .

When people choose a Victim mindset, they complain, blame, and make excuses, and they have little energy left over to solve their problems. As a result, they typically remain stuck where they are, telling their sad story over and over to any poor soul who will listen. (Ever hear of a "pity party"?) In this way, Victims exhaust not only their own energy but often drain the energy of the people around them.

By contrast, when people choose a Creator mindset, they use their words and thoughts to improve a bad situation. First, they accept responsibility for creating their present outcomes and experiences, and their words reflect that ownership. Next, they plan and take positive actions to improve their lives. *Ownership* and a *plan*. In this way, Creators energize themselves and the people around them.

Whenever you feel yourself slipping into Victim language, ask yourself: What do I want in my life—excuses or results? What could I think, say, and do right now that would get me moving toward the outcomes and experiences I want?

Blaming . . . is a pastime for losers. There's no leverage in blaming. Power is rooted in self-responsibility.

Nathaniel Branden

JOURNAL ENTRY   5

In this activity, you will practice the language of personal responsibility. By learning to translate Victim statements into Creator statements, you will master the language of successful people.

1 Draw a line down the middle of a journal page. On the left side of the line, copy the 10 Victim statements found below.

2 On the right side of the line, translate the Victim statements into the words of a Creator. The two keys to Creator language are taking ownership of a problem and taking positive actions to solve it. *Ownership* and a *plan*. When you respond as if you are responsible for a bad situation, then you are empowered to do something about it (unlike Victims, who must wait for someone else to solve their problems). Use the translations on pages 53–54 as models.

3 Write what you have learned or relearned about how you use language: Is it your habit to speak as a Victim or as a Creator? Do you find yourself more inclined to blame yourself, blame others, or seek solutions? Be sure to give examples. What is your goal for language usage from now on? How, specifically, will you accomplish this goal? Your paragraph might begin, *While reading about and practicing Creator language, I learned that I . . .*

Remember to DIVE DEEP!

Victim Language	Creator Language
1. If they'd do something about the parking on campus, I wouldn't be late so often.	1.
2. I'm failing my online class because the site is impossible to navigate.	2.
3. I'm too shy to ask questions in class even when I'm confused.	3.
4. She's a lousy instructor. That's why I failed the first test.	4.
5. I hate group projects because people are lazy and I always end up doing most of the work.	5.
6. I wish I could write better, but I just can't.	6.
7. My friend got me so angry that I can't even study for the exam.	7.
8. I'll try to do my best this semester.	8.
9. The financial aid form is too complicated to fill out.	9.
10. I work nights so I didn't have time to do the assignment.	10.

The way you use words has a tremendous impact on the quality of your life. Certain words are destructive; others are empowering.

Susan Jeffers

If you are in shackles, "I can't" has relevance; otherwise, it is usually a roundabout way of saying "I don't want to," "I won't," or, "I have not learned how to." If you really mean "I don't want to," it is important to come out and say so. Saying "I can't" disowns responsibility.

Gay Hendricks & Kathlyn Hendricks

ONE STUDENT'S STORY

ALEXSANDR KANEVSKIY, *Oakland University, Michigan*

When I began college, I was unmotivated and chose to blame others for my problems and my shortcomings. I was so much smarter than everyone that I didn't need to do all the work that everyone else did; at least that's what I thought. My favorite pastime was staring blankly at a television, rather than attending lecture or doing assigned homework. I figured everything would take care of itself without my interference. I had carried this uninhibited laziness with me through high school and it, unfortunately, translated into my college career. It was then that the gravitas of my situation hit me; at my current rate I was going to be dismissed from school. I was placed on academic probation my sophomore year and unless I improved, I was out.

This was when I first laid my eyes and hands on the *On Course* book. I didn't think much of it at first; just another guide for the misguided, full of backwards theories and advice that wouldn't help me, or anyone else. But from the first reading, I noticed that this book was different. It used different language, language that didn't bore me or induce disinterest. What's funniest, though, was that one of the first journals that I was assigned had the most profound impact on my changing as a student. Just as *On Course* used innovative and interesting language to teach, this journal was all about changing my own language. Rather than use language that blames others or is blatantly negative, that journal taught me to use positive Creator language. I needed to think and speak in a language that searched for answers and solutions, not a language that kept me unmotivated and helpless. When I rephrased my thinking and speaking, the rest of life followed. All of a sudden, responsibility was in my own hands and the solutions that I needed, but was afraid to search out, became much clearer. Now that I knew there were, in fact, answers and solutions, I didn't look to blame those around me. I realized that it was up to me to find these solutions, that they would not magically appear before my eyes and that nobody else would find them for me. My faults and shortcomings became more apparent than ever, and my arrogance was startling. I saw that I was not smart enough to be exempt from school and from the work of my fellow students. They all searched for solutions and held themselves responsible for these solutions; I never realized this because I had never yearned for these solutions, and therefore never had responsibility.

I stopped expecting solutions to come to me naturally and started to work, rather than fall asleep at the television. Positive Creator language was only the first step, but what I took from this first lesson carried through to every other lesson in class and in life. I found that I was newly interested in my classes; homework became a pleasure because each assignment was yet another opportunity to learn. Rather than fall asleep at the television, I now fell asleep after studying. And probation? That became a thing of the past. Even in basketball (my sport of choice) I started to take more of an interest in passing, rather than scoring, and helping my teammates, instead of blaming them for mistakes. Amongst my friends I am now known as the "problem solver," which is just as surprising to me as it is to them. They've noticed a definite change, and I am glad to advise them to read my *On Course* book so that maybe they too will find a lesson that sparks their own improvement. *On Course* provided me with valuable steppingstones that have made me into a student and person who cares enough to take responsibility for his language and his actions, doing what needs to be done in order to succeed in school and in the outside world.

Making Wise Decisions

FOCUS QUESTIONS   How can you improve the quality of the decisions you make? How can you take personal responsibility for the outcomes and experiences in your life?

Life is a journey with many opportunities and obstacles, and each one requires a choice. Whatever you are experiencing in your life today is, to a great extent, the result of your past choices. More important, whatever you'll experience in the future will be fashioned greatly by the choices you make from this moment on.

This is an exciting thought. If we can make wiser choices, we can more likely create the future we want. On the road to a college degree, you will face important choices such as these:

Shall I . . .

- major in business, science, or creative writing?
- work full-time, part-time, or not at all?
- drop a course that bores me or stick it out?
- experiment with alcohol and drugs?
- study for my exam or go out with friends?

The sum of these choices, plus thousands of others, will determine your degree of success in college and in life. Doesn't it seem wise, then, to develop an effective strategy for choice management?

The end result of your life here on Earth will always be the sum total of the choices you made while you were here.

Shad Helmstetter

Peter Mueller/Condenaststore Collliection

THE WISE CHOICE PROCESS

In the face of any challenge, you can make a responsible decision by answering the six questions of the Wise Choice Process. This process, you might be interested to know, is a variation of a decision-making model that is used in many career fields. For example, nurses learn a similar process for helping patients that is abbreviated ADPIE. These letters stand for Assess, Diagnose, Plan, Implement, and Evaluate. Counselors and therapists in training may learn a similar process for solving personal problems. This process was described in 1965 by William Glasser in his book *Reality Therapy*.

And the *NASA Systems Engineering Handbook* says, "Systems engineering [. . .] consists of identification and quantification of system goals, creation of alternative system design concepts, performance of design trades, selection and implementation of the best design, verification that the design is properly built and integrated, and post-implementation assessment of how well the system meets (or met) the goals." In layperson's terms, systems engineers use their version of the Wise Choice Process to achieve their goals.

You are about to learn a decision-making system that will empower you to take greater responsibility for creating your life as you want it to be . . . despite the inevitable challenges that life presents.

> My choice; my responsibility; win or lose, only I hold the key to my destiny.
>
> Elaine Maxwell

1. **What's My Present Situation?** Begin by identifying your problem or challenge, being sure to define the situation as a Creator, not as a Victim. The important information here is "What exists?" (not "Whose fault is it?"). Quiet your Inner Critic, that self-criticizing voice in your head: *I am a total loser in my history class.* Likewise, ignore your Inner Defender, that judgmental voice that blames everyone else for your problems: *My history instructor is the worst teacher on the planet.* Instead, rely on your Inner Guide, your wise, impartial inner voice that tells the truth as best it can. Consider only the objective facts of your situation, including how you feel about them. For example:

   I stayed up all night studying for my first history test. When I finished taking the test, I hoped for an A. At worst, I expected a B. When I got the test back, my grade was a D. Five other students got A's. I feel depressed and angry.

   By the way, sometimes when we accurately define a troublesome situation, we immediately know what to do. The problem wasn't so much the situation as our muddy understanding of it.

> I am the cause of my choices, decisions, and actions. It is I who chooses, decides, and acts. If I do so knowing my responsibility, I am more likely to proceed wisely and appropriately than if I make myself oblivious of my role as source.
>
> Nathaniel Branden

2. **How Would I Like My Situation to Be?** You can't change the past, but if you could create your desired outcome in the future, what would it look like?

   I get A's on all of my future tests.

3. **What Are My Possible Choices?** Create a list of possible choices that you *could* do, knowing you aren't obligated to do any of them. Compile your list without judgment. Don't say, "Oh, that would never work." Don't even say, "That's a great idea." Judgment during brainstorming stops the creative flow.

Move from judgments to possibilities, discovering as many creative options as you can. Give yourself time to ponder, explore, consider, think, discover, conceive, invent, imagine. Then dive even deeper. If you get stuck, try one of these options. First, take a different point of view. Think of someone you admire and ask, "What would that person do in my situation?" Or, pretend your problem belongs to someone else, and he asks you what you should do. What advice would you offer? Third, incubate. That is, set the problem aside and let your unconscious mind work on a solution while you do other things. Sometimes a great option will pop into your mind while you are brushing your hair, doing math homework, or even sleeping. Your patience will often pay off with a helpful option that would have remained invisible had you accepted the first idea that came to mind or, worse, given up.

A person defines and redefines who they are by the choices they make, minute to minute.

Joyce Chapman

- *I could complain to my history classmates and anyone else who will listen.*
- *I could drop the class and take it next semester with another instructor.*
- *I could complain to the department head that the instructor grades unfairly.*
- *I could ask my successful classmates for help.*
- *I could ask the instructor for suggestions about improving my grades.*
- *I could read about study skills and experiment with some new ways to study.*
- *I could request an opportunity to retake the test.*
- *I could take all of the online practice quizzes.*
- *I could get a tutor.*

4. **What's The Likely Outcome of Each Possible Choice?** Decide how you think each choice is likely to turn out. If you can't predict the outcome of one of your possible choices, stop this process and gather any additional information you need. For example, if you don't know the impact that dropping a course will have on your financial aid, find out before you take that action. Here are the possible choices from Step 3 and their likely outcomes:

Destiny is not a matter of chance; it is a matter of choice. It is not a thing to be waited for; it is a thing to be achieved.

William Jennings Bryan

- *Complain to history classmates: I'd have the immediate pleasure of criticizing the instructor and maybe getting others' sympathy.*
- *Drop the class: I'd lose three credits this semester and have to make them up later.*
- *Complain to the department head: Probably she'd ask if I've seen my instructor first, so I wouldn't get much satisfaction.*
- *Ask successful classmates for help: I might learn how to improve my study habits; I might also make new friends.*
- *Ask the instructor for suggestions: I might learn what to do next time to improve my grade; at least the instructor would learn that I want to do well in this course.*
- *Read about study skills: I would probably learn some strategies I don't know and maybe improve my test scores in all of my classes.*
- *Request an opportunity to retake the test: My request might get approved and give me an opportunity to raise my grade. At the very least, I'd demonstrate how much I want to do well.*

- *Take all of the online practice quizzes: This action wouldn't help my grade on this test, but it would probably improve my next test score.*
- *Get a tutor: A tutor would help, but it would probably take a lot of time.*

5. **WHICH CHOICE(S) WILL I COMMIT TO DOING?** Now create your plan. Decide which choice or choices will likely create your desired outcome; then commit to acting on them. If no favorable option exists, consider which choice leaves you no worse off than before. If no such option exists, then ask which choice creates the least unfavorable outcome. And remember that not making a choice is a choice.

I'll talk to my successful classmates, make an appointment with my instructor and ask him to explain what I can do to improve, and I'll request an opportunity to retake the test. I'll read the study skills sections of On Course and implement at least three new study strategies. If these choices don't raise my next test score to at least a B, I'll get a tutor.

Each situation will dictate the best options. In this example, if the student had previously failed four tests instead of one, the best choice might be to drop the class. Or, if everyone in the class were receiving Ds and Fs, and if the student had already met with the instructor, a responsible option might be to see the department head about the instructor's grading policies.

6. **WHEN AND HOW WILL I EVALUATE MY PLAN?** At some future time you will want to assess your results. To do so, compare your new situation with how you want it to be (as you described in Step 2). If the two situations are identical (or close enough), you can call your plan a success. If you find that you are still far from your desired outcome, you have some decisions to make. You might decide that you haven't implemented your new approach long enough, so you'll keep working your plan. Or you may decide that your plan just isn't working, in which case you'll return to Step 1 and work through Step 5 to design a plan that will work better. However, you're not starting completely over because this time you're smarter than you were when you began: Now you know what doesn't work.

After my next history test, I'll see if I have achieved my goal of getting an A. If not, I'll revise my plan.

Here's the bottom line: Our choices reveal what we *truly* believe and value, as opposed to what we *say* we believe and value. When I submissively wait for others to improve my life, I am being a Victim. When I passively wait for luck to go my way, I am being a Victim. When I make choices that take me off course from my future success just to increase my immediate pleasure (such as partying instead of studying for an important test), I am being a Victim. When I make choices that sacrifice my goals and dreams just to reduce my immediate discomfort (such as dropping a challenging course instead of spending extra hours working with a tutor), I am being a Victim.

However, when I design a plan to craft my life as I want it, I am being a Creator. When I carry out my plan even in the face of obstacles (such as when

> What we really mean by free will, of course, is the visualizing of alternatives and making a choice between them.
>
> Jacob Bronowski

> The principle of choice describes the reality that I am in charge of my life. I choose it all. I always have, I always will.
>
> Will Schutz

the campus bookstore runs out of a book that I need for class and I keep up with my assignments by reading a copy the instructor has placed on reserve in the library), I am being a Creator. When I take positive risks to advance my goals (such as asking a question in a large lecture class even though I am nervous), I am being a Creator. When I sacrifice immediate pleasure to stay on course toward my dreams (such as resisting the urge to buy a new cell phone so I can reduce my work hours to study more), I am being a Creator.

No matter what your final decision may be, the mere fact that you are defining and making your own choices is wonderfully empowering. By participating in the Wise Choice Process, you affirm your belief that you *can* change your life for the better. You reject the position that you are merely a Victim of outside forces, a pawn in the chess game of life. You insist on being the Creator of your own outcomes and experiences, shaping your destiny through the power of wise choices.

One's philosophy is not best expressed in words; it is expressed in the choices one makes. In the long run, we shape our lives and we shape ourselves. The process never ends until we die. And, the choices we make are ultimately our own responsibility.

Eleanor Roosevelt

JOURNAL ENTRY / 6

In this activity, you will apply the Wise Choice Process to improve a difficult situation in your life. Think about a current problem, one that you're comfortable sharing with your classmates and teacher. As a result of this problem, you may be angry, sad, frustrated, depressed, overwhelmed, or afraid. Perhaps this situation has to do with a grade you received, a teacher's comment, or a classmate's action. Maybe the problem relates to a job, a relationship, or money. The Wise Choice Process can help you make an empowering choice in any part of your life.

1 Write the six questions of the Wise Choice Process and answer each one as it relates to your situation.

The Wise Choice Process

1. What's my present situation? (Describe the problem objectively and completely.)
2. How would I like my situation to be? (What is your ideal future outcome?)
3. What are my possible choices? (Create a long list of specific choices that might create your preferred outcome.)
4. What's the likely outcome of each possible choice? (If you can't predict the likely outcome of an option, stop and gather more information.)
5. Which choice(s) will I commit to doing? (Pick from your list of choices in Step 3.)
6. When and how will I evaluate my plan? (Identify the specific date and criteria by which you will determine the success of your plan.)

2 Write what you learned or relearned by doing the Wise Choice Process. Be sure to Dive Deep. You might begin: *By doing the Wise Choice Process, I learned that I . . .*

Remember, you can enliven your journal by adding pictures you found, drawings of your own, or quotations or song lyrics that appeal to you.

When I see all the choices I really have, it makes the world a whole lot brighter.

Debbie Scott, student

ONE STUDENT'S STORY

FREDDIE DAVILA, *The Victoria College, Texas*

During my first semester of college I noticed a trend among my fellow students. Every time an assignment was due, many of them came to class with excuses instead of their completed work. I took this behavior personally because I had made time to complete all of my homework and prepare for class. I find it extremely disrespectful to the instructors and to those who come to class to learn whenever college students act like helpless children.

Also during my first semester, I happened to be taking "Strategies for Success," a class that introduced me to the *On Course* textbook. When I was invited to identify an important lesson worth sharing in a "One Page of Wisdom" assignment, I felt I needed to explain what I had learned throughout the

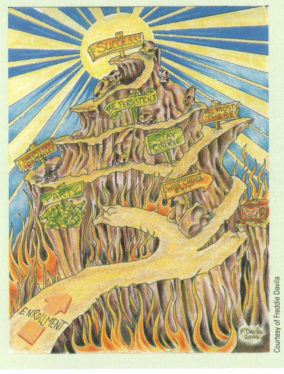

Courtesy of Freddie Davila

semester the best way I knew how—through art. I looked back at the Wise Choice Process and the Responsibility Model for inspiration. As I did the preliminary sketches, I kept in mind the excuses I had heard students use over the last few months. I wanted my art to show that by making excuses, they were acting like Victims and were only hurting themselves.

I hope some of the students in my class saw themselves in the drawing; my goal was to make people think about their self-sabotaging habits and bad choices that stand in the way of their success. The road to success is filled with tough obstacles and tempting distractions, but by making wise choices at critical forks in the road, students on the journey will find success to be their ultimate destiny.

PERSONAL RESPONSIBILITY / at Work

I found that the more I viewed myself as totally responsible for my life, the more in control I seemed to be of the goals I wanted to achieve.

Charles J. Givens, entrepreneur and self-made multimillionaire

A student once told me she'd had more than a dozen jobs in three years. "Why so many jobs?" I asked.

"Bad luck," she replied. "I keep getting one lousy boss after another." *Hmmmm*, I wondered. *Twelve lousy bosses in a row? What are the odds of that?*

Responsibility is about ownership. As long as I believe my career success belongs to someone else (like "lousy" bosses), I'm operating from a Victim mindset, and my success is unlikely. Victims give little effort to choosing or preparing for a career. Instead, they allow influential others (such as parents and teachers) or circumstances to determine their choice of work. They complain about the jobs they have, make excuses for why they haven't gotten the jobs they want, and blame others or their own permanent flaws for their occupational woes. By contrast, Creators know that the foundation of success at work (as in college) is accepting this truth: *By our choices, we are each the primary creators of the outcomes and experiences of our lives.*

Accepting responsibility in the work world begins with consciously choosing your career path. You alone can decide what career is right for you. That's why Creators explore their career options thoroughly, match career requirements with their own talents and interests, consider the consequences of choosing each career (such as how much education the career requires or what the employment outlook is), and make informed choices. Choose your career wisely because few things in life are worse than spending 8 hours a day, 50 weeks a year, working at a job you hate.

Taking responsibility for your work life also means planning your career path to keep your options open and your progress unobstructed. For example, you could keep your career options open in college by taking only general education courses while investigating several possible fields of work. Or you could eliminate a financial obstacle by getting enough education—such as a dental hygiene degree—to support yourself while pursuing your dream career—such as going to dental school.

In short, Creators make use of the power of wise choices. They believe that there is always an option that will lead them toward the careers they want, and they take responsibility for creating the employment they want. Instead of passively waiting for a job to come to them, they actively go out and look. One of my students lost a job when the company where she worked closed. She could have spent hours in the cafeteria complaining about her bad fortune and how she could no longer afford to stay in school. Instead she created employment for herself by going from store to store in a mall asking every manager for a part-time job until one said, "Yes." In the time she could have wasted in the cafeteria complaining about her money problems, she solved them with positive actions.

When it comes to finding a full-time career position, Creators continue to be proactive. They don't wait for the perfect job opening to appear in their local paper or on an Internet job site. They don't wait for a call from an employment agency. They know that employers prefer to hire people they know and like, so Creators do all they can to get known and liked by employers in their career field. They start by researching companies that need their talents and for which they might like to work.

Then, they contact potential employers directly. They don't ask if the employer has a job opening. Instead, they seek an informational interview: "Hi, I've just gotten my degree in accounting, and I'd like to make an appointment to talk to you about your company. . . . What's that? You don't have any positions open at this time? No problem. I'm just gathering information at this point, looking for where my talents might make the most contributions. Would you have some time to meet with me this week? Or would next week be better?"

Creators go to these information-gathering interviews prepared with knowledge about the company, good questions to ask, and a carefully prepared résumé. At the end of the meeting they ask if the interviewer knows employers who might need their skills. They call all of the leads they get and use the referral as an opening for a job interview: "I was speaking with John Smith at the Ajax Company, and he suggested that I give you a call about a position you have open." A friend of mine got an information-gathering interview and wowed the personnel manager with her professionally prepared résumé and interviewing skills; even though the company

▶

continued PERSONAL RESPONSIBILITY | at Work

"had no openings" when she first called, two days after the interview, she was offered a position.

Accepting responsibility not only helps you *get* a great job, it makes it possible to *excel* on the job. Employers love responsible employees. Wouldn't you? Instead of complaining, blaming, making excuses, and thus creating an emotionally draining work environment, responsible employees create a positive workplace where absenteeism is low and work production is high. Instead of repeating ineffective solutions to problems, proactive employees seek solutions, take new actions, and try something new. They pursue alternative routes instead of complaining about dead ends. Creators show initiative instead of needing constant direction, and they do their best work even when the boss isn't looking. Creators are willing to go the extra mile, and this effort pays off handsomely. As someone once said, "There is no traffic jam on the extra mile." If you run into a challenge while preparing for a career, seeking a job, or working in your career, don't complain, blame, or make excuses. Instead, ask yourself a Creator's favorite question: "What's my plan?"

TECH TIPS: Personal Responsibility

Locus of Control is the scientific term that describes the degree to which you believe that that your outcomes and experiences are the result of your choices or of forces outside your control, such as luck or powerful others. In other words, measuring locus of control is a way to measure the degree to which you take responsibility for your life. To further assess yourself on this important success factor, do an Internet search for "locus of control test." The first test of this kind was created by psychologist Julian Rotter in 1966, and you can still find his tests posted online, along with a number of others.

Ahoona.com is an online tool that walks you through a process of making decisions. Funded by a grant from the National Science Foundation, this site was created by Dr. Ali Abbasa, a college professor who teaches decision analysis. The decision-making process asks you for important information such as goals, pros and cons, alternatives, and uncertainties. At each step of the decision-making process, it provides information about how to think more deeply. Tools used include pro/con, decision trees, and weight and rate. There is also a social media option that allows you to invite friends or anyone in the world to weigh in on your decision. *(Web)*

ChoiceMap is an app designed to help make difficult decisions. It asks you to describe your decision and possible options (e.g., *What subject should I major in: biology, English, or math?*) and the factors influencing your decision (e.g., difficulty, time to degree, your interest level, employment outlook). Then you weight the personal importance of each factor and apply the ratings to each option. Choice-Map's algorithm rates each option, showing how close it comes to being your perfect choice. Use the app to help you make decisions ranging from what to have for breakfast to who to marry. While this app does show your "best" options, you are, of course, responsible for your final choice. No fair complaining later that "The app made me do it." *(iOS)*

DecisionBuddy, like ChoiceMap, is an app that breaks down the decision-making process into little steps that guide you to your final choice. *(Android)*

Note: All of the above are free, but some may offer upgraded features for a fee.

Change Your Inner Conversation

FOCUS QUESTION   How can you raise your self-esteem by changing your self-talk?

Imagine this: Three students schedule an appointment with their instructor to discuss a project they're working on together. They go to the instructor's office at the scheduled time, but he isn't there. They wait 45 minutes before leaving. As you learn what they do next, which student do you think has the strongest self-esteem?

Student 1, feeling discouraged and depressed, spends the evening watching television while neglecting assignments in other subjects. Student 2, feeling insulted and furious, spends the evening complaining to friends about the horrible instructor who stood them up. Student 3, feeling puzzled about the mix-up, emails the instructor to see what happened and to set up another meeting; while waiting for a response, this student spends the evening studying for a test in another class.

Which student has the strongest self-esteem?

It is the mind that maketh good or ill, That maketh wretch or happy, rich or poor.

Edmund Spenser

THE CURSE OF STINKIN' THINKIN'

How is it that three people can have the same experience and respond to it so differently? According to psychologists like Albert Ellis, the answer lies in what each person believes caused the event. Ellis suggested that different responses can be understood by realizing that the activating event (A) plus our beliefs (B) equal the consequences (C) (how we respond). In other words, A + B = C. For example:

Self-esteem can be defined as the state that exists when you are not arbitrarily haranguing and abusing yourself but choose to fight back against those automatic thoughts with meaningful rational responses.

Dr. Thomas Burns

Activating Event	+ Beliefs	= Consequence
Student #1: Instructor didn't show up for a scheduled conference.	My instructor thinks I'm dumb. I'll never get a college degree. I'm a failure in life.	Got depressed and watched television all evening.
Student #2: Same.	My instructor won't help me. Teachers don't care about students.	Got angry and spent the night telling friends how horrible the instructor is.
Student #3: Same.	I'm not sure what went wrong. Sometimes things just don't turn out the way you plan. There's always tomorrow.	Emailed the instructor to see what happened and to set up a new appointment; then studied for another class.

Ellis suggests that our upsets are caused not so much by our problems as by what we *think* about our problems. When our thinking is full of irrational beliefs—what Ellis calls "stinkin' thinkin'"—we feel awful even when the circumstances don't warrant it. So, how we *think* about the events in our lives is the key issue. Problems may come and go, but our "stinkin' thinkin'" stays with us. As the old saying goes, "Everywhere I go, there I am."

Stinkin' thinkin' isn't based on reality. Rather, these irrational thoughts are the automatic chatter of the Inner Critic (keeper of Negative Beliefs about the self) and the Inner Defender (keeper of Negative Beliefs about other people and the world).

So what about our three students and their self-esteem? It's not hard to see that Student 1, who got depressed and wasted the evening watching television, has low self-esteem. This student is thrown far off course simply by the instructor's not showing up. A major cause of this self-defeating reaction is the Inner Critic's harsh self-judgments. Here are some common self-damning beliefs held by Inner Critics:

I'm dumb.	I'm unattractive.
I'm selfish.	I'm lazy.
I'm a failure.	I'm not college material.
I'm incapable.	I'm weak.
I'm not as good as other people.	I'm a lousy parent.
I'm worthless.	I'm unlovable.

People dominated by their Inner Critic often misinterpret events, inventing criticisms that aren't there. A friend says, "Something came up, and I can't meet you tonight." The Inner Critic responds, "I screwed up again! I'll never have any friends!"

The activating event doesn't cause the consequence; rather, the judgmental chatter of the Inner Critic does. A strong Inner Critic is both a cause and an effect of low self-esteem.

What about Student 2, the one who spent the evening telling friends how horrible the instructor was? Though perhaps less apparent, this student's judgmental response also demonstrates low self-esteem. The finger-pointing Inner Defender is merely the Inner Critic turned outward and is just as effective at getting the student off course. Here are some examples of destructive beliefs held by an Inner Defender:

People don't treat me right, so they're rotten.
People don't act the way I want them to, so they're awful.
People don't live up to my expectations, so they're the enemy.
People don't do what I want, so they're against me.
Life is full of problems, so it's terrible.
Life is unfair, so I can't stand it.
Life doesn't always go my way, so I can't be happy.
Life doesn't provide me with everything I want, so it's unbearable.

People dominated by their Inner Defender imagine personal insults and slights in neutral events. A classmate says, "Something came up, and I can't meet you tonight." The Inner Defender responds, "Who do you think you are, anyway? I can find someone a lot better to study with than you!"

The activating event doesn't cause the angry response; rather, the judgmental chatter of the judgmental Inner Defender does. A strong Inner Defender is both a cause and an effect of low self-esteem.

Only Student 3 demonstrates high self-esteem. This student realizes he doesn't know why the instructor missed the meeting. He doesn't blame himself, the instructor, or a rotten world. He considers alternatives: Perhaps the instructor got sick or was involved in a traffic accident. Until he finds out what happened and decides what to do next, this student turns his attention to an action that will keep him on course to another goal. The Inner Guide is concerned with positive results, not judging self or others. A strong Inner Guide is both a cause and an effect of high self-esteem.

DISPUTING IRRATIONAL BELIEFS

How, then, can you avoid stinkin' thinkin'?

First, you can become aware of the chatter of your Inner Critic and Inner Defender. Be especially alert when events in your life go wrong, when your desired outcomes and experiences are thwarted. That's when we are most likely to complain, blame, and excuse. That's when we substitute judgments of ourselves or others for the positive actions that would get us back on course.

Once you become familiar with your inner voices, you can begin a process of separating yourself from your Inner Critic and Inner Defender. To do this, practice disputing your irrational and self-sabotaging beliefs. Here are four effective ways to dispute:

- **Offer evidence that your judgments are incorrect:** *My instructor emailed me last week to see if I needed help with my project, so there's no rational reason to believe he won't help me now.*

- **Offer a positive explanation of the problem:** *Sure my instructor didn't show up, but he may have missed the appointment because of a last-minute crisis.*

- **Question the importance of the problem:** *Even if my instructor won't help me, I can still do well on this project, and if I don't, it won't be the end of the world.*

- **If you find that your judgments are true, instead of continuing to criticize yourself or someone else, offer a plan to improve the situation:** *If I'm honest, I have to admit that I haven't done well in this class so far From now on I'm going to attend every class, take good notes, read my assignments two or three times, and work with a study group before every test.*

According to psychologist Ellis, a key to correcting irrational thinking is changing a "must" into a preference. When we think "must," what follows in our thoughts is typically awful, terrible, and dreadful. For example, my Inner Defender's belief that an instructor "must" meet me for an appointment or he is an awful, terrible, dreadful person is irrational; I'd certainly "prefer" him to meet me for an appointment,

> Replacing a negative thought with a positive one changes more than just the passing thought—it changes the way you perceive and deal with the world.
>
> Dr. Clair Douglas

> Does it help to change what you say to yourself? It most certainly does. . . . Tell yourself often enough that you'll succeed and you dramatically improve your chances of succeeding and of feeling good.
>
> Drs. Bernie Zilbergeld & Arnold A. Lazarus

but his not meeting me does not make him horrible—in fact, he may have a perfectly good reason for not meeting with me. As another example, my Inner Critic's belief that I "must" pass this course or I am an awful, terrible, dreadful person is irrational; I'd certainly "prefer" to pass this course, but not doing so does not make me worthless—in fact, not passing this course may lead me to something even better. Believing irrationally that I, another person, or the world "must" be a particular way, Ellis says, is a major cause of my distress and misery.

STEREOTYPE THREAT

Social psychologist Claude Steele of Stanford University has identified a kind of stinkin' thinkin' that afflicts cultural groups: *stereotype threat*. A stereotype is a generalization about members of a particular group. For example, *African Americans are all excellent in sports but they aren't good students . . . or women are all terrific at taking care of children but they are poor at math and science.* Stereotype threat is a fear that your behavior in a particular situation—such as taking a math test—might confirm a negative stereotype about a cultural group to which you belong. The resulting anxiety causes a self-fulfilling prophesy, and you do, indeed, perform down to the stereotype rather than up to your ability.

As an example of the effect of stereotype threat, Steele and his colleagues showed that when race was emphasized, African-American college students did less well than their white classmates on a standardized test. However, when race was not emphasized, African-American students' scores were equivalent to those of white students. Further studies have shown that the academic success of many cultural groups fall prey to stereotype threat, including Latinos, females in math, and students of working-class backgrounds.

Here's how stinkin' thinkin' seems to contribute to stereotype threat. Let's say a female student sits down to take a math test. That's the activating event. Next come her beliefs: She knows the stereotype—women aren't good at math. She doesn't want to be lumped into or reinforce that stereotype. She becomes anxious, distracted, and can't remember all she studied. The result is a self-fulfilling prophesy. She doesn't do as well on the test as she is capable of, and the culprit is her stinkin' thinkin'.

Besides causing immediate problems in test situations, stereotype threat may even cause people to avoid the threat area altogether. A woman may avoid majoring in math and science. A white man may reject playing basketball. A working-class student may lose motivation and drop out of college.

The strategies for disputing that were mentioned earlier can also be applied to stereotype threat. A woman may **offer evidence that the stereotype is wrong**: *I did pretty well in math and science in high school . . . and I just read that four women recently won Nobel Prizes in science and mathematics.* A white man may **question the importance of the stereotype**: *I may not be the best player on the basketball team, but so what . . . it's great fun.* A working-class student may **offer a plan to address the stereotype**: *My English teacher told us her parents were migrant farm workers; I'm going to talk to her about how she kept herself motivated to get a college degree.*

Y ou mainly make yourself needlessly and neurotically miserable by strongly holding absolutist irrational beliefs, especially by rigidly believing unconditional shoulds, oughts, and musts.

Albert Ellis

E veryone experiences stereotype threat. We are all members of some group about which negative stereotypes exist, from white males and Methodists to women and the elderly.

Claude M. Steele

Another way to reduce the negative impact of stereotype threat has been suggested by psychologists Michael Johns, Toni Schmader, and Andy Martens in a study at the University of Arizona. They gave a math test to one group of students and found that female students performed worse than the men. Before giving the math test to a second group, they told students briefly about how stereotype threat could negatively affect the performance of women. Specifically, they announced, "It's important to keep in mind that if you are feeling anxious while taking this test, this anxiety could be the result of these negative stereotypes that are widely known in society and have nothing to do with your actual ability to do well on the test." In this second round of tests, female students did as well as the men. It seems that simply knowing about stereotype threat can reduce its power.

The guiding principle in this section is simple: Choose wisely the thoughts you allow to occupy your mind. Avoid letting automatic, negative thoughts or negative stereotypes undermine your self-esteem or your results. Evict stinkin' thinkin' and replace it with thoughts that empower.

When a woman mathematician enters a room, attends a meeting, goes to a conference, or applies for a job, the first thing that is noticed is that she is a woman . . . As a result, many women talk about feeling 'guilty until proven innocent.'

Claudia Henrion

JOURNAL ENTRY / 7

In this activity, you will practice disputing the judgments of your Inner Critic and your Inner Defender. As you become more skilled at seeing yourself, other people, and the world more objectively and without distracting judgments, your self-esteem will thrive.

1 Write a sentence expressing a recent problem or event that upset you. Think of something troubling that happened in school, at work, or in your personal life. For example, *I got a 62 on my math test.*

2 Write a list of three or more criticisms your Inner Critic (IC) might level against you as a result of this situation. Have your Inner Guide (IG) dispute each one immediately. Review the four methods of disputing described in the section Disputing Irrational Beliefs. You only need to use one of them for each criticism. For example,

IC: You failed that math test because you're terrible in math.

IG: It's true I failed the math test, but I'll study harder next time and do better. This was only the first test, and I now know what to expect next time.

3 Write a list of three or more criticisms your Inner Defender (ID) might level against someone else or life as a result of this situation. Have your Inner Guide (IG) dispute each one immediately. Again use one of the four methods for disputing. For example,

ID: You failed that math test because you've got the worst math instructor on campus.

IG: I have trouble understanding my math instructor, so I'm going to make an appointment to talk with him in private. John ▶

JOURNAL ENTRY **7** *continued*

really liked him last semester, so I bet I'll like him, too, if I give him a chance.

4 **Make a choice—write about one of the following:**

A. **Write what you have learned or relearned about changing your inner conversation.** Your journal entry might begin: *In reading and writing about my inner conversations, I have discovered that . . . .* Wherever possible, offer personal experiences or examples to explain what you learned.

B. One instructor said about this journal entry: "While I understand the importance of having students change their inner conversations, I don't think they ever actually apply what they write in their journals to the challenging situations in their lives. In other words, there's a big gap between what they learn and what they do." **Write a reply to this instructor expressing your opinion about her concern.**

ONE STUDENT'S STORY

DOMINIC GRASSETH, *Lane Community College, Oregon*

Enrolling in college at the age of 28 was very intimidating to me. Having dropped out of high school at 15, I had a real problem with confidence. Even though I had a GED and was earning a decent living as a car salesman, I still doubted that I was smart enough to be successful in college. I finally took the leap and enrolled because I want a career where I don't have to work 12 hours a day, six days a week and never see my family. However, by the second week of the semester, I found myself falling back into old habits. I was sitting in the back of the classroom, asking what homework was due, and talking through most of the class. Negative thoughts constantly ran through my mind: *The teachers won't like me. I can't compete with the*

18-year-olds right out of high school. I don't even remember what a "verb" is. I can't do this.

Then in my College Success class, we read Chapter 2 of *On Course* about becoming a Creator and disputing "stinkin' thinkin'." I realized I had taken on the role of the Victim almost my whole life, and I was continuing to do it now. One day I was on my porch when I caught myself thinking my usual negative thoughts. It occurred to me that I was the only one holding me back, not the teachers, not the other students, not math, not English. If I wanted to be successful in college, I had to quit being scared. I had to change my thinking. So I made a deal with myself that any time I caught myself thinking negatively, I would rephrase

the statement in a way that was more positive. I started to truly pay attention to the thoughts in my head and question the negative things I was telling myself. After that I began sitting up front in my classes and participating more. I've always been kind of scattered, so I started using a calendar and a dry-erase board to keep track of what I had to do.

What amazes me is that I didn't really make that big of a change, yet I finished the semester with a 4.0 average! All I did was realize that what I was saying to myself was my underlying problem. I am responsible for my thoughts, and the choice about whether or not to succeed is mine. These days when I have a ridiculous thought going through my mind and I change it, I smile. It's very empowering.

Photo: Courtesy of Dominic Grasseth.

Discovering
Self-Motivation

Successful Students . . .

▶ **create inner motivation,** providing themselves with the passion and drive to persist toward their goals and dreams, despite all obstacles.

▶ **design a compelling life plan,** complete with motivating goals and dreams.

▶ **commit to their goals and dreams,** visualizing the successful creation of their ideal future.

Struggling Students . . .

▶ **have little sense of passion and drive,** often quitting when difficulties arise.

▶ **tend to invent their lives as they live them.**

▶ **wander aimlessly from one activity to another.**

Once I accept responsibility for creating my own life, I must choose the kind of life I want to create.

I'm motivated to create the outcomes and experiences I've chosen for my life.

CASE STUDY IN CRITICAL THINKING / Popson's Dilemma

Fresh from graduate school, Assistant Professor Popson was midway through his first semester of college teaching when he began to get discouraged. Long gone were the excitement and promise of the first day of class. Now, only about two-thirds of his students were attending, and some of them were barely holding on. When Popson asked a question during class, the same few students answered every time. The rest stared off in bored silence. One student always wore a knit cap with a slender cord slithering from under it to a smartphone in his shirt pocket. With 10 or even 15 minutes remaining in a class period, students would start stuffing notebooks noisily into their backpacks or book bags. Only one student had visited him during office hours, despite Popson's numerous invitations. And when he announced one day that he was canceling the next class to attend a professional conference, a group in the back of the room pumped their fists in the air and hooted with glee. It pained Popson to have aroused so little academic motivation in his students, and he began asking experienced professors what he should do.

Professor Assante said, "Research says that about 70 percent of students enroll in college because they see the degree as their ticket to a good job and fat paycheck. And they're right. College grads earn nearly a million dollars more in their lives than high school grads. Show them how your course will help them graduate and prosper in the work world. After that, most of them will be model students."

Professor Buckley said, "Everyone wants the freedom to make choices affecting their lives, so have your students design personal learning contracts. Let each one choose assignments from a list of options you provide. Let them add their own choices if they want. Even have them pick the dates they'll turn in their assignments. Give them coupons that allow them to miss any three classes without penalty. Do everything you can to give them choices and put them in charge of their own education.

Once they see they're in control of their learning and you're here to help them, their motivation will soar."

Professor Chang said, "Deep down, everyone wants to make a difference. I just read a survey by the Higher Education Research Institute showing that two-thirds of first-year students believe it's essential or very important to help others. Find out what your students want to do to make a contribution. Tell them how your course will help them achieve those dreams. Even better, engage them in a service learning project. When they see how your course can help them live a life with real purpose, they'll be much more interested in what you're teaching."

Professor Donnelly said, "Let's be realistic. The best motivator for students is grades. It's the old carrot and stick. Start every class with a quiz and they'll get there on time. Take points off for absences and they'll attend regularly. Give extra points for getting assignments in on time. Reward every positive action with points and take off points when they screw up. When they realize they can get a good grade in your class by doing what's right, even the guy with the smartphone will get involved."

Professor Egret said, "Most people work harder and learn better when they feel they're part of a team with a common goal, so help your students feel part of a community of learners. Give them interesting topics to talk about in pairs and small groups. Give them team assignments and group projects. Teach them how to work well in groups so everyone contributes their fair share. When your students start feeling like they belong and start caring about one another, you'll see their academic motivation go way up."

Professor Fanning said, "Your unmotivated students probably don't expect to pass your course, so they quit trying. Here's my suggestion: Assign a modest challenge at which they can all succeed if they do it. And every student *has* to do it. No exceptions. Afterward, give students specific feedback on what they did well and what they can do to improve. Then give them a slightly more challenging assignment and repeat the cycle again and again. Help them *expect* to be successful by *being* successful. At some point they're going to say, 'Hey, I can do this!' and then you'll see a whole different attitude."

Professor Gonzales said, "Learning should be active and fun. I'm not talking about a party; I'm talking engaging students in educational experiences that teach deep and important lessons about your subject. Your students should be thinking, 'I can't wait to get to class to see what we're going to do and learn today!' You can use debates, videos, field trips, group projects, case studies, learning games, simulations, role plays, guest speakers,

visualizations . . . the possibilities are endless. When learning is engaging and enjoyable, motivation problems disappear."

Professor Harvey said, "I've been teaching for 30 years, and if there's one thing I've learned, it's this: You can't motivate someone else. Maybe you've heard the old saying, 'When the student is ready, the teacher will arrive.' You're just wasting your energy trying to make someone learn before they're ready. Maybe they'll be back in your class in five or ten years and they'll be motivated. But for now, just do the best you can for the students who *are* ready."

Listed below are the eight professors in this story. Based on your experience, rank the quality of their advice on the scale below. Give a different score to each professor. Be prepared to explain your choices.

Best advice ◄   ► Worst advice

Professor	What Motivates Students
___ **Professor Assante**	Good job and fat paycheck
___ **Professor Buckley**	Freedom to make choices
___ **Professor Chang**	Desire to make a difference
___ **Professor Donnelly**	Good grades
___ **Professor Egret**	Feel part of a community
___ **Professor Fanning**	Expectation of being successful
___ **Professor Gonzalez**	Learning that is engaging and enjoyable
___ **Professor Harvey**	Can't motivate someone else

DIVING DEEPER

Is there an approach not mentioned by one of the eight professors that would be even more motivating for you?

Creating Inner Motivation

FOCUS QUESTIONS   How important do educators think motivation is to your academic success? What determines how motivated you are? What can you do to keep your motivation consistently high this semester . . . and beyond?

Recently, two extensive surveys asked college and university educators to rank factors that hinder students' success and persistence. These surveys were done by American College Testing (ACT) and the Policy Center on the First Year of College. In both surveys, educators identified *lack of motivation* as the number one barrier to students' success in college.

There are three things to remember about education. The first is motivation. The second is motivation. The third is motivation.

Terrell Bell, former U.S.
Secretary of Education

Lack of motivation has various symptoms: students arriving late to class or being absent, assignments turned in late or not at all, work done sloppily, appointments missed, offers of support ignored, and students not participating in class discussions or activities, to name just a few. But the most glaring symptom of all is the enormous number of students who vanish from college within their first year. According to ACT, about one-third of students in U.S. four-year public colleges and universities fail to return for their second year. In public two-year colleges, it's even worse: Nearly *half* of first-year students don't make it to a second year. Despite these grim statistics, you can be among those who stay and thrive in higher education!

A FORMULA FOR MOTIVATION

The study of human motivation—exploring why we do what we do—is extensive and complex. However, one formula explains much about academic motivation: $V \times E = M$.

Today's theories about motivation emphasize the importance of factors within the individual, particularly the variables of expectancy and value. Students' motivations are strongly influenced by what they think is important (value) and what they believe they can accomplish (expectancy).

K. Patricia Cross

In this formula, "V" stands for value. In terms of your education, value is determined by the benefits you believe you'll obtain from seeking and obtaining a college degree. The greater the benefits you assign to college outcomes and experiences, the greater will be your motivation. The greater your motivation, the higher the cost you'll be willing to pay in terms of time, money, effort, frustration, inconvenience, and sacrifice. Take a moment to identify the score that presently represents the value you place on seeking and obtaining a college education. Choose a number from 0 to 10 (where "0" represents no perceived value and "10" represents an extremely high perceived value).

Having rated the value you place on achieving a college education, consider for a moment how your deep culture influenced your rating. Some cultural beliefs will boost your motivation, giving you staying power when the going gets rough. For example, most Chinese mothers place a high value on education, according to researcher Ruth K. Choa. They are quite willing to make big sacrifices to help their children succeed in school. Parents of middle- and upper-class students in North America are also known to place a high value on education. When parents in a culture demonstrate with words and deeds that they value education, the odds are great their children will as well.

Conversely, some cultures devalue formal education, thus lowering academic motivation. Working-class culture in North America often encourages its members to leave school in favor of a job and paycheck. Once the majority on campus, men now represent only about 43 percent of enrollment at North American colleges. It appears that to a growing number of men, "school is not cool." Some minorities, anthropologist John Ogbu observed, put little effort into academics in order to avoid the cultural stigma of acting "white." In a dominant culture that prizes education, such mindsets put members of these cultures in a painful dilemma. To do well in school goes against their culture, but to do poorly in school handicaps their future. Bottom line: To keep your motivation high, you'll need to have a clear sense of the personal value to you of a college degree.

In the formula $V \times E = M$, the "E" stands for expectation. In terms of your education, expectation is determined by how likely you think it is that you can earn a college degree with a reasonable effort. To make that calculation, you need to weigh your abilities (how good a student you are and how strong your previous education is) against the difficulty of achieving your goal (how challenging the courses are that you will need to take and how much you are willing to sacrifice to be successful). Take a moment to identify the score that presently represents your personal expectation of being able to complete a college degree with a reasonable effort. Choose a number from 0 to 10 (where "0" represents no expectation of success and "10" represents an extremely high expectation of success).

Once again, consider how cultural influences may have swayed your expectations of success in college. If your rating is high, consider whether your score reflects the expectation of your parents or others in your culture. Studies show that many middle- and upper-class students in North America, as well as Asian-American students, have internalized high expectations for achieving academic success. However, members of other cultures may not have the same beliefs to lift their motivation. See if you can spot a self-defeating generalization about a group to which you belong because of your race, religion, sex, economic class, age, ethnicity, ability, or geographical region. For example, a young woman in my writing class once told me she knew she was going to fail. It was only the first day of the class and I asked her why she thought that. "I'm from the country," she said, "and people from the country can't write." I asked where she had learned that. "My fifth-grade teacher told us," she replied. And her tone said, "There, that *proves* it."

Research shows that teacher expectations influence students' own expectations of academic success. Fortunately, many teachers hold very high expectations for their students. Sadly, some instructors hold low expectations for all students, while some hold low expectations just for students of a particular culture. If you've had such a teacher, or encounter one in college, don't allow a Victim mindset to buy into disempowering stereotypes such as people from the country can't write, or women can't learn math, or students with learning disabilities aren't college material, or older students have lost the ability to learn. Instead, employ a Creator mindset, set your own high expectations, and live up to them.

There is evidence that the time for learning various subjects would be cut to a fraction of the time currently allotted if the material were perceived by the learner as related to his own purposes.

Carl Rogers

Students tend to internalize the beliefs teachers have about their ability and they rise and fall in achieving the level of expectation of their teachers.

Lynn Kell Spradlin

In a nutshell, the V × E = M formula says that your level of motivation in college is determined by multiplying your value score by your expectation score. For example, if the value you place on a college degree is high (say, a 10), but your expectation of success in college is low (say, a 1), then your motivation score will be very low (10). Similarly, if you put little value on a college degree (say a 2), even if your expectation for success in college is high (say, a 9), then once more, your motivation score will be very low (18). In either case, your low score suggests that you probably won't do what is required to succeed in college: to make goal-directed choices consistently, to give a high-quality effort regularly, and to persist despite inevitable obstacles and challenges. Sadly, then, you'll likely join the multitude of students who exit college long before earning a degree.

Probably you see where all of this leads. To stay motivated in college, first, you need ways to raise (or keep high) the **value** you place on college, including the academic degree you'll earn, the knowledge you'll gain, and the experiences you'll have while enrolled. Second, you need ways to raise (or keep high) the **expectation** you have of being successful in college while making what you consider to be a reasonable effort. Throughout *On Course*, you'll encounter literally hundreds of skills that, when mastered, will contribute greatly to your expectations for success in college.

For now, however, we are going to focus on value. Only you can determine how much value a college education holds for you, but let's look at some of the benefits that others have attributed to achieving a degree beyond high school.

VALUE OF COLLEGE OUTCOMES

One of the most widely recognized benefits of a college degree is increased earning power. According to recent U.S. Census Bureau data, high school graduates earn an average of $1.2 million dollars during their working lives. However, if you complete a two-year associate's degree, that lifetime total goes up another $400,000. If you complete a four-year bachelor's degree, you can add another $500,000. That means college graduates earn nearly one million dollars more in their lifetimes than those who end their formal education with a high school degree. Think what that additional money could do to help you and the people you love live a good life.

Not only does a college degree offer increased earnings, it also opens doors to employment in many desirable professions. Six out of every 10 jobs now require some postsecondary education and training, according to data reported by the ERIC Clearinghouse on Higher Education. The U.S. Department of Labor reports that the number of jobs requiring advanced skills now grows at twice the rate of those requiring only basic skills.

A college degree confers many additional benefits. According to the Institute for Higher Education Policy and the Carnegie Foundation, college graduates enjoy . . .

- higher savings levels.
- improved working conditions.
- increased personal and professional mobility.

F or learning to take place with any kind of efficiency, students must be motivated. To be motivated, they must become interested. And they become interested when they are actively working on projects which they can relate to their values and goals in life.

Gus Tuberville, former president, William Penn College

- improved health and life expectancy.
- improved quality of life for offspring.
- better consumer decision making.
- increased personal status.
- more hobbies and leisure activities.

College grads also become more open-minded, more cultured, more rational, more consistent, and less authoritarian. As a bonus, these benefits are passed on to their children.

Additionally, attaining a college degree can bring personal satisfaction and accomplishment. I once had a 76-year-old student who inspired our class with her determination "to finally earn the college degree that I cheated myself out of more than 50 years ago." Another valuable outcome of a college degree is the pride and esteem that many enjoy when they walk across the stage to receive their hard-earned diploma. And for some, a college degree is an essential step toward fulfilling a personal vision; such was true for my college roommate who, for as long as he could remember, dreamed of being a doctor (and today he is one).

For some people, long-term goals are too distant to be motivating. They do get fired up, however, by short-term goals they can nearly touch, such as outcomes they can create during this semester. Table 3.1 shows the short-term goals that one of my students chose for himself, along with his reasons why.

> The value of a college education is not the learning of many facts but the training of the mind to think.
>
> Albert Einstein

TABLE 3.1 One Student's Desired Outcomes

Desired Outcomes	Value
Earn a grade point average (GPA) of 3.8 or better and make the Dean's List this semester.	A high GPA will look great on my transcript when I apply for a job. Also, it will give me a real boost of self-confidence.
In my English class, write at least one essay that contains no more than two nonstandard grammar errors.	I want to be able to write without worrying that someone who reads my work is going to think I'm stupid or illiterate.
In my Student Success class, learn at least three strategies for managing my time more effectively.	I feel overwhelmed and stressed with all I need to do, and learning how to manage my time better will lower my stress level.
Get an A in my accounting class.	I want a career in accounting, so doing well in this course is the first step toward success in my profession.
Make three or more new friends.	My friends from high school all went to other colleges or they're working. I want to make new friends here so I'll have people to hang out with on the weekends.

VALUE OF COLLEGE EXPERIENCES

Value isn't found only in outcomes; it's also found in experiences. In fact, all human beings manage their emotions by doing their best to maximize positive experiences and minimize negative ones. What, for example, is the value of playing an intramural sport, attending a movie, belonging to a fraternity or sorority, dancing, playing a video game, or hanging out with friends? Primarily, all are choices to manage our inner experiences. If done in excess, any one of these choices can get us off course from our desired outcomes. But done in moderation, all of these activities (and many others) can create a positive experience and contribute greatly to academic motivation. That's because if you're enjoying the journey called college, you're much more likely to persist until you reach the destination called graduation.

So, what are your desired experiences in college? If someday in the future you were to tell someone that college was one of the best experiences of your life, what specifically would you have experienced? Many will say "fun." Fair enough. Then make fun happen. Your challenge is to experience fun while staying on course to academic success. And you can do it! Consider these options for fun: Join a club, play a sport, get to know a classmate, attend a party, learn something new that really interests you. Here are other experiences that my students desired: respect, relaxation, connection, self-confidence, an open mind, quiet reflection, passion for learning, total engagement, full-out participation, inspiration, challenge, courage, spirit of the group, self-acceptance, joy, pride, freedom, and an "Aha."

One of the students in my college success class said he wanted to experience "creativity." As an alternative to the final project, he proposed to write a rap song about the success principles he'd learned in our class. I told him he had my permission as long as he agreed to "rap" his project to our class on the last day of the semester. Little did I know that he was a professional rapper with a couple of CDs to his credit. As promised, he (and his whole group) showed up on the last day of the semester, handed out the words to "The College Success Rap," and treated us all to a rousing course finale. Best of all, he did a great job of demonstrating that he had learned many of the key principles of success, helping his classmates learn them even more deeply. Afterward he said, "Man, that was a great experience!"

Table 3.2 lists the desired experiences that another of my students identified for herself, along with her reasons why.

German philosopher Friedrich Nietzsche once said, "He who has a *why* to live for can endure almost any *how*." He affirms that few obstacles can stop us when we understand the personal value we place on the outcomes and experiences of our journey. Discover your own motivation and your chances for success soar!

Setting specific goals helps learners in at least three ways: The goals focus attention on important aspects of the task; they help motivate and sustain task mastery efforts; and they serve an information function by arming learners with criteria that they can use to assess and if necessary adjust their strategies as they work.

Jere Brophy

What ultimately counts most for each person is what happens in consciousness: the moments of joy, the times of despair added up through the years determine what life will be like. If we don't gain control over the contents of consciousness we can't live a fulfilling life.

Mihaly Csikszentmihaly

TABLE 3.2 One Student's Desired Experiences

Desired Experiences	Value
Fun	My brother dropped out of college because he said it was all work and no play. I know I'm going to have to work hard in college, but I want to have fun, too. I think if I'm enjoying myself, that'll make all the assignments more bearable.
Academic confidence	I've never done particularly well in school, although my teachers have always said I could be a good student if I applied myself more. I want to feel just as smart as any other student in my classes.
Excitement about learning	I didn't really like my classes in high school. I want to get excited about learning in at least one course, so I look forward to the homework and sometimes the class time goes so fast I can't believe when it's over.
Personal confidence	I have always been a shy person, and I want to become more outgoing so I can do well on future job interviews and be more assertive in my career so I get the promotions I deserve.

He who puts in four hours of "want to" will almost always outperform the person who puts in eight hours of "have to."

Roger von Oech

JOURNAL ENTRY / **8**

In this journal entry, you'll identify your desired outcomes and experiences for this course and/or this semester. Developing clarity on what you want to create this semester will help you stay motivated and on course until the end. Use the student examples earlier in this section as models, but of course record your own desired outcomes, experiences, and reasons.

1 In your journal, create an empty table like Table 3.1. Fill in three or more of your own desired *outcomes* for this course and/or this semester. Next to each, explain why you value achieving that outcome. Remember, "outcomes" are those things you will take *away* with you at the end of the semester (such as a grade or something you learn). At this point, you don't have to know HOW you will achieve these outcomes; you only need to know WHAT you want and WHY.

2 In your journal, create an empty table like Table 3.2. Fill in three or more of your desired *experiences* for this course and/or this semester. Next to each, explain why you value having that experience. Remember, "experiences" are those things you will have *during* this semester (such as fun or a sense of community). Once again, all that matters here is WHAT you would like to experience and WHY. At this time, you don't need to worry about HOW. ▶

Success isn't a result of spontaneous combustion. You must set yourself on fire.

Arnold H. Glasow

3 **Using the formula of V × E = M, write about your level of moti-**
vation to be successful in college. Begin as follows: *The value*
I place on being a success in college is ___ [0–10] and my expecta-
tion of being a success in college is ___ [0–10]. Multiplied together,
this gives me an achievement motivation score of ___ [0–100].
Then continue by explaining your score and identifying specific
actions you can do to raise it (or keep it high).

Remember, dive deep. When you explore your motivation at a deep
level, you improve your chances of having an important insight that can
change your life for the better. So dive deep and discover what really
motivates you.

ONE STUDENT'S STORY

CHEE MENG VANG, *Inver Hills Community College, Minnesota*

When I got to college, my biggest challenge was staying motivated. I was always going out clubbing with my friends, older sisters, and cousins. I was also shooting pool and hanging out with friends until late at night. I was lazy all the time and couldn't concentrate. I missed classes, fell behind in my homework, and tried to do everything at the last minute. This caused a lot of problems for me, like getting Ds on my tests and quizzes. I felt like whatever happened to me was out of my control. I was feeling down and filled with dissatisfaction.

One night I was in a club, watching people drinking and dancing, and I thought, "This is getting boring. I'm tired and this isn't taking me anywhere at all." It was a good thing that College Success was part of my full-time student schedule. Our book was called *On Course*, and it helped me big time. It taught me to see myself as the primary cause of my outcomes and experiences and to find my desires that cause me to act. I was so stupid because my desire was right in front of me. There are so many reasons why it is important that I do well in college. My parents came to the United States from Laos, and all they ever wanted was a better life for their kids. It was hard for them in a new country, and we never had very much money. I realized I was being a loser and letting them down. Also, I am the first man in my family to go to college and my lovely five little brothers look up to me. I need to show them what a good role model their big brother can be. I want a career that will allow me to help my family, and when I have children, I don't want to be a dad working in McDonald's. My dream is to be a pharmacist, but I was headed in the wrong direction.

I come from a poor family, and I don't ever want to be like that in the future, so I had to make changes right away. I stopped going out to clubs and started taking responsibility. I became more outgoing in class. I studied two hours or more every day. I started getting As and Bs on my tests and quizzes. I finished the semester by raising my D grades to Bs. As you can see, I've gone from being a lazy, unmotivated guy to a responsible, outgoing, I-control-my-destiny man. Now I don't feel like a victim any more. I've actually started to feel like a hero to my parents, my little brothers, and even to the small community where we live.

Designing a Compelling Life Plan

FOCUS QUESTIONS If your life were as good as it could possibly be, what would it look like? What would you have, do, and be?

While growing up, Joan dreamed of becoming a famous singer. Following high school, she started performing in night clubs. She married her manager, and the two of them lived in a motor home, driving from town to town in pursuit of singing jobs. After exhausting years on the road, Joan recorded a song. It didn't sell, and her dream began to unravel. Marital problems complicated her career. Career problems complicated her marriage. Joan grew tired of the financial and emotional uncertainty in her life. Finally, in frustration, she divorced her husband and gave up her dream of singing professionally.

> Your goals are the road maps that guide you and show you what is possible for your life.
>
> Les Brown

Although disappointed, Joan started setting new goals. She needed to earn a living, so she set a short-term goal to become a hairdresser. After graduating from cosmetology school, Joan saved enough money to settle some debts, buy a car, and pay for a new long-term goal. She decided to go to a community college (where I met her) and major in dental hygiene.

Two years later, Joan graduated with honors and went to work in a dentist's office. Lacking a dream that excited her, Joan chose another long-term goal: earning her bachelor's degree. Joan worked days in the dentist's office and at night she attended classes. After a few years, she again graduated with honors.

Then, she set another long-term goal: earning her master's degree. Earlier in her life, Joan had doubted that she was "college material." With each academic success, her confidence grew. "One day I realized that once I set a goal, it's a done deal," Joan said.

This awareness inspired her to begin dreaming again. As a child, Joan had always imagined herself as a teacher, but her doubts had always steered her in other directions. Master's degree now in hand, she returned to our college to teach dental hygiene. A year later, she was appointed department chairperson. In only seven years, Joan went from a self-doubting first-year student to head of our college's dental hygiene department. Despite obstacles and setbacks, she continued to move in a positive direction, ever motivated by the promise of achieving personally valuable goals and dreams.

> The most important thing about motivation is goal setting. You should always have a goal.
>
> Francie Larrieu Smith

ROLES AND GOALS

According to psychologist Brian Tracy, many people resist setting life goals because they don't know how. Let's eliminate this barrier so you, like Joan, can experience the heightened motivation that accompanies personally meaningful goals.

First, think about the roles you have chosen for your life. A life role is an activity to which we regularly devote large amounts of time and energy. For example, you're presently playing the role of college student. How many of the following roles are you also playing: friend, employee, employer, athlete,

CATHY   **by Cathy Guisewite**

One day Alice came to a fork in the road and saw a Cheshire cat in a tree. "Which road do I take?" she asked. "Where do you want to go?" was his response. "I don't know," Alice answered. "Then," said the cat, "it doesn't matter."

Lewis Carroll

brother, sister, church member, son, daughter, roommate, husband, wife, partner, parent, grandparent, tutor, musician, neighbor, volunteer? Do you play other roles as well? Most people identify four to seven major life roles. If you have more than seven, you may be spreading yourself too thin. Consider combining or eliminating one or more of your roles while in college. If you have identified fewer than four roles, assess your life again. You may have overlooked a role or two.

Once you identify your life roles, think about your long-term goals for each one. Identify what you hope to accomplish in this role in the next 2 to 5 or even 10 years. For example, in your role as a student, 10 years from now will you have a 2-year associate of arts (A.A.) degree? A 4-year bachelor of arts (B.A.) or bachelor of science (B.S.) degree? Will you have attended graduate school to earn a master of arts (M.A.) or master of science (M.S.) degree? Or gone even farther to obtain a doctor of philosophy (Ph.D.) degree, a medical doctor (M.D.) degree, or a doctor of jurisprudence (J.D.) law degree? Any of these future academic goals could be yours.

HOW TO SET A GOAL

To be truly motivating, a goal needs five qualities. You can remember them by applying the DAPPS rule. "DAPPS" is an acronym, a memory device in which each letter of the word stands for one of five qualities: Dated, Achievable, Personal, Positive, and Specific.

Dated

Motivating goals have specific deadlines. A short-term goal usually has a deadline within a few months (like your semester's desired outcomes set in Journal Entry 8). A long-term goal generally has a deadline as far in the future as 1 year, 5 years, even 10 years (such as the goal you have for your most advanced academic degree). As your target deadline approaches, your motivation typically increases. This positive energy helps you finish strong. If you don't meet your deadline, you have an opportunity to examine what went wrong and create a new plan. Without a deadline, you might stretch the pursuit of a goal over your whole life, never reaching it.

Achievable

Motivating goals are challenging but realistic. It's unrealistic to say you'll run a marathon (26+ miles) next week if your idea of a monster workout has been opening and closing the refrigerator. Still, if you're going to err, err on the side of optimism. When you set goals at the outer reaches of your present ability, stretching to reach them causes you to grow. Listen to other people's advice, but trust yourself to know what is achievable for you. Apply this guideline: "Is achieving this goal at least 50 percent believable to me?" If so and you *really* value it, go for it!

Personal

Motivating goals are your own. They aren't thrust upon you by someone else. Be aware of pressure to conform to the expectations of others. Maybe you have a passion for graphic design but your parents want you to major in business so you can join the family business. Also be aware of subtle pressure to conform to the norms of your culture at the expense of what you want. For example, all cultures create expectations about what men and women *should* do, and, interestingly, gender-role stereotypes are similar across cultures. If you're a woman who wants to be an engineer, don't set a goal to be a dental hygienist. If you're a man who wants to be a kindergarten teacher, don't set a goal to be a lawyer. You don't want to be on your deathbed some day and realize you have lived someone else's life. Trust that you know better than anyone else what you want.

Positive

Motivating goals focus your energy on what you *do* want rather than on what you *don't* want. So translate negative goals into positive goals. For example, a negative goal not to fail a class becomes a positive goal to earn a grade of B or better. I recall a race car driver explaining how he miraculously kept his spinning car from smashing into the concrete racetrack wall: "I kept my eye on the track, not the wall." Likewise, focus your thoughts and actions on where you *do* want to go rather than where you *don't* want to go, and you, too, will stay on course.

Specific

Motivating goals state outcomes in specific, measurable terms. It's not enough to say, "My goal is to do better this semester" or "My goal is to work harder at my job." How will you know if you've achieved these goals? What specific, measurable evidence will you have? Revised, these goals become, "I will complete every college assignment this semester to the best of my ability" and "I will volunteer for all offerings of overtime at work." Being specific keeps you from

Goals are dreams with a deadline.

Napoleon Hill

I always wanted to be somebody, but now I realize I should have been more specific.

Lily Tomlin

fooling yourself into believing you've achieved a goal when, in fact, you haven't. It also helps you make choices that create positive results.

Through the years, I've had the joy of working with students who have had wonderful and motivating long-term goals: becoming an operating room nurse, writing and publishing a novel, traveling around the world, operating a refuge for homeless children, marrying and raising a beautiful family, playing professional baseball, starting a private school, becoming a college professor, swimming in the Olympics, managing an international mutual fund, having a one-woman art show, becoming a fashion model, getting elected state senator, owning a clothing boutique, and more. How about you? What do you *really* want?

DISCOVER YOUR DREAMS

Perhaps even more than goals do, dreams fuel our inner fire. They give our lives purpose and guide our choices. They provide motivating energy when we run headlong into an obstacle. When Candy Lightner's daughter was killed by a drunk driver, she transformed this tragedy into her dream to stop drunk driving, and her dream became the international organization Mothers Against Drunk Driving (MADD). I found my dream only after 20 years of college teaching: My passion is empowering students with the beliefs and behaviors essential for living a rich and personally fulfilling life. Although it's difficult to define a dream, they're grand in size and fueled by strong emotions. Unlike goals, which usually fit into one of our life roles, dreams often take over our lives, inspire other people, and take on a life of their own. That's why I sometimes wonder if people have dreams or if dreams have people.

T he future belongs to those who believe in the beauty of their dreams.

Eleanor Roosevelt

If you presently have a big dream, you know how motivating it is. If you don't have a big dream, you're certainly in the majority. Most people have not found a guiding dream, yet they can still have great lives. College, though, offers a wonderful opportunity to discover or expand your dreams. You'll be exposed to hundreds, even thousands, of new people, ideas, and experiences. With each encounter, be aware of your energy. If you feel your voltage rise, pay attention. Something within you is getting inspired. If you're fortunate enough to find such a dream, consider the pithy advice of philosopher Joseph Campbell: "Follow your bliss."

YOUR LIFE PLAN

Wise travelers use maps to locate their destination and identify the best route to get there. Similarly, Creators identify their goals and dreams and the most direct path there. In creating such a life plan, it helps to start with your destination in mind and work backwards. If you have a dream, accomplishing it becomes your ultimate destination. Or maybe your destination is the accomplishment of one or more long-term goals for your life roles. Because you can't complete a long journey in one step, your short-term goals become stepping-stones, and each one completed brings you closer to the achievement of a long-term goal or dream.

Take a look at a page of a life plan that one student, Pilar, designed for herself. Although Pilar recorded her dream, not everyone will be able to do that. Her full life plan includes a page for each of her life roles, all of them with the same dream. Obviously, some life roles are going to make a more significant contribution to her dream than others. Notice that each long- and short-term goal adheres to the DAPPS rule.

MY DREAM: *I help families adopt older children (10 years old or older) and create home environments in which the children feel loved and supported to grow into healthy, productive adults.*

MY LIFE ROLE: *College student*

MY LONG-TERM GOALS IN THIS ROLE:

1. *I earn an associate of arts (A.A.) degree by June 2016.*
2. *I earn a bachelor of arts (B.A.) degree by June 2018.*
3. *I earn a master of social work (M.S.W.) degree by June 2020.*

MY SHORT-TERM GOALS IN THIS ROLE (THIS SEMESTER):

1. *I achieve an A in English 101 by December 18.*
2. *I write a research paper on the challenges of adopting older children by November 20.*
3. *I achieve an A in Psychology 101 by December 18.*
4. *I learn and apply five or more psychological strategies that will help my family be happier and more loving by November 30.*
5. *I achieve an A in College Success by December 18.*
6. *I dive deep in every* On Course *journal entry, writing a minimum of 500 words for each one.*
7. *I learn five or more new success strategies and teach them to my younger brothers by November 30.*
8. *I take at least one page of notes in every class I attend this semester.*
9. *I turn in every assignment on time this semester.*
10. *I learn to use a computer well enough to prepare all of my written assignments by October 15.*

This is the first page of Pilar's six-page life plan. She wrote a similar page for each of her other five life roles: sister, daughter, friend, athlete, and employee at a group home for children.

What is significant about a life plan is that it can help us live our own lives (not someone else's) as well as possible.

Harriet Goldhor Lerner

We . . . believe that one reason so many high-school and college students have so much trouble focusing on their studies is because they don't have a goal, don't know what all this studying is leading to.

Muriel James & Dorothy Jongeward

Consciously designing your life plan, as Pilar did, has many benefits. A life plan defines your desired destinations in life and charts your best route for getting there. It gives your Inner Guide something positive to focus on when the chatter of your Inner Critic or Inner Defender attempts to distract you. And, like all maps, a life plan helps you get back on course if you get lost.

Perhaps most of all, a life plan is your personal definition of a life worth living. With it in mind, you'll be less dependent on someone else to motivate you. Your most compelling motivation will be found within.

Many people fail in life, not for lack of ability or brains or even courage but simply because they have never organized their energies around a goal.

Elbert Hubbard

I started getting successful in school when I saw how college could help me achieve my dreams.

Bobby Marinelli, student

JOURNAL ENTRY 9

In this activity, you will design one or more parts of your life plan. To focus your thoughts, glance back at Pilar's life plan and use it as a model.

1 **Title a new page in your journal: MY LIFE PLAN. Below the title, complete the part of your life plan for your role as a student.**

My Dream: [If you have a compelling dream, describe it here. If you're not sure what your dream is, you can simply write, "I'm searching."]

My Life Role: Student

My Long-Term Goals in This Role: [These are the outcomes you plan to achieve as a student in the next 2 to 10 years, or even longer if necessary.]

My Short-Term Goals in This Role: [These are the outcomes you plan to achieve as a student this semester; each one achieved brings you closer to your long-term goals as a student. To begin your list of short-term goals, you can write the same desired outcomes that you chose in **Journal Entry 8**; then add other short-term goals as appropriate.]

Remember to apply the DAPPS rule, making sure that each long- and short-term goal is Dated, Achievable, Personal, Positive, and Specific. With this in mind, you may need to revise the desired outcomes that you transfer here from **Journal Entry 8**.

YOUR CHOICE: If you wish, repeat this process for one or more of your other life roles: employee, parent, athlete, and so on. The more roles you plan, the more complete your vision of life will be. Taken together, these pages map your route to a rich, personally fulfilling life.

At this time you don't have to know how to achieve your goals and dreams, so don't even think about the method. All you need to know is what you want. In the following chapters, you'll learn dozens of powerful strategies for turning your life plan into reality. For now, keep your eye on your destination!

2 **Write about what you have learned or relearned by designing your life plan.** In particular, identify any impact this effort has had on your level of motivation to do well in college this semester, or do well in any other parts of your life.

My older brother had always been my closest friend. When I was a junior in high school, he committed suicide, and I was the one who found his body. That is something no one should ever have to experience. The image haunted me, and my life took a bad turn. Sometimes I felt angry. Other times I felt numb. Even though I had a 3.7 average in high school and made the all-conference baseball team, I was just going through the motions of life. I quit thinking about long-term goals or anything like that. I felt like giving up, and I lost any sense of a future.

When I got to college, I wasn't thinking about what I wanted in life or where I planned on going. The journal assignments in *On Course* changed that. They made me reflect on things I have done in my life and things that have happened to me. I found out I was never really organized with anything I did; I was always going with the flow and living in the moment. Any goals I had were short-term ones I knew I could easily reach. Even though I received a baseball scholarship to play in college, I never really challenged myself to see what I could accomplish. I would always do my work and get good grades, but I never thought about how that would affect my future.

When I first started writing the journals, I would only write about half a page. I just wanted to get them done. Then I realized they were helping me figure out how to improve my life. That's when I started writing two or three pages. Sometimes I would reread my journals at night to see what my progress was. I've never written anything that affected my life like these journals. I went from writing as little as possible to taking my time and seeing what I could get out of each one.

As I wrote my way through the course, I realized that Victim thinking was dragging me down. I began taking responsibility for my own actions in every situation instead of blaming others for my own bad choices. I also realized that my life is my own and I want to live it for me. The course forced me to think seriously about who I am, what I want to do, and how I can achieve it. For the first time I have a plan for my life.

We have a family friend who is a police chief, and he told me about his work. What he said gave me the feeling that law enforcement was something I would enjoy doing. I want to help people and that's what he does every day. I have decided to complete my A.A. degree and then transfer to Kansas University to major in Criminal Justice with a minor in Psychology. After I get experience in local law enforcement, I plan on switching to the federal side, such as ATF, DEA, or Homeland Security.

In the future, I also plan on being a husband and a father. I will do my very best to shape my children in the positive way this class has shaped me. Life isn't easy. People go through struggles. I will teach them to not just dream, but to make plans, to set goals and keep themselves focused!

I'm happy with the way I live now. I'm organized, have a daily routine, and have future goals in mind. I have changed as an individual over the course of this semester by exploring deep down and finding out who I really want to be. I'm more outgoing, focused and responsible because of this course. I'm not only a better individual but a better writer. I didn't expect this course to change my life, but I've done a complete 180. I've gone from just going through the motions to having goals that I want to achieve. I'm feeling happier. I'm where I want to be in life.

Photo: Courtesy of Brandon Beavers.

Committing to Your Goals and Dreams

FOCUS QUESTIONS   Do you start new projects (such as college) with great enthusiasm, only to lose motivation along the way? How can you keep your motivation strong?

Many people doubt they can achieve what they truly want. When a big, exciting goal or dream creeps into their thoughts, they shake their heads. "Oh, sure," they mumble to themselves, "how am *I* going to accomplish that?"

In truth, you don't need to know how to achieve a goal or dream when you first think of it. What you do need is an unwavering commitment, fueled by a strong desire. Once you promise yourself that you will do whatever it takes to accomplish your goals and dreams, you often discover the method for achieving them in the most unexpected ways.

> Always bear in mind that your own resolution to succeed is more important than any one thing.
>
> Abraham Lincoln

COMMITMENT CREATES METHOD

A commitment is an unbending intention, a single-mindedness of purpose that promises to overcome all obstacles, regardless of how you may feel at any particular moment. During the summer between my sophomore and junior years in college, I learned the power of commitment.

That summer, I used all of my savings to visit Hawaii. While there, I met a beautiful young woman, and we spent 12 blissful days together.

One of my desires was to have a wonderful love relationship, so I promised to return to Hawaii during Christmas break. However, back in college 6,000 miles away, my commitment was sorely tested. I had no idea how, in just three months, I could raise enough money to return to Hawaii. Committed to my dream, though, I spent weeks inventing and rejecting one scheme after another. (Though I didn't realize it at the time, I was actually using the Wise Choice Process to find my best option.)

> When you have a clear intention, methods for producing the desired results will present themselves.
>
> Student Handbook, University of Santa Monica

Then one day, I happened upon a possible solution. I was glancing through *Sports Illustrated* magazine when I noticed an article written by a student-athlete from Yale University. Until that moment, all I'd had was a commitment. When I saw that article, I had a plan. A long shot, yes, but a plan, nonetheless: Maybe the editors of *Sports Illustrated* would buy an article about the sport I played, lightweight football. Driven by my commitment, I worked on an article every evening for weeks. Finally, I dropped it in the mail and crossed my fingers.

A few weeks later, my manuscript came back, rejected. On the printed rejection form, however, a kind editor had handwritten, "Want to try a rewrite? Here's how you might improve your article. . . ."

I spent another week revising the article, mailed it directly to my encouraging editor, and waited anxiously. Christmas break was creeping closer. I had just about given up hope of returning to Hawaii in December.

Then one day my phone rang, and the caller identified himself as a photographer from *Sports Illustrated*. "I'll be taking photos at your football game this weekend. Where can I meet you?"

And that's how I learned that my article had been accepted. Better yet, *Sports Illustrated* paid me enough money to return to Hawaii. I spent Christmas on the beach at Waikiki, with my girlfriend on the blanket beside me.

Suppose I hadn't made a commitment to return to Hawaii? Would reading *Sports Illustrated* have sparked such an outrageous plan? Would I, at 20 years of age, have ever thought to earn money by writing a feature article for a national magazine? Doubtful!

What intrigues me as I recall my experience is that the solution for my problem was there all the time; I just couldn't see it until I made a commitment.

By committing to our dreams, we program our brains to look for solutions to our problems and to keep us going when the path gets rough. Whenever you're tempted to look for motivation outside yourself, remember this: Motivation surges up from a *commitment* to a passionately held purpose.

> Once a commitment is made without the option of backing out, the mind releases tremendous energy toward its achievement.
>
> Ben Dominitz

VISUALIZE YOUR IDEAL FUTURE

Human beings seek to experience pleasure and avoid pain. Put this psychological truth to work for you by visualizing the pleasure you'll derive when you achieve your goals or dreams.

Cathy Turner explained how she visualized her way to winning two Olympic gold medals in speed skating: "As a little girl, I used to stand on a chair in front of the mirror and pretend I had won a gold medal. I'd imagine getting the medal, I'd see them superimposing the flag across my face just like they did on TV, and I would start to cry. When I really did stand on the podium, and they raised the American flag, it was incredible. I was there representing the United States, all of the United States. The flag was going up and the national anthem was being played, and there wasn't a mirror in front of me and it wasn't a chair I was standing on. I had dreamt that for so long. All my life. And my dream was coming true right then and there."

To make or strengthen your commitment to achieve success in college, do what Cathy Turner did. Visualize yourself accomplishing your fondest goal and imagine the delight you'll experience when it actually happens. Let this desired outcome and the associated positive experiences draw you like a magnet toward a future of your own design.

> From my own experience, there is no question that the speed with which you are able to achieve your goals is directly related to how clearly and how often you are able to visualize your goals.
>
> Charles J. Givens

Some years ago, I happened to glance at a three-ring notebook carried by one of my students. Taped to the cover was a photo showing her in a graduation cap and gown.

"Have you already graduated?" I asked.

"Not yet. But that's what I'll look like when I do."

"How did you get the photo?"

"My sister graduated from college a few years ago," she explained. "After the ceremony, I put on her cap and gown and had my mother take this picture. Whenever I get discouraged about school, I look at this photo and imagine myself walking across the stage to receive my diploma. I hear my family cheering for me, just like we did for my sister. Then I stop feeling sorry for myself and get back to work. This picture reminds me what all my hard work is for."

A few years later at her graduation, I remember thinking, "She looks just as happy today as she did in the photo. Maybe happier."

Life will test our commitments. To keep them strong in times of challenge, we need a clear picture of our desired results. We need a motivating mental image that, like a magnet, draws us steadily toward our ideal future.

The power of visualizing makes sense when you remember that getting anywhere is difficult if you don't know where you're going. A vivid mental image of your chosen destination keeps you on course even when life's adversities conspire against you.

> I see a Chicago in which the neighborhoods are once again the center of our city, in which businesses boom and provide neighborhood jobs, in which neighbors join together to help govern their neighborhood and their city.
>
> Harold Washington, Chicago's first black mayor

HOW TO VISUALIZE

Here are four keys to an effective visualization.

1. **Relax.** Visualizing seems to have the most positive impact when experienced during deep relaxation. One way to accomplish deep relaxation is to breathe deeply while you tighten muscle groups one by one from the tips of your toes to the top of your head.

2. **Use Present Tense.** Imagine yourself experiencing success *now*. Therefore, use the present tense for all verbs: *I am walking across the stage to receive my diploma.* OR *I walk across the stage.* (Not past tense: *I was walking across the stage*; and not future tense: *I will be walking across the stage.*)

3. **Use All Five Senses.** Imagine the scene concretely and specifically. Use all of your senses. What do you see, hear, smell, taste, touch?

4. **Feel the Feelings.** Events gain power to motivate us when accompanied by strong emotions. Imagine your accomplishment to be just as grand and magnificent as you wish it to be. Then feel the excitement of your success.

> Visualization takes advantage of what almost might be called a "weakness" of the body; it cannot distinguish between a vivid mental experience and an actual physical experience.
>
> Dr. Bernie Siegel

Psychologist Charles Garfield notes that athletes have used visualizations to win sports events; psychologist Brian Tracy writes about salespeople using visualizations to succeed in the business world; and Dr. Bernie Siegel, a cancer specialist, has even chronicled patients improving their health with visualizations.

Finally, consider this: the act of *keeping* your commitment may be as important, if not even *more* important, than achieving a particular goal or dream. In this way, you raise your expectations for the success of future commitments, knowing that when you make a promise to yourself, you keep it.

So, create lofty goals and dreams. And, from deep within you, commit to their achievement.

JOURNAL ENTRY / 10

In this activity, you will visualize the accomplishment of one of your most important goals or dreams. Once you vividly picture this ideal outcome, you will have strengthened your commitment to achieve it, and you will know how to do the same thing with all of your goals and dreams.

1 **Write a visualization of the exact moment in the future when you are experiencing the accomplishment of your biggest goal or dream in your role as a student.** Describe the scene of your success as if it is happening to you *now*. For example, if your desire is to graduate from a four-year university with a 4.0 average, you might write, *I am dressed in a long, blue robe, the tassel from my graduation cap tickling my face. I look out over the thousands of people in the audience, and I see my mother, a smile spreading across her face. I hear the announcer call my name. I feel a rush of adrenaline, and chills tingle on my back as I take my first step onto the stage. I see the college president smiling, reaching her hand out to me in congratulations. I hear the announcer repeat my name, adding that I am graduating with highest honors, having obtained a 4.0 average. I see my classmates standing to applaud me. Their cheers flow over me, filling me with pride and happiness. I walk. . . .*

For visual appeal, consider also drawing a picture of your goal or dream in your journal. Or cut pictures from magazines and use them to illustrate your writing. If you are writing your journal on a computer, consider adding digital images that depict your visualization. (If you don't know how, ask someone for help.) Allow your creativity to support your dream.

Remember the four keys to an effective visualization:

1. **Relax** to free your imagination.

2. Use **present-tense verbs** . . . describe the experience as if you are talking to someone on the phone at the very moment you are doing it. *I am going through the door....*

3. Use all **five senses**. What do you see, hear, smell, taste, and feel (touch)?

4. Include **emotion**. Imagine yourself feeling fantastic in this moment of grand accomplishment. You deserve to feel fantastic!

Read your visualizations often. Ideal times are right before you go to sleep and when you first awake in the morning. You may even wish to record your visualizations and listen to them often.

Until one is committed there is hesitancy, the chance to draw back, always ineffectiveness. Concerning all acts of initiative (and creation), there is one elementary truth, the ignorance of which kills countless ideas and splendid plans: that the moment one definitely commits oneself, then Providence moves too. All sorts of things occur to help one that would never otherwise have occurred. A whole stream of events issues from the decision, raising in one's favour all manner of unforeseen incidents and meetings and material assistance, which no man could have dreamt would have come his way.

William Hutchison Murray, Scottish mountaineer

ONE STUDENT'S STORY

JAMES TERRELL, *Appalachian State University, North Carolina*

Coming to Appalachian State University was a bit overwhelming for me. It meant that I would be seven hours away from my family. It also meant that I could not just go home whenever I wanted to. In the first week of school, I felt okay and was so glad to be on my own and making my own decisions. Things started to change quickly when I realized that I had to make some important decisions, the ones that my parents usually helped me make. In the back of my mind I kept thinking, I cannot ask them for help because I am on my own now. I began to get a little depressed because I missed my family, and things were not easy for me. I was ready to quit and enroll in a community college nearer home because I felt that the professors expected too much out of me. I was nearly at the point of telling my parents I was ready to come home because I really did not know why I was here.

That's when we began talking about accepting self-responsibility in my Access Seminar class. In this lesson, things started to become clear to me. I learned about the different voices everyone has inside of them. I began to realize that it was my Inner

Guide talking to me and helping me to stay on course when I was ready to give up. Also, I noticed it was my Inner Critic that was criticizing everything I did to try to stay on course. I had opposing forces trying to get to me.

I continued to listen to my Inner Guide, but I realized there was still something missing. The next week in the class we talked about creating inner motivation. As we began this lesson, I realized that the reason I was struggling was because I lacked motivation. I did not have a goal in mind that would help me stay on track. This chapter helped me realize that I needed a goal and a dream to stay focused, and in class, we began to do activities that helped us visualize them. In addition to our written journals, our teachers told us to draw a picture of our dreams and to brainstorm obstacles that we might face on the way to our dreams. Before this, I knew I wanted to be a lawyer, and that was about it. Some people would be happy just knowing they wanted to be a lawyer when they finished college. I needed to know a little more, so I visualized various steps to becoming a lawyer. First, I pictured myself graduating from Appalachian State

with a degree in political science, next I was graduating from Campbell University with a law degree, and then I saw myself moving to California, where I became a successful entertainment lawyer, living with my family in a nice neighborhood. As I visualized each part of my dream, everything became clear to me. I learned through reading this chapter and talking with the teachers that having our dreams written or drawn on paper can help us stay motivated.

I now feel more confident about staying in school. Every time I go into some of my hard classes, I just keep the mental picture of the day I enter law school and the dream I have plastered inside my head. Every time I get stressed or feel overwhelmed, I just look at the picture of my dream on the wall. I say to myself, "James, did you think this was going to be an easy road to your dream?" Every time the answer is "no," but now I know I'm not going to quit just because of obstacles. I look forward to the next four years of my life because I know that this course has taught me the basics of what I need to know to be a successful college student. I am now encouraged to help other people learn what I have learned, so they can be successful too.

Photo: Courtesy of James Terrell.

SELF-MOTIVATION / at Work

> Figure out what kind of job would make you happiest because the kind that would make you happiest is also the one where you will do your best and most effective work.
>
> *Richard Bolles, career expert, author of What Color Is Your Parachute?*

One of the most important choices you will ever make is whether to seek a job, a career, or a calling. When you have a *job*, you work for a paycheck. When you have a *career*, you work for the enjoyment and satisfaction you earn from your daily efforts . . . and you also get paid, possibly very well. A *calling* is a deeply felt commitment to the work for its own sake. With a calling, you feel that you are contributing to yourself, your loved ones, and to some part of humanity. I've had all three, and I assure you, a career is a great improvement on a job.

And a calling is even better; it makes life a whole lot sweeter. If you want to feel motivated to get up and go to work 50 weeks a year, you'll definitely want to choose a career. Better yet, find your calling.

College is a great place to prepare for a career. But, to stay self-motivated, you'll want to match your career choice and college major with your unique interests, talents, and personality. I once had a student who was majoring in accounting because he'd heard that accountants make a lot of money. He saw no problem with the fact that he hated math. He thought he was preparing for a career when in fact he was preparing for a job.

Some of the most motivated students in higher education are those who see college as the next logical step on the path to their career goals.

SEEKING CREATORS

Candidates must demonstrate self-motivation, a strong sense of purpose, and effective goal-setting abilities.

Sometimes these are younger students who are pursuing a lifelong dream of working in a particular profession. More often they are older students who've grown weary of working at uninspiring jobs and have come to college to prepare for rewarding careers. These self-motivated students are the ones who not only make the most of their education but who also enjoy the journey.

If you have a dream of a particular career, stay open to the possibility of finding something even more suited for you. If you're not yet sure what you want to do, keep exploring. The answer will probably reveal itself to you, and when it does, your life will change. One student I knew went from barely getting Cs and Ds to earning straight As when she discovered her passion to be a kindergarten teacher.

Use your life-planning skills to design a motivating career path for yourself, identifying the long- and short-term goals that will act as steppingstones to your success. Using the DAPPS rule that you learned in this chapter, you might create a career path like this:

2 years: I've received my A.A. degree in accounting with high honors and, by thoroughly researching accounting firms nationally, I've chosen five firms that look promising to work for after earning my B.A. degree.

5 years: I've earned my B.A. in accounting with high honors, and I'm employed in an entry-level accounting position in a firm of my choice earning $50,000 or more per year.

10 years: I own my own accounting firm, and I'm earning $150,000 or more per year, contributing to the financial prosperity and security of my clients.

Keep in mind that there is more to choosing an employer than how much money you're offered.

Choosing an employer whose purpose and values are compatible with your own will assist you greatly to stay motivated. By reading a company's mission statement, you can find out what it claims are its purpose and values. For example, suppose you wanted to work in retail sales or marketing for one of the giant office products companies. Here is the mission statement for Staples:

Slashing the cost and hassle of running your office! Our vision is supported by our core values: C.A.R.E.

- *Customers*—Value every customer
- *Associates*—Support them as valuable resources
- *Real Communications*—Share information with people when they need it
- *Execution*—Achieve our business goals

Now, here is the mission statement for a major competitor, Office Depot:

Office Depot's mission is to be the most successful office products company in the world. Our success is driven by an uncompromising commitment to:

- *Superior Customer Satisfaction:* A company-wide attitude that recognizes that customer satisfaction is everything.

- *An Associate-Oriented Environment:* An acknowledgment that our associates are our most valuable resource. We are committed to fostering an environment where recognition, innovation, communication, and the entrepreneurial spirit are encouraged and rewarded.

- *Industry-Leading Value, Selection, and Services:* A pledge to offer only the highest-quality merchandise available at everyday low prices, providing customers with an

outstanding balance of value, selection, and services.

- *Ethical Business Conduct:* A responsibility to conduct our business with uncompromising honesty and integrity.

- *Shareholder Value:* A duty to provide our shareholders with superior Return-On-Investment.

Based on their mission statements, which company do you think has a purpose and value system that would create a more motivating work environment for you?

Once you actually begin your search for a position in your chosen career, your goal-setting abilities and visualizing skills will help you stay motivated. You can expect to make dozens of contacts with potential employers for each one that responds with interest to your inquiry. One way to keep yourself motivated during your search is to set a goal of making a specific number of contacts each week. *Goal: I will send a letter of inquiry and my résumé to 10 or more potential employers each week.* In this way, you focus your energy on what you have control over—your own actions.

Additionally, take a few minutes each day to visualize yourself already in the career of your choice; see your office, your coworkers, and imagine yourself doing the daily activities of your career. This mental movie will reduce anxieties and remind you of the purpose for your hard work. Visualizing yourself in your ideal career will help keep you motivated when you encounter delays and disappointments on the path to your goal.

When you actually begin your career, self-motivation strategies will become extremely important to your success. You can't read many employment ads without noticing how many businesses are seeking employees who are "self-motivated."

The ad might say "Must work well on own" or "Seeking a self-starter," but you know what such buzz words really mean. These employers want a worker who is able to take on a task and stick with it until completion despite obstacles or setbacks. Who wouldn't want a self-motivated worker? If you were an employer, wouldn't you?

Finally, your ability to set goals in your career is critical to your success. Goals and quotas are inevitable for those in sales positions, but many employers require all of their workers to set goals and create work plans. Your ability to set effective goals will not only help you excel at achieving goals for yourself, but also for your team, office, and company. As you move up in responsibility, your ability to coach others to set goals will be a great asset to the entire organization.

You will likely be working 30, 40, or even more years. Your ability to discover inner motivation will have a great deal to do with the quality of the outcomes and experiences you create during all of these years.

TECH TIPS: Self-Motivation

42Goals allows you to set and track numerous goals. Log your progress and create charts to show your movement toward goals over time. By making your page public, you can share your progress with friends. *(Web, Android, and iOS)*

Mindbloom asks you to imagine that you are a tree. Each leaf on this tree represents an important element in your life (e.g., Career, Health, Relationships, Finances). For each leaf (important life area) you choose actions to improve that area. As you perform these actions, your tree flourishes. In essence, goal setting becomes a game to get your tree (a metaphor for your life) to prosper and grow. You can add inspirational quotes, images, and music. *(Web, Android, and iOS)*

stickK.com uses incentives and accountability to motivate users to achieve a goal. You create a commitment contract by setting a goal and a deadline. For example, "I will study for at least 20 hours every week." Then—and this part is optional—you create the stick (of "carrot and stick" fame). For example, for your stick you could provide your credit card and agree to pay $50 to a group you despise if you don't achieve your goal. (As of this writing, the website claims nearly 20 million dollars are "on the line" as sticks.) If you want, pick a referee who decides if you achieved your goal. You can also link in friends to encourage you. *(Web)*

DoSomething.org might be just what you're looking for if you want to ignite your passion for helping others and (as the site says) "make the world suck less." If you're looking for a service learning project for a class you're taking, this site provides hundreds of options. Claiming 3.3 million youthful (13–25 years old) members, DoSomething offers members an opportunity to join campaigns to improve life on planet Earth, addressing problems of poverty, violence, and environment, among many. *(Web)*

Note: All of the above are free, but some may offer upgraded features for a fee.

Write a Personal Affirmation

FOCUS QUESTIONS   What personal qualities will you need to achieve your dreams? How can you strengthen these qualities?

Certain personal qualities will be necessary to achieve your goals and dreams. For example, if you desire a happy family life, you'll need to be loving, supportive, and communicative. To discover the cure for cancer, you'll need to be creative, persistent, and strong-willed.

Think of the short- and long-term goals you have for your education. What are the personal qualities you'll need to accomplish them? Will you need to be intelligent, optimistic, articulate, responsible, confident, goal-oriented, mature, focused, motivated, organized, hard-working, curious, honest, enthusiastic, self-nurturing?

The potential for developing all of these personal qualities, and more, exists in every healthy human being. Whether a particular person fulfills that potential is another matter.

During childhood, a person's judgment of his or her personal qualities seems to be based mostly on what others say. If your friends, family, or teachers told you as a child that you're smart, you probably internalized this quality and labeled yourself "smart." But if no one said you are smart, perhaps you never realized your own natural intelligence. Worse, someone important may have told you that you are dumb, thus starting the negative mind chatter of your Inner Critic.

How we become the labels that others give us is illustrated by a mistake made at a school in England. A group of students at the school were labeled "slow" by their scores on an achievement test. Because of a computer error, however, their teachers were told these children were "bright." As a result, their teachers treated them as having high potential. By the time the error had been discovered, the academic scores of these "slow" students had risen significantly. Having been treated as if they were bright, the kids started to act bright. Perhaps, like these children, you have positive qualities waiting to blossom.

As adults, we can consciously choose what we believe. As one of my psychology professors used to say, "In your world, your word is law." In other words, my thoughts create my reality, and then I act according to that reality (regardless of its accuracy). For example, suppose I'm taking a large lecture class and I keep getting confused. Students sitting around me ask questions when they're confused, but I don't because, well, I've just never been comfortable asking questions in a large lecture hall—that's just the way I am. I'm shy. My Inner Defender is fine with this explanation because it protects me from doing something uncomfortable. Or maybe it's part of my deep culture to refrain from

We are what we imagine ourselves to be.

Kurt Vonnegut, Jr.

We continue to be influenced by our earliest interactions with our parents. We hear their voices as our own internal self-talk. Those voices function like posthypnotic suggestions. They often govern our lives.

John Bradshaw

questioning authority figures such as an instructor. The trouble is, the questions I don't ask keep popping up on tests, and I'm about to fail the course if I don't do something different.

Another part of me, my Inner Guide, knows I'd benefit from being bolder. In fact, if I want to pass this course, I *have* to be bolder! So I try an experiment. I start telling myself, *I am bold . . . I am bold . . . I am bold*. Of course, life keeps giving me chances to test my claim. A few class sessions later, I have another question, but I don't ask it. This time, though, I'm keenly aware of what I did: I took the wimpy way out. Undaunted, I continue my experiment, thinking, *I am bold . . . I am bold . . . I am bold*. The next time I have a question, I wait until after class and ask a fellow student. A little better, but still not *bold*. Then one day in class, I'm totally confused. *I am bold*. I shoot my hand in the air. Gulp. The professor calls on me, I ask my question, she answers, and, amazingly enough, I live to tell about it. Better yet, I get the answer correct on the next test. And best of all, my action finally corresponds with my claim. I came to a fork in the road (one I know so well), I consciously chose the bold path, I got the answer I needed, and I realize: My new thought generated new behaviors that, in turn, changed my outcomes and experiences for the better. And, if I did it once, I can do it again. Any time I need to. Any time I *choose* to!

> I was saying "I'm the greatest" long before I believed it.
>
> Muhammad Ali

CLAIMING YOUR DESIRED PERSONAL QUALITIES

An effective way to strengthen desired qualities is to create a personal affirmation. An affirmation is a statement in which we claim desired qualities as if we already have them in abundance. Here are some examples:

- I am a bold, joyful, generous man.
- I am a confident, creative, selective woman.
- I am a spiritual, wise, and curious man, finding happiness in all that I do.
- I am a supportive, organized, and secure woman, and I am creating harmony in my family.

Affirmations help us breathe life into personal qualities that we choose to strengthen. One of my colleagues recalls that whenever she made a mistake as a child, her father would say, "I guess that proves you're NTB." "NTB" was his shorthand for "not too bright." Imagine her challenge of feeling intelligent when she kept getting that message from her father! Today, she doesn't even need her father around; her Inner Critic is happy to remind her that she's NTB. She could benefit from an affirmation that says, "I am VB (very bright)."

> To adopt new beliefs, we can now systematically choose affirming statements, then consciously live in them.
>
> Joyce Chapman

What limiting messages did you receive as a child? Perhaps others said you were "homely," "stupid," "clumsy," or "always screwing up." If so, today you can create an affirmation that empowers your desired qualities. For example, you could say, "I am a beautiful, intelligent, graceful woman, turning any mistake into a powerful lesson."

"Mother, am I poisonous?"

Frank Modell/Cartoonbank.com

Some people report that their positive affirmations seem like lies. The negative messages from their childhood (chanted today by their Inner Critics) feel more like the truth. If so, try thinking of your affirmation as prematurely telling the truth. You may not feel beautiful, intelligent, or graceful when you first begin claiming these qualities, but, just as the "slow" children at the English school responded positively to being treated as bright, with each passing day you can behave your way into proving the truth of your chosen qualities. Using affirmations is like becoming your own parent: You acknowledge the positive qualities that no one has thought to tell you about . . .

until now. And then, most important, you act on them, changing your outcomes and experiences in the process.

LIVING YOUR AFFIRMATION

Of course, simply creating an affirmation is insufficient to offset years of negative programming. Affirmations need reinforcement to gain influence in your life. Here are three ways to empower your affirmation: Repeat . . . Dispute . . . Align.

1. **Repeat Your Affirmation.** In this way you'll remember the qualities you have chosen to strengthen. One student repeated her affirmation during workouts on a rowing machine. The steady pace of the exercise provided the rhythm to which she repeated her affirmation. What would be a good occasion for you to repeat your affirmation?

2. **Dispute Your Inner Critic.** Realize that you already possess the qualities you desire. You already *are* creative, persistent, loving, intelligent . . . whatever. These are your natural human qualities waiting to be re-empowered. To confirm this reality (and quiet your Inner Critic), simply recall a specific event (or many) in your past when you displayed a quality that is in your affirmation.

3. **Align Your Words and Deeds.** At each choice point, be what you affirm. If you say that you're "bold," make a bold choice. If you claim that you're "organized," do what an organized person does. If you assert that you're "persistent," keep going even when you don't feel like it. At some point, you'll have the evidence to assert, "Hey, I really am bold, organized, and persistent!" Your choices will prove the truth of your affirmation and your new outcomes and experiences will be the reward.

So, decide which personal qualities will help you stay on course to your goals and dreams and prepare to write a personal affirmation that will help you bring them forth!

M y "Born to Lose" tattoo was written on my mind long before it was written on my arm. Now I'm telling myself I'm "Born to Win."

Steve R., student

A ffirmations have to be supported by the behavior that makes them happen.

Charles Garfield

JOURNAL ENTRY | **11**

In this activity, you will create a personal affirmation. If you repeat your affirmation often, it will help you make choices that will strengthen the personal qualities needed to achieve your goals and dreams.

1 **Write a one-sentence statement of one of your most motivating goals or dreams in your role as a student.** You can simply copy one that you wrote in Journal Entry 10 (or create a new one if you prefer).

2 **Write a long list of personal qualities that would help you achieve this educational goal or dream.** Use adjectives such as *persistent, intelligent, hard-working, loving, articulate, organized, friendly, confident, relaxed,* and so on. Write as many qualities as possible.

3 **Circle the three qualities on your list that seem the most essential for you to achieve your goal or dream as a student (the one you identified in Step 1).**

4 **Write three versions of your personal affirmation.** Do this by filling in the blanks in sentence formats A, B, and C below. Fill the blanks with the three personal qualities you circled in Step 3 above. NOTE: Use the same three personal qualities in each of the three formats.

Format A: I am a _____, _____, _____ **man/woman.**

Example: I am a strong, intelligent, persistent woman.

Format B: I am a _____, _____, _____ **man/woman,** _____ing _____.

Example: I am a strong, intelligent, persistent woman, creating my dreams.

Format C: I am a _____, _____, _____ **man/woman, and I** _____.

Example: I am a strong, intelligent, persistent woman, and I love life.

Don't copy the examples; create your own unique affirmation.

5 **Circle or highlight the sentence from Step 4 that you like best.** Say or think your preferred affirmation to yourself until you can do so without looking at your written words. This repetition helps you to begin taking ownership of your affirmation and desired qualities.

6 **Write three paragraphs—one for each of the three qualities in your affirmation.** In each of these paragraphs, write about a specific experience when you displayed your desired quality. For example, if one of your desired qualities is persistence, tell a story about a time in your life when you were persistent (even a little bit!). Write the story like a scene from a book, with enough specific details that readers will feel as though they are seeing what you experienced. Your paragraph might begin: *The first quality from my affirmation is. . . . A specific experience in my life when I demonstrated that quality was. . . .*

You can add creativity to your journal by adding pictures or key words that you found, your own original drawings, or quotations or song lyrics that appeal to you.

An affirmation is self-talk in its highest form.

Susan Jeffers

The practice of doing affirmations allows us to begin replacing some of our stale, worn out, or negative mind chatter with more positive ideas and concepts. It is a powerful technique, one which can in a short time completely transform our attitudes and expectations about life, and thereby totally change what we create for ourselves.

Shakti Gawain

When I began dreading every day at work, I knew it was time for a change. I was working in our family's restaurant, and I never had time for myself. Also, I could see how the long hours were aging my mother. I enjoyed keeping the books for the restaurant, so I thought I might like to be an accountant. My mother agreed that I would probably be good at it.

So I enrolled at Chaffey College and took an introductory accounting course. I was anxious because 10 years earlier I had attended college and got a bunch of Fs and Ws. My GPA was only 0.91 back then, but at the time, I didn't care. I had a job making decent money, so what did I need college for? I wasn't motivated, and my grades showed it. However, when I got a B in the accounting course this time, I was ecstatic.

My feeling of accomplishment didn't last long, though. My past low grades caught up to me, and I was placed on the highest level of academic probation. I was just one step from being officially dismissed from the college, and my B in accounting wasn't nearly enough to pull up my GPA from years long past. I felt the heaviness of this burden weighing me down. I felt defeated and reluctantly enrolled in a mandatory guidance class. The class would temporarily protect me from being dismissed and provide a year for me to raise my GPA above 2.0. Along with the Guidance class, I took two accounting classes and one math class.

On the first day of the Guidance class, I looked around at my peers. They looked very young, and I immediately felt out of place. Negative thoughts swirled in my head: *You can't do this. You messed up too much in the past. Do you really think you can raise your GPA enough to be able to stay in school? You're older than most of these students, and you're in a Guidance class with them?* My thoughts shouted how inadequate I was. My Inner Critic was the only voice I heard, though I didn't have a name for it at the time. As the semester progressed, I learned about the different inner voices we hear in our heads. I learned to identify which voice I heard, and I began to harness the voice of my Inner Guide telling me to stay motivated. Then I read about believing in myself and writing a personal affirmation. If I didn't believe in myself, I knew I was going to repeat my previous failures in college. I couldn't let that happen. That's when I came up with an affirmation to help me believe in myself. I would often think or say aloud: *I am capable, loved, valued, wise to learn from my mistakes, and I will persevere by never giving up on myself.* Whenever I heard my Inner Critic's voice, I replaced it with the words of my affirmation.

Throughout the semester, I repeated my affirmation hundreds of times. I spoke these words enough to begin believing them. I used my affirmation to reduce the panic I felt before final exams. It also helped me complete a major project in accounting using Excel. Along with the other tools I learned in the course, I know my affirmation has paid off. I finished my Guidance class with an A+, I earned an overall GPA of 3.785, and I got off probation. All of the knowledge I gained from reading *On Course* and implementing it in my life has contributed to a very successful semester. I know I will reach my goals because this time I am better equipped with tools from the book and I know how to be a successful student. I may have begun my college education many years ago being a straight F student, but I choose to no longer be that unmotivated student. After all, "I am capable, loved, valued, wise to learn from my mistakes, and I will persevere by never giving up on myself."

Photo: Courtesy of Tina Steen.

Mastering
Self-Management

Successful Students . . .

▶ **act on purpose,** choosing deeds that move them on course to their goals and dreams.

▶ **employ self-management tools,** regularly planning and carrying out purposeful actions.

▶ **develop self-discipline,** showing commitment, focus, and persistence in pursuing their goals and dreams.

Struggling Students . . .

▶ **wait passively or wander from one unpurposeful activity to another.**

▶ **live disorganized, unplanned lives,** constantly responding to the whims of the moment.

▶ **quit or change course when their actions don't lead to immediate success.**

Once I accept responsibility for choosing and creating the life I want, the next step is taking purposeful actions that will turn my desires into reality.

I am taking all of the actions necessary to achieve my goals and dreams.

CASE STUDY IN CRITICAL THINKING   The Procrastinators

Two students from Professor Hallengren's English composition class sat in the cafeteria discussing the approaching deadline for their fourth essay.

"There's no way I can get this essay done on time," Tracy said. "I've turned in every essay late, and I still owe him a rewrite on the second one. Professor Hallengren is going to be furious!"

"You think you're in trouble!" Ricardo said. "I haven't even turned in the last essay. Now I'm going to be two essays behind."

"How come?" Tracy asked. "I would have thought a young guy right out of high school would have all the time in the world."

"Don't ask me where my time goes," Ricardo answered, shrugging. "Deadlines keep sneaking up on me, and before I know it, I'm weeks behind. I live on campus, and I don't even have to commute. But something always comes up. Last weekend I was going to write that other English essay and then study for my sociology test, but I had to go to a wedding out of state on Saturday. I was having such a good time, I didn't drive back until Monday morning. Now I'm even further behind."

"So that's why you missed English class on Monday," Tracy said. "Professor Hallengren lectured us because so many students were absent."

"I know I miss too many classes. One time I stayed home because I didn't have my essay ready. And sometimes I stay up late talking to my girlfriend on the phone or playing video games. Then I can't get up in the morning."

"My situation is different," Tracy said. "I'm in my 30s and I'm a single mother. I have three kids: five, seven, and eight. I work 20 hours a week, and I'm taking four courses. I just can't keep up with it all! Every time I think I'm about to catch up, something goes wrong. Last week one of my kids got sick. Then my refrigerator broke, and I had to work overtime for money to get it fixed. Two weeks ago they changed my schedule at work, and I had to find new day care. All my professors act like their class is all I have to do. I wish! The only way I could do everything is give up sleeping, and I'm only getting about five hours a night as it is."

"What are you going to do?" Ricardo asked.

"I don't think I can make it this semester. I'm considering dropping all of my classes."

"Maybe I should drop out, too."

1. **Who do you think has the more challenging self-management problem, Ricardo or Tracy? Be prepared to explain your choice.**
2. **If this person asked for your advice on how to do better in college, what specific self-management strategies would you recommend that he or she adopt?**

DIVING DEEPER

Which person's situation, Ricardo's or Tracy's, is more like yours? Explain the similarities and identify what you do to keep up with all of the things you need to do.

Acting on Purpose

FOCUS QUESTIONS   Have you ever noticed how much highly successful people accomplish? How do they make such effective use of their time?

Creators do more than dream. They have developed the skill of translating their desired outcomes into purposeful actions. They make a plan and then take one step after another . . . even when they don't *feel* like it . . . until they achieve their objective. Goals and dreams set your destination, but only persistent, purposeful actions will get you there.

Thomas Edison did more than dream of inventing the light bulb; he performed more than 10,000 experiments before achieving his goal. Martin Luther King, Jr., did more than dream of justice and equality for people of all races; he spoke and organized and marched and wrote. College graduates did more than dream of their diplomas; they attended classes, read books, wrote essays, conferred with instructors, rewrote essays, formed study groups, did library research, asked questions, went to support labs, sought out tutors, and much, much more!

When we consider the accomplishments of successful people, we may forget that they weren't born successful. Most achieved their success through the persistent repetition of purposeful actions. Creators apply a powerful strategy for turning dreams into reality: **Do important actions first, preferably *before* they become urgent.**

HARNESS THE POWER OF QUADRANT II

The significance of **importance** and **urgency** in choosing our actions is illustrated in the chart of the Quadrant II Time Management System® (from Stephen Covey's book *The 7 Habits of Highly Effective People*) on the next page. This chart shows that our actions fall into one of four quadrants, depending on their importance and urgency.

Only you can determine the importance of your actions. Sure, others (such as friends and relatives) will have their opinions, but they don't really know what you value. If an action will help you achieve what you value, then it's *important* and you'd be crazy not to do it. Sadly, though, many people fill their time with unimportant actions, thus sabotaging their goals and dreams.

Likewise, only you can determine the urgency of your actions. Sure, others (such as instructors and counselors) will set deadlines for you, but these external finish lines won't be motivating unless you make them personally important. If meeting an approaching deadline will help you achieve something you value, it's *urgent,* and you'd be crazy not to meet that deadline. Sadly, though, many people miss important, urgent deadlines, thus sabotaging their goals and dreams.

I've heard all sorts of excuses from students who "couldn't" get an assignment in on time. However, when I asked, "Could you have met the deadline if it was worth one million dollars?" their answer was almost always, "Sure, but it wasn't."

Do not confuse a creator with a dreamer. Dreamers only dream, but creators bring their dreams into reality.

Robert Fritz

I am personally persuaded that the essence of the best thinking in the area of time management can be captured in a single phrase: organize and execute around priorities.

Stephen Covey

So now we know the real problem. It wasn't that they "couldn't" meet the deadline. They just didn't make the deadline valuable enough to do what needed to be done. Creators choose their own goals and meet deadlines (even those set by others) because it's what *they* want, because it's important to creating the life *they* desire.

As you read on about the four quadrants, ask yourself, "In which quadrant am I choosing to spend most of my time?" The choice you make will dramatically affect the outcomes and experiences you create.

- **QUADRANT I ACTIONS (Important and Urgent)** are important activities done under the pressure of nearing deadlines. These are critical actions that must be done *now* or the consequences may be grim. One of my friends in college began his junior paper (the equivalent of two courses) just three days before it was due. He claimed that success in college was *important* to him, and the impending deadline certainly made this assignment *urgent*. He worked on the paper for 72 hours straight, finally turning it in without proofreading. Although he squeaked by this time, he fell deeper and deeper into his pattern of procrastination. In our senior year he failed too many courses and was dismissed by the university. When you act on low priorities and neglect high priorities, you sabotage your goals and dreams. At the last minute, procrastinators dive desperately into Quadrant I to handle an action that has always been important but is now desperately urgent. People who spend their lives in Quadrant I are constantly dashing about putting out brush fires in their lives. They frantically create modest achievements in the present while sacrificing extraordinary success in the future. Worse, Quadrant I is the one in which people experience stress, develop ulcers, and flirt with nervous breakdowns.

- **QUADRANT II ACTIONS (Important and Not Urgent)** are important activities done *without* the pressure of looming deadlines. These actions move you a step closer to a personally valuable outcome or experience.

N̲ot all of your daily activities are of equal importance, and your mission is to organize and prioritize all activities into a working plan.

Charles J. Givens

I̲t is not enough to be busy … the question is: What are we busy about?

Henry David Thoreau

	Urgent	**Not Urgent**
Important	**Quadrant I** *Example:* Staying up all night cramming for an 8:00 A.M. test.	**Quadrant II** *Example:* Creating a study group in the first week of the semester.
Not Important	**Quadrant III** *Example:* Attending a hastily called meeting that has nothing to do with your goals.	**Quadrant IV** *Example:* Mindlessly watching television until 4:00 A.M.

When you engage in an important activity with time enough to do it well, you can create your greatest dreams. Lacking urgency, Quadrant II actions are easily postponed. Almost all of the suggestions in this book belong in Quadrant II. For example, you could postpone forever keeping a journal, using the Wise Choice Process, adopting the language of Creators, discovering and visualizing your dreams, designing a life plan, and creating personal affirmations. However, when you do take purposeful actions such as these, you create a rich, full life. Quadrant II is where you will find Creators.

- **QUADRANT III ACTIONS (Not Important and Urgent)** are unimportant activities done with a sense of urgency. How often have you responded to the demand of your ringing phone only to be trapped in a long, unwanted conversation? Or you agree to something because you can't bring yourself to say "no"? When we allow someone else's urgency to talk us into an activity unimportant to our own goals and dreams, we have chosen to be in Quadrant III.

- **QUADRANT IV ACTIONS (Not Important and Not Urgent)** are simply time wasters. Everyone wastes some time, so it's not something to judge yourself for, though your Inner Critic may try. Instead, listen to your Inner Guide. Become more conscious of your choices, and minimize wasting the irreplaceable hours of each day. A college professor I know surveyed his classes and found that many of his students watch more than 40 hours of television per week. That's the equivalent of a full-time job without pay or benefits!

A study in 1961 showed that students in higher education studied an average of 25 hours per week. Twenty years later, in 1981, college students' study time had dropped to 20 hours per week. By 2003, the average dropped again to only 13 hours of studying per week. These numbers help explain why so many capable students get off course in college. It's difficult to learn complex subjects with so little time spent in Quadrants I and II.

WHAT TO DO IN QUADRANTS I AND II

So what do Quadrant I and II actions look like? In college, Creators attend class regularly. They take good notes. They do all assignments to the best of their ability. They schedule conferences with their instructors. They create study groups. They organize their notes and study them often. They predict questions on upcoming tests and carry the answers on 3 × 5 study cards. No external urgency motivates them to take these purposeful actions. They create their own urgency by a strong commitment to their valued goals and dreams.

By contrast, Victims spend much of their time in Quadrants III and IV, where they repeat unproductive actions such as complaining, blaming, excusing, and wasting time. Not surprisingly, they move farther and farther off course each day.

If you want to know which quadrant you are in at any moment, ask yourself this question: "Will what I'm doing now positively affect my life one year from today?" If the answer is "yes," you are in Quadrant I or II. If the answer is "no," you are probably in Quadrant III or IV.

While it is true that without a vision the people perish, it is doubly true that without action the people and their vision perish as well.

Johnetta B. Cole, former president, Spelman College

A vision without a task is but a dream, a task without a vision is drudgery, a vision and a task is the hope of the world.

From a church in Sussex, England, ca. 1730

Creators say "no" to Quadrant III and Quadrant IV activities. Sometimes the choice requires saying "no" to other people: *No, I'm not going to be on your committee this semester. Thank you for asking.* Sometimes this choice requires saying "no" to themselves: *No, I'm not going to sleep late Saturday morning. I'm going to get up early and study for the math test. Then I can go to the movies with my friends without getting off course.*

When we say "no" to Quadrants III and IV, we free up time to say "yes" to Quadrants I and II. Imagine if you spent just 30 additional minutes each day taking purposeful actions. Think how dramatically that one choice could change the outcome of your life!

Remember to reread the visualization of your dream (**Journal Entry 10**) often to help you stay motivated. Also, remember to say your affirmation (**Journal Entry 11**) each day to remind you of the personal qualities that will keep you on course to your dreams! These are both great Quadrant II actions.

JOURNAL ENTRY / 12

In this activity, you will assess the degree to which you are acting on purpose. *Your* purpose! As you spend more time in Quadrants I and II, you will notice a dramatic improvement in the results you are creating.

1 **Write a list of 15 or more specific actions you have taken in the past two days.** (The actions are *specific* if someone could have recorded you doing them with a video camera.)

2 **Using an entire journal page, draw a four-quadrant chart like the example in the article.**

3 **Write each action from your list in Step 1 in the appropriate quadrant on your chart.** After each action, put the approximate amount of time you spent in the activity. For example, Quadrant IV might be filled with actions such as these:

1. Watched TV (2 hours)
2. Phone call to Terry (1 hour)
3. Watched TV (3 hours)
4. Went to the mall and wandered around (2 hours)
5. Hung out in the cafeteria (2 hours)
6. Played video game (4 hours)

4 **Write about what you have learned or relearned concerning your use of time. And as a result, what will you do that you have not been doing?** Effective writing anticipates questions that a reader may have and answers these questions clearly. To dive deep in this journal entry, answer questions such as the following:

- What exactly did you discover after analyzing your time?
- In which quadrant do you spend the most time?
- What specific evidence did you use to draw this conclusion?
- If you continue using your time in this way, are you likely to reach your goals and dreams? Why or why not?
- What most often keeps you from taking purposeful actions?
- How do you feel about your discoveries?
- What different choices, if any, do you intend to make about how you use time?

When I started college as a freshman engineering student, I knew I would have a little trouble with the transition from high school to college. What I didn't know was that my main challenge would come from distractions. There's a mall only five minutes from campus, and when my friends wanted to hang out there, I wouldn't say no. Other times we'd play video games, or go out to dinner, or watch television. There was always something to distract me and no one to tell me to get to work. I was an A/B student in high school, and I was used to things coming easy to me. In college there's a lot more work and it's definitely not work you can do in five minutes and be done like in high school. I always found some excuse not to do my work, and then I'd try to do it the day it was due. I remember waiting until about 30 minutes before my first chemistry test to start studying. When my grades started dropping, I realized I needed to change, but I wasn't sure how.

That's when we read about self-management in the *On Course* book. In class we did an activity where we divided a paper into four quadrants. Then we put what we had done the last two days onto those quadrants. I only had a few things in Quadrants I and II (Important).

But Quadrant IV (Unimportant) was full. I realized I was studying only about 3 hours a week, but I was going to the mall about 5 hours, watching movies and television about 6 to 10 hours, playing video games about 20 hours, and surfing the Internet about 30 hours. I had never had a high-speed connection before, and things like YouTube and Facebook were consuming a good part of my life.

Now that I had figured out my problem, I needed a solution. I started by hanging up the quadrants in my room with my wasted time on them. I then put up another blank quadrant chart next to it. I decided to try new ways to manage my time over the next week and keep track of how I spent my time every day. I set a goal to reduce my time in Quadrants III and IV to no more than 20 hours per week and increase my time in Quadrants I and II up to 30 or 40 hours. At first I tried to completely cut out everything that was a waste of time, but I found myself stressed out. I was studying so much I thought my brain would explode, and I couldn't remember what I was studying. Then I tried getting all of my work done before I did anything that could be seen as a waste of time. But, again I was unable to focus on my work. Then

I found the strategy that has helped. I put my schedule on a dry erase board and I adjust it to what I have going on that week. I make sure that I put both work and leisure time on the schedule. Also, if I have something important going on, like a test, I write it on my schedule in bold letters so I don't forget. Essentially I have made a reusable planner.

This strategy has helped me out a lot since I put it into effect. When I filled in the quadrants at the end of the first week, I was about halfway to my goals. Toward the end of the semester, I tracked my time again, and I reached my goals. My new system makes me more aware of what I'm choosing to do. I spend less time on the Internet, and I learned to say no. I remember when a bunch of my friends wanted to go to the movies the night before I had a math test. They asked me to go at least 10 times, but I stayed home and studied. I actually did really well on the test. Probably the best choice I made was taking my video games home. Since I started writing my important work on the whiteboard, I've missed almost no assignments and my grades have improved in every class. I have found a strategy that arranges my time so that I can get my important work done and still have time for fun things. My reusable planner has helped me a lot in my freshman year, and I plan to keep using it throughout college.

Photo: Courtesy of Jason Pozsgay.

Creating a Leak-Proof Self-Management System

FOCUS QUESTIONS   How can you devote more time to creating the outcomes and experiences that matter most to you?

At the beginning of a class, I asked my students to pass in their assignments. A look of panic came over one man's face. "What assignment?" he moaned. "You mean we had an *assignment* due today?" On another day, I overheard a student ask a friend: "Did you study for the math test today?" "No," the friend replied, "I didn't have time." Not long ago, a student told me, "I'm doing fine in my classes, but that's because I'm letting the rest of my life go down the drain."

Time is the coin of your life. It is the only coin you have, and only you can determine how it will be spent.

Carl Sandburg

Do these situations sound familiar? Do important actions leak through your hands like water? Do you sometimes give a half-hearted effort on important tasks . . . or finish them late . . . or not even do them at all? Do you neglect one important role in your life to do well in another? It's no easy matter getting everything done, especially if you're adding college to an already demanding life. But there are proven tools that can help you work more effectively and efficiently.

Typically these are called *time management* tools, but the term is misleading because no one can actually manage time. No matter what we mortals do, time just keeps on ticking. What we *can* manage, however, is ourselves. More specifically, we can manage the choices we make within the time we have every day.

TIME AND CULTURE

As with so many aspects of life, cultures differ in their beliefs and attitudes about time. In some cultures, such as Latino and Native American cultures, people tend to be relaxed and informal about time. In such a culture, arriving late for an appointment may not be considered a blunder or an insult. However, members of mainstream North American culture—including higher education—usually view time differently. A common saying is "Time is money." Both are saved, budgeted, invested, spent, and wasted. Time is considered a valuable resource, and how you use it shapes not only your outcomes and experiences but the judgments that others make of you as well.

Unlike many people in dominant culture who may find their days and their lives driven by appointment books, calendars, and to-do lists, Latino cultural values do not emphasize rigid adherence to schedules.

Lynn Kell Spradlin

A wise choice in college is to assume that your instructors take a serious view of time-sensitive choices such as attending classes, completing homework, and keeping appointments. Instructors will often list in their course syllabus the penalties for offenses. Even if your grade isn't lowered by such choices, you can assume that your reputation with the instructor has been harmed.

One of the keys to your success in college, then, is having a leak-proof self-management system. This is the system in which you record, organize, prioritize, and store all of your important actions. Then you complete one important task after another to the best of your ability. In short, **the secret to effective self-management is making choices that maximize the time you spend in Quadrants I and II.** These are the quadrants, you'll recall, where all of your actions are important because they help you achieve your desired outcomes and experiences.

Understand that there's no self-management system that is right for everyone. Rather, there are many tools with which to experiment. You'll know you've found your best self-management system when you start achieving more of your desired outcomes and experiences with less stress. As a bonus, when you find the self-management approach that feels right for you, your expectations of success in college (and elsewhere) will go up because now you'll be confident you can get the required work done. Below are six of the best tools for making sure you spend the bulk of your time creating a great future. You can choose to get organized by using paper versions of these tools, or you can find apps for your smartphone or websites that perform the same functions electronically.

WEEKLY CALENDAR: FOR TRACKING RECURRING SCHEDULED EVENTS

Some of the things you need to do happen every week, maybe even on the same day and at the same time. Examples include classes, study time, sports-team practice, commuting, work, and recreation. An ideal tool created for managing such actions is a **Weekly Calendar** (page 115). On your weekly calendar, record all of your commitments that happen at the same time every week. The value of recording classes, sports-team practice, commuting, and work hours on your calendar is probably obvious. However, you may wonder why you should schedule study times. After all, there's no teacher, coach, or boss counting on you to show up to study. Think again. There is someone *very* important waiting for you to show up. *You!* If you're really serious about being a success in college, job number one is learning. And the key to learning is studying. One of the quickest ways to sabotage your college success is to think, *I'll study whenever I have free time.* Study time doesn't just happen. You need to *make* it happen. Schedule it and do it! As a rule of thumb, schedule two hours of study time for each hour of class time you have each week. For example, if you have 12 class hours each week, set aside 24 hours on your weekly calendar to study. If you choose to do something instead of studying at a scheduled time, make sure the substitute activity is more important. *Much more important.* And do this only on rare occasions. Once you get in the habit of trading study time for Quadrant III or IV activities, you're going to be off course in college in no time.

MONTHLY CALENDAR: FOR TRACKING ONE-TIME SCHEDULED EVENTS

Of course, many important actions occur only once, and that date might be far in the future. These actions will happen on a specific day and probably at a

I think that learning about and using time is a very complicated kind of learning. Many adults still have difficulty with it.

Virginia Satir

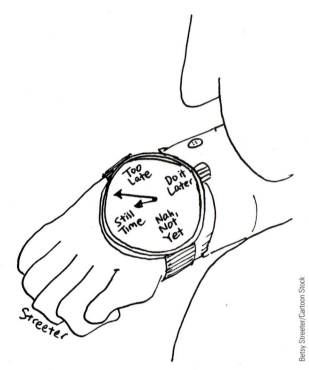

Betsy Streeter/Cartoon Stock

specific time. If you miss it, it's gone forever. For such actions, a **Monthly Calendar** (page 116) provides a chronological list of your upcoming Quadrant I and II commitments, appointments, and assignments. Use it to record one-time events such as a tutoring session or conference with an instructor. Also put on your calendar the due dates of tests, research papers, final exams, projects, lab reports, and quizzes. With a monthly planner, one glance will show you all of your one-time events in the days, weeks, even months to come. Never again will you moan the Victim's lament: *What do you mean that's due today?*

In place of paper calendars, many people keep their appointment schedule on a smartphone. Smartphones are actually handheld computers that can do a lot more than merely store your calendar. Depending on the model, a smartphone can also record contact information (address and phone numbers), play music, send and receive text messages, take photos and videos, surf the Internet, and allow you to download and respond to email. A smartphone can even be programmed to send you a reminder about an appointment or deadline. Free electronic calendars are offered by a number of Internet sites (simply do an Internet search for "online calendar"). A unique advantage of these services is that most allow you to create calendars that can be accessed and updated by members of a group. If you have a project group, a study team, or a large family, an online calendar service might be just the right tool for managing your collective schedules.

Scheduling purposeful actions on your calendar is one thing; actually doing them is quite another. Once you have chosen your priorities, let nothing keep you from completing them other than a rare emergency or special opportunity. Make a habit of saying "no" to unscheduled, low-priority alternatives found in Quadrants III and IV.

In college I learned how to manage more tasks than anyone could possibly finish. Literally. We learned how to keep a lot of balls in the air at the same time. You couldn't study for every class every day, so you had to decide what could be put off till later. The experience taught us to set priorities.

Dennis Hayes, Hayes Microcomputer Products

NEXT ACTIONS LIST: FOR TRACKING ONE-TIME UNSCHEDULED EVENTS

Some important actions don't need to happen on a specific day. They just need to be done as soon as possible. A **Next Actions List** (page 117) records everything you need to do "next" (as opposed to a calendar, where you schedule actions on a particular day and time). Whenever you have some free time that you might otherwise waste, your next actions list provides Quadrant I or II actions to complete. Here's how to use one:

1. Write your life roles and corresponding goals, which you defined in Chapter 3, in the shaded boxes. This first step makes your Next Actions List more effective than a mere to-do list by ensuring

that your actions are directed at the accomplishment of *all* of your important goals.

2. List Quadrant I (Important and Urgent) actions for each of your goals. For example, if your short-term goal for Math 107 is to earn an A, your list might contain actions like these:

Role: Math 107 student

Goal: Grade A

- *Read pages 29–41 and do problems 1–10 on page 40.*
- *Study 2 hours or more for Friday's test on Chps. 1–3.*

Each of these actions is **important,** and each is relatively **urgent.** As with a goal set with the DAPPS rule, be specific. Vague items such as *Do homework* provide little help when the time comes to take action. Much more helpful are specific tasks such as *Read pages 29–41 and do problems 1–10 on page 40.*

3. List Quadrant II (Important and Not Urgent) actions under each of your goals. For example, your list for Math 107 might continue with actions like these:

- *Make appointment with Prof. Finucci and ask her advice on preparing for Friday's test.*
- *Reschedule appointment with math lab tutor.*
- *Meet with study group and compare answers on practice problems.*

These Quadrant II behaviors are the sorts of activities that struggling students seldom do. You could go through the entire semester without doing any of these purposeful actions because none of them is urgent. But when you consistently choose Quadrant II actions, this decision makes a big difference in the results you create.

Whenever you have free time during the day, instead of slipping unconsciously into Quadrants III or IV, check your Next Actions List for purposeful actions. As you complete an action, cross it off your list. As you think of new important actions, add them to your list under the appropriate role. A bonus of keeping a Next Actions List is that it eliminates the burden of remembering numerous small tasks, freeing your brain to do more creative and critical thinking.

TRACKING FORM: FOR TRACKING ACTIONS THAT NEED TO BE REPEATED NUMEROUS TIMES

Some goals are achieved by repeating particular actions consistently over time. A **Tracking Form** (on page 118) helps you coordinate many oft-repeated actions that are all directed at a common goal. Elite athletes typically use some form of this tool to plan and monitor their training. In college, a Tracking Form is ideal for helping you plan and take actions that will help

> Asking "What's the next action?" undermines the victim mentality. It presupposes that there is a possibility of change, and that there is something you can do to make it happen.
>
> David Allen

> All the best work is done the way ants do things—by tiny untiring and regular additions.
>
> Lefcadio Hearn

you succeed in a challenging course. Suppose, for example, you decide to use a Tracking Form to help you gain a deep understanding of sociology and earn an A in the course. One helpful outer (physical) action might be "Read the textbook one or more hours." A possible inner (mental) action is "Say my affirmation five or more times." So, you write these two actions in the appropriate left-hand column, and put the dates of the next 14 days at the top of the check-box columns.

Each day that you take these actions, you check the appropriate box, and at the end of 14 days you'll see exactly what you have (or have not) done to achieve your goal. One of my students commented, "Before I used the Tracking Form, I thought I was studying a lot. Now I realize I'm not studying enough." She started studying more, and her grades improved dramatically. A Tracking Form keeps your Inner Defender from fooling you into thinking you're doing what's necessary to stay on course when, in fact, you're not.

WAITING-FOR LIST: FOR TRACKING COMMITMENTS THAT OTHERS HAVE MADE TO YOU

Your progress toward a goal will sometimes stall while you wait for someone else to get back to you. Maybe you're waiting to hear from a librarian about when a book you need has become available. Maybe you're waiting to hear from friends about whether they're going to join you at the basketball game on Friday night. Maybe you're waiting for an instructor to tell you whether you can change the topic of your term paper. Each of these items should go on your **Waiting-For List**, along with the date it's added. Glance over the list daily. When an item has been on the list a while, contact the appropriate person and give them a nudge. With this tool, you'll dramatically reduce the number of times your goals get stuck waiting for someone else to take action on something important to you.

PROJECT FOLDER: FOR TRACKING AND MANAGING PROGRESS TOWARD A LARGE GOAL

Some goals take many actions to achieve. For each multistep project, create a separate **Project Folder**. Suppose your speech instructor assigns a group presentation. Everything related to that large task goes in one folder: the handout describing the assignment, the names and contact information for all group members, a Next Actions List for this project, assignments for each group member, the email address of someone you heard about who knows how to make great PowerPoint slides, research materials you've collected for your part of the presentation, a list of helpful websites, and YouTube videos that might enliven your presentation. Every time you get more information related to this presentation, it goes in the Project Folder. Never again will you utter those woeful words: "I know it's here somewhere."

To keep track of your progress, put a Next Actions List on the outside of the folder. Use this tool to record all of the actions you (or others, if it's a group

How much of human life is lost in waiting?

Ralph Waldo Emerson

project) are tasked to do. You might even put a due date for each of these actions so you keep the project moving toward completion.

THE REWARDS OF EFFECTIVE SELF-MANAGEMENT

Some people resist using a written self-management system. "These forms and charts are for the anally retentive," one student objected. "Everything I need to do, I keep right here in my head." I know this argument well, because I used to make it myself. Then one day, one of my mentors replied, "If you can remember everything you need to do, I guess you're not doing very much." Ouch.

I decided it wouldn't kill me to experiment with self-management tools. Over time, I came up with my own combination of the tools we've been examining. And over more time, my tools migrated more and more into my computer and smartphone. In the process I became aware of how I'd been wasting precious time. With my old self-management system (mostly depending on my memory, with an occasional "note to self"), the best I did was remember to do what was important and urgent. The worst I did was forget something vital. Then I'd waste time cleaning up the mess I'd made.

With my present self-designed system, I almost always complete my Quadrant I actions on time. I also spend large chunks of time in Quadrant II, where I take important actions before they become urgent. I'm better at keeping commitments to myself and to others. I'm less likely to go off course. Relieved of remembering every important task I need to do, my mind is free to think more creatively and boldly. And, most of all, my written self-management system helps me carry out the persistent, purposeful actions necessary to achieve my goals and dreams.

If you're already achieving all of your greatest goals and dreams, then keep using your present self-management system because it's working! However, if your Inner Guide knows you could be more successful than you are now, then maybe it's time to implement a new approach to managing your choices. You'll rarely meet a successful person who doesn't use some sort of written self-management system, whether in the world of work or in college. In fact, researchers at the University of Georgia found that students' self-management skills and attitudes are even better predictors of their grades in college than their Scholastic Aptitude Test (SAT) scores.

Consistently using a written self-management system is a habit that takes time to establish. You may begin with great energy, only to find later that a week has gone by without using it. No need for self-judgment. Instead, simply examine where you went astray and begin your plan anew. Experiment until you find the system that works best for your personality and creates the outcomes and experiences you desire. In time, you will excel at using your personally designed written self-management system. And then watch how much more you accomplish!

When the seniors in the College Board study were asked what contributed to a successful and satisfying career in college, 73 percent said the "ability to organize tasks and time effectively."

Tim Walter & Al Siebert

When people with whom you interact notice that without fail you receive, process, and organize in an airtight manner the exchanges and agreements they have with you, they begin to trust you in a unique way.

David Allen

JOURNAL ENTRY / **13**

In this activity, you'll explore how you could improve your present self-management system. By using time more effectively and efficiently, you'll complete a greater number of important actions and maximize your chances of attaining your goals and dreams.

1 **Write about the system (or lack of system) that you presently use to decide what you will do each day.** There is no "wrong" answer, so don't let your Inner Critic or Inner Defender get involved. Consider questions such as how you know what homework to do, when to prepare for tests, what classes to attend, and what instructor conferences to go to. How do you track what you need to do in other roles, such as your social or work life? Why do you currently use this approach? How well is your system working (giving examples wherever possible)? How do you *feel* while using this approach to self-management (e.g., stressed, calm, energized, frantic, etc.)?

2 **Write about how you *could* use or adapt the self-management tools in this chapter to create a leak-proof self-management system and improve your outcomes and experiences. Or, if you do not want to use or adapt any of these tools, explain why.** Consider the Weekly Calendar, the Monthly Calendar, the Next Actions List, the Tracking Form, the Waiting-For List, and the Project List. How might you use them separately or in combination? How could you use a smartphone, computer, or other technology in your self-management system? How might you use self-management tools not mentioned here that you may know about? In short, invent your own system for managing your choices that you think will maximize the quality of your outcomes and experiences.

I used to wonder how other students got so much done. Now that I'm using a planner, I wonder how I settled for doing so little.

John Simmons, student

Weekly Planner for the Week of _____

	Monday	Tuesday	Wednesday	Thursday	Friday	Saturday	Sunday
7:00 AM							
7:30 AM							
8:00 AM							
8:30 AM							
9:00 AM							
9:30 AM							
10:00 AM							
10:30 AM							
11:00 AM							
11:30 AM							
12:00 PM							
12:30 PM							
1:00 PM							
1:30 PM							
2:00 PM							
2:30 PM							
3:00 PM							
3:30 PM							
4:00 PM							
4:30 PM							
5:00 PM							
5:30 PM							
6:00 PM							
6:30 PM							
7:00 PM							
7:30 PM							
8:00 PM							
8:30 PM							
9:00 PM							
9:30 PM							
10:00 PM							
10:30 PM							
11:00 PM							

Notes:

Monthly Calendar

Monday	Tuesday	Wednesday	Thursday	Friday	Saturday	Sunday

Month _____

Next Actions List

Role:
Goal:

Role:
Goal:

Role:
Goal:

Role:
Goal:

Role:
Goal:

Telephone calls

Miscellaneous actions

Role:
Goal:

Tracking Form

Role:

Dream:

Long-term goal:

Short-term goals (to be accomplished this semester):

      1.

      2.

      3.

      4.

OUTER (Physical) Action Steps

Dates:

INNER (Mental) Action Steps

Dates:

ALLYSA LEPAGE, *Sacramento City College, California*

When the fall semester began, I wasn't sure how I was going to fit everything into my schedule. In addition to taking three college courses, I was waitressing 24 hours a week, taking dance classes, teaching dance classes to kids, spending time with my boyfriend, doing housework and errands, hanging out with friends from three different groups (high school, college, and church), and rehearsing two evenings a week for an annual December musical at Memorial Auditorium, an event that draws thousands of people. I'd stay up late to get my homework done, then wake up exhausted. I was struggling in math, and in my heart I knew I could be doing better in my other classes. I'd

forget to turn in homework, I was skimping on preparation for my dance classes, I wasn't calling friends back, and I'd forget to bring costumes and makeup to rehearsals for the musical. I was sick all the time with colds and headaches. I was seriously stressed and not doing full justice to anything.

Before I lost all hope, my Human Career Development class went over self-management tools. I developed my own system and started writing down everything I needed to do. I keep a big calendar by my bed so I see it in the morning, and I carry a smaller calendar in my purse. My favorite tool is a list of everything I have to do put into categories. I make a new list every

day and put important things at the top so it's okay if I don't get to the ones on the bottom. My system helps me see what my priorities are and get them done first so I don't feel so scattered.

By doing important things first, I began having more focus, not rushing as much, and getting more done. Of course I had to let a few lower-priority things go for a while, like doing housework and spending as much time with some of my friends. I started getting more sleep, completing my homework, and getting As on all of my tests while doing everything else that I needed to do. After a while, I began to accomplish so much more and I realized that I *do* have enough time to fit all of the important things into my schedule. In fact, every once in a while now I actually find myself with a luxury I haven't had in a long while—free time.

Developing Self-Discipline

FOCUS QUESTIONS   Do you find yourself procrastinating, even on projects that mean a great deal to you? How can you keep taking purposeful actions even when you don't feel like it?

Every semester, perfectly capable students abandon their goals and dreams. Somewhere along the path, they get distracted and stop . . . or they wander off in another direction.

"Hey," their instructors want to shout, "You're going the wrong way. The goals and dreams you say you want are over here! Keep coming this way. You can do it!"

Maybe these students believe college is a sprint, over in a flash. Not so. Like most grand victories, college is a marathon with many hurdles along the way. It may take only 30 seconds to stride proudly across the stage to receive your college diploma. However, it will have taken you thousands of persistent small steps performed over years to get there.

Self-discipline is self-caring.

Dr. M. Scott Peck

In a word, success takes self-discipline—the willingness to do whatever has to be done, whether you feel like it or not, until you reach your goals and dreams. Every January, athletic clubs are wall-to-wall with people who made New Year's resolutions to get in shape. You know what happens. A month later, the crowds are gone, reminding us that getting and staying in shape takes commitment, focus, and persistence.

So it goes with every important goal we set. Our actions reveal whether we have the self-discipline to stay on course in the face of tempting alternatives. Most students want to be successful, but *wanting* and *doing* are worlds apart. Hanging out with friends is easier than going to class. Watching television is easier than reading a challenging textbook. Partying is easier than doing research at the library.

Many people choose instant gratification. Few choose the far-off rewards of persistent and purposeful actions. Many begin the journey to their dreams; few finish. Yet all we need to do is put one foot in front of the other . . . again and again and again. A journey of a thousand miles may begin with a single step, but many more had better follow.

Self-discipline has three essential ingredients: **commitment**, **focus**, and **persistence**. In Journal Entry 10, you explored how to strengthen your commitment. Now we'll take a look at focus and persistence.

To be disciplined or non-disciplined is a choice you make every minute and every hour of your life. Discipline is nothing more than the process of focusing on any chosen activity without interruption until that activity is complete.

Charles J. Givens

STAYING FOCUSED

Distractions constantly tug at our minds, and, like an unruly child, the unfocused mind dashes from one distraction to another. Everyone has experienced losing focus for a minute, an hour, even a day. But struggling students lose focus for weeks and months at a time. They start arriving late, skipping classes, doing sloppy work, ignoring assignments. They take their eyes off of the prize and forget why they are in college.

For many students, the time to beware of losing focus is at midterm. The excitement of the new semester has been replaced by the never-ending list of assignments. That's when Inner Defenders start offering great excuses to quit: *I've got boring teachers; my schedule stinks; I'm still getting over the flu; next semester I could start all over.* And Inner Critics chime in with practiced self-judgments: *I never could do math; I'm not as smart as my classmates; I'm too old; I'm too young; I'm not really college material.*

You always have to focus in life on what you want to achieve.

Michael Jordan

Your Inner Guide, however, knows that winners stay focused and finish strong. They complete the semester with a bang, not a snivel. Their efforts go up as the semester winds down. Your Inner Guide can help you regain focus by addressing one question: *What are my goals and dreams?* If you need a reminder, revisit your life plan in Journal Entry 9 and the visualization of your biggest academic goals or dream in Journal Entry 10. If your goals and dreams don't motivate you to keep taking purposeful actions right to the finish line, then perhaps you need to rethink where you want to go in life.

Calvin and Hobbes   by Bill Watterson

BEING PERSISTENT

If focus is self-discipline in thought, then persistence is self-discipline in action. Here's the question your Inner Guide can ask when you slow down or quit: "Do I love myself enough to keep going?" After all, you are the one who'll benefit most from the accomplishment of your goals and dreams . . . and you're the one who will pay the price of disappointment if you fail.

Here's the thing, though. Although failure is certain if you quit, success isn't guaranteed simply because you persist. Sometimes wisdom requires more than simply repeating the same thing over and over and expecting a better result. If Plan A isn't working, don't quit. But also don't keep doing what isn't working! Change your approach. Move on to Plan B. Or C or D, if necessary.

One of my students learned just how powerful persistence and a willingness to try something different can be. When Luanne enrolled in my English 101 class, she had taken and failed the course three times before. She had actually developed some good writing skills, but she definitely needed to master Standard English to pass the course. "I know," she said, "that's what all my other teachers told me." She paused, took a deep breath and added, "At least I'm not a quitter."

I asked Luanne why she was going to college. As she told me about her dream to work in television, her eyes sparkled. I asked if mastering standard grammar would help her achieve her dream. She hesitated, perhaps nervous about where her answer might lead.

Finally she said, "Yes."

"Great! So, what's one action that, if repeated every day for a month or more, would improve your grammar?" She needed to discover a Quadrant II activity and make it a new habit.

"Probably studying my grammar book."

I handed her a **32-Day Commitment Form** (located in this chapter following Journal Entry 14). "Okay, then, I'm inviting you to make a commitment to

P erhaps the most valuable result of all education is the ability to make yourself do the thing you have to do, when it ought to be done, whether you like it or not; it is the first lesson that ought to be learned; and however early a man's training begins, it is probably the last lesson that he learns thoroughly.

Thomas Henry Huxley

study your grammar book for 32 days in a row. You can put a check on this form each day that you keep your promise to yourself. Will you do it?"

"I'll try."

"C'mon, Luanne. You've been *trying* for three semesters. My question is, 'Will you commit to studying grammar for 30 minutes every day for the next 32 days?'"

She paused again. Her choice at this moment would surely affect her success in college, and probably the outcome of her life.

"Okay," she said, "I'll do it."

And she did. Each time I passed the writing lab, I saw Luanne working on grammar. She was there so often the tutors started joking about charging her rent.

But that's not all Luanne did. She attended every English class. She completed every writing assignment. She met with me to discuss her essays. She created flashcards with her problem sentences on one side and corrections on the other. In short, Luanne was taking the persistent actions of a self-disciplined student.

As mentioned earlier, to receive a passing grade in English 101, students had to pass one of two exit exam essays graded by other instructors. The first exam that semester brought Luanne some good news: She had gotten her highest score ever. But there was the usual bad news as well: Both exam graders said her grammar errors kept them from passing her.

Luanne was at another important choice point. Did she have the self-discipline to persist in the face of discouraging news? Would she quit or finish strong?

"Okay," she said finally, "show me how to correct my errors." We reviewed her essay, sentence by sentence. The next day she went to the writing lab earlier; she left later. She rewrote the exam essay for practice, and we went over it again. Applying self-discipline, Luanne's mastery of standard grammar continued to improve.

That semester, the second exit exam was given on the Friday before Christmas. In order to finalize grades, all of the English 101 instructors met that evening to grade the essays. I promised to call Luanne with her results.

The room was quiet except for rustling papers as two dozen English instructors read one essay after another. At about 10 p.m. that night, I received my students' graded essays. I looked quickly through the pile and found Luanne's. She had passed! As I dialed the phone to call her, Luanne's previous instructors told others about her success.

"Merry Christmas, Luanne," I said into the phone, "you passed!"

I heard her delight, and at that moment, two dozen instructors in the room began to applaud.

AVOIDING PROCRASTINATION

Imagine you have a math test tomorrow, but instead of studying, you watch television all evening. Chances are, you're procrastinating. Suppose you need to

---

The major difference I've found between the highly successful and the least successful is that the highly successful stick to it. They have staying power. Everybody fails. Everybody takes his knocks, but the highly successful keep coming back.

Sherry Lansing, former CEO, Paramount Pictures

A dream doesn't become reality through magic; it takes sweat, determination, and hard work.

Colin Powell

have an uncomfortable conversation with an instructor, but you keep avoiding him. Chances are, you're procrastinating. What if you have a paper to write for English class, but the night before you reorganize your closet instead? Chances are, you're procrastinating.

Procrastination is postponing something until later. Why do we do that? Usually because whatever we're postponing causes us discomfort. And that becomes a real problem when the action we're putting off is important. When a Quadrant I and II action is unpleasant, procrastination urges us to hang out in Quadrant III or IV. *I don't feel like doing my chemistry homework tonight. I'll do it tomorrow. Today I'll try out my new video game.* Procrastination has good intentions: protecting us from pain. But too often when we procrastinate we undermine our desired outcomes and experiences. That's why procrastination is one of the biggest—and trickiest—enemies of self-discipline…and, therefore, our success.

Dan Ariely is a professor of psychology and behavioral economics. One of his interests is examining behaviors that seem irrational, such as those that move us away from our stated goals rather than toward them. In his book *Predictably Irrational*, he describes an experiment he conducted to

1. understand student procrastination and
2. discover solutions to this self-sabotage.

Here's what Professor Ariely did. For each of three classes, he assigned the same three major papers for homework. For all three classes, he announced the same penalty for a late paper: a 1 percent drop in grade for each day late. The assignments and penalty for lateness were the same for all three classes, but how a paper was determined "late" was different.

For Class 1, Ariely gave students three firm deadlines. All students were required to turn in their papers in weeks 4, 8, and 12 or face the announced penalty. No exceptions.

For Class 2, Ariely invited each student to choose his or her deadlines for turning in the papers. Once they chose their three deadlines, however, they could not change them. As with Class 1, they would receive the announced penalty if a paper were late.

For Class 3, Ariely told students they could turn in their three papers whenever they felt like it. There were no deadlines. They would be penalized only for a paper that was handed in after the course ended.

When the course was over, Professor Ariely computed the average grade in each of the three classes. Which class do you think had the highest average grade? And what can you learn from the results about overcoming procrastination?

It turns out that Class 1, with three firm deadlines given by the professor, got the best grades. Class 2, with the opportunity to set their own deadlines, got the second best grades. And Class 3, with totally open deadlines, got the poorest grades.

Ariely concluded that most of his students overcame procrastination best when they had strict deadlines set by an authority (Class 1). Students who were encouraged to set their own deadlines (Class 2) avoided procrastination better than students left totally without deadlines (Class 3).

Why do we procrastinate? In other words, why do we often allow the things that matter most to be at the mercy of things that matter least? Perhaps the most common reason is that certain important tasks are unpleasant.

Hyrum W. Smith

You must give up something in the immediate present—comfort, ease, recognition, quick rewards—to attract something even better in the future . . .

Pat Riley

Ariely noticed something interesting, however, when he looked more closely at Class 2 (students who each chose their own three deadlines). Most of the students in this class spread their deadlines over the semester and earned grades as good as the grades of students in Class 1 (students with teacher-mandated deadlines). But some students in this class spaced their deadlines very little, and a few didn't spread them out at all. Ariely noted that the papers of these latter students appeared rushed and poorly written, receiving low scores even before any penalties for lateness. As a result, these students pulled down the average grades in their class.

Ariely's conclusion? Pre-commitments are a great way to avoid giving in to the temptation of procrastination. Here's what he means. To give our self-discipline a boost, we need to plan ahead and make a commitment that out-smarts our tendency to postpone discomfort. For example, if we have trouble tackling a big project, we can use a 32-day commitment to get us to do a little each day. If we have trouble saving money, we can arrange to have our employer take out a small amount from every pay check and place it in a savings account. If we can't resist ice cream before going to bed, we can make sure there is none in the refrigerator. If we resist studying a challenging subject, we can create or join a study team of dedicated students who won't let us off the hook.

So, what important action have you been putting off? And what pre-commitment plan could you put in place today that will help you create the tomorrow you want?

The secret of getting ahead is getting started. The secret of getting started is breaking your complex overwhelming tasks into small manageable tasks, and then starting on the first one.

Mark Twain

My Daddy used to ask us whether the teacher had given us any homework. If we said no, he'd say, "Well, assign yourself." Don't wait around to be told what to do. Hard work, initiative, and persistence are still the nonmagic carpets to success.

Marian Wright Edelman

JOURNAL ENTRY / 14

In this activity, you will apply self-discipline by planning and carrying out a 32-day commitment that will help you achieve a goal in college. Making and keeping a 32-day commitment has a number of benefits. First, it guarantees that you spend significant time on task, which is essential to college success. Second, a 32-day commitment automatically provides distributed practice, one of the keys to deep and lasting learning. And third, it helps you make visible progress toward your goal, thus raising your expectations of success and your motivation to persist.

1 From your life plan in Journal Entry 9, copy one of your most important and challenging short-term goals from your role as a *student*.

2 Write and complete the following sentence stem three or more times: I WOULD MOVE STEADILY TOWARD THIS GOAL IF EVERY DAY I . . . .

Write three or more different physical actions that *others can see you do* and that you can do every day of the week, including weekends. So you wouldn't write, "I am motivated" or "I attend class." Others cannot see your motivation, and you can't attend class every day for 32 days straight. Instead, if your short-term goal is to earn an A in

English, you might complete the sentence with specific actions such as these:

1. **I WOULD MOVE STEADILY TOWARD THIS GOAL IF EVERY DAY**

   I spent at least 15 minutes doing exercises in my grammar book.

2. **I WOULD MOVE STEADILY TOWARD THIS GOAL IF EVERY DAY**

   I wrote at least 200 words in my journal.

3. **I WOULD MOVE STEADILY TOWARD THIS GOAL IF EVERY DAY**

   I revised one of my previous essays, correcting the grammar errors that my teacher marked.

Chances are, all of these actions will fall in Quadrant II.

3 On a separate page in your journal, create a 32-Day Commitment Form or attach a photocopy of the one following this Journal Entry. Complete the sentence at the top of the form ("Because I know. . . .") with ONE action from your list in Step 2. For the next 32 days, put a check beside each day that you keep your commitment.

4 Make a choice—write about one of the following:

A. **Describe your thoughts and feelings as you begin your 32-day commitment.** Develop your journal paragraphs by asking and answering readers' questions, such as, How self-disciplined have you been in the past? What is your goal? What were some possible actions you considered? What action did you choose for your 32-day commitment? How will this action, when performed consistently, help you reach your goal? What challenges might you experience in keeping your commitment? How will you overcome these challenges? How do you feel about undertaking this commitment? What is your prediction about whether or not you will succeed in keeping your 32-day commitment? If you miss a day, what will be your inner conversation?

B. Imagine that your *On Course* class has an anonymous online discussion board. (That is, students can post messages online for the class to read, but no one can tell who wrote them unless they sign their name.) One student posts, "I missed day four of my 32-day commitment, and now I feel terrible about myself. I'm great about keeping promises to everyone else, but I'm not so good about keeping commitments to myself." A second student writes, "I missed two days of my 32-day commitment already, but it doesn't bother me at all. It's just a stupid homework assignment. What difference does it make?" **Write a response that you imagine your instructor might write to the two anonymous students.**

IMPORTANT: If you miss a day on your 32-Day Commitment Form, don't judge yourself or offer excuses. Simply ask your Inner Guide what got you off course, learn the lesson that is available, renew your commitment to yourself, and start over at Day 1.

Becoming a world-class figure skater meant long hours of practice while sometimes tolerating painful injuries. It meant being totally exhausted sometimes, and not being able to do all the things I wanted to do when I wanted to do them.

Debi Thomas

32-Day Commitment

Because I know that this commitment will keep me on course to my goals, I promise myself that every day for the next 32 days I will take the following action:

_____

_____

_____

Day 1		Day 17	
Day 2		Day 18	
Day 3		Day 19	
Day 4		Day 20	
Day 5		Day 21	
Day 6		Day 22	
Day 7		Day 23	
Day 8		Day 24	
Day 9		Day 25	
Day 10		Day 26	
Day 11		Day 27	
Day 12		Day 28	
Day 13		Day 29	
Day 14		Day 30	
Day 15		Day 31	
Day 16		Day 32	

ONE STUDENT'S STORY

HOLT BOGGS, *Belmont Technical College, Ohio*

I was a first-year student and enjoying college, but I was having a hard time in my electronics class. The teacher lectured about things like current, watts, volts, and resistance, and even though I read the book, took notes in class, and asked questions, I still wasn't understanding what I needed to. When I got back my first test, I didn't fail but I did pretty badly. I was scared because, if this is what the first test was like, how hard would the rest of them be? This was a new experience for me because I never had to study much to do well in school. I knew that I had to try something different if I was going to pass electronics.

In my Student Learning and Success class, I read about the 32-day commitment, and I decided to give it a try. I decided to read one section from my electronics book twice every day for 32 days. I figured that if I read the section twice, maybe I would understand it better the second time around. However, as the semester went on, I still wasn't doing so hot. At times I felt like quitting my commitment because, even though I was reading every section twice, I still wasn't getting it. By midterm, I was ahead of the class in the book, and when the instructor taught the section, it was all review for me. Then one day he was putting examples on the board, and I realized, "Hey, I know this stuff." Since I already understood most of the material,

I had time to focus on the things that I didn't understand. Everything that was still blurry to me he made clear. On the next chapter test, I got a 93, and in the end I passed the class with a B.

It's amazing what doing one little thing for 32 days can do for you. I never would have thought committing 32 days to reading a section from my book twice would help so much. Before, I'd say, "Yeah, I read it," but I was only skimming. When I read it a second time, I picked up things that I missed the first time through and I really understood what I was reading. In the end, the 32-day commitment was able to help me pass my electronics class, but even more important, this experience gave me a lot more confidence. Now I know that I can pass all of the challenging classes on the way to my degree.

SELF-MANAGEMENT / at Work

Success in business requires training and discipline and hard work. But if you're not frightened by these things, the opportunities are just as great today as they ever were.

David Rockefeller, former chairman, Chase Manhattan Bank

Success in the workplace—as in college—means converting your goals into a step-by-step plan. Then you need the self-discipline to spend the majority of your time doing what is important, preferably before it becomes urgent. Here in the realm of action, doers separate themselves from dreamers. Folks in business often refer to this aspect of success as "doing diligence."

In college, "doing diligence" is wise because the effort usually nets you good grades, and a high GPA impresses potential employers with both your intelligence and your work ethic. But getting good grades isn't all you can do in college to stand out in a job interview. Here are some other Quadrant II actions that will look great on your résumé:

- Gain experience in your career field through part-time jobs, volunteer work, internships, or cooperative-education experiences.

- Demonstrate leadership qualities through your involvement with the student government.

▶

- Create a portfolio of your best college work.
- Join clubs or activities that relate to your future career.

Wise choices like these offer employers something that distinguishes you from all of the other applicants for the job.

When it comes time to search for a position in your field, your effective self-management skills will once more serve you well. Consider using the **Tracking Form** to direct your outer and inner action steps toward your employment goal. The **Next Actions List** is a great tool for keeping track of essential one-time actions such as returning calls or sending thank-you notes after an interview. **Weekly and Monthly Calendars** help you avoid the embarrassment of arriving late or having to cancel a job interview because of a scheduling conflict. **Waiting-For Lists** enable you to follow up with requests you have made, such as a reference letter you haven't received. A **Project Folder** for each job you apply for keeps all of the information about that position in one place. All of these tools allow you to monitor your use of time, assuring that you spend the bulk of your time productively in Quadrants I and II.

As you begin your career search, consider doing the following outer action steps:

- Develop a list of careers that interest you.
- Make a list of potential employers in each career.
- Attend a résumé-writing workshop.
- Write a résumé and cover letter to showcase the talents and experiences you offer an employer.
- Personalize each cover letter to fit the job you're applying for.
- Develop your telephone skills.
- Participate in mock interviews where others ask you likely questions.

Your college's career center or a career development course can help you take these job-search actions effectively.

Searching for employment can get discouraging, and you would be wise to take some inner actions to maintain a positive attitude. You could create an affirmation as a mental pick-me-up. For example, "I am enthusiastically taking all of the actions necessary to find the ideal position to start my career." Or "I optimistically send out 10 job inquiries each week." If you find an important action difficult to do (such as calling employers to see if they have unadvertised openings), you could visualize yourself doing it and having the experience go extraordinarily well.

Once you move into your career, your self-management skills will become essential for accomplishing all you have to do. Notice how many people at your workplace carry planners, either paper or electronic. If you don't already have a planner that works for you, experiment to see if one will help you to manage the avalanche of tasks that will come your way in a new position. There's no one-size-fits-all self-management system for everyone, but there is one self-management system that will fit you. And it's your responsibility to find or invent it.

At the beginning of your career, tasks will likely take you twice as long to do as they will after a few years of practice. So not only do you need to manage your next actions list, you'll also need to make some sacrifices to get them all done. People with a "job" mentality sometimes stop short of getting all of their work done because work inevitably leaks into their personal time. They work only until their "shift" is over. On the other hand, people with a "career" mentality know that sometimes they'll need to stay late or take work home. They have the discipline to work until the task is done. Of course, these folks have to find a balance that allows them to have a personal life as well. One important thing to know is that the workload is always heavy at the beginning of a career, and this is the time when you establish your reputation as someone who can be counted on to get the job done.

TECH TIPS: Self-Management

Google Calendar, among many free online resources offered by Google, can be accessed from any device with Internet access. Calendars may be shared so that two or more people can access and update the same calendar. Ideal for project teams at school and busy families at home. *(Web, Android, and iOS)*

Evernote is a powerful electronic notebook that makes it easy to record and organize all of your lists and notes. You can create to-do lists, record voice reminders, and organize your daily schedule. You can even add websites to your notes. *(Web, Android, and iOS)*

Any.do, Workflowy, and **Todoist** are list-making and task-management tools with different features. Any.do, for example, can send you an email reminder before your tasks are due, while Workflowy basically just lets you create lists and sub-lists in an outline format. They all offer the option to collaborate with classmates, friends, and loved ones to accomplish things together. You may wish to experiment with their different approaches to see which works best for you. *(Web, Android, and iOS)*

Myhomeworkapp provides a student planner that offers the ability to track assignments, projects, and tests. *(Web, Android, and iOS)*

Joesgoals.com is a simple website that works very much like an electronic Tracking Form. You plug in goals, track each action you take toward the goals, and earn points as you take positive actions. *(Web)*

Focusboosterapp.com is a desktop digital timer that helps you avoid distractions and stay on task. You set the timer for, say, 25 minutes and then focus diligently on one task until the timer goes off. Then you reward your efforts as you choose. *(Web)*

RescueTime uses another method to help you stop wasting time online. You can set it to track your time on websites and applications (for example, Facebook), generate a weekly email report on how you spend your time, and even limit the time you can spend in certain places if you choose. If you often find yourself in Quadrants III and IV, this could be a big help. *(Web, Android)*

Dontbreakthechain is an online way to track a 32-day (and beyond!) commitment. Simply set a goal to take (or not take) a certain action that will help you achieve a personal, academic, or professional goal. Every day you keep your commitment, you go to the website and click the date on the calendar. The calendar puts the date in a red block . . . and over time a chain of red blocks is formed. The longer the chain, the closer you are to your victory. *(Web, Android, and iOS)*

iStudiez, My Study Life, and **myHomework** are digital planners that give you the ability to track your tasks, assignments, projects, and tests. *(Web, Android, and iOS)*

Note: All of the above are free, but some may offer upgraded features for a fee.

BELIEVING IN YOURSELF

Develop Self-Confidence

FOCUS QUESTIONS   In which life roles do you feel most confident? In which do you experience self-doubt? What can you do to increase your overall self-confidence?

On the first day of one semester, a woman intercepted me at the classroom door. "Can I ask you something?" she said. "How do I know if I'm cut out for college?"

"What's your opinion?" I asked.

"I think I'll do okay."

"Great," I said.

She stood there, still looking doubtful. "But . . . my high school counselor said. . . ." She paused.

"Let me guess. Your counselor said you wouldn't do well in college? Is that it?"

She nodded. "I think he was wrong. But how do I know for sure?"

Indeed! How *do* we know? There will always be others who don't believe in us. What matters, however, is that we have confidence in ourselves. Self-confidence is the core belief that *I CAN*, the unwavering trust that I can successfully do whatever is necessary to achieve my realistic goals and dreams.

Ultimately, it matters little whether someone else thinks you can do something. It matters greatly whether *you* believe you can. Luck aside, you'll probably accomplish just about what you believe you can. In this section we'll explore three effective ways to develop greater self-confidence.

> If people don't feel good about themselves and believe that they'll win a championship, they never will.
>
> Tara VanDerveer, former head coach of the NCAA Championship Stanford University women's basketball team

CREATE A SUCCESS IDENTITY

Are you confident that you can tie your shoes? Of course. And yet there was a time when you weren't. So how did you move from doubt to confidence? Wasn't it by practicing over and over? You built your self-confidence by stacking one small victory upon another. As a result, today you have confidence that you can tie your shoes every time you try. By the same method, you can build a success identity in virtually any endeavor.

> Success brings its own self-confidence.
>
> Lillian Vernon Katz

The life of Nathan McCall illustrates the creation of a success identity under difficult circumstances. It also shows how a Creator mindset can help you overcome any feelings you have of being "different," such as not being part of the mainstream culture. McCall grew up in a Portsmouth, Virginia, ghetto where he faced prejudice and racism. His involvement with crimes and violence led to imprisonment. After his release, McCall attended college and studied journalism. As you might imagine, one of his greatest challenges was self-doubt. But he persevered, tackling each challenge as it came—one more test passed, one more course completed. After graduation, he got a job with a newspaper, and over the years he steadily rose to the position of bureau chief. Recalling his accumulated successes, McCall wrote in his journal, "These experiences solidify my belief that I can do anything I set my mind to do. The possibilities are boundless." Boundless indeed! McCall went from street-gang member and prison inmate to successful and respected reporter for the *Washington Post,* later author of a *New York Times* bestseller, and then became a faculty member at Emory University in Georgia.

Genuine self-confidence results from a history of success, and a history of success results from persistently taking purposeful actions. That's why a 32-day commitment (Journal Entry 14) is not only an effective self-management tool but also a great way to start building a success identity. After we experience success in one area of our lives, self-confidence begins to seep into every corner of our being, and we begin to believe *I CAN*.

CELEBRATE YOUR SUCCESSES AND TALENTS

A friend showed me a school assignment that his eight-year-old daughter had brought home. At the top of the page was written: *Nice job, Lauren. Your spelling is very good. I am proud of you.* What made the comments remarkable is this: The teacher had merely put a check on the page; Lauren had added the compliments herself.

At the age of eight, Lauren has much to teach us about building self-confidence. It's great when someone else tells us how wonderful our successes and talents are. But it's even more important that we tell ourselves.

One way to acknowledge your success is to create a success deck: Every day, write at least one success (big or small) on an index card. Add it to your growing stack of successes and read through the deck every day. Or post the cards on a wall where you'll be reminded often of your accomplishments: *Got an 86 on history test. . . . Attended every class on time this week. . . . Exercised for two hours at the gym.* In addition to acknowledging your successes, you can celebrate them by rewarding yourself with something special—a favorite dinner, a movie, a night out with friends.

VISUALIZE PURPOSEFUL ACTIONS

We can also strengthen our self-confidence, as well as our abilities, by visualizing purposeful actions done well, especially actions outside our comfort zone. Psychologist Charles Garfield once performed an experiment to determine the impact of visualizations on a group of people who were afraid of public speaking. These nervous speakers were divided into three subgroups:

Group 1 read and studied how to give public speeches, but they delivered no actual speeches.

Group 2 read about speechmaking and also gave two talks each week to small audiences of classmates and friends.

Group 3 read about effective speaking and gave one talk each week to small groups. This group also watched videotapes of effective speakers and, twice a day, *mentally rehearsed* giving effective speeches of their own.

Research studies show that people who have high self-esteem regularly reward themselves in tangible and intangible ways. . . . By documenting and celebrating their successes, they insure that these successes will reoccur.

Marsha Sinetar

Peak performers develop powerful mental images of the behavior that will lead to the desired results. They see in their mind's eye the result they want, and the actions leading to it.

Charles Garfield

Experts on public speaking, unaware of the experiment, evaluated the effectiveness of these speakers both before and after their preparation. Group 1 did not improve at all. Group 2 improved significantly. Group 3, the group that had visualized themselves giving excellent speeches, improved the most.

When I first introduce the idea of visualizing to my students, many are skeptical. In particular, young male students are often outspoken. "That's just *stupid*," one basketball player said. Two things helped change the minds of many. First, they were intrigued to learn that world-class athletes use mental imagery to improve their skills. Three examples are basketball legend Michael Jordan, golf great Tiger Woods, and tennis superstar Roger Federer. Second, like me, many skeptics became believers after they gave visualization a serious try. My conversion occurred after I dramatically improved my backhand in racquetball. I got a book with still pictures showing each step of a perfect backhand. For weeks, I imagined those steps in my mind . . . and then practiced them on the court. My "aha" came the day that one of my backhands smacked the front wall with the crack of a pistol (instead of my usual marshmallow hitting a pillow).

Mentally rehearsing purposeful actions will not only help you improve your ability to do the action but will also reduce associated fears. Suppose you're feeling anxious about an upcoming test. Your Inner Critic is probably visualizing a disaster: *As soon as I walk into the exam room, my pulse starts racing, I start sweating, I start feeling weak, and my mind goes totally blank. I fail!*

What if you visualized a more positive experience? You could imagine yourself taking the test confidently, creating an ideal outcome. Your revised mental movie might look like this: *I walk into the exam fully prepared. I've attended all of my classes on time, done my very best work on all of my assignments, and studied effectively. Feeling confident, I find a comfortable seat and take a few moments to breathe deeply, relax, and focus myself. I concentrate on the subject matter of this test. I release all my other cares and worries, feeling excited about the opportunity to show how much I have learned. The instructor walks into the room and begins handing out the exams. I know that any question the instructor asks will be easy for me to answer. I glance at the test and see questions that my study group and I have prepared for all semester. Alert and aware, I begin to write. Every answer I write flows easily from the storehouse of knowledge I have in my mind. I work steadily and efficiently, and, after finishing, I check my answers thoroughly. I hand in the exam with a comfortable amount of time remaining, and as I leave the room, I feel a pleasant weariness. I am confident that I have done my very best.*

Because you choose the movies that play in your mind, why not choose to star in a movie in which you successfully complete purposeful actions?

Creators know there are many choices that will strengthen self-confidence. When we consciously choose options such as creating a success identity, celebrating our successes and talents, and visualizing the successful completion of purposeful actions, we will soon be able to say with supreme confidence: *I CAN.*

Mental practice is also referred to as "visualization" or "imagery rehearsal." We start with 20 to 30 minutes of relaxation training, followed by the visualization of some aspect of the athlete's game that needs improvement. It's the mental equivalent of physical practice.

Dr. Richard Suinn,
Sports Psychologist to
Olympic athletes

If we picture ourselves functioning in specific situations, it is nearly the same as the actual performance. Mental practice helps one to perform better in real life.

Dr. Maxwell Maltz

JOURNAL ENTRY   15

In this activity, you will practice ways to increase your self-confidence. Self-confident people *expect* success, which in turn strengthens their motivation and fuels their energy. If what they are doing isn't working, they don't quit. Instead, they switch to Plan B (or C or D) and persist. Then they finish strong, consistently giving their best to achieve their goals and dreams! In this way, the very success they want and expect often becomes a reality.

Make a choice: Do two of the following four actions:

1 **List the successes you have created in your life.** The more successes you list, the more you will strengthen your self-confidence. Include small victories as well as big ones.

2 **List your personal skills and talents.** Again, the longer your list, the more you will strengthen your self-confidence. What are you good at doing? What would your friends say are your skills and talents? Don't overlook talents that you use daily. No talent is too insignificant to acknowledge. If listing your personal skills and talents makes you uncomfortable, recall the old saying, "It ain't bragging if it's true!"

3 **List positive risks that you have taken in your life.** When did you stretch your comfort zone and do something despite your fear?

4 **Write a visualization of yourself successfully doing an important action that you presently have some resistance about doing.** For example, maybe you fear asking a question in your biology lecture or you're nervous about going to a scheduled job interview. Remember to use the four keys to effective visualizing discussed in Journal Entry 10:

1. **Relax.**
2. **Use present-tense verbs.**
3. **Be specific and use many senses.**
4. **Feel the feelings.**

As a model for your writing, reread the positive visualization that appears in the article right before this journal entry.

I wanted to be the best dentist that ever lived. People said, "But she's a woman; she's colored," and I said, "Ha! Just you wait and see."

Bessie Delany, dentist and author

If you have no confidence in self, you are twice defeated in the race of life. With confidence, you have won even before you have started.

Marcus Garvey

Have you ever walked into a classroom feeling like everyone is staring at you? When you get called upon to read aloud to the class, does your heart beat like a bass drum that you hope others can't hear? When someone talks to you, do you sweat and stumble over your words and end up feeling like a complete fool? I never wanted to admit that lack of confidence was a problem for me, but in school I was always the person who was extremely shy and quiet, always keeping to myself, trying to be invisible. When someone asked me a question, I would attempt to answer, but I would lower my eyes and my voice would get very quiet, making it hard to hear what I was saying. The other person probably thought I was rudely ignoring them. The first day of class in college, as I was looking around at all of the students coming in, I realized the biggest obstacle I had to face was me. My low self-confidence, low self-esteem, and my extreme quietness were going to be a huge challenge.

When I had decided to attend college, I was a little scared, but I had plenty of love and support from my family and was excited to attend. I knew my grades wouldn't be a problem, as I have really good study habits. Due to health issues, I attended high school through an independent study program. I was able to graduate with good grades, but I never had to be around anyone except my teacher.

I lacked social skills with people my own age, but I always had my homework done early and for all of my hard work, I graduated three months early. The first day in college, however, I was a nervous wreck, wondering if I had made a huge mistake by enrolling. The teachers announced that we would be doing group activities, partnering with others, reading aloud, and forming study groups to strengthen our skills. I panicked, and all I could do was tell myself not to give up. As the days passed, I said little or nothing during my classes. In my English class, I partnered with Annette, a woman who befriended me the first day despite my quietness. The class uses the *On Course* book, and we started learning strategies that could help us. I was still nervous, but after reading about some of the strategies, I decided to take more actions to get the most out of my college education and experience. I became determined to prove to myself and everyone else that I could succeed in college.

In order to create what *On Course* calls a "success identity," I made a 32-day commitment to be more outspoken. One promise I made was to talk to at least three people every day. Another was to read out loud in front of the class without having to be asked by my teachers. I also decided to volunteer more in class and share more of my work without being embarrassed. I decided to ask more questions during and after class as well as offer help to my classmates. I even asked my teachers and classmates for written feedback about my efforts to be more self-confident and participate actively in class. Not only did they give me this feedback, some even wrote me inspirational praise.

I'm very proud of myself for all of the changes I've made and that I'm still making every day. I am inspired to continue to grow and reach my full potential, and I'm grateful to all of the people who have been so kind to me and helped me see that I can do it. During the semester, we were asked to write an essay about what we had learned in the course, and my teacher announced that students would be able to read their essays in front of the Copper Mountain College Board of Trustees. I was so proud of the progress I had made that I was the second student in the class to volunteer. As I read my speech, I felt my confidence growing and was even able to make a good amount of eye contact with my audience. After my speech was done, I thanked everyone and as I walked back to my spot I started crying, knowing I had accomplished my goal. Thanks to learning *On Course* strategies and receiving encouragement and motivation from my family, teachers, friends, and classmates, today I have stronger self-confidence and a more positive outlook on my future than ever before.

Photo: Courtesy of Ashley Freeman.

Employing Interdependence

Successful Students . . .

▶ **develop mutually supportive relationships,** recognizing that life is richer when giving to and receiving from others.

▶ **strengthen relationships with active listening,** showing their concern for the other person's thoughts and feelings.

▶ **respect cultural differences,** understanding how to achieve success in a world of increasing diversity.

Struggling Students . . .

▶ **remain dependent, codependent, or independent** in relation to others.

▶ **listen poorly,** demonstrating little desire to understand another person's perspective.

▶ **judge those who are different** as inappropriate, lacking, wrong, or bad.

Once I accept responsibility for taking purposeful actions to achieve my goals and dreams, I then develop mutually supportive relationships that make the journey easier and more enjoyable.

I am employing interdependence in my relationships.

CASE STUDY IN CRITICAL THINKING | Professor Rogers's Trial

Professor Rogers thought her Speech 101 students would enjoy role-playing a real court trial as their last speech for the semester. She also hoped the experience would teach them to work well in teams, a skill much sought after by employers. So, she divided her students into groups of six—a team of three defense attorneys and a team of three prosecuting attorneys—and provided each group with court transcripts of a real murder case. Using evidence from the trial, each team would present closing arguments for the case, after which a jury of classmates would render a verdict. Each team was allowed a maximum of 24 minutes to present its case, and all three team members would receive the same grade.

After class, **Anthony** told his teammates, **Sylvia** and **Donald**, "We'll meet tomorrow at 4:00 in the library and plan a defense for this guy." Sylvia felt angry about Anthony's bossy tone, but she just nodded. Donald said, "Whatever," put headphones on, and strolled away singing louder than he probably realized.

"Look," Anthony said to Sylvia at 4:15 the next day, "we're not waiting for Donald any more. Here's what we'll do. You go first and take about 10 minutes to prove that our defendant had no motive. I'll take the rest of the time to show how it could have been the victim's brother who shot him. I want an A out of this."

Sylvia was furious. "You can't just decide to leave Donald out. Plus, what about the defendant's fingerprints on the murder weapon! We have to dispute that evidence or we'll never win. I'll do that. And I'll go last so I can wrap up all the loose ends. I want to win this trial."

The defense team met twice more before the trial. Donald came to only one of the meetings and spent the entire time texting his girlfriend. He said he wasn't sure what he was going to say, but he'd have it figured out by the day of the trial. Anthony and Sylvia argued about which evidence was most important and who would speak last. At one point, another student threatened to call security when Sylvia lost her temper and started shouting at Anthony that no one had elected him the leader. Sylvia glared at the complaining student and then at Anthony, and without another word, stomped out of the library.

The day before the trial, Anthony went to Professor Rogers. "It's not fair that my grade depends on my teammates. Donald couldn't care less what happens, and Sylvia is always looking for a fight. I'll present alone, but not with them."

"If you were an actual lawyer," Professor Rogers replied, "do you think you could go to the judge and complain that you aren't getting along with your partners? You'll have to figure out how to work as a team. The trial goes on as scheduled, and all three of you will get the same grade."

On the day of the trial, the three student prosecutors presented one seamless and persuasive closing argument. Then Anthony leapt up, saying, "I'll go first for my team." He spoke for 21 minutes, talking as fast as he could to present the entire case, including an explanation of how the defendant's fingerprints had gotten on the murder weapon. Sylvia, greatly flustered, followed with a 7-minute presentation in which she also explained how the defendant's fingerprints had gotten on the murder weapon. At that point, Professor Rogers announced that the defense was already 4 minutes over their time limit. Donald promised to be brief. He assured the jury that the defendant was innocent and then read three unconnected passages from the transcript as "proof." His presentation took 75 seconds. The jury of fellow students deliberated for 5 minutes and unanimously found the defendant guilty. Professor Rogers gave all members of the defense team a D for their speeches.

Listed below are the characters in this story. Rank them in the order of their responsibility for the group's grade of "D." Give a different score to each character. Be prepared to explain your answer.

Most responsible ▶ ① ② ③ ④ ◀ Least responsible

___ **Professor Rogers**   ___ **Sylvia**

___ **Anthony**   ___ **Donald**

DIVING DEEPER

Imagine that you have been assigned to a group project in one of your college courses and that the student whom you scored above as most responsible for the group's grade of D (Anthony, Sylvia, or Donald) is in your group. What positive actions could you take to help your group be a success despite this person?

Creating a Support System

All of us make a choice—often unconsciously—about the kinds of relationships we have with other people. And that choice has a huge impact on our success in college and beyond.

People generally engage in four kinds of relationships. The kinds we choose most often reveal the beliefs we have about ourselves and other people. Which of the following sounds most like you?

- *I can't achieve my goals by myself, so I choose to be* **dependent**.
- *I make helping other people achieve their goals more important than achieving my own goals, so I choose to be* **codependent**.
- *By working hard, I can get some of what I want all by myself, so I choose to be* **independent**.
- *I know I can get some of what I want by working alone, but I'll accomplish more and have more fun if I give and receive help, so I choose to be* **interdependent**.

In which of these ways do you usually relate to others? More important, which choice will best help you achieve your goals and dreams?

A SIGN OF MATURITY

Moving from dependence or codependence to independence is a major step toward maturity. An exciting part of the college experience for many students is their newfound freedom and independence. And there are certainly times when independence is the best choice.

However, Creators know that life is often easier and more enjoyable when people collaborate. They are quite capable of being *in*dependent when going it alone is the best choice. But they can also be *inter*dependent when it is necessary or more

> Dependent people need others to get what they want. Independent people can get what they want through their own effort. Interdependent people combine their own efforts with the efforts of others to achieve their greatest success.
>
> Stephen Covey

> We are all interdependent. Do things for others—tribe, family, community—rather than just for yourself.
>
> Chief Wilma Mankiller

effective to work with others. Creators maximize their results in college by seeking assistance from instructors, classmates, librarians, advisors, counselors, community services, and family members, to name just a few. They know that choosing *inter*dependence—at the right times—demonstrates the greatest maturity of all.

Consider my student Martha. Two weeks before the end of a semester, she announced to our class, "I just came today to say goodbye. I have to withdraw from college because my babysitter moved. My baby's only two, and I can't find anyone I trust to stay with her. I wanted to say how much I'll miss you all."

A concerned silence followed Martha's announcement. Her quiet, solid presence had made her a favorite with classmates.

Then one of the women in the class said, "My kids are grown, and this is the only class I'm taking this semester. I can watch your child for the next few weeks if that would help you get through the semester. The only thing is, you'll need to bring your baby to my house because I don't have a car."

"I don't have a car either," Martha said. "Thanks anyway."

"Wait a minute," a young man said. "I have a car. I'll drive you and your child back and forth until the semester's over. It's only two weeks!"

Martha sat for a moment, stunned. "Really? You'd do that for me?" In three minutes, Martha's fate had changed from dropping out of school to finishing the semester with the help of two classmates.

Interdependence can help you stay on course in college and support your success in ways you can't even imagine now. By contrast, codependence is among the most destructive relationships. Codependent people are motivated not by their own successes, but by someone else's approval or dependence upon them. Codependent people abandon their own dreams and even endure abuse to keep the approval of others.

John was a bright fellow who had been in college for seven years without graduating. During a class discussion, he related an experience he said was typical of him: He'd been studying for midterm test in history when a friend called and asked for help with biology. John had already passed biology. John set aside his own studies and spent the evening tutoring his friend. The next day John failed his history exam. In his journal, he wrote, "I've learned that in order to be successful, I need to make my dreams more important than other people's approval. I have to learn to say 'no.'" Codependent people like John often spend time in Quadrant III, engaged in activities that are important to someone else but unimportant to their own goals and dreams.

With codependence, dependence, and independence, giving and receiving are out of balance. The codependent person *gives* too much. The dependent person *takes* too much. The independent person seldom gives *or* receives. By contrast, the interdependent person finds a healthy balance of giving and receiving, and everyone benefits. That's why building mutually supportive relationships is one of the most important Quadrant II behaviors you'll ever undertake.

My experience is that most students choose independence far more often than interdependence. Perhaps they think asking for help reveals them as weak.

> Nobody but nobody can make it out here alone.
>
> Maya Angelou

> Taking on responsibilities that properly belong to someone else means behaving irresponsibly toward oneself.
>
> Nathaniel Branden

Or they don't feel worthy of the help. Whatever the cause, they avoid using the many resources their colleges provide to help them succeed. Let's consider some choices you can make to create a support system that will help you not only achieve your goals in college but make the journey less stressful as well.

SEEK HELP FROM YOUR INSTRUCTORS

Building positive relationships with your college instructors is a powerful Quadrant II action that can pay off handsomely. Your instructors have years of specialized training. You've already paid for their help with your tuition, and all you have to do is ask.

    If you haven't already, find out your professors' office hours and make an appointment. Arrive prepared with questions or requests, and you'll likely get good help. As a bonus, by getting to know your instructors, you may find a mentor who will help you in college and beyond.

GET HELP FROM COLLEGE RESOURCES

Nearly every college spends a chunk of tuition money to provide support services for students, but these services go to waste unless you use them. Do you know what support services your college offers, where they are, and how to use them? If you completed your College Smart-Start Guide in Chapter 1, you have a list that you may want to expand now.

Confused About Future Courses to Take?

Get help from your advisor or someone in the academic advisement center. Among other things, advisors can help you decide on a major and create a multiyear academic plan that includes all of your required courses and their prerequisites. As you may recall from Chapter 1, such a plan is called a *long-term educational plan*.

Academic Problems?

Get help from your college's learning or tutoring center. Many colleges offer help with reading, writing, and math. Additional sources of academic assistance might include a science learning center or a computer lab. Your college may also have a diagnostician who tests students for learning disabilities and can suggest ways of overcoming them.

Money Problems?

Get help from your college's financial aid office. Money is available in grants and scholarships (which you don't pay back), loans (which you do pay back, usually at low interest rates), and student work programs (which offer jobs on campus). Your college may also have a service that can locate an off-campus

Until recently, the "old girls" did not know how the "old boys'" network operated…. Women now know that, besides hard work and lots of skill, the move to the top requires a supportive network.

June E. Gabler

For every one of us that succeeds, it's because there's somebody there to show you the way out. The light doesn't always necessarily have to be in your family; for me it was teachers and school.

Oprah Winfrey

job, perhaps one in the very career field you want to enter after graduation. Revisit the "Money Matters" section in Chapter 1 for detailed information about addressing money problems.

Personal Problems?

No man is an island, entire of itself; every man is a piece of the continent, a part of the main.

John Donne

Get help from your college's counseling office. Trained counselors are available at many colleges to help students through times of emotional upset. It's not unusual for students to experience personal challenges during college. Creators seek assistance.

Health Problems?

Get help from your college's health service. Many colleges have doctors who see students at little or no cost. Health-related products may be available inexpensively or even for free. Your college may even offer low-cost health insurance for students.

My driving belief is this: great teamwork is the only way to reach our ultimate moments, to create the breakthroughs that define our careers, to fulfill our lives with a sense of lasting significance.

Pat Riley, former professional basketball coach

Problems Deciding on a Career?

Get help from your college's career office. There you can take aptitude tests, discover job opportunities, discover careers you've never heard of, learn to write or improve your résumé, and practice effective interviewing skills.

Problems Getting Involved Socially at Your College?

Get help from your college's student activities office. Here you'll discover athletic teams, trips, choirs, dances, service projects, student professional organizations, the college newspaper, the campus literary magazine, clubs, and more. All are just waiting for you to get involved.

CREATE A PROJECT TEAM

If you're tackling a big project, why not create a team to help? A project team is formed to accomplish one particular task. In business, when a project needs attention, an *ad hoc* committee is formed. *Ad hoc* is Latin for "toward this." In other words, an ad hoc committee comes together for the sole purpose of solving one problem. Once the task is complete, the committee disbands.

I never did anything alone. Whatever was accomplished in this country was accomplished collectively.

Golda Meir

One of my students created a project team to help her move. More than a dozen classmates volunteered, including a fellow who provided a truck. In one Saturday morning, the team packed and delivered her possessions to a new apartment. Without the help, how long would the move have taken her, how much would it have cost, and how much stress would it have caused her?

What big project do you have that would benefit from the assistance of others? The only barrier standing between you and a project team is your stubborn independence.

START A STUDY GROUP

In the late 1970s and early 1980s, a mathematics graduate student at the University of California, Berkeley, showed the value of academic study groups. Uri Treisman had noticed that successful students in calculus met outside of class and, among other things, talked about solving math problems. Struggling students didn't. As a result of this observation, Treisman created a program for struggling calculus students. His approach encouraged these students to gather for the purpose of talking about mathematics and solving challenging problems. The program was so successful that it has since been offered at many other colleges and universities. You can create a variation of Triesman's program in any course you want. Simply start a study group with some of your classmates. A study group differs from a project team in two ways. First, a study group is created to help everyone on the team excel in a particular course. Second, a study group meets many times throughout a semester. In fact, some study groups are so helpful that their members stay together throughout college.

None of us is as smart as all of us.

Ken Blanchard

Study groups offer a number of benefits. Participation increases your active involvement with the course content, which in turn leads to deeper learning and higher grades. The resulting academic success raises your expectations for success and increases your level of motivation. Study group participation helps you develop the skill of working with a group, a skill much sought after by employers. And some study group members may become your lifelong friends. Here are three suggestions for maximizing the value of your study group:

1. **Choose Only Creators.** As the semester begins, make a list of potential study group members: classmates who attend regularly, come prepared, and participate actively. Also watch for that quiet student who doesn't say much but whose occasional comments reveal a special understanding of the subject. After the first test or essay, find out how the students on your list performed and invite three or four of the most successful to study with you.

Alone we can do so little; together we can do so much.

Helen Keller

2. **Choose Group Goals.** Regardless of potential, a study group is only as effective as you make it. Everyone should agree upon common goals. You might say to prospective study group members, "My goal in our math class is to master the subject and earn an A. Is that what you want, too?" Team up with students whose goals match or exceed your own.

3. **Choose Group Rules.** The last step is establishing team rules. Pat Riley, one of the most successful professional basketball coaches ever, had his players create a "team covenant." Before the season, they agreed on the rules they would follow to stay on course to their goal of a championship. Your team should do the same. Decide where, how often, and at what time you'll meet. Most important, agree on what will happen during the meetings.

Many study groups fail because they turn into social gatherings. Yours will succeed if you adopt rules like these:

Rule 1: We meet in the library every Thursday afternoon from one to three o'clock.

Rule 2: All members bring their favorite study materials, including 20 new questions with answers and sources (e.g., textbook page or class notes).

Rule 3: All study materials are discussed and all written questions are asked, answered, and understood before any socializing.

One of my students took this advice and started a study group in his anatomy and physiology class, a course with a high failure rate. At the end of the semester, he proudly showed me a thank-you card signed by the other four members of his group. "We couldn't have done it without you," they wrote. "Thanks for *making* us get together!" Defying the odds, everyone in the group had passed the course.

The people you spend time with will dramatically affect your outcomes and experiences in college. If they place little value on learning or a college degree, it's challenging to resist their negative influence. However, if you associate with highly committed, hard-working students, their encouragement can motivate you to stay on course to graduation even when the road gets rough. A student in my class actually moved when he realized that "friends" from his old neighborhood spent most of their time putting down his efforts to get a college degree. When it comes to selecting your "group" in college, be sure to choose people who want out of life what you do.

Start a contact list of the people you meet in college. You might even want to write a few notes about them: their major or career field, names of family members, hobbies, interests, and especially their strengths. Keep in touch with these people during and after college.

Creators develop mutually supportive relationships in college that continue to support them for years—even for a lifetime. Don't get so bogged down with the daily demands of college that you fail to create an empowering support network.

THE DIFFERENCE BETWEEN HEAVEN AND HELL

A story is told of a man who prayed to know the difference between heaven and hell. An angel came to take the man to see for himself. In hell, the man saw a huge banquet table overflowing with beautifully prepared meats, vegetables, drinks, and desserts. Despite this bounty, the prisoners of hell had withered, sunken looks. Then the man saw why. The poor souls in hell could pick up all the food they wanted, but their elbows would not bend, so they could not place the food into their mouths. Living amidst all that abundance, the citizens of hell were starving.

Coming together is a beginning, staying together is progress, and working together is success.

Henry Ford

If people around you aren't going anywhere, if their dreams are no bigger than hanging out on the corner, or if they're dragging you down, get rid of them. Negative people can sap your energy so fast, and they can take your dreams away from you, too.

Earvin (Magic) Johnson

Then the angel whisked the man to heaven, where he saw another endless table heaped with a similar bounty of splendid food. Amazingly, just as in hell, the citizens of heaven could not bend their elbows to feed themselves.

"I don't understand," the man said. "Is heaven the same as hell?"

The angel only pointed. The residents of heaven were healthy, laughing, and obviously happy as they sat together at the banquet tables. Then the man saw the difference.

The citizens of heaven were feeding each other.

No matter what accomplishments you make, somebody helps you.

Althea Gibson Darben

JOURNAL ENTRY / **16**

In this activity, you will explore your beliefs and behaviors regarding giving and receiving.

1 **Write and complete the following ten sentence stems:**

1. A specific situation when someone assisted me was . . .

2. A specific situation when I assisted someone else was . . .

3. A specific situation when I made assisting someone else more important than my own success and happiness was . . .

4. When someone asks me for assistance I usually feel . . .

5. When I think of asking someone else for assistance I usually feel . . .

6. What usually gets in the way of my asking for help is . . .

7. If I often asked other people for assistance . . .

8. If I joyfully gave assistance to others . . .

9. If I gratefully accepted assistance from others . . .

10. One goal that I could use assistance with today is . . .

2 **Write about two (or more) choices you could make to create a stronger support system for yourself in college.** Consider the choices you could make to overcome the challenges and obstacles to your success. Consider also any resistance you may have about taking steps to create a support system. Dive deep as you explore each choice fully.

Individually, we are one drop.

Together, we are an ocean.

Ryunosuke Satoro

ONE STUDENT'S STORY

MITCH MULL, *Asheville-Buncombe Technical Community College, North Carolina*

The biggest challenge to my success has always been me. Any time I had a problem, I would try to solve it on my own because I didn't want people to think less of me. I probably got this belief from my father, who is very independent. While pursuing an A.A. degree in Horticulture at Haywood Community College a few years ago, I dropped many classes because I was reluctant to ask for help from fellow students or the instructors. I was able to graduate, but only barely.

Later, while working with a landscaping company, I decided to return to school to advance my career in horticulture. I needed some credits to enter a bachelor's program, so I enrolled at Asheville-Buncombe Technical College. In my first semester, I registered for a night chemistry class and an online student success course. When I registered, I was asked if I really wanted to take the chemistry course. They said it's the most dropped class every semester. With that news, I knew I needed to change my strategies to do better, but I didn't know what I was doing wrong. In the first week of the success course, we took the *On Course* self-assessment, and I scored lowest on interdependence. Needless to say, I wasn't surprised.

The book convinced me that being overly independent and solitary in my studies isn't always a good thing and could possibly keep me from achieving my goals. I decided to commit myself to being more interdependent. I started showing up early for chemistry which, as I had been warned, was very challenging. I asked the instructor for assistance on homework that I couldn't understand. He'd take a minute to write out an equation on the board or help me see how to get it. After he aimed me in the right direction, it would often click for me. There were other chemistry students who came to class early and hung around outside. When I overheard them discussing the course, I joined them. It soon turned into a study group, which further helped me to come out of my shell. The online forums in our success class were also good stepping stones towards my opening up to others. The online discussions helped me overcome the shyness or nervousness that caused me to avoid most interactions. In both classes I made new friends that I may not have even talked to before. Instead of struggling as I had at Haywood, I got As in both of my classes. Without the success class and *On Course*, I probably would have struggled with chemistry or dropped it.

Interdependence has also helped me professionally. Working as a supervisor for a local landscape company, I always thought I needed to tackle every task by myself so I'd get praise from my bosses for being efficiently independent. But a lot of times I wasn't achieving the results that my bosses wanted.

Employing interdependence was hard for me at first but has become easy. Almost any time I ask for help, I receive it. Recently, I was trying to repair an irrigation line break. I've made the same type of repair many times alone, but it normally took a lot of time. This time, I asked a fellow supervisor to help keep water pumped out of the hole as I made the repair. If I hadn't asked for help, it would have taken much longer and the repair may have even failed. Then I would have had to fix it again, and my boss wouldn't have been happy. I've also been helping others as much as possible. Some mornings, the nursery manager gets behind in loading trucks, and I pitch in to ensure all the loads are ready before our crews arrive. I've also been working closer with the secretaries to make sure all time logs are returned on time and tracking down any that are missing. There have been big improvements in all these relationships since I've been employing interdependence!

After completing my courses at A-B Tech, I transferred to North Carolina A&T as a junior in Agricultural Education. I'm still working full-time with the landscaping company while going to school part-time. I have about a year left to get my bachelor's degree, and then I plan on getting a master's with the goal of working in a state cooperative extension program. At NC A&T, I have all As and only one B. I was never a big fan of asking for help, but I must say that the benefits of interdependence have made me a believer.

Photo: Courtesy of Mitch Mull.

Strengthening Relationships with Active Listening

FOCUS QUESTIONS   Do you know how to strengthen a relationship with active listening? What are the essential skills of being a good listener?

Once we have begun a mutually supportive relationship, we naturally want the relationship to grow. Books on relationships abound, suggesting untold ways to strengthen a relationship. At the heart of all of these suggestions is a theme: We must show that we value the other person professionally, personally, or both.

Many ways exist to demonstrate another's value to us. Some of the most powerful methods include keeping promises, giving honest appreciation and approval, resolving conflicts so that both people win, staying in touch, and speaking well of someone when talking to others. However, for demonstrating the high esteem with which you value another person, there may be no better way than active listening.

Few people are truly good listeners. Too often, we're thinking about what we want to say next. Or our thoughts dash off to our own problems, and we ignore what the other person is saying. Or we hear what we *thought* the person was going to say rather than what he or she actually said.

Good listeners, by contrast, clear their minds and listen for the entire message, including words, tone of voice, gestures, and facial expressions. No matter how well one person communicates, unless someone else listens actively, both the communication and the relationship are likely to go astray. Imagine the potential problems created if good listening skills are absent when an instructor says to a class, "I need to change the date of the final exam from next Monday to the previous Friday. I just found out that I need to turn in my final grades on Monday." Suppose a student assumes that the instructor said the exam will be moved to the *following* Friday (instead of the *previous* Friday). When that student shows up on the "following" Friday, not only will the exam be long over, but the instructor will have turned in the final course grades as well. Talk about an unpleasant surprise!

Listening actively means accepting 100 percent responsibility for receiving the same message that the speaker sent, uncontaminated by your own thoughts or feelings. That's why active listening begins with empathy, the ability to understand the other person as if, for that moment, you *are* the other person. To empathize doesn't mean that you necessarily agree. Empathy means understanding what the other person is thinking and feeling. And you actively reveal this understanding.

With active listening, you send this message: *I value you so much that I am doing my very best to see the world through your eyes.*

When people talk, listen completely. Most people never listen.

Ernest Hemingway

For the lack of listening, billions of losses accumulate: retyped letters, rescheduled appointments, rerouted shipments, breakdowns in labor management relations, misunderstood sales presentations, and job interviews that never really get off the ground.

Michael Ray & Rochelle Myers

HOW TO LISTEN ACTIVELY

Active listening is a learned skill. You will become an excellent listener if you master the following four steps:

Step 1: Listen to Understand

Listening isn't effective when you're simply waiting for the first opportunity to insert your own opinion. Instead, focus fully on the speaker, activate your empathy, and listen with the intention of fully understanding what the other person thinks and feels.

Step 2: Clear Your Mind and Remain Silent

Don't be distracted by judgmental chatter from your Inner Critic and Inner Defender. Clear your mind, stay focused, and be quiet. Let your mind listen for thoughts. Let your heart listen for the undercurrent of emotions. Let your intuition listen for a deeper message hidden beneath the words. Let your companion know that you are actively listening. Sit forward. Nod your head when appropriate. Offer verbal feedback that shows you are actively listening: *Mmmmm . . . I see . . . Uh huh. . . .*

Step 3: Ask the Person to Expand or Clarify

Don't make assumptions or fill in the blanks with your own experience. Invite the speaker to share additional information and feelings:

- *Tell me more about that.*
- *Could you give me an example?*
- *Can you explain that in a different way?*
- *How did you feel when that happened?*
- *What happened next?*

Step 4: Reflect the Other Person's Thoughts and Feelings

Don't assume you understand. In your own words, restate what you heard, both the ideas and the emotions. Then verify the accuracy of your understanding:

- To a classmate: *Sounds like you're really angry about the instructor's feedback on your research paper. To you, his comments seem more sarcastic than helpful. Is that it?*
- To a professor: *I want to be clear about the new date for the final exam. You're postponing the exam from Monday to the following Friday. Have I got it right?*

Notice that reflecting adds nothing new to the conversation. Don't offer advice or tell your own experience. Your goal is merely to understand.

USE ACTIVE LISTENING IN YOUR COLLEGE CLASSES

Active listening not only strengthens relationships with people, it strengthens our understanding of new concepts and helps us learn. In class, successful students clear their minds and prepare to hear something of value. They reflect the

---

Active listening, sometimes called reflective listening, involves giving verbal feedback of the content of what was said or done along with a guess at the feeling underneath the spoken words or acts.

Muriel James & Dorothy Jongeward

If I were to summarize in one sentence the single most important principle I have learned in the field of interpersonal relations, it would be this: Seek first to understand, then to be understood.

Stephen Covey

instructor's ideas, confirming the accuracy of what they heard. When confused, they ask the instructor to expand or clarify, either in class or during the instructor's conference hours. Using a Creator mindset, these students actively listen to understand. And, ultimately, they record their understanding in their notes. Obviously, the more accurate the information is in your class notes, the more you will learn when studying.

So, choose today to master active listening. You'll be amazed at how much this choice will improve your relationships, your learning, and your life.

W hat few people realize is that failure to be a good listener prevents us from hearing and retaining vital information, becoming a roadblock to personal and professional success.

Jean Marie Stine

JOURNAL ENTRY   17

In this activity, you will practice the skill of active listening by writing out a conversation with your Inner Guide. As discussed earlier, thoughts are dashing through our minds much of the time. Writing a conversation with your Inner Guide applies this knowledge in a new and powerful way. First, it helps us become more aware of the thoughts that are guiding our choices. Second, writing this conversation encourages us to sort through confusion and find a positive solution. Third, it reminds us that we are not our thoughts and we can change them whenever doing so would benefit us. And, finally, writing this conversation with our Inner Guide gives us practice with an important mental skill used by highly intelligent and adaptive people: *metacognition.*

Metacognition is the skill of thinking about our thinking. Developing metacognition helps us see where our thinking is flawed. It allows us to change our thinking to achieve better outcomes and experiences. If you've ever talked to yourself while working on a problem, you were probably using metacognition. You may find writing this dialogue to be a new (and perhaps unusual) experience. However, the more you practice, the more you'll see what a valuable success skill it is to have a conversation with yourself as an active listener. And, of course, becoming an active listener with others will strengthen those relationships immeasurably.

1 Write a conversation between you (ME) and your Inner Guide (IG) about a problem you are facing in college. Label each of your IG's responses with the listening skill it uses: silence, expansion, clarification, reflection (remember to reflect feelings as well as thoughts). Let your IG demonstrate the skills of active listening without giving advice.

Here's an example of the beginning of such a conversation:

ME: I've been realizing what a difficult time I have asking for assistance.

IG: Would you like to say more about that? (Expansion)

ME: Well, I've been having trouble in math. I know I should be asking more questions in class, but . . . I don't know, I guess I feel dumb because I can't do the problems myself.

IG: You seem frustrated that you can't solve the math problems without help. (Reflection)

ME: That's right. I've always resisted that sort of thing.

D r. Eliot's listening was not mere silence, but a form of activity. Sitting very erect on the end of his spine with hands joined in his lap, making no movement except that he revolved his thumbs around each other faster or slower, he faced his interlocutor and seemed to be hearing with his eyes as well as his ears. He listened with his mind and attentively considered what you had to say while you said it. . . . At the end of an interview the person who had talked to him felt that he had his say.

Henry James about Charles W. Eliot, former president of Harvard University

▶

JOURNAL ENTRY / 17 *continued*

IG: What do you mean by "that sort of thing"? **(Clarification)**

ME: I mean that ever since I can remember, I've had to do everything on my own. When I was a kid, I used to play alone all the time.

IG: Uh-huh. . . . **(Silence)**

ME: As a kid, I never had anyone to help me. And I don't have anyone to help me now.

IG: So, no one is available to help you? Is that how it seems? **(Reflection)**

ME: Well, I guess I could ask Robert for help. He seems really good in math, but I'm kind of scared to ask him.

IG: What scares you about asking him? **(Expansion)** . . . etc.

Imagine that the conversation you create here is taking place over the phone. Don't hang up until you've addressed all aspects of the problem and know what your next action step will be. Let your Inner Guide demonstrate how much it values you by being a great listener.

2 **Write what you learned or relearned about active listening during this conversation with your Inner Guide and what changes, if any, you will make in your communications**. Remember to dive deep to discover a powerful insight. When you think you have written all you can, see if you can write at least one more paragraph.

ONE STUDENT'S STORY

TEROA PASELIO, *Windward Community College, Hawaii*

I grew up in the shadow of my older brother. I was just the little sister of Lafaele Paselio, the all-star football jock, who was one of the popular kids in school. I was never in the spotlight. I felt unimportant. I had no identity of my own. A potato with nothing on it is pretty bland, and that's how I felt. It was really depressing because I knew I have so much to offer.

Stepping into college wasn't as exciting for me as it probably is for most people. Sure it was a new journey, a new experience, but for me, it was just another place to be called Lafaele's little sister. My brother had just finished a year at Windward Community College in Kaneohe, Hawaii, and everyone there knew who he was. Now I was once again in his shadow. Even though my brother had transferred to a university in San Diego, California, I knew I was bound to fall into the same situation I had experienced throughout my life. Once again, I was just Lafaele's little sister.

In my Introduction to College class, we learned tips on how to succeed in college. The class had assignments to write journal entries from the *On Course* book. A journal that was particularly meaningful for me was the one where you wrote a conversation between you and your Inner Guide. Your Inner Guide was supposed to use good listening skills to help you come up with a solution to a problem. It was funny because while I was doing that journal I realized I had the solution right in front of my face, and the conversation with my Inner Guide brought it out. I realized I am in charge of my life. It doesn't matter what others think of me. I fell in love with who I am and what I can do with my life. There are things I'm good at that Lafaele's not good

▶

at. I love my music, and I want to be a high school teacher.

I also saw how good listening skills will help me be the kind of teacher I want to be. I want to make students believe that they matter. I want them to feel important. Some of my teachers have really listened to me and made me feel that I matter. A teacher who doesn't listen sends the message that what the student thinks isn't important. That the *student* isn't important. I remember when I disagreed with my philosophy teacher one time, and he told me to explain

why. Then he kept interrupting me and telling me I was wrong without even letting me explain myself. That made me feel angry, and I'm never going to be like him. I'm going to listen to people. I tell my friends if I interrupt you, tell me to stop. I want to listen to the people in my life so they know that what they say is important to me.

With the help of the Introduction to College class, I learned that I can find answers to the problems I face. I just have to listen to my Inner Guide, to myself. It is my choice to let the fact that

I am Lafaele's sister get to me or not. I can now say that the person I am today is a lot stronger than the person I was yesterday. I don't have to be the bland potato any more. I am Teroa Paselio, that's it! No one's sister, no one's cousin, no one's namesake, but Teroa Paselio! After writing that journal, I walked into school on Monday singing to myself "I'm feeling like a star, you can't stop my shine!" I can definitely say I'm no longer living in anyone's shadow.

Photo: Courtesy of Teroa Paselio.

Respecting Cultural Differences

FOCUS QUESTIONS What are some keys to achieving success in a world of increasing diversity?

Virtually anywhere you go these days, you encounter people different from you. And that's a trend you can expect to grow. The Pew Research Center predicts major changes in race and ethnicity in the United States between now and 2050. Whites will decrease from 67 to 47 percent of the population. Latino/a Americans will increase from 14 to 29 percent. African Americans will remain constant at 13 percent. And Asian Americans will increase from 5 to 9 percent. Other ethnicities such as Native Americans and Arab Americans will add even more to the growing diversity of North America.

College enrollment already reflects these changes, according to the *Chronicle of Higher Education*. In the past 40 years, entering White students decreased from 90.9 to 73.1 percent. Simultaneously, African American students increased from 7.5 to 11 percent. Four decades ago, Asians and Latinos/as combined made up only 0.6 percent of new students in higher education, but today the percent of Asians has increased to 8.9 and Latinos to 9.7.

Visible differences such as skin color are relatively easy to identify. Others may be less obvious but no less important. These differences include religion, economic class, mental and physical ability, sexual orientation, age, military experience, and learning preferences, to name just a few. If you add deep-culture differences in beliefs, values, attitudes, and norms, the list of possible differences between any two people is long, indeed.

I am an American; free born and free bred, where I acknowledge no man as my superior, except for his own worth, or as my inferior, except for his own demerit.

Theodore Roosevelt

Much has been written about the challenges of interacting effectively with people who are different. If you search "diversity" at Amazon.com, you'll get links to nearly 17,000 books. If you search "diversity" at Google.com, you'll get more than 230 million results! The complexity of creating harmony in diverse populations has also been explored in college courses, professional journals, newspapers, magazines, conferences, and workshops. The problems explored in these forums range from misunderstandings stemming from differences in cultural beliefs, attitudes, norms, and rules to the horrors of hate crimes, ethnic cleansings, and genocide.

Addressing the complexities of deeply ingrained prejudice and oppression of minorities is beyond the scope of a book about college success. My hope is that people empowered by the strategies in this book, like you, will find satisfaction in living up to their potential instead of tearing down the lives of others. And if you are a student who faces prejudice and unfair treatment, my hope is that you will feel empowered to stand in opposition to such injustices. Whether you consider yourself a member of a cultural majority or minority, your success very likely depends on your ability to interact effectively with people who are different from you. In higher education, for example, someone different from you may be your instructor, tutor, counselor, advisor, or classmate. In the workplace, someone different from you may be your employer, supervisor, manager, customer, or coworker.

By themselves, differences are not a problem. But add to them the human tendency to judge, fear, and (in some cases) harm people who are different, and you have the perfect recipe for conflict between individuals, groups, and nations. The antidote is to replace judgments with respect.

There are certainly moral arguments to be made for treating everyone with respect, but there is a very practical reason as well. Today, more than ever before, everyone's success is affected by their ability to interact effectively with people who are different from them. Judgments lead to fear, misunderstanding, conflict, discrimination, oppression, and even war. By contrast, respect leads to cooperation, compassion, learning, empowerment, success, and peace. Your choice to judge or show respect will have a profound effect on the outcomes and experiences of your life and those with whom you interact.

> Tolerance, inter cultural dialogue and respect for diversity are more essential than ever in a world where peoples are becoming more and more closely interconnected.
>
> Kofi Annan, former Secretary-General of the United Nations

SHOWING RESPECT

Here are some ways you can show respect to people who are different from you. They range from the simple to the complex:

1. **Pronounce Names Correctly.** There are few things more personal to us than our names. In her book, *Stealing Buddha's Dinner*, Bich Minh Nguyen tells of her shame when Americans pronounced her Vietnamese name "bitch" instead of "Bick." The internationalization of sports is helping mainstream North Americans hear the pronunciation of unfamiliar names such as Yani Tseng (Taiwanese professional golfer), Daisuke Matsuzaka (Japanese professional baseball player), Siyar Bahadurzada (Afghan mixed martial artist), and Ndamukong Suh (professional football player

whose father is from Cameroon). When you meet someone with an unfamiliar name, simply say, "I want to be sure I'm pronouncing your name correctly. Would you please say it for me?"

2. **Use the Preferred Term for a Person's Cultural Group.** Close in importance to our names is the name of our cultural group. Thus, using preferred terminology conveys the same sort of respect as does pronouncing a person's name correctly. Complicating the issue, members of some cultures may differ in their preference. So, once again, if in doubt, ask.

For example, *Latino* and *Latina* are terms preferred by many members of this cultural group. However, some may prefer "Hispanic," a term that others reject as having been thrust upon them by the U.S. Census Bureau. Also, avoid using terminology that excludes a group. For example, if you say to a group of people, "You're welcome to bring your husband or wife," you have excluded gay people and singles living together. Instead, simply say "husband, wife, or partner." When it comes to people with disabilities, remember that the disability is not the person, so separate the two by presenting the person first. Instead of a "disabled person," say "a person with differing abilities." Some members of majority groups get annoyed by this extra effort to come up with the preferred terminology, and they judge it as "political correctness." However, like our personal names, the terms we prefer for our cultural groups are personal as well, and honoring that preference shows respect.

3. **Learn Nonverbal Behaviors.** Experts in communication say that as much as 90 percent of the message we send is conveyed nonverbally. That's why it's essential to know that two nonverbal languages can be as different as two verbal languages. Here are a few examples:

> **Gestures:** Circling your thumb and forefinger in North America means "Everything is great . . . A-Ok." In some South American countries, however, this is an obscene gesture. A two-handed handshake in North America emphasizes one's pleasure when greeting someone. But in Saudi Arabia such a gesture is offensive because Saudis consider one's left hand to be unclean.

> **Space:** In North American culture, we tend to stand about three to four feet apart when speaking to most people. However, people in some South American and Arabic cultures stand much closer to one another in conversation. I once saw two male students talking after class. One was from Saudi Arabia, the other from the United States. Every time the Saudi student stepped closer, the American stepped back. During a 5-minute conversation, they covered about 15 feet in their cross-cultural dance. It was humorous to watch, but I wonder if either or both felt disrespected with no idea why.

> **Eye Contact:** For many North Americans, eye contact during a conversation generally conveys interest and respect. However, in Asian

[E]thnic group members pay very serious attention to the ways in which they label themselves and are labeled by others. Finding out what term is preferable is a matter of respect. . .

Jerry V. Diller

When it comes to nonverbal language, we often mistakenly assume that our systems of communicating nonverbally are all the same.

David Matsumoto and
Linda Juang

cultures such as Korea and Japan, eye contact is considered rude and disrespectful. Imagine the potential misunderstandings in a conversation between an instructor and student from these different cultures.

So whether the difference is in gestures, space, eye contact, or other body language, we can be respectful by realizing that others may speak a different nonverbal language.

4. **See People as Individuals (Not Stereotypes).** The human mind is a pattern-making device. We want to generalize about life to understand, explain, and predict. Knowing that a particular instructor is "easy" or "hard," for example, helps us make decisions about such things as how much to study for a final exam. Unfortunately, once our minds grab onto a generalization, we want to apply it even if it's wrong or doesn't apply in this situation. This is the problem with stereotypes. A stereotype is a generalization about a group of people based on limited or even faulty evidence. Once we accept a generalization as true, we have a tendency to apply it to all individuals we encounter from that group. If you want to see examples of stereotypes you hold about others, simply complete the following sentence stems with the first thought that comes to mind:

Women are...	Southerners are...
Republicans are...	White men are...
Jews are...	Asians are...
Black men are...	Rich people are...
Muslims are...	College instructors are...

Stereotypes about any group disrespect individuals from that group, denying them their uniqueness. Knowing cultural tendencies—for example, whether a culture is individualistic or collectivistic—may help to explain why a member of that culture did what he or she did. But using a stereotype to try to predict what a person will do insults that person's uniqueness. As one example of how to employ this idea, don't assume someone either fits a stereotype or can speak for a whole culture: "Emiko, you people are all good in math, right?" Ouch. Instead of stereotyping, see each person for the unique individual he or she is. Just like you.

5. **Avoid the Right/Wrong Game.** Human beings are judgment machines. We think what we do is right, so anything different must be wrong. When we play the Right/Wrong Game with people whose culture is different from ours, it has a fancy name: *ethnocentrism*. Ethnocentrism is the belief that the way *we* do things is superior to the way *they* do things.

Sheena Iyengar, a Columbia University business professor, tells of an experience she had with ethnocentrism. At a restaurant in Japan, she ordered green tea with sugar. The waiter replied, "One does not put

> It is nearly impossible to grow up in a society and not take on its prejudices. Consequently, it is not a matter of whether one is biased. We all are. Rather, it is a question of what negative racial attitudes one has learned so far and what, from this moment on, one is willing to do about them.
>
> Jean Moule

sugar in green tea." She replied that she knows Japanese people do not put sugar in their green tea, but she likes to put sugar in her green tea. Because of her insistence, the waiter passed on her request to the restaurant manager. After a few minutes, the manager came to her table, apologized, and explained that the restaurant could not serve green tea with sugar because it had no sugar. Because she could not have her green tea the way she preferred, Dr. Iyengar ordered a cup of coffee. The coffee was delivered along with two packets of sugar! Sure, there's a certain humor to the story . . . but beneath it all, there's disrespect. My way is better than your way . . . I'm right . . . you are wrong! How often do we disrespect—or even harm—someone because we insist on being right?

6. **Avoid Microaggressions.** You think of yourself as a good person. You'd never participate in acts of blatant racism. Yet you may unintentionally disrespect people who are different from you through microaggressions. Microaggressions are brief slights and insults that send demeaning messages to members of minority groups. Jean Moule, an African American professor at Oregon State University, shares some personal examples: "A man saw my face as I walked into the store and unconsciously checked his wallet. On the street, a woman catches my eye a half a block away and moves her purse from the handle of her baby's stroller to her side as she arranges the baby's blanket. In the airport, a man signals to his wife to move her purse so it is not over the back of her chair, adjacent to the one I am moving toward. . . . I believe these are examples of 'blink of the eye' racism." The hidden message in each person's response is that African Americans are criminals.

> I see a huge irony. While hate crimes receive the most attention, the greatest damage to the life experiences of people of color is from racial microaggression.
>
> Derald Wing Sue

Here's another example. A female student is in a math study group with three men who ignore her efforts to contribute to the discussion of homework problems. The hidden message is that women can't do math. Asian American college professor Derald Wing Sue notes that he is often complimented for speaking English so well. A third-generation American, Sue replies, "I hope so. I was born here." The hidden message is that he will always be a foreigner in the country of his birth.

What makes microaggressions challenging to address is twofold. The senders are often unaware of their bias and the receivers aren't sure if the slight was deliberate. If you believe you were the recipient of a microaggression, use the assertiveness skills you'll learn later in this chapter to address the insult. And if someone tells you that he or she was insulted by something you said or did (a microaggression), set your Inner Defender aside. Use the listening skills you practiced earlier to learn how you can be more respectful of others.

7. **Advocate for Respect.** Oppression comes in many guises. Sometimes it shows up as a joke that makes fun of someone who is different. Sometimes oppression escalates to a bigoted comment about

something like someone's race, religion, or sexual orientation. Realize that your silence will be interpreted as agreement with these prejudiced views. Be a voice for respect by letting others know that you don't approve of such comments. (You'll learn some great strategies for being assertive later in this chapter.)

Sadly, oppression will sometimes escalate to acts of cruelty and violence. Recent examples on college campuses include a swastika scrawled on a bathroom wall near a Jewish studies center, signs in bathrooms that said "Death to Fags," and the stabbing of a Nigerian-born student body president. No one can—or should have to—learn in an environment of fear. College offers an opportunity to encounter many points of view so that you can choose the ones that will best support you to create a great life. Don't allow others to deny you or your fellow students of that opportunity because of their prejudices and biases. If you witness or are the target of such hate crimes, report them to campus officials. Follow up to see that something is done. And, in the spirit of interdependence, consider requesting help from a group that has experience dealing with hate crimes, such as the Southern Poverty Law Center and the Anti-Defamation League. These and other groups that promote social justice can be found via an Internet search.

Interacting effectively with people from different cultures can be challenging. However, in a world that is becoming more diverse with each passing day, showing respect for others—and insisting upon it for yourself—will help you achieve your goals and dreams while helping others to do the same.

All that is necessary for the triumph of evil is that good men do nothing.

Edmund Burke

You demand respect and you'll get it. First of all, you give respect.

Mary J. Blige

JOURNAL ENTRY 18

❶ **Describe a time when you felt disrespected**. Present the experience as if it is a scene from a novel. Describe the setting where the event took place. Explain who was there. Show what they did and said. Explain how you felt.

❷ **Describe the same experience a second time, but this time revise what people said and did in a way that would have left you feeling fully respected.** In this revision of history, have everyone speak and behave in ways that would have changed the outcomes and experiences for the better, leaving you feeling fully respected.

INTERDEPENDENCE / at Work

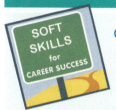

Over 90 percent of us who work for a living do so in organizations, and the ability to function effectively as a member of a team is usually an imperative of success.

Nathaniel Branden, psychologist

You may have noticed that many employment ads say, "Looking for a team player" or "Must relate well to others." Few abilities have more impact on your success at work than your ability to interact well with supervisors, peers, subordinates, suppliers, and customers. And enhancing this ability starts now.

SEEKING CREATORS

Candidates must demonstrate interdependence, a team orientation, and a strong ability to work cooperatively with others.

Someday you'll probably ask former professors or employers to write you a letter of recommendation. What they write on that future day will depend on the relationships you're building with them now. Are you someone who works well with others? Someone who completes assignments and does them with excellence? Attends classes regularly and on time? Is respectful of others? Self-aware? Responsible?

A former student called me with a request that I write her a recommendation. After much thought, I said no. Based on her performance in my class, I could not honestly write anything that would help her chances of getting hired. Sadly, when she was "blowing off" my course, she hadn't anticipated the day when she would need me to speak well of her to a potential employer.

In the work world, most people must interact well with others to keep their jobs or to advance. In college, one way to continue developing effective interdependence is by participating actively in study groups. Learning to work collaboratively now will contribute to your success tomorrow (not to mention that your grades will likely be higher).

As you begin a search for your ideal job, one of the best sources of information about what a career is *really* like is someone who is doing it now. By conducting information-gathering interviews with enough people who are working in your chosen profession, you'll learn about qualifications, employment outlook, work conditions, and salaries. If you don't know anyone in the career of your choice, be a Creator and ask people you know for referrals. If that fails, try the Yellow Pages or an online search. Call a company you find there, ask for the Public Information Office, and explain the information you're seeking. Besides the information you may uncover, who knows who might be impressed with your professional approach to job hunting!

The same information-gathering strategy is helpful when it comes to learning important information about a particular employer you may be considering. Talk to people who work at the company and find out from the inside what it's really like. For example, if you find the company's mission statement appealing, ask employees if the company backs up those words with actions. Of course, it's important to talk to a number of people to avoid being swayed by one or two biased opinions.

Many people limit their job search to employment agencies and advertised positions, jobs listed in the "visible" marketplace. However, some career specialists estimate that as many as 85 to 90 percent of the available jobs are unlisted and found only by uncovering them in the "invisible" marketplace. Creators discover these unpublished openings by networking. Do that by seeking informational interviews with possible employers, and ask them if they

EMPLOY TEAMWORK

know of others who might have a job for which you'd qualify. Additionally, you can ask friends and acquaintances if they know of positions that are available where they work. Ask professors if they've heard of job openings. Ask at church and club meetings. Ask all of these folks to spread the word that you're looking for a position. You never know who might help you discover an opening that would be ideal for you. A great job might become visible only because you asked a friend who asked a coworker who asked his sister who asked her boss who said, "Sure, we've got a job like that. Have the person call me."

Another great strategy during a job search is to develop a support group, especially one made up of other job seekers. Support groups not only provide emotional support when disappointments (and your Inner Critic) strike, they can also give you helpful suggestions and practice at essential skills. For example, support groups can critique your résumé and cover letters. They can help you practice your interviewing skills. Someone in your support group may share an experience that can teach you a valuable lesson. For instance, if someone reports going blank when an interviewer asked,

"Do you have any questions for me?" you'll learn to prepare questions to ask at your own interviews.

Okay, let's say you've gotten your dream position in the company you wanted. Teamwork continues to have a big impact on your work life. The *Harvard Business Review* reported a study that discovered why some scientists at Bell Labs in New Jersey were considered "stars" by their colleagues. Interestingly, the stars had done no better academically than their less successful colleagues. In fact, the study found that the stars and their coworkers were very similar when measured on IQ and personality tests. What distinguished the stars was their strong networks of important colleagues. When problems struck, the stars always had someone to call on for advice, and their requests for help were responded to quickly. Interdependence transformed good scientists into stars.

I once asked a very successful investment banker (he retired at the age of 35) how important networking was in his profession. "Well, there's networking up here," he said, holding his hand as high as he could reach, "and then there's everything else down here." He dropped his hand to within inches of the floor. "In this business, you either build relationships or you fail."

One last suggestion about interdependence could apply anywhere on your career path, but is particularly important once you are in your job: Find a mentor. A mentor is someone further along in his or her career development and willing to guide and help newer employees like you. Keep your eyes open for someone successful whose qualities you admire. You can create an informal mentoring relationship by making choices that put you into frequent contact with this person, or you can create a formal relationship by actually asking the person to be your mentor. With wisdom born of experience, a mentor can help keep you on course to career success.

TECH TIPS: Interdependence

OpenStudy is for students who want to connect with learners studying the same subjects that they are. In addition to working with groups, you can also ask questions and (according to the site) expect an answer in about five minutes. The site says it has 1 million student members from 160 countries and 190 study groups. If you haven't found the right peers at your college with whom to study, this site could be your solution. *(Web, iOS)*

ThinkBinder.com also offers the opportunity to create online study groups where you can share course notes, files, and links as well as chat and collaborate on a whiteboard. You can create and/or start any number of study groups, so you could have one for every course you are taking. *(Web)*

Rcampus.com is another source for online groups where students can share files, send messages, and study together. A member can create any number of study groups, and each group comes with its own home page and message center. The person who creates the group then invites others to join by giving them the Group ID and access code. *(Web)*

Koofers.com helps students find internships. After you complete an online job profile, Koofers shares this information with companies looking for students qualified for either an internship or full-time career opportunity. *(Web)*

The **Project Implicit website (implicit. harvard.edu)** gives you an opportunity to uncover your hidden biases about people in numerous categories including age, religion, sexuality, skin color, weight, and disabilities. You might be surprised at your results—I was. The project is the work of scientists at a number of universities worldwide, including Harvard. *(Web)*

Dropbox, Box, and **Copy** are file-sharing services that allow you to easily share large files with fellow students and across multiple devices. *(Web, Android, and iOS)*

Google Hangouts allows you to meet with classmates for distance-learning/online study groups. *(Web, Android, iOS)*

Note: All of the above are free, but some may offer upgraded features for a fee.

Be Assertive

BELIEVING IN YOURSELF

FOCUS QUESTION   How can you communicate in a style that strengthens relationships, creates better results, and builds strong self-esteem?

On rare occasions, we may encounter someone who doesn't want us to achieve our goals and dreams. Much more often, though, we run across folks who are too busy, too preoccupied, or couldn't care less about helping us. Meeting such people is especially likely in a bureaucracy such as a college or university. How we communicate our desires to them has a profound impact not only on the quality of the relationships and results we create, but on our self-esteem as well.

According to family therapist Virginia Satir, the two most common patterns of ineffective communication are **placating** and **blaming.** Both perpetuate low self-esteem.

Once a human being has arrived on this earth, communication is the largest single factor determining what kinds of relationships she or he makes with others and what happens to each in the world.

Virginia Satir

- **Placating.** Victims who placate are dominated by their Inner Critic. They place themselves below others, protecting themselves from the sting of criticism and rejection by saying whatever they think will gain approval. Picture placators on their knees, looking up with a pained smile, nodding and agreeing on the outside, while fearfully hiding their true thoughts and feelings within. "*Please, please approve of me*," they beg as their own Inner Critic judges them unworthy. To gain this approval, placators often spend time in Quadrant III doing what is urgent to others but unimportant to their own goals and dreams. Satir estimated that about 50 percent of people use placating as their major communication style.

- **Blaming.** Victims who blame are dominated by their Inner Defender. They place themselves above others, protecting themselves from disappointment and failure by making others fully responsible for their problems. Picture them sneering down, a finger jabbing judgmentally at those below. Their Inner Defender snarls, "*You never . . . Why do you always . . . ? Why don't you ever . . . ? It's your fault that. . . .*" Satir estimated that about 30 percent of people use blaming as their major communication style.

Either passively placating or aggressively blaming keeps Victims from developing mutually supportive relationships, making the accomplishment of their dreams more difficult. The inner result is damaged self-esteem.

LEVELING

Learning to perceive the truth within ourselves and speak it clearly to others is a delicate skill, certainly as complex as multiplication or long division, but very little time is spent on it in school.

Gay & Kathlyn Hendricks

What, then, is the communication style of Creators? Some have called this style *assertiveness*: honestly expressing opinions and requests. Satir calls this communication style *leveling*. Leveling is characterized by a simple, yet profound, communication strategy: asserting the truth as you see it.

Creators boldly express their personal truth without false apology or excuse, without harsh criticism or blame. Leveling requires a strong Inner Guide and a commitment to honesty. Here are three strategies that promote leveling:

1. **Communicate Purposefully.** Creators express a clear purpose even in times of emotional upset. If a Creator goes to a professor to discuss a disappointing grade, she will be clear whether her purpose is to (1) increase her understanding of the subject, (2) seek a higher grade, (3) criticize the instructor's grading ability, or accomplish some other option. By knowing her purpose, she has a way to evaluate the success of her communication. The Creator states purposefully, *When I saw my grade on this lab report, I was very disappointed. I'd like to go over it with you and learn how to improve my next one.*

I speak straight and do not wish to deceive or be deceived.

Cochise

2. **Communicate Honestly.** Creators candidly express unpopular thoughts and upset feelings in the service of building mutually supportive relationships. The Creator says honestly, *I'm angry that you didn't meet me in the library to study for the sociology test as you agreed.*

3. **Communicate Responsibly.** Because responsibility lies within, Creators express their personal responsibility with I-messages. An I-message allows creators to take full responsibility for their reaction to anything another person may have said or done. An effective I-message has four elements:

A statement of the situation:	*When you . . .*
A statement of your reaction:	*I felt/thought/decided . . .*
A request:	*I'd like to ask that you . . .*
An invitation to respond:	*Will you agree to that?*

Let's compare Victim and Creator responses to the same situation. Imagine that you feel sick one day and decide not to go to your history class. You phone a classmate, and she agrees to call you after class with what you missed. But she never calls. At the next history class, the instructor gives a test that was announced the day you were absent, and you fail it. Afterward, your classmate apologizes: "Sorry I didn't call. I was swamped with work." What response do you choose?

Placating: *Oh, don't worry about it. I know you had a lot on your mind. I probably would have failed the test anyway.*

Blaming: *You're the lousiest friend I've ever had! After making me fail that test, you have some nerve even talking to me!*

Leveling: *I'm angry that you didn't call. I realize that I could have called you, but I thought I could count on you to keep your word. If we're going to be friends, I need to know if you're going to keep your promises to me in the future. Will you?*

Notice that the leveling response is the only one of the three that positively addresses the issue, nurtures a relationship of equals, and demonstrates high self-esteem.

MAKING REQUESTS

Making effective requests is another demonstration of both assertiveness and high self-esteem. Creators know they can't reach their greatest goals and dreams alone, so they ask for help. The key to making effective requests is applying the DAPPS rule. Whenever possible, make your requests **D**ated, **A**chievable, **P**ersonal, **P**ositive, and—above all—**S**pecific. Here are some translations of vague Victim requests to specific, clear Creator requests:

> We should replace our alienating, criticizing words with "I" language. Instead of, "You are a liar and no one can trust you," say, "I don't like it when I can't rely on your words—it is difficult for us to do things together."
>
> **Ken Keyes**

Victim Requests	Creator Requests
1. I'm going to be absent next Friday. It sure would be nice if someone would let me know if I miss anything.	1. John, I'm going to be absent next Friday. Would you be willing to call me Friday night and tell me what I missed?
2. I don't suppose you'd consider giving me a few more days to complete this research paper?	2. I'd like to request an extension on my research paper. I promise to hand it in by noon on Thursday. Would that be acceptable?

When you make specific requests, the other person can respond with a clear "yes" or "no." If the person says "no," all is not lost. Try negotiating:

1. *If you can't call me Friday night, could I call you Saturday morning to find out what I missed?*

2. *If Thursday noon isn't acceptable to you, could I turn my paper in on Wednesday by 5:00?*

A Creator seeks definite yes or no answers. Victims often accept "maybe" or "I'll try" for fear of getting a "no," but it's better to hear a specific "no" and be free to move on to someone who will say "yes."

One of my mentors offered a valuable piece of advice: "If you go through a whole day without getting at least a couple of 'no's,' you aren't asking for enough help in your life."

SAYING "NO"

Saying "no" is another tool of the assertive Creator. When I think of the power of saying "no," I think of Monique. One day after class she took a deep breath, sighed, and told me she was exhausted. She complained that everyone at her job kept bringing her tasks to do. As a result, she had virtually no social life, and she was falling behind in college. She wanted advice on how to manage her time better.

"Sounds like you're working 60 hours a week and doing the work of two people," I observed. She nodded modestly. "Here's an outrageous thought: The next time someone at work brings you more to do, say 'no.'"

"That sounds so rude."

"Okay then, say, 'I'm sorry, but my schedule is full, and I won't be able to do that.'"

"What if my boss asks? I can't say 'no' to her."

"You can say, 'I'll be glad to take that on. But since I have so many projects already, I'll need you to give one of them to someone else. That way I'll have time to do a good job on this new project.'"

Monique agreed to experiment with saying "no." The next time I saw her, she was excited. "I sent my boss a memo telling her I had too much work and I couldn't take on the latest project she had assigned me. Before I'd even talked to her about the memo, one of my coworkers came by. He said our boss had sent him to take over some of my projects. Not only did I not get the new project, I got rid of two others. I just might be able to finish this semester after all."

Monique's voice had a power that hadn't been there before. With one "no" she had transformed herself from exhausted to exhilarated. That's the power of a Creator being assertive.

If you go to somebody and say, "I need help," they'll say, "Sure, honey, I wish I could," but if you say, "I need you to call so-and-so on Tuesday, will you do that?" they either will say yes or they'll say no. If they say no, you thank them and say, "Do you know someone who will?" If they say yes, you call on Wednesday to see if they did it. You wouldn't believe how good I've gotten at this, and I never knew how to ask anybody for anything before.

Barbara Sher

When two people are relating maturely, each will be able to ask the other for what he or she wants or needs, fully trusting that the other will say "no" if he or she does not want to give it.

Edward Deci

JOURNAL ENTRY | 19

In this activity, you will explore assertiveness. This powerful way of being creates great results, strengthens relationships, and builds self-esteem.

❶   **Make a choice—write about one of the following (A or B):**

A.   **Write three different responses to the instructor described in the following situation.** Respond to the instructor by (1) placating, (2) blaming, and (3) leveling. For an example of this exercise, refer to the dialogues in the section above titled "Leveling."

Situation: You register for a course required in your major. It is the last course you need to graduate. When you go to the first class meeting, the instructor tells you that your name is NOT on the roster. The course is full, and no other sections of the course are being offered. You've been shut out of the class. The instructor tells you that you'll have to postpone graduation and return next semester to complete this required course.

Remember, in each of your three responses, you are writing what you would actually say to the instructor—first as a placator, second as a blamer, and third as a leveler.

B.   **Think about one of your most challenging academic goals. Decide who could help you with this goal. Write a letter to this person and request assistance.** You can decide later whether or not you will send the letter.
Here are some possibilities to include in your letter:

- Tell the person your most challenging academic goal for this semester.

- Explain how this goal is a stepping stone to your dream.

- Describe your dream and explain its importance to you.

- Identify your obstacle, explaining it fully.

- Discuss how you believe this person can help you overcome your obstacle.

- Admit any reluctance or fear you have about asking for assistance.

- Request *exactly* what you would like this person to do for you and persuade him or her to give you helpful assistance.

Remember, for effective requests, use the DAPPS rule.

❷   **Write what you have learned or relearned about being assertive.** How assertive have you been in the pursuit of your goals and dreams? How has this choice affected your self-esteem? What changes do you intend to make in communicating (placating, blaming, leveling), making requests, and saying "no"? Be sure to dive deep!

When things really get difficult, all I can say is, ask for help.

Dr. Bernie Siegel

I returned fall quarter feeling broken. I had hoped some time off would help my marriage and my mental state. But I felt exhausted and overwhelmed. I barely slept or ate. I was grinding my teeth and having nightmares. In class, I daydreamed because I didn't really want to be there. I already have a bachelor's degree from Wilmington College, but I'm back in school because I want to be a nurse. In the past, my GPA has always been high. But because of challenges in my marriage, studying was no longer on my A list. Maybe not even on my B or C list. I had to read an assignment several times to get it, and I was definitely not doing my best work. When I got a C on the first test in Anatomy and Physiology, I panicked. The worst part was pretending everything was okay. I couldn't ask for help or admit the level of suffering. Not me. Instead, I smiled my best Pollyanna grin and went through the motions to keep up the appearance of a healthy life.

I was taking PSYC 1108: College Success because the previous term someone had come into my English class and raved about it. *That sounds like a course I could use*, I thought. In the first week, I took the self-assessment. Ouch. Kick a girl while she's down. I scored remarkably low in interdependence. I was shocked that creating a support system was so important. I'd always valued my independent nature. But I knew I had to do something different. I had to start somewhere.

So I started by asking for help. At first, it made me feel like vomiting. But it got easier. I trusted *On Course* and decided there must be benefits to interdependence. With practice, it got more comfortable. Now, it's wonderful. I began by asking students who were doing well in Anatomy and Physiology to start a study group. We would meet and go over what we covered in class. They told me about strategies they use to memorize all the bones we had to know. We made study cards and I carried them everywhere. I even started asking for help from coworkers at the hospital where I work. I usually did all of the patient charting, but I started asking others to share the task.

Next, I practiced the art of saying "no." I was raised to say "yes," followed by "please." Saying "no" took some work. I literally broke out in hives at first. I took allergy medicine and kept trying. I've gotten so good at it that now I say it every day, usually followed by "thank you." My mom is famous for calling me and asking me to pick up something at the store. I finally told her I had to choose activities that were important to my goals, like studying my nursing courses. I even said "no" to cleaning my house all the time. I prefer a clean house, but saying no to cleaning means I can say yes to more important things. The results have been life-changing.

I also made a conscious effort to tell people how I truly feel. Living as my authentic, quirky self feels right. Many relationships where I was doing all the work have disappeared. For example, I asked my husband to help more around the house. He got angry at first, but I told him how important it is to me to get help so I can succeed in school and become a nurse. Now he helps more than he used to. I've finally made living the life that I want a priority, and the people who really care about me are glad.

I am so happy and grateful that I signed up for this course. Also, that I took it seriously and dove deep. I was off course in September, but the New Year is looking brighter. When I got my grades at the end of the quarter, I had all As. My marriage is way better and my husband tells me I've changed. He doesn't say how, but I can tell that he likes me better now. This process didn't happen overnight. The journal entries were a valuable tool to inspire healing. While writing the journals, I felt very reserved at first. But soon I realized that I had something to say. I was hearing my voice again . . . *my* voice! Hearing my voice was like running into an old friend. There was a moment when I giggled. I thought, "I remember you. I like you. Where have you been, my old friend?"

Photo: Courtesy of Amy Acton.

Gaining
Self-Awareness

Successful Students . . .

▶ **recognize when they are off course.**

▶ **identify their self-defeating patterns of thought, emotion, and behavior.**

▶ **rewrite their outdated scripts,** revising limited core beliefs and self-defeating patterns.

Struggling Students . . .

▶ **wander through life unaware of being off course.**

▶ **remain unaware of their self-defeating patterns of thought, emotion, and behavior.**

▶ **unconsciously persist in making choices based on outdated scripts,** finding themselves farther and farther off course with each passing year.

Despite all of my efforts to create success in college and in life, I may still find myself off course. Now is the perfect time to identify and revise the inner obstacles to my success.

I am consciously choosing core beliefs and habit patterns that support my success.

CASE STUDY IN CRITICAL THINKING — Strange Choices

"Do your students make really strange choices?" **Professor Assante** asked.

The other professors looked up from their lunches. "What do you mean?" one asked.

"At the beginning of each class, I give short quizzes that count as 50 percent of the final grade," Professor Assante replied. "One of my students comes late to every class, even though I keep telling her there's no way she can pass the course if she keeps missing the quizzes. But she still keeps coming late! What is she thinking?"

"That's nothing," **Professor Buckley** said. "I've got a really bright student who attends every class and offers great comments during discussions. But the semester is almost over, and he still hasn't turned in any assignments. At this point, he's too far behind to pass. Now that's what I call a strange choice."

"You think that's strange," **Professor Chang** said, "I'm teaching composition in the computer lab. Last week I sat down next to a woman who was working on her essay, and I suggested a way she could improve her introduction. I couldn't believe what she did. She swore at me, stormed out of the room, and slammed the door."

Professor Donnelly chimed in. "Well, I can top all of you. In my philosophy class, participation counts for one-third of the final grade. I've got a student this semester who hasn't said a word in 12 weeks. Even when I call on him, he just shakes his head and says something under his breath that I can't hear. One day after class, I asked him if he realized that if he didn't participate in class discussions, the best grade he could earn is a D. He just mumbled, 'I know.' Now there's a choice I don't get!"

"How about this!" **Professor Egret** said. "I had a student last semester with a B average going into the final two weeks. Then he disappeared. This semester, I ran into him on campus, and I asked what happened. 'Oh,' he said, 'I got burned out and stopped going to my classes.' 'But you only had two more weeks to go. You threw away 13 weeks of work,' I said. You know what he did? He shrugged his shoulders and walked away. I wanted to shake him and say, 'What is wrong with you?'"

Professor Fanning said, "Talk about strange choices. Last week I had four business owners visit my marketing class to talk about how they promote their businesses. Near the end of the period, a student asked if the business owners had ever had problems with procrastination. While the panelists were deciding who was going to answer, I joked, 'Maybe they'd rather answer later.' Okay, it was weak humor, but most of the students chuckled, and then one panelist answered the question. The next day I got a call from the dean. The student who'd asked about procrastination told him I'd mocked her in front of the whole class, and now she's going to drop out of college. I had videoed the class, so I asked her if she'd be willing to watch the recording. Later she admitted I hadn't said what she thought I had, but she still dropped out of school. What is it with students today and their bizarre choices?"

Listed below are the six professors' students. Choose the one you think made the strangest choice and speculate on why this student made the choice. Dive deeper than obvious answers such as "He's probably just shy." Why do you suppose he is shy? What past experiences might have made him this way? What might the inner conversation of his Inner Critic and Inner Defender sound like? What emotions might he often feel? What beliefs might he have about himself, other people, or the world? In what other circumstances (e.g., work, relationships, health) might a similar choice sabotage his success?

 ▶ ① ② ③ ④ ⑤ ⑥ ◀

____ **Professor Assante's** student

____ **Professor Buckley's** student

____ **Professor Chang's** student

____ **Professor Donnelly's** student

____ **Professor Egret's** student

____ **Professor Fanning's** student

DIVING DEEPER

Recall a course you once took in which you made a choice that your instructor might describe as "strange." Explain why you made that choice. Dive deep, exploring what *really* caused your choice.

Recognizing When You Are Off Course

FOCUS QUESTIONS   In which of your life roles are you off course? Do you know how you got there? More important, do you know how to get back on course to your desired outcomes and experiences?

Take a deep breath, relax, and consider your journey so far.

You began by accepting personal responsibility for creating your life as you want it. Then you chose personally motivating goals and dreams that give purpose and direction to your life.

Next, you created a self-management plan and began taking effective actions. Most recently, you developed mutually supportive relationships to help you on your journey. Throughout, you have examined how to believe in yourself.

Despite all these efforts, you may still be off course—in college, in a relationship, in your job, or somewhere else in your life. You just aren't achieving your desired outcomes and experiences. Once again, you have an important choice to make. You can listen to the blaming, complaining, and excusing of your Inner Critic and Inner Defender. Or you can ask your Inner Guide to find answers to important questions such as . . .

- What habits do I have that sabotage my success?
- What beliefs do I have that get me off course?
- How can I consistently make wise choices that will create a rich, personally fulfilling life?

C onsider this: If at first you don't succeed, something is blocking your way.

Michael Ray & Rochelle Myers

THE MYSTERY OF SELF-SABOTAGE

Self-sabotage has probably happened to everyone who's set off on a journey to a better life. Consider my student Jerome. Fresh from high school, Jerome said his dream was to start his own accounting firm by his 30th birthday. He set long-term goals of getting his college degree and passing the C.P.A. (certified public accountant) exam. He set short-term goals of earning As in every class he took during his first semester. He developed a written self-management system and demonstrated interdependence by starting a study group. But at semester's end, the unthinkable happened: Jerome failed Accounting 101!

Wait a minute, though. Jerome's Inner Guide has more information. You see, Jerome made some strange choices during his first semester. He skipped his accounting class three times to work at a part-time job. On another day, he didn't attend class because he was angry with his girlfriend. Then he missed two Monday classes when he was hung over from weekend parties. He was late five times because parking was difficult to find. Jerome regularly put off doing homework until the last minute because he was so busy. He didn't hand in an important assignment because he found

P rogressively we discover that there are levels of experience beneath the surface, beneath our consciousness, and we realize that these may hold the key both to the problems and the potentialities of our life.

Ira Progoff

it confusing. And he stopped going to his study group after the first meeting because . . . well, he wasn't quite sure why. As the semester progressed, Jerome's anxiety about the final exam grew. The night before, he stayed up late cramming, then went to the exam exhausted. During the test, his mind went blank.

Haven't you, too, made choices that worked against your goals and dreams? Haven't we all! We take our eyes off the path for just a moment, and some invisible force comes along and pulls us off course. By the time we realize what's happened—if, in fact, we ever do—we can be miles off course and feeling miserable.

What's going on around here, anyway?

UNCONSCIOUS FORCES

One of the most important discoveries in psychology is the existence and power of unconscious forces in our lives. We now know that experiences from our past linger in our unconscious minds long after our conscious minds have forgotten them. As a result, we're influenced in our daily choices by old experiences we don't even recall.

Dr. Wilder Penfield of the Montreal Neurological Institute found evidence that our brains may retain nearly every experience we have ever had. Dr. Penfield performed brain surgery on patients who had local anesthesia but were otherwise fully awake. During the operation, he stimulated brain cells using a weak electric current. At that moment his patients reported re-experiencing long-forgotten events in vivid detail.

Further research by neuroscientist Joseph LeDoux suggests that a part of our brains called the amygdala stores emotionally charged but now unconscious memories. The amygdala, like a nervous watchman, examines every new experience and compares it to past experiences. When a key feature of a new event is similar to a distressing event from the past, it declares a match. Then, *without our conscious knowledge*, the amygdala hijacks our rational thought processes. It causes us to respond to the present event as we learned to respond to the past event. The problem is, the outdated response is often totally inappropriate in our present situation. By the time the amygdala loosens its grip on our decision-making power, we may have made some very bad choices.

If many of the forces that get us off course are unconscious, how can we spot their sabotaging influence? By analogy, the answer appears in a fascinating discovery in astronomy. Years ago, astronomers developed a mathematical formula to predict the orbit of any planet around the sun. However, one planet, Uranus, failed to follow its predicted orbit. Astronomers were baffled as to why Uranus was "off course." Then the French astronomer Leverrier proposed an ingenious explanation: The gravitational pull of an invisible planet was getting Uranus off course. Sure enough, when stronger telescopes were invented, the planet Neptune was discovered, and Leverrier was proven correct.

In the entire history of science, it is hard to find a discovery of comparable consequence to the discovery of the power of unconscious belief as a gateway—or an obstacle—to the hidden mind, and its untapped potentialities.

Willis Harman

We know from surgical experiences that electrical stimulation delivered to the temporal area of the brain elicits images of events that occurred in the patient's past. This is confirmation that such memories are "stored," but in most instances they cannot be voluntarily recollected. Thus, all of us "know" more than we are aware that we know.

Richard Restak, M.D.

Here's the point: Like planets, we all have invisible Neptunes tugging at us every day. For us, these invisible forces are not in outer space. They exist in inner space, in our unconscious minds. As with Uranus, the first clue to spotting the existence of these unconscious forces is recognizing that we are off course. So, be candid. Where are you off course in your life today? School? Relationships? Work? Health? Finances? Elsewhere? What desired outcomes and experiences are you moving away from instead of toward? What goals and dreams seem to be slipping away? Self-awareness allows you to identify that you are off course. Only then can you start making wiser choices that will get you back on course to the life you want to create.

I learned that I could not look to my exterior self to do anything for me. If I was going to accomplish anything in life, I had to start from within.

Oprah Winfrey

JOURNAL ENTRY / 20

Everyone gets off course at times, but only those who are self-aware can make a course correction to improve their lives.

1 **Write about a time when you were off course and took effective actions to get back on course.** Examples include ending an unhealthy relationship, entering college years after high school, changing careers, stopping an addiction, choosing to be more assertive, or changing a negative belief or bias you held about yourself, other people, or the world. Dive deep in your journal entry by asking and answering questions such as the following:

- In what area of my life was I off course?
- What choices had I made to get off course?
- What changes did I make to get back on course?
- What challenges did I face while making this change?
- What personal strengths helped me make this change?
- What benefits did I experience as a result of my change?
- If I hadn't made this change, what would my life be like today?

2 **Write about an area of your life in which you are off course today.** If you need help in identifying an area, review your desired outcomes and experiences from Journal Entry 8 and your goals and dreams from Journal Entry 9. Explain which area of your life is furthest from the way you would like it to be. What choices have you made that got you off course? What will be the effect on your life if you continue to stay off course?

The fact that you've made positive changes in the past is a good reminder that you have the personal strengths to make similar changes whenever you wish. All you need is the awareness that you're off course and the motivation to make new choices.

The truth is that our finest moments are most likely to occur when we are feeling deeply uncomfortable, unhappy, or unfulfilled. For it is only in such moments, propelled by our discomfort, that we are likely to step out of our ruts and start searching for different ways or truer answers.

M. Scott Peck, M.D.

I was in the emergency room when it hit me how far off course I was. My friend Matt had driven me to the emergency room because the Student Health Center couldn't supply the antibiotics I needed for a bad sore throat. As we sat in the waiting room talking, I told Matt that I was failing math, and I broke down and cried. I told him I was doing things in college that I had never done at home. When I was in high school, my parents were very strict. They didn't let me go out late during the week, and they'd wake me up in the morning to make sure I went to school. But in college, no one cares if you stay out all night or even if you get up and go to class. I had adopted "Why not?" as my motto, and I started doing things I knew I shouldn't be doing. My weekends had become a blur of boys and parties, and I had even started partying during the week. The parties I went to in high school were mostly small girls' nights, nothing like the drunken fraternity parties I was going to on campus. In high school I was one of the smart kids, and even though I hardly ever studied, I was an honor student. But college was different. I was doing terrible in math and not much better in biology. It was a shock to not do as well as I had in high school.

I started getting a bleak outlook on life, and I didn't really want to be at the university. I had no idea what I wanted to major in. I thought of myself as lazy and irresponsible. I remember telling one of my friends that I should just get married, have kids, and then I'd probably be divorced by 40. After that I'd spend the rest of my life in a lousy job, struggling to survive. I felt like I couldn't do anything right. I don't know why I let everything bother me so much, but I felt awful.

Talking with Matt in the emergency room, I started realizing how lonely I felt in college. I missed my family, especially my sister. I wasn't getting along with my roommate, and we competed about everything: going out, boys, drinking, staying up late, playing video games, you name it. A lot of the students at my university are really into playing *Halo*. I tried to fit in, but I'm no good at video games. At my school, if you're not in engineering, they tease you nonstop. One time a guy picked up my *On Course* book and starting teasing me about the class. "So what do you do in that class," he asked, "sit around and talk about your *feelings*?" I didn't bother saying that the course helped me think things out, things I wouldn't have thought about, like all of the mistakes I was making.

That day in the emergency room was my wake up call. Sitting there talking with Matt, I not only realized that I was way off course, I also realized that deep down I didn't believe in myself, and therefore I couldn't take actions today to improve my tomorrow. After that, I realized I had to make some dramatic changes. I got a new roommate, stopped partying, buckled down, and passed my math class. That was two years ago. Today I'm a junior and my life is very different. I've found a major that I love, I just finished an internship that was great, and my GPA is 3.4. Making positive changes isn't always easy. But my life started to get better that day in the emergency room when I took a good look at myself and realized just how far off course I was.

Photo: Courtesy of Sarah Richmond.

Identifying Your Scripts

FOCUS QUESTIONS   What habit patterns in your life get you off course? How did these habit patterns develop?

Once you realize you're off course, you need to figure out how to get back on course. This can be tricky. The forces pulling us off course are often just as invisible to us as the planet Neptune was to Leverrier and his fellow observers of outer space.

As observers of inner space, psychologists seek to identify what they can't actually see: the internal forces that divert human potential into disappointment. In various psychological theories, these unconscious inner forces have been called names such as ego defenses, conditioned responses, programs, mental tapes, blind spots, schemas, and life-traps.

The term I like best to describe our unconscious internal forces was coined by psychologist Eric Berne: **scripts**. In the world of theater, a script tells an actor what words, actions, and emotions to perform onstage. When the actor gets a cue from others in the play, he doesn't make a choice about his response. He responds automatically as his script directs. Performance after performance, he reacts the same way to the same cues.

Responding automatically from a dramatic script is one sure way to succeed as an actor. However, responding automatically from a *life* script is one sure way to struggle as a human being.

> A psychological script is a person's ongoing program for his life drama which dictates where he is going with his life and how he is to get there. It is a drama he compulsively acts out, though his awareness of it may be vague.
>
> Muriel James & Dorothy Jongeward

ANATOMY OF A SCRIPT

Everyone has scripts. I do, your instructors do, your classmates do, you do. Some scripts have helped us achieve our present success. Other scripts may be getting us off course from our goals and dreams. Becoming aware of our unique personal scripts helps us make wise choices at each fork in the road, choices that help us create the life we want.

Scripts are composed of two parts. Closest to the surface of our awareness reside the directions for how we are to think, feel, and behave. **Thought patterns** include habitual self-talk such as *I'm too busy, I'm good at math, People different from me are a threat, I always screw up, The way we do things around here is the right way so all other ways must be wrong, I can't write.* **Emotional patterns** include habitual feelings such as anger, excitement, anxiety, sadness, and joy. **Behavior patterns** include habitual actions such as smoking cigarettes, criticizing others, arriving on time, never asking for help, and exercising regularly. When people know us well, they can often predict what we will say, feel, or do in a given situation. This ability reveals their recognition of our patterns.

Deeper in our unconscious mind lies the second, and more elusive, part of our scripts, our **core beliefs**. Early in life, we form core beliefs about the world (e.g., *The world is safe* or *The world is dangerous*), about other people (e.g., *People can be trusted* or *People can't be trusted*), and about ourselves (e.g., *I'm worthy* or *I'm unworthy*). Though we're seldom aware of our core beliefs, these unconscious judgments dictate what we consistently think, feel, and do.

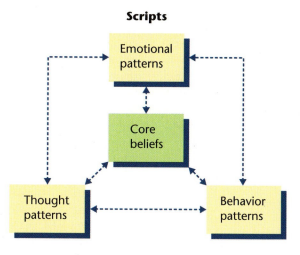

Scripts

Emotional patterns

Core beliefs

Thought patterns

Behavior patterns

These beliefs become the lenses through which we see the world. Whether accurate or distorted, our beliefs dictate the choices we make at each fork in the road. What do you believe that causes you to make choices that other people think are strange? More important, what do you believe that keeps you from creating the outcomes and experiences you want?

HOW WE WROTE OUR SCRIPTS

P arents, deliberately or unaware, teach their children from birth how to behave, think, feel, and perceive. Liberation from these influences is no easy matter.

Eric Berne

Though no one knows exactly how we wrote our life scripts as children, reasonable explanations exist. One factor seems to be **how others responded to us**. Imagine this scene: You're two years old. You're feeling lonely and hungry, and you begin to cry. Your mother hurries in to pick you up. "There, there," she croons. "It's all right." She hugs you, feeds you, sings to you. You fall asleep full and content. If this happens often enough, what do you suppose you'd decide about the world, about other people, about yourself? Probably you'd believe *The world is kind; People will help me; I am lovable*. In turn, these beliefs would dictate your thoughts, emotions, and behaviors. With positive beliefs such as these at the core of your scripts, very likely you'd develop optimistic thought patterns (e.g., *If I ask, I'll get help*), positive emotional patterns (e.g., joy and enthusiasm), and empowering behavior patterns (e.g., asking for what you want).

Now imagine the same childhood scene with a different response. You cry but no one comes. You scream louder, but still no one comes. Finally you abandon hope that anyone will respond. You cry yourself to sleep, alone and hungry. Imagine also that being ignored happens often. You'd probably develop core beliefs such as *The world doesn't care about me; People won't help me; I'm not important*. You could very well develop pessimistic thought patterns (e.g., *I'm alone*), negative emotional patterns (e.g., anxiety and anger), and passive behavior patterns (e.g., not asking for what you want).

Now, imagine this scene one more time. As you're crying for attention and food, an adult storms into your room, screams "Shut up!" and slaps your face. After a few wounding experiences like this, you may decide *The world is a dangerous and painful place; People will hurt me; I'm unlovable!* These beliefs may lead to defensive thought patterns (e.g., *People are out to get me*), defensive emotional patterns (e.g., fear and rage), and defensive behavior patterns (e.g., immediately fighting or fleeing at the first sign of danger). Imagine how easily these patterns could get you off course later in life.

T he hearts of small children are delicate organs. A cruel beginning in this world can twist them into curious shapes. The heart of a hurt child can shrink so that forever afterward it is hard and pitted as the seed of a peach.

Carson McCullers

A second factor that seems to shape our scripts is **what significant adults said to us**. What did they say about the world: Is it safe or dangerous? What did they say about other people, especially those who are different from us: Can they be trusted or not? And, perhaps most important, what did important adults say about us? Psychologists have a term for qualities that tell us how we "are" or "should be": **attributions**. Common attributions tell us to be *good, quiet, rebellious, devoted, helpful, athletic, sexy, tough, independent, dependent, invisible, macho, dominant, competitive, smart, shy,* or *confident*.

Psychologists also have a term for the qualities that tell us what we "are not" or "should not be": **injunctions**. Common injunctions include *don't be yourself,* *don't talk back, don't feel, don't think, don't be intimate, don't say no, don't say yes, don't get angry, don't trust people who are different from you, don't show your feelings, don't love yourself, don't be happy, don't be weak, don't believe in yourself, don't exist.*

A third way we seem to write our scripts is by **observing the behavior of significant adults**. Children notice, *What did important adults do? If it's right for them, it's right for me.* When children play, we see them trying on adult behaviors, conversations, and emotions. It doesn't take a detective to figure out where they learned them. From significant adults we learn not only our unique personal scripts but our cultural programs as well. For example, some cultures believe we shape our future through our choices, whereas other cultures believe our future is determined by forces beyond our control. Some cultures place emphasis on future accomplishments, whereas others focus on the present or past. Some cultures are very time conscious, whereas others are more casual about time. Some cultures encourage individuality, whereas others place family and community above all other concerns. Each belief is deeply embedded in the culture and becomes the lens through which its members see the world, influencing their choices, whether they are aware of the beliefs or not.

In these ways we each develop our personal scripts and cultural programs. Each is comprised of core beliefs and their resulting patterns of thoughts, feelings, and behaviors. At critical choice points, especially when we are under stress, we unconsciously default to our personal scripts and cultural programs for guidance.

The good news about our unconscious scripts and programs is that their intention is always positive—always to minimize our pain, always to maximize our pleasure. They help us adapt to the family and society in which we are born. Many of us made it through the mental, emotional, and physical challenges of growing up with the help of our childhood scripts and programs. Some of us would not have survived without them.

But, as you might guess, there is bad news as well: When we make unconscious choices as adults, we often get off course. That's because the scripts and programs we developed in childhood often do not apply to the situations of our present lives. Imagine an adult who can't stop playing a role he or she learned years ago for a grade school play! Many of us do the equivalent of this in our daily lives.

To others, a choice I make may seem strange. To me, it makes perfect sense. The important issue, though, is: Do my habitual choices help or hinder me in the pursuit of the life I want to create? To answer this question, I need to take three steps. First, I need to become aware of my Neptunes, that is, my unconscious beliefs, attitudes, biases, norms, prejudices, and values. Second, I need to assess which of my mindsets help and which hinder me in the pursuit of my goals and dreams. And finally, I need to keep and strengthen the habits that help me while revising or replacing the ones that hinder me. And it all starts with self-awareness.

By the time we are adults, we have learned many cultural rules of behavior and have practiced those rules so much that they are second nature to us. Much of our behavior as adults is influenced by these learned patterns and rules, and we are so well practiced at them that we engage in these behaviors automatically and unconsciously.

David Matsumoto & Linda Juang

The more you are keenly aware of your misery-creating thoughts, feelings, and behaviors, the greater your chances are of ridding yourself of them.

Albert Ellis

SELF-DEFEATING HABIT PATTERNS

Though our unconscious scripts are as invisible to us as the planet Neptune was to early astronomers, we can often see their influence in our lives. Put a check next to any of the following patterns of thought, emotion, and behavior that are often true of you. These habits may reveal the presence of personal scripts or cultural programs that get you off course. In particular, see if you can identify any habits that may have gotten you off course in the area you wrote about in Journal Entry 20.

☐ **1.** I waste a lot of time doing unimportant things (e.g., television, video games).

☐ **2.** I wonder if I'm "college material."

☐ **3.** I easily get upset (e.g., angry, sad, anxious, depressed, guilty, frustrated).

☐ **4.** I hang out with people who don't support my academic goals.

☐ **5.** I believe that most people don't like me.

☐ **6.** I often turn in college assignments late.

☐ **7.** I worry that people stereotype me because of a cultural group (race, religion, sex, economic class, age, etc.) to which I belong rather than seeing me for who I really am.

☐ **8.** I worry excessively about doing things perfectly.

☐ **9.** I think most of my classmates are smarter than I am.

☐ **10.** I quit things that are important to me.

☐ **11.** I allow a person in my life to treat me badly.

☐ **12.** I don't believe I deserve success as much as other people do.

☐ **13.** I miss more college classes than I should.

☐ **14.** I'm very critical of myself.

☐ **15.** I wait until the last minute to do important college assignments.

☐ **16.** I don't ask questions in class or participate in class discussions.

☐ **17.** I often break promises I have made to myself or others.

☐ **18.** I am addicted to something (e.g., caffeine, alcohol, cigarettes, soft drinks, video games, social networking websites, drugs).

☐ **19.** I experience severe test anxiety.

☐ **20.** I feel uncomfortable about asking for help.

☐ **21.** I have strong negative feelings about a particular group of people who are different from me.

☐ **22.** I often side-talk or daydream in my college classes.

☐ **23.** I seldom do my best work on college assignments.

☐ **24.** I am very critical of other people.

☐ **25.** I get extremely nervous when I speak to a group.

☐ **26.** I keep promising to study more in college, but I don't.

The grooves of mindlessness run deep. We know our scripts by heart.

Ellen J. Langer

☐ **27.** I get my feelings hurt easily.

☐ **28.** I am a loner.

☐ **29.** I am uncomfortable being around people who are different from me.

☐ **30.** I get defensive when someone gives me feedback that I did something wrong.

☐ **31.** I . . . _____

☐ **32.** I . . . _____

Are you aware of any other of your patterns—mental, emotional, or behavioral? If so, add them to the list.

> It is not true that life is one damn thing after another—it's one damn thing over and over.
>
> Edna St. Vincent Millay,
> American poet

JOURNAL ENTRY / 21

In this activity, you will explore self-defeating patterns in your life that may reveal unconscious scripts. You're about to embark on an exciting journey into your inner world! There you can discover—and later revise—the invisible forces that have gotten you off course from your goals and dreams.

1 **Write about one of your self-defeating *behavior* patterns.** Choose a behavior pattern that you checked on the list or identify a self-defeating behavior that isn't on the list but that you do often. Remember, a behavior is something someone else can see you do. Develop your journal paragraphs by anticipating questions that someone reading it might have about this behavior pattern. (Even you might have questions when you read your journal 10 years from now.) For example,

- What exactly is your self-defeating behavior pattern?
- What are some specific examples of when you did this behavior?
- What may have caused this habit?
- What undesirable effects has it had on your life?
- How would your life be improved if you changed it?

One student began by writing, "One of my self-defeating behavior patterns is that I seldom do my best work on college assignments. For example, in my biology lab. . . ."

2 **Repeat Step 1 for one of your self-defeating *thought* patterns or for one of your self-defeating *emotional* patterns.** Once again, choose a pattern that you checked on the list or identify a habit that isn't on the list but that you often think or feel. You might begin, *One of my self-defeating thought patterns is that I often wonder if I am smart enough to be successful in college. I especially think this during exams. For example, last Thursday I . . . Or . . . One of my self-defeating emotional patterns is that I often feel frustrated. For example. . . .*

> All serious daring starts from within.
>
> Eudora Welty

ONE STUDENT'S STORY

JAMES FLORIOLLI, *Foothill College, California*

At different points in my life I've given up when I ran into a challenge. As a child, I loved baseball, but when I got hit in the face with a ball, I stopped playing. In school, I started having problems with my writing skills, and I was diagnosed with a learning disability. I got all kinds of accommodations, even more than I deserved, and I started goofing off. I convinced myself that success was getting the best grades possible with the least amount of work. After high school, college didn't seem like a viable option, so I joined the Marine Corps Reserve. Boot camp was even harder than I thought it would be. Once again, I used the minimum amount of effort necessary to complete each task, and I failed to achieve the level of success in the Marines that I could have. When I left the Marines to get a civilian job, I defined success as getting maximum compensation for minimum effort.

I got a job at the phone company and at first it seemed perfect. I'm very well paid for very little effort. However, this situation isn't as rewarding as

I thought it would be. After a few years I began to want a greater challenge. I knew I needed an education to advance in the workplace, so I started taking college courses part-time. For the first year I avoided classes that involved a lot of writing, as I was still intimidated by past failures in this area. But when poor writing began to affect my grades in other courses, I decided to take a composition class. In that class we read *On Course*, and in the chapter about self-awareness, I began to see how negative scripts could cause problems. I started wondering if there was a script contributing to the frustration I was feeling in my life. An idea kept coming up that at first I was unwilling to accept. I had always thought of myself as a hard worker, but looking back on my life I could not deny there were challenges I had run away from. When baseball had required extra work to get past my fear of the ball, I quit. When school stopped coming easily to me, I quit. When I realized how hard I'd have to work to be a success in the Marines, I quit. Seeing

this pattern was powerful for me. Finally, I felt like I understood how I ended up in the situation I am in. I realized that I'll do anything to avoid feeling bad. If I feel down in any way, I'm willing to throw everything out the window to feel better. In the past, I have doubted myself and been afraid to take risks. I overvalued security and undervalued me. I need to believe I am capable of accomplishing anything I want to.

Soon I have to pick my college major. One option is to get a computer science degree and continue working at the phone company. This would probably lead to the greatest profit and security. Or, I could choose a major that would prepare me for my dream job working in the front office of a professional baseball team. Obviously, going for my dream would be very difficult and call for a large initial pay cut. Knowing I have an issue with not following through on my most challenging commitments, I need to set my goals very carefully. No matter what I choose, I hope that when everything is said and done I will be proud of what I have accomplished. This will mean I have successfully revised my negative script of running from important challenges in my life.

Rewriting Your Outdated Scripts

FOCUS QUESTIONS   How can you revise self-defeating scripts that keep you from achieving your full potential?

Once, in a writing class, I was explaining how to organize an essay when a student named Diana told me she didn't understand. She asked if I'd write an explanation on the board.

Earlier in the class, we'd been talking about the differences between left-brain and right-brain thinking. We'd discussed how the left side of the brain deals with logical, organized information, while the right side deals with more creative, intuitive concepts. "No problem," I said to Diana, "I hear your left brain crying out for some order. Let's see if I can help."

As I turned to write on the blackboard, she screamed, "You have no right to talk to me that way!"

I was stunned. Talk about a strange response! I took a deep breath to compose myself. "Maybe we could talk about this after class," I said.

THE IMPACT OF OUTDATED BELIEFS

Diana and I did talk, and I learned that she was in her late 30s, a single mother of an 8-year-old daughter. Our conversation wandered for a while; then Diana mentioned that she had always disliked school. In elementary school, she had consistently gotten low grades, while her sister consistently earned As. One day, when Diana was about 12, she overheard her father and mother talking about her poor report card. "I don't know what we're going to do with Diana," her father said. "She's the *half-brain* of the family." (Do you see it yet . . . what got Diana upset with me?)

Diana accepted as a fact other people's belief that she couldn't think or learn. She developed patterns of thoughts, emotions, and behaviors that supported this belief. She decided that school was a waste of time (thought), she exploded when anyone questioned her about schoolwork (emotion), and she was often absent (behavior). Diana barely graduated from high school, then got a menial job that bored her.

For nearly 20 years, Diana heard her Inner Critic (sounding much like her father) telling her that something was wrong with her brain. Finally, another inner voice began to whisper, *Maybe—just maybe. . . .* Then one day she took a big risk and enrolled in college.

"So what happens?" she said, getting angry again. "I get a teacher who calls me a *half-brain*! I knew this would happen. I ought to just quit."

I used my best active listening skills: I listened to understand. I reflected both her thoughts and her anger. I asked her to clarify and expand. I allowed long periods of silence.

Finally, her emotional storm subsided. She took a deep breath and sat back.

I waited a few moments. "Diana, I know you think I called you a 'half-brain.' But what I actually said was *left* brain. Remember we had been talking in class about the difference between left-brain and right-brain thinking? Two different approaches to planning your essay? I was talking about that."

"But I *heard* you!"

"I know that's what you *heard*. But that isn't what I *said*. I've read two of your essays, and I know your brain works just fine. What really matters, though, is what *you* think! You need to believe in your own intelligence. Otherwise, you'll always be ready to hear people call you a 'half-brain' no matter what they really said. Worse, you'll always believe it yourself."

> We don't see things as they are, we see them as we are.
>
> Anais Nin

> We are what we think. All that we are arises with our thoughts. With our thoughts, We make the world.
>
> Buddha

Imagine how difficult it is to make wise choices when you hold the core belief "I am a half-brain." Diana had come within an inch of dropping out of college, of abandoning her dreams of a college degree. And all because of her childhood script.

DOING THE REWRITE

Until we revise our limiting scripts, we're less likely to achieve some of our most cherished goals and dreams. That's why realizing we're off course can be a blessing in disguise. By identifying the self-defeating patterns of thought, emotion, and behavior that got us off course, we may be able to discover and revise the underlying core beliefs that are sabotaging our success.

Diana stuck it out and passed English 101. She persevered and graduated with an Associate of Arts degree in early childhood education. When I spoke to her last, she was working at a nursery school and talking about returning to college to finish her bachelor's degree. Like most of us, she'll probably be in a tug of war with her scripts for the rest of her life. But now, at least, she knows that she, and not her scripts, can be in charge of making her choices.

One of the great discoveries about the human condition is this: We are not stuck with our personal scripts or cultural programming. We can re-create ourselves. We can keep what works and change what doesn't. By revising outdated scripts, we can get back on course and dramatically improve the outcomes and experiences of our lives.

In developing our own self-awareness many of us discover ineffective scripts, deeply embedded habits that are totally unworthy of us, totally incongruent with the things we really value in life.

Stephen Covey

JOURNAL ENTRY / **22**

In this activity, you'll practice revising your scripts, thus taking greater control of your life. As in Journal Entry 17, you'll once again be writing a conversation with your Inner Guide, a critical thinking skill that empowers you to become your own best coach, counselor, mentor, and guide through challenging times. This practical application of critical thinking greatly enhances your self-awareness, helping you take greater responsibility for making the wise choices necessary to create your desired outcomes and experiences.

1 Write a dialogue with your Inner Guide that will help you revise your self-sabotaging scripts.

Have your Inner Guide ask you the following 10 questions. After answering each question, let your Inner Guide use one or more of the active listening skills to help you dive deeper:

- **Silence** (demonstrating that you are paying close attention to the speaker)

- **Reflection** (expressing in your own words what you think the speaker is saying and feeling)

- **Expansion** (requesting examples, evidence, and experiences)
- **Clarification** (asking for an explanation)

Ten questions from your Inner Guide:

1. In what area of your life are you off course?
2. What self-defeating **thought patterns** of yours may have contributed to this situation?
3. What different thoughts could you choose to get back on course?
4. What self-defeating **emotional patterns** of yours may have contributed to this situation?
5. What different emotions could you choose to get back on course?
6. What self-defeating **behavior patterns** of yours may have contributed to this situation?
7. What different behaviors could you choose to get back on course?
8. What limiting **core beliefs** of yours (about the world, other people, or yourself) may have led you to adopt the self-defeating patterns that we've been discussing?
9. What different beliefs could you choose to get back on course?
10. As a result of what you've learned here, what new behaviors, thoughts, emotions, or core beliefs will you adopt?

A sample dialogue follows.

Sample Dialogue with Your Inner Guide

IG: In what area of your life are you off course? (Question 1)

ME: My grades are terrible this semester.

IG: Would you say more about that? **(Expansion)**

ME: In high school I got mostly As and Bs even though I played three sports. My goal this semester is to have at least a 3.5 grade point average, but the way things are going, I'll be lucky if I even get a 2.0.

IG: What self-defeating **thought patterns** of yours may have contributed to this situation? (Question 2)

ME: I guess I tell myself I shouldn't have to work hard to get good grades in college.

IG: Why do you think that? Is there a deeper meaning? **(Clarification)**

ME: If I have to study hard, then I must not be very smart.

IG: That's a good awareness! What different thoughts could you choose to get back on course to your goal of getting at least a 3.5 average? (Question 3)

It is a marvelous faculty of the human mind that we are also able to stop old programming from holding us back, anytime we choose to. That gift is called conscious choice.

Shad Helmstetter

> Until you make the unconscious conscious, it will direct your life and you will call it fate.
>
> Carl Jung

> Whatever we believe about ourselves and our ability comes true for us.
>
> Susan L. Taylor, former editor-in-chief, *Essence* magazine

JOURNAL ENTRY | **22** | *continued*

ME: I could remind myself that going to college is like moving from the minor leagues to the major leagues. The challenge is a lot greater, and I better start studying like a major league student or I'm not going to succeed.

IG: What self-defeating **emotional patterns** of yours may have contributed to this situation? (Question 4)

ME: I get really frustrated when I don't understand something right away.

IG: So you want to understand it immediately. **(Reflection)**

ME: Absolutely. When I don't get it right away, I switch to something else.

IG: That's understandable since everything came so easy to you in high school. What different emotion could you choose to get you back on course to your goal of a 3.5 GPA? (Question 5)

ME: I could do the same thing I do in basketball when the coach asks me to shut down the other team's top scorer. I can psych myself up and push myself to study harder. My college degree is worth a lot more to me than winning a basketball game.

IG: What self-defeating **behavior patterns** of yours may have contributed to this situation? (Question 6)

ME: Like I said before, I get frustrated when I don't understand something right away, and then I put it aside. I always plan to come back to it later, but usually I don't.

IG: Are there any other self-defeating behaviors you can think of? **(Expansion)**

ME: I don't ask my teachers for help or go to the tutoring center either. I guess I hate asking for help. It's like admitting that I'm not very smart.

IG: There's that concern again about not being smart enough. **(Reflection)**

ME: I hadn't realized my Inner Critic is so loud!

IG: Now you can prove your Inner Critic wrong. What different behaviors could you choose to get back on course to your goal? (Question 7)

ME: I could ask my teachers for more help and go to the tutoring center. Also, when I set homework aside, I could write on my calendar when I'm going to work on it again. I'm really good about doing things that I write down.

IG: I like it! What limiting **core beliefs** of yours (about the world, other people, or yourself) may have led you to adopt the self-defeating patterns that we've been discussing? (Question 8)

ME: This conversation has made me realize I have some doubts about whether I'm as smart as I think I am. Maybe I don't believe

▶

I can really succeed in college unless studying comes easy for me. Maybe I got a little spoiled and lazy in high school.

IG: What different core belief could you choose to get back on course to your goal? (Question 9)

ME: I can succeed in college if I'm willing to do the work . . . and give it my best.

IG: That's great! Do the work and do your best! As a result of what you've learned here, what new behaviors, thoughts, emotions, or core beliefs will you commit to? (Question 10)

ME: When I feel like putting an assignment aside, I'll work on it for at least 15 more minutes. Then, if I stop before I'm finished, I'll write on my calendar when I'm going to work on it again and I'll go back and finish it later. If I'm still having trouble with the assignment, I'll ask my professor for help. And I'll keep reminding myself, "Do the work and do my best." If that doesn't help, I'll be back to talk to you some more. I *will* get a 3.5 average! Thanks for listening.

ONE STUDENT'S STORY

ANNETTE VALLE, *The Victoria College, Texas*

Mrs. Turner, my seventh-grade math teacher, lives in my head. I haven't seen her in more than 30 years, but I can still picture her on the day I went up to her desk at the front of the room. She had fair skin, long brown hair, and hazel eyes. I can see her elbows on her big wooden desk, her eyes staring off into the distance, clicking the nail of a finger against the nail on her thumb. When I asked her to help explain the math, she turned and waved my paper at me and told me I was too stupid to learn math. All these years later, I can still hear her words. *I have no idea why you even come to this class, Annette. You're never going to pass math. You're just stupid.* Then she dismissed me with a wave of her hand.

I grew up in Houston, Texas, in the 1970s. College was something that rich, smart people did. It wasn't an option for poor Hispanic children living in the barrio. In our neighborhood, no one talked about going to college. Conversations were about drug dealers, drive-bys, and the latest girl who'd been beaten up by her husband. Our biggest goal in life was to survive. Like many of my friends, I dropped out of school. I got married at 15 and had two children by the time I was 17. After my brother got his GED in the military in 1980, he talked me into getting a GED, too. That diploma qualified me for higher-paying jobs, like working security in a chemical plant or loading ATM machines. But they were all boring jobs that required physical labor, and I wasn't very happy.

Now fast forward to 2005. That's when I was diagnosed with rheumatoid arthritis. The doctor said I couldn't work at physical jobs anymore, and I became eligible for a rehabilitation program that offered an opportunity for me to attend college. When I started my first semester at the age of 46, I was overwhelmed and scared. The campus seemed huge. I was intimidated by all of the young students and the academic requirements that I didn't understand. The teachers said, "Here's your syllabus," but I had no idea what a "syllabus" was. My English teacher told us to do our research paper in MLA format, but I had no idea what that meant either. I didn't want to ask because I figured everyone else knew. So I pretended I knew, too. I walked around campus with my head down and watched the cement. If I had a problem and someone didn't say, *Can I help you?* I would just try to figure it out on my own.

One of my courses was called Strategic Learning, where we read *On Course*. In this class I learned to overcome my fears and accept every challenge placed before me. It helped me become armed with the belief that the choices I make and the strategies I use are what will determine what happens to me. I learned to combat the scripts in my head that were saying *You're not smart enough; You can't do this; You'll never be a good college student.* I replaced those negative thoughts with *I can do this; I will do whatever it takes to get the work done; Only I can change my path.* It's a good thing I had this class, because I was also taking math. Mrs. Turner was still in my head telling me I was stupid and would never pass math. Instead of giving in like I had when I was in her class, I tried my newly learned strategies with determination. One thing I did was take inspirational quotations from *On Course* and write them on my workspace wall at home. When I feel like giving up, I read them out loud. Then I remind myself that I am just as smart as my younger classmates and I can accomplish my dreams just as well as they can. I'm willing to do whatever it takes, even if that means spending 40 hours a week in tutoring. Maybe I'll never be a great math student, but I did pass the course.

I'm now in my fourth semester in college, and I walk across campus with my head up. When I see another student who's confused, I offer to help. I've even used some of the *On Course* techniques to encourage other students who have the same obstacles I had. The course made me a stronger person and helped me change my life. Still, I get sad when I realize that I believed Mrs. Turner for so long. I wasted a lot of years listening to her criticisms in my mind, and for a long time let her steal my thunder of achievement.

Photo: Courtesy of Annette Valle.

SELF-AWARENESS / at Work

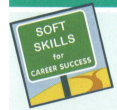

Looking inward is the first place we need to look to find our own direction, not the last.

Clarke G. Carney & Cinda Field Wells in Career Planning

Many people spend more time choosing a movie than choosing their career. As a result, the unlucky ones later dread going to work, perhaps for the rest of their lives! Creators, by contrast, devote time and effort to one of life's most important Quadrant II activities: conscious career planning. As a result, many of them actually enjoy going to work.

Conscious career planning requires self-awareness. How else can you find a match between you and the thousands of career possibilities open to you? A place to start your planning is taking an inventory of your **hard skills**. Hard skills are the special-knowledge skills that you've learned to do throughout your life. They include such abilities as swimming, writing, programming computers, playing racquetball, solving mathematics problems, building a house, creating a budget, giving a speech, drawing blood, writing a business plan, designing a garden, cooking lasagna, backpacking, playing chess, and reading. You probably learned many of your hard skills from a teacher, coach, mentor, or book. These skills can typically be video recorded, and they tend to be applicable only in limited and specific situations; for example, writing a business plan isn't a skill of much value when you're programming computers. To begin your inventory of hard skills, ask yourself, "What talents have gotten me compliments, recognition, or awards? In which school courses have I received good grades?

SEEKING CREATORS

Candidates must demonstrate self-awareness, self-confidence, and positive work and life habits.

When did I feel fully alive, extremely capable, or very smart, and what skills was I using at the time?" Finding a match between your hard skills and the requirements of a career is essential for success.

Continue your self-assessment with an inventory of your **soft skills** (sometimes referred to as "necessary skills"). Soft skills are the ones you have developed to cope with life. They include the ones you're exploring in this book: making responsible choices, motivating yourself, being industrious, developing mutually supportive relationships, demonstrating self-awareness, finding lessons in every experience, managing your emotions, and believing in yourself. Many of these soft skills you learned unconsciously as you faced life's challenges. Usually, they are attitudes and beliefs, so they can't be videoed for playback. They are as invisible as oxygen but just as important to the quality of your life. Unlike hard skills, soft skills tend to be helpful in any career; for example, feeling confident is valuable whether you are an accountant, computer programmer, or nurse. To create an inventory of your soft skills, ask yourself, "What personal qualities have earned me compliments? What accomplishments am I proud of, and what inner qualities helped me achieve them?" Finding a match between your soft skills and the demands of a career further increases your chances of rising to the top of your profession.

To create a third component of your self-assessment, identify your **personal preferences**. To do so, go to your college's career center and ask to take one of the well-known interest inventories: the *Strong Interest Inventories* (SII), the *Self-Directed Search* (SDS), or the *Myers-Briggs Type Indicator®* (MBTI®) instrument. These tools help you discover personal preferences and suggest possible college majors and career choices that will match your interests. An additional tool, the *Holland Code,* places you in one of six personality types and

▶

suggests possible careers for each. Which of the following personality types sounds most like you?

Realistic personalities prefer activities involving objects, tools, and machines. Possible careers: mechanic, electrician, computer repair, civil engineer, forester, industrial arts teacher, dental technician, farmer, carpenter.

Investigative personalities prefer activities involving abstract problem solving and the exploration of physical, biological, and cultural phenomena for the purpose of understanding and controlling them. Possible careers: chemist, economist, detective, computer analyst, doctor, astronomer, mathematician.

Artistic personalities prefer activities involving self-expression, using words, ideas, or materials to create art forms or new concepts. Possible careers: writer, advertising manager, public relations specialist, artist, musician, graphic designer, interior decorator, inventor.

Social personalities prefer activities involving interaction with other people to inform, train, develop, help, or enlighten them. Possible careers: nurse, massage therapist, teacher, counselor, social worker, day-care provider, physical therapist.

Enterprising personalities prefer activities involving the persuasion and management of others to attain organizational goals or economic gain. Possible careers: salesperson, television newscaster, bank manager, lawyer, travel agent, personnel manager, entrepreneur.

Conventional personalities prefer activities involving the application of data to bring order out of confusion and develop a prescribed plan. Possible careers: accountant, computer operator, secretary, credit manager, financial planner.

The research of Dr. John Holland, creator of the Holland Code, shows that people tend to be satisfied in careers that are compatible with their personality type, and people are less satisfied when the match isn't there. Becoming aware of your interest preferences and personality type improves your chances of finding a satisfying career match.

Another important area of self-knowledge is your scripts, those that support your success and especially those that don't. For example, what beliefs do you hold that might keep you from pursuing or succeeding in your chosen career? If one of your scripts is to distrust other people, then it will be difficult for you to develop the support systems that will enhance your success. This awareness allows you to make a conscious choice about revising the script. Remember, since you wrote your script originally, you can rewrite it in the service of a successful career.

Self-awareness in the workplace will also help you notice when your self-sabotaging habits get you off course. For example, you'll stop arriving at meetings late; instead, you'll arrive a few minutes early. You'll stop interrupting when others are talking; instead, you'll listen actively. You'll stop acting as if you know all the answers; instead, you'll ask others for their opinions. In short, you'll become conscious of converting destructive behaviors into constructive behaviors. If you've ever had bosses or coworkers who demonstrate any of these negative behaviors, you'll know how you wished they would become aware of what they were doing and change.

To summarize, cultivating the soft skill of self-awareness will help you choose a career that you will enjoy and bring out the behaviors, beliefs, and attitudes that will help you to excel in that profession.

TECH TIPS: Self-Awareness

Self-awareness inventories abound on the Internet. To take one, do an Internet search for "self-awareness test" or "self-awareness inventory." For example, you'll find one at Wisc-online.com, a collaborative effort by the 16 colleges in the Wisconsin Technical College system. Search the site for "Self-Awareness" to take a 24-question test.

Zenify (not to be confused with a drink by the same name) is an app for your mobile device that is designed to help you move out of auto-pilot and become more aware of what you are thinking, doing and feeling in every moment. The app delivers seven levels of assignments on a schedule you choose. Most assignments arrive as a text message, though some contain pictures or music. Assignments ask you to focus your awareness on various aspects of your life, including thoughts, emotions, relationships, parents, and friends. *(Android, iOS; free)*

Queendom.com is a website with many self-assessment tests and quizzes that help you learn about yourself. You'll find many other tests on this site that relate to the inner qualities presented in *On Course*, including self-awareness, self-esteem, assertiveness, procrastination, listening skills, anxiety, depression, anger management, and emotional intelligence. *(Web; brief reports on your results are free; extended reports require a paid membership)*

Write Your Own Rules

BELIEVING IN YOURSELF

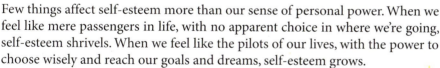

FOCUS QUESTIONS   What personal rules do you have that dictate the choices you make daily? Which of these rules help you create high self-esteem?

Few things affect self-esteem more than our sense of personal power. When we feel like mere passengers in life, with no apparent choice in where we're going, self-esteem shrivels. When we feel like the pilots of our lives, with the power to choose wisely and reach our goals and dreams, self-esteem grows.

Unconscious personal scripts and cultural programs can steal our sense of personal power and drag down our self-esteem. When these unconscious forces take over, we essentially give up control of our lives. Then we make those strange choices that can push us far off course and leave us wondering, "How the heck did I get over here?" Consider, for example, the cultural tradition of *marianism* in which Latinas are expected to follow rules such as these: *Place the needs of your husband and family above your own, Never criticize your husband, Remain faithful to your marriage regardless of the cost, Never share personal problems with others.* If a Latina has consciously accepted these rules as her own, she will gladly make the personal sacrifices needed, and she will achieve the outcomes

I think you're going to be very surprised to discover that you may be living by rules of which you're not even aware.

Virginia Satir

and experiences of her choosing. In fact, her sense of cultural pride may very well give her self-esteem a powerful boost. However, if she unconsciously lets these rules dictate her choices, she may feel helpless and angry at the life she is living. Imagine, for example, trying to earn a college degree if you are forever setting aside your dreams to help others achieve what they want. Only when you consciously accept, revise, or replace some cultural rules are you likely to feel completely at peace with yourself. The same, of course, is true of the rules embedded in your personal scripts.

As psychologist Virginia Satir pointed out, we are all living by rules, but the important issue is *Have we chosen our own rules?* To answer that question, you'll want to identify and preserve any empowering rules that are keeping you on course. Then you'll want to become conscious of and revise any rules that are holding you back. Finally, you'll want to write new rules that will support you in achieving even greater victories. That's what former First Lady Eleanor Roosevelt did. Here are some of the life rules she created to guide her choices: *Do whatever comes your way as well as you can. Think as little as possible about yourself; think as much as possible about other people. Since you get more joy out of giving joy to others, you should put a good deal of thought in the happiness that you are able to give.*

> As a member of the Sikh faith, I was constantly keeping track of so many rules: what to wear, what to eat, forbidden behaviors, and my duties to my family. When I added it all up, there wasn't much left for me to decide—so many of my decisions had been made for me.
>
> Sheena Iyengar

THREE SUCCESS RULES

I have polled thousands of college instructors, and they consistently identify three behaviors that their most successful students do consistently. As you'll see, these rules apply just as well to creating great outcomes in other life roles such as your career and relationships. Consider, then, these three rules as the foundation of your personal code of conduct.

Rule 1: I Show Up

Commit to attending every class from beginning to end. Someone once said that 90 percent of success is simply showing up. Makes sense, doesn't it? How can you be successful at something if you're not there? Studies show a direct correlation between attendance and grades (as one measure of success). At Baltimore City Community College, a study found that, on average, as absences went up, grades went down, especially in introductory courses. A study by a business professor at Arizona State University showed that, on average, his students' grades went down one full grade for every two classes they missed. If you can't get motivated to show up, maybe you need new goals and dreams.

> The most important thing is to have a code of life, to know how to live.
>
> Hans Selye, M.D.

Rule 2: I Do My Best Work

Commit to doing your best work on all assignments, including turning them in on time. You'd be amazed at how many sloppy assignments instructors see. But it isn't just students who are guilty. A friend in business has shown me hundreds of job applications so sloppily prepared that they begged to be tossed in the trash. Doing your best work on assignments is a rule that will propel you to success in all you do.

Rule 3: I Participate Actively

Commit to getting involved. College, like life, isn't a spectator sport. Come to class prepared. Listen attentively. Take notes. Think deeply about what's being said. Ask yourself how you can apply your course work to achieve your goals and dreams. Read ahead. Start a study group. Ask questions. Answer questions. If you participate at this high level, you couldn't keep yourself from learning even if you wanted to.

Some students resist adopting these three basic rules of success. They say, "But what if I get sick? What if my car breaks down on the way to class? What if . . .?" I trust that by now you recognize the voice of the Inner Defender, the internal excuse maker.

Of course something may happen to keep you from following your rules. Each rule is simply your strong *intention*. Each rule identifies an action you believe will help you achieve your desired outcomes and experiences. So you *intend* to be at every class from beginning to end. You *intend* to do your very best work and turn assignments in on time. You *intend* to participate actively. Your promise *to yourself* is never to break your own rules for a frivolous reason. However, you'll always break your own rules if something of a higher value (like your health) demands it. At each fork in the road, the key to your success is being aware of which choice leads to the future you want. When you are a Creator, you make each choice uncontaminated by the past (your scripts), informed by your own rules of conduct, and ultimately determined by which option, in that moment, will best support the achievement of your goals and dreams.

CHANGING YOUR HABITS

Exceptional students not only follow these three basic rules of success, they also create their own rules for college and life. By choosing personal rules, they commit to replacing their limiting scripts and cultural constraints with consciously chosen habits. Here are a few of my own life rules:

- I keep promises to myself and others.
- I seek feedback and make appropriate course corrections.
- I respect others by arriving on time.
- I do my very best work on all projects important to me.
- I play and create joy.
- I care for my body with exercise, healthy food, and good medical care.
- I am kind.

Do I follow these rules every day of my life? Unfortunately, no. And when I don't, I soon see myself getting off course. Then I can recommit to following my self-chosen rules and avoid sabotaging the life I want to create.

Once we follow our own rules long enough, they're no longer simply rules. They become habits. And once our positive actions, thoughts, and feelings become habits, few obstacles can block the path to our success.

> People who lead a satisfying life, who are in tune with their past and with their future—in short, people whom we would call "happy"—are generally individuals who have lived their lives according to rules they themselves created.
>
> **Mihaly Csikszentmihalyi**

> What is hateful to you do not to your neighbor. That is the entire Law; all the rest is commentary.
>
> **The Talmud**

I'll give you the Four Rules of Success:

1. Decide what you want.
2. Decide what you want to give up in order to get what you want.
3. Associate with successful people.
4. Plan your work and work your plan.

Blair Underwood, actor

In this activity, you will write your own rules for success in college and in life. By following your own code of conduct, you will more likely stay on course toward your greatest dreams.

To focus your mind, ask yourself, "What do successful people do consistently? What are their thoughts, attitudes, behaviors, and beliefs?"

1 Title this journal entry "MY PERSONAL RULES FOR SUCCESS IN COLLEGE AND IN LIFE." Below that, write a list of your own rules for achieving your goals in college. List only those actions to which you're willing to commit to do consistently. You might want to print your rules on certificate paper and post them where you can see them daily (perhaps right next to your affirmation). Consider adopting the following as your first three rules:

1. I show up.
2. I do my very best work.
3. I participate actively.

2 Write your thoughts and feelings about which of your personal rules is the most important to your success in college and in life, and why.

What if one of your rules was: I dive deep! How much would that rule improve your results in college and in life?

ONE STUDENT'S STORY

BRANDEÉ HUIGENS, *Northeast Iowa Community College, Iowa*

I was never a drinker in high school, but when I turned 21, I started going out to bars with my friends. I found that "liquor courage" made me feel better about myself. When I was drinking, I was funny, had a great time, and I was happy. Then I started having blackouts. One time I woke up in my truck, surrounded by policemen, and I had no idea how I had gotten there or where I had been. Another time, I woke up in my bed and there were traffic citations all over the place. I found out later that I had spent the night in jail and the police had sent me home in a cab, but what made it worse was that I didn't remember a second of it. I had always gotten good grades before, but now I started missing my college classes. I wasn't doing as well as I wanted, especially in my nursing classes, like microbiology. I felt crappy and started putting even more pressure on myself. Then I would drink and it made me feel better, almost like a good friend. Trouble was, I'd wake up the next day and my life was falling apart. People were telling me that I could get a medical withdrawal, and I started thinking about dropping out of college.

Looking back on it now, I realize that I had completely lost control of my inner core. I've never been a quitter, though, and I started using my journal entries for this course to figure out my challenges and how to fix them. My entries would run on for five or six pages as I poured myself emotionally into my writing. I was excited because it was a way to express myself positively. About halfway through the semester, I made a new rule for myself and told my class about it: *I will abstain from drinking alcohol.* From day one, it was a rule that took over my life, and I decided to track it with a 32-Day Commitment. To support my change, I started going to AA meetings and I got a counselor at the Substance Abuse Services Center. I reread my journals for inspiration, and every day in this class we'd share how we were doing on our commitments. Of course there were times I was tempted to drink, but I successfully completed my 32 days, and then I just kept going. In the last six months, I have abstained from drinking every day but one.

Today, I think about how powerful it was to write that little sentence and make a new rule for myself. It set so many other things in motion. Some are obvious, like I got sober and stopped having blackouts. My final grades were awesome, and I even got a B in micro, the hardest course I ever took. I also got a new perspective on grades. I always wanted to be perfect so I could get approval from my family, but now I see a B as a success instead of a failure. Perhaps most of all, I learned that in trying to please everyone else but me, I had lost focus on what is important to me and all I want to accomplish. Now I've created an assertiveness rule. I've starting speaking up for myself and saying "no," and I can feel my confidence and self-esteem getting stronger. From this class and from the people I shared it with, I have learned how to stand up for myself. My inner core is not fully complete, but the seed has been planted and it is definitely starting to grow.

Adopting
Lifelong Learning

Successful Students . . .

▶ **develop a learning orientation to life,** seeking new learning experiences that offer valuable lessons and strengthen their learning "muscles" for future challenges.

▶ **discover their preferred ways of learning,** utilizing strategies that allow them to maximize their learning of valuable new information and skills.

▶ **employ critical thinking,** using probing questions and higher-order reasoning skills to evaluate complex situations, make wise choices, and solve important problems.

Struggling Students . . .

▶ **avoid new learning experiences,** believing they have a fixed amount of intelligence that may not be up to the challenge.

▶ **often experience frustration,** boredom, or resistance when their instructors don't teach the way they prefer to learn.

▶ **use poor thinking skills** that result in confusion, unsound judgment, enduring problems, and even exploitation by others.

As a Creator, I take personal responsibility for learning all of the information, skills, and life lessons necessary to achieve my goals and dreams.

I learn valuable lessons from every experience I have.

One September morning, on their first day of college, two dozen first-year students made their way into the biology laboratory. They sat down, six at a lab table, and glanced about for the professor. Because this was their first college class, most of the students were a bit nervous. A few introduced themselves. Others kept checking their watches.

At exactly nine o'clock, the professor, wearing a crisply pressed white lab coat, entered the room. "Good morning," he said. He set a white plate in the middle of each table. On each plate lay a small fish.

"Please observe the fish," the professor said. "Then write down your observations." He turned and left the room.

The students looked at each other, puzzled. This was *bizarre!* Oh, well. They took out scrap paper and wrote notes such as, *I see a small fish.* One student added, *It's on a white plate.*

Satisfied, they set their pens down and waited. And waited. For the entire class period, they waited. A couple of students whispered that it was a trick. They said the professor was probably testing them to see if they'd do something wrong. Time crawled by. Still they waited, trying to do nothing that would get them in trouble. Finally, one student mumbled that she was going to be late for her next class. She picked up her books and stood. She paused. Others rose as well and began filing out of the room. Some looked cautiously over their shoulders as they left.

When the students entered the biology lab for their second class, they found the same white plates with the same small fish already waiting on their laboratory tables. At exactly nine o'clock, the professor entered the room. "Good morning. Please take out your observations of the fish," he said.

Students dug into their notebooks or book bags. Many could not find their notes. Those few who could held them up for the professor to see as he walked from table to table.

After visiting each student, the professor said, "Please observe the fish. Write down all of your observations."

"Will there be a test on this?" one student asked. But the professor had already left the room, closing the door behind him. Frustrated, the student blurted, "Why doesn't he just tell us what he wants us to know?"

The students looked at one another, more puzzled. They peered at the fish. Those few who had found their notes glanced from the fish to their notes and back again. Was the professor crazy? What else were they supposed to notice? It was only a stupid fish.

About then, one student spied a book on the professor's desk. It was a book for identifying fish, and she snatched it up. Using the book, she quickly discovered what kind of fish was lying on her plate. She read eagerly, recording in her notes all of the facts she found about her fish. Others saw her and asked to use the book, too. She passed the book to other tables, and her classmates soon found descriptions of their fish. After about 15 minutes the students sat back, very pleased with themselves. Chatter died down. They waited. But the professor didn't return. As the period ended, all of the students carefully put their notes away.

The same fish on the same white plate greeted each student in the third class. The professor entered at nine o'clock. "Good morning," he said. "Please hold up your observations." All of the students held up their notes immediately. They looked at each other, smiling, as the professor walked from table to table, looking at their work. Once again, he walked toward the door. "Please . . . *observe* the fish. Write down *all* of your observations," he said. And then he left.

The students couldn't believe it. They grumbled and complained. *This guy is nuts. When is he going to teach us something? What are we paying tuition for, anyway?* Students at one table, however, began observing their fish more closely. Other tables followed their example.

The first thing all of the students noticed was the biting odor of aging fish. A few students recorded details about the fish's color that they had failed to observe in the previous two classes. They wondered if the colors had been there originally or if the colors had appeared as the fish aged. Each group measured its fish. They poked it and described its texture. One student looked in its mouth and found that he could see light through its gills. Another student found a small balance beam, and each group weighed its fish. They passed around someone's pocket knife. With it, they sliced open the fish and examined its insides. In the stomach of one fish they found a smaller fish. They wrote quickly, and their notes soon overflowed onto three and four sheets of paper. Finally someone shouted, "Hey, class was over 10 minutes ago." They carefully placed their notes in three-ring binders. They said good-bye to their fish, wondering if their finny friends would be there on Monday.

They were, and a vile smell filled the laboratory. The professor strode into the room at exactly nine o'clock. The students immediately thrust their notes in the air. "Good morning," the professor said cheerfully, making his way from student to student. He took longer than ever to examine their notes. The students shifted anxiously in their chairs as the professor edged ever closer to the door. How could they endure the smell for another class period? At the door, the professor turned to the students. "All right," he said. "Now we can begin."

—*Inspired by Samuel H. Scudder, "Take This Fish and Look at It" (1874)*

Based on what you observed in this biology class, rate the professor on the scale below. Be prepared to explain your rating.

Terrible ▶   ◀ Excellent

DIVING DEEPER

If you had been in this biology lab class, what lessons about college and life would you have learned from the experience? When you think you have discovered one life lesson, dive deeper and find another, even more powerful lesson. And then another and another.

Developing a Learning Orientation to Life

FOCUS QUESTION How can you maximize your learning in college and in life?

"Uh-oh," I thought. "I am in big trouble!"

I was 18 years old at the time, but I recall that scary moment as if it were yesterday. I was about to start my first semester in college. Our entire class was on campus for orientation, and one task was to choose our first-semester classes. I was sitting with one of my new roommates exploring course descriptions. John was going down the reading list for a literature course we were considering. "I've read this book," he said, ticking the title with the tip of his pen, "and this one . . . and this one. . . . and this one . . . and this one." Like many of my classmates, John had gone to a private high school. I had gone to a public high school. John had read every book on the list. I had never even *heard* of the books on the list. That's when I thought: "Uh-oh . . . I am in big trouble!"

In that moment, I made an unconscious and unfortunate choice. I went into survival mode: *I just want to survive the next four years and graduate.* As a result, I filled my schedule with courses I thought would be easy. One course turned out to be more difficult than I thought, so I dropped it. During classes, I seldom spoke, afraid I would say something stupid. At the end of my first semester, I breathed a sigh of relief. I had passed all of my courses. My grades were much lower than they had been in high school, but I had survived. For the next seven semesters, I avoided taking classes with a professor who had a reputation of being "hard." When it came time to pick a major, I chose the one a friend told me was the easiest. My grades crept steadily upward as I got better and better at playing the grade game. After four years, I achieved my goal. I graduated. By most standards I was a success in college. But was I?

GROWTH MINDSETS AND FIXED MINDSETS

It turns out that psychologist Carol Dweck and others have studied the way I approached learning as an undergraduate. Apparently my approach is fairly common. Psychologists call it a "fixed mindset." The opposite is a "growth mindset." As I describe these mindsets, see if they sound familiar.

Learners with a **fixed mindset** believe people are born with a fixed amount of ability and talent. When it comes to intelligence, they've either got it or they don't. If they do well in school, it's because they're smart. If they don't do well in school, it's because they aren't. Dweck found that students with a fixed mindset prefer tasks they can already do well. New challenges are threatening because they fear their intelligence may not be up to the task. Thus, when they encounter a challenge, they tend to avoid it or quit as a method of self-protection. Mistakes and failures scare them because, in their mindset, such outcomes reflect poorly on their fixed level of intelligence. I've seen students complete all of the courses they need to graduate except one. That course is inevitably in the subject they fear: perhaps math, writing, or a foreign language. When students with a fixed mindset experience a challenge, setback, or failure, their inner chatter judges them (*I'm just not smart enough*) and they may give up. Does this sound like Victim behavior to you?

By contrast, learners with a **growth mindset** believe that intelligence is like a muscle—it gets stronger the more it's used. Interestingly, this mindset is consistent with what we know about how the brain learns. The more we exercise our brains, the more neural networks are created and the "smarter" we become.

Too many students are hung up on grades and on proving their worth through grades. Grades are important, but learning is more important.

Carol Dweck

. . . a miracle is just a shift in perception.

Marianne Williamson

(See "Becoming an Active Learner" in *A Toolbox for Active Learners* for more on this.) A growth mindset encourages us to accept challenges, to work hard, to learn from mistakes, to change course if needed, and to keep going despite setbacks and failures. Learners in this mindset believe their hard work and persistence can overcome initial difficulties in mastering a subject or a skill. If what they are doing isn't working, their Inner Guide explains, "I didn't work hard enough" or "There's a better way to do it," or both. They accept responsibility and they make a new plan. I trust that by now you recognize the response of a Creator.

Dweck has tested her theory about fixed and growth mindsets on students from preschool through college. One was an experiment with pre-med students at an Ivy League university. These students were taking a very challenging course in organic chemistry. The stakes were high because their grade in the course would play a big role in whether or not they got into medical school. Students with a growth mindset distinguished themselves from students with a fixed mindset in three important ways: (1) they enjoyed the course more, (2) they bounced back more effectively from setbacks such as poor test scores, and (3) their final grades were higher.

Psychologist Joshua Aronson and colleagues also tested Dweck's theory. They asked Stanford University students to be pen pals with local middle school students and help the younger students stay in school. The experimenters asked the Stanford students to tell their young pen pals things such as "Humans are capable of learning and mastering new things at any time in their lives." In other words, the Stanford students were encouraging their young pen pals to adopt a growth mindset. What the experimenters actually wanted to see was what impact expressing a growth mindset might have on the Stanford students. When later compared to a control group, the Stanford students in the experiment earned higher grades and reported more often that they enjoyed their academic work.

Dweck and others have explored what causes some people to adopt a fixed mindset while others take on the more empowering growth mindset. One explanation is that fixed mindsets result when important adults (e.g., parents or teachers) praise us for our intelligence: *You did so well in math. You're obviously very smart!* The message here is that success is the result of being smart. The problem is, now we're nervous about trying something new. After all, if we fail that means we're not smart enough ... and we believe there's no way to get more "smarts." By contrast, a growth mindset is more likely to develop when important adults praise us for our effort (rather than our intelligence): *You did so well in math. You're obviously a hard worker!* The message here is that success is the result of effort. Armed with this belief, we're more likely to respond positively to future challenges because we're confident we can work harder if the outcome or experience is worth it.

Like other mindsets, fixed and growth mindsets seem to be shaped by deep-culture beliefs. For example, Japanese and Chinese parents are more likely to attribute success to a strong effort (growth mindset). They believe that all students can learn if they work hard enough. By contrast, North American parents are more likely to attribute success to inborn intelligence or ability (fixed mindset). This cultural belief shows up in the American educational system where "gifted" students are given enriched academic programs.

> The purpose of learning is growth, and our minds, unlike our bodies, can continue growing as we continue to live.
>
> Mortimer Adler

> If there is no dark and dogged will, there will be no shining accomplishment; if there is no dull and determined effort, there will be no brilliant achievement.
>
> Chinese proverb

If you've developed a growth mindset, you have a core belief that will help you achieve success in college and beyond. However, if you realize you've developed a fixed mindset, you aren't stuck with it. You can revise your mindset.

HOW TO DEVELOP A GROWTH MINDSET

Here are four ways to develop or strengthen a growth mindset.

Think of Your Brain As a Muscle. Like a muscle, the more you use your brain, the "smarter" and more capable it becomes. The technical term is *neuroplasticity*. Neuroplasticity is the ability of your brain to use new experiences to revise old neural networks and create new ones. This is how learning happens. Once you understand this concept, you'll realize that—with mental effort—your brain is designed to grow and change. The idea that each human brain has a fixed capacity belongs on the scrap heap of faulty beliefs along with "the world is flat." Just because you may be challenged to learn something today doesn't mean that you can't learn it. Because of your brain's neuroplasticity, effort and persistence combined with effective study strategies are the keys to effective learning. For more information about this concept, see "Becoming an Active Learner" in *A Toolbox for Active Learners*.

It's never too late to change your mindset. Mindsets are beliefs—powerful ones and ones that shape our motivation—but beliefs can be changed.

Carol Dweck

Set Learning Goals . . . As Well As Performance Goals. When I was an undergraduate, I set performance goals. My main goal was to see my grade point average improve every semester. I achieved that goal, but I paid a price. To assure success, I played it safe, wasting many learning opportunities. I avoided courses that might have introduced me to a whole new world. I steered clear of "hard" professors who might have become mentors or guides. By studying only to get grades, I learned just enough to pass tests. Sure, I got a degree and, with it, a ticket into the world of employment . . . but at what cost? Don't misunderstand, there's nothing wrong with setting a goal to get good grades. Obviously, good grades are the means to many future goals, such as a job or graduate school. But there is something wrong if our *only* goal is to earn a grade. Such a goal limits our potential. It keeps us from developing knowledge, skills, and wisdom that could help us create a richer, more personally fulfilling life. The solution is to combine both kinds of goals. *Performance goals* provide you with measurable accomplishments (like grades), whereas *learning goals* offer knowledge and skills you can use for the rest of your life.

We now accept the fact that learning is a lifelong process of keeping abreast of change. And the most pressing task is to teach people how to learn.

Peter Drucker

So, what would a learning goal look like? Suppose you're taking a writing class. A performance goal would be to earn an A in the course. A *learning* goal would be to master three ways to write an effective introductory paragraph. Suppose you want to lose weight. A performance goal would be to weigh 150 pounds by June 30. A learning goal would be to learn three important principles of good nutrition. Suppose you're taking an organic chemistry course. A *performance* goal would be to finish reading your textbook by December 1. A *learning* goal would be to master the ability to read challenging content for at least 20 minutes without losing focus. Notice that performance goals usually give us a defined (often measurable) outcome. By contrast, learning goals help us grow, giving us skills and abilities we can use to achieve future performance goals. Whereas my *performance* goal might be to achieve *x*, my *learning goal* might be to learn five strategies to help me do *x*. Those same five strategies may also help me to achieve other goals for the rest of my life. Take a look back to the goals you set in Journal Entry 9 and see what kind of goals you created there. If they are mostly performance goals, consider adding a couple of learning goals.

Seek Feedback. Feedback is essential to learning. Luckily, life offers us helpful feedback every day. Sadly, many ignore it . . . especially those with a fixed mindset. At first, feedback taps us politely on the shoulder. If we pay no attention, feedback shakes us vigorously. If we continue to ignore it, feedback may knock us to our knees, creating havoc in our lives. This havoc might be failing out of school or getting fired from a job. There's usually plenty of feedback long before the failure or firing if we will only heed its message. Your Inner Defender may see feedback as a threat, but your Inner Guide knows it is vital for success.

> Once you embrace unpleasant news, not as a negative but as evidence of a need for change, you aren't defeated by it. You're learning from it.
>
> **Bill Gates**

In college, think of yourself as an airplane pilot and your instructors as your personal air traffic controllers. When they correct you in class or write a comment on an assignment or give you a grade on a test, what they are really saying is, *You're on course, on course . . . whoops, now you're off course, off course . . . okay, that's right, now you're back on course.* Airplane pilots appreciate such feedback. Without it, they might not get to their destination. They might even crash. Likewise, effective learners welcome their instructors' feedback and use it to stay on course. They heed every suggestion that instructors offer on assignments; they understand the message in their test scores; they request clarification of any feedback they don't understand; and they ask for additional feedback. Maybe the idea of paying attention to feedback sounds obvious to you, but I can't tell you how many students I've known who made the same mistakes over and over, ignoring both my feedback and the reality that when you keep doing what you've been doing, you'll keep getting what you've been getting.

> All human beings are periodically tested by the power of the universe . . . how one performs under pressure is the true measure of one's spirit, heart, and desire.
>
> **Spike Lee**

Everywhere in life, heeding feedback is vital to creating the life you want. The feedback may be something said by friends, lovers, spouses, parents, children, neighbors, bosses, coworkers, and even strangers. Or it may be more subtle, coming in the form of an unsatisfying relationship, a boring job, blackouts from drinking too much, or runaway credit card debt. Any areas of discomfort or distress are red flags of warning: *Hey, wake up! You're headed away from your desired outcomes and experiences. You're off course!* And that awareness leads to a fourth way for developing a growth mindset.

Change Course When Needed. It's one thing to realize you are off course. It's quite another to do something about it. Course correction takes courage. You need to admit that what you are doing isn't working, seek alternatives, abandon the familiar, and to walk into the unknown. Victims stay stuck. Creators learn, change, and grow.

One of my off-course students was feeling overwhelmed by all she had to do, and then she made a course correction, changing the way she tackled large projects. In her journal she wrote, "When I break a huge task into chunks and do a little bit every day, I can accomplish great things."

Another off-course student discovered he was an expert at blaming his failures in college on other people: his boss, his teachers, his parents, his girlfriend. He decided to change and hold himself more responsible. He learned, "In the past I have spent more energy on getting people to feel sorry for me than I have on accomplishing something worthwhile."

A third off-course student was filled with hate for her father, who she felt had abandoned her, and then she decided to change. She forgave him and moved on with her life. She wrote, "Spending all of my time hating someone leaves me little time to love myself."

A fourth off-course student realized how little effort and care he put into everything he did, including his college assignments. He discovered, "I'm always looking for ways to cut corners, to get out of doing what's necessary. It doesn't work. I have to do my best in order to be successful."

And one more off-course student realized that the only goal he'd ever set in school was to get good grades. As a graduate student, he discovered, "When I focus on learning, my grades take care of themselves. Better yet, I learn things I can use to improve the quality of my life!" He regretted all of the learning he had missed out on, but he got excited by all there still is to learn. He started taking courses that excited him. He found new ways to apply what he was learning and created a whole new life for himself. He was grateful that he had given himself the gift of a major course correction, one that changed his outcomes and experiences. In case you haven't guessed, I was this off-course student.

We seldom move toward our goals and dreams in a straight line. With constant course corrections, however, we improve our chances of getting there eventually. And along the way, the University of Life offers us exactly the lessons we need to develop our full potential. We only have to listen, learn, change, and grow.

> The capacity to correct course is the capacity to reduce the differences between the path you are on now and the optimal path to your objective....
>
> Charles Garfield

> To me, earth is a school. I view life as my classroom. My approach to the experiences I have every day is that I am a student, and that all my experiences have something they can teach me. I am always asking myself, "What learning is available for me now?"
>
> Mary Hulnick, vice president, University of Santa Monica

JOURNAL ENTRY | 24

In this activity, you will explore course corrections you have made or that you need to make to improve your outcomes and experiences.

Make a choice—write about one of the following:

(A) Describe an important course correction you have made in the past. Explain how you became aware that you were off course, what you did to change course, and how your efforts turned out. Most important, what did you learn from this experience?

(B) Identify where you are presently off course and offer a plan for making a course correction. Explain an aspect of your life (e.g., college, social life, finances, spirituality) that is off course. Describe the feedback you received—from inside or outside of you—informing you that you're off course. What will you do differently to get on course? Most important, what lesson do you think the University of Life wants you to learn from this situation?

> If we don't change direction soon, we'll end up where we're going.
>
> Professor Irwin Corey

JESSIE MAGGARD, *Urbana University, Ohio*

The first friends I made in college were my teammates on the soccer team. After practice we started riding around, shopping, and going to parties. We almost never talked about school or personal problems. To them, play time was more important. I wasn't getting much sleep and I was exhausted all the time. I didn't feel like studying, and when I went to class, I wasn't learning much. Then a couple of things happened that shook me up. First, my English teacher handed back a paper and told me it wasn't very good. I thought all day about what she said and it really bothered me. I'm the first person in my family to go to college, and I started worrying about whether I was going to make it. If I was doing poorly in a class that I thought was easy, what would happen in more difficult classes? Second, I learned that my parents were getting divorced. I tried talking about my feelings with some

of my teammates, but they just listened and didn't say anything. I might as well have been talking to a wall, and I realized they weren't really interested in my problems.

The *On Course* book talks about how easy it is to get off course even when you want to be successful. That is so true. By the time soccer season ended, I was *way* off course and I knew I had to make some serious changes. At first I spent more time by myself. I wrote out a schedule and started to get more organized. Then I slowly began spending more time with people in my dorm, and over time I developed friendships with six amazing people who have really touched me. Doing well in school is important to them, too. We started studying together, and my grades began to improve. I even got comments from my teachers about how I had changed. Still, I felt weighed down by my parents' divorce and it was a huge distraction from

my schoolwork. One of my new friends had gone through her parents' divorce, and she gave me tips on how she had gotten through it. She encouraged me to sit down with my parents and talk about my feelings. I did, and it helped so much to talk with them and understand why they had fallen out of love with each other.

Through all of this, I've learned that when you get off course, you have to do something different. My soccer friends had different goals. I'm not trying to put them down. Their goals weren't bad; they just weren't my goals. My goal is to get my degree and teach kindergarten, and when I was hanging out with my soccer friends, I was headed in the wrong direction. I totally changed my peer group, and now I am back on course. I know I'm the only person who can change my life. I just need the courage to stand up for myself. At the time, changing seemed so difficult, but now in the big picture, it seems so easy.

Photo: Courtesy of Jessie Maggard.

Discovering Your Preferred Ways of Learning

I t is very natural to teach in the same way we learn. It may be difficult for us to believe that others could learn in a way that is foreign and difficult for us.

Carolyn Mamchur

FOCUS QUESTIONS What is your preferred way of learning? What can you do when your instructor doesn't teach the way you prefer to learn?

Today, we're well into the information age. That means staying on course to our goals and dreams requires learning vast amounts of information, facts, theories, and skills. Once you master the CORE Learning System explained in *A Toolbox for Active Learners*, all that learning should be easy, right? Not quite.

You see, in addition to learning approaches that are common to us all, each of us has our own preferred learning experiences. Each of us has our own favored ways of taking in and deeply processing our learning experiences. Each of us has our own preferred ways of creating meaning from the rush and jumble of information we encounter in college, at work, at home, and everywhere else in life. Knowing how *you* prefer to learn gives you a great advantage everywhere in life, but especially in college when you get an instructor who doesn't teach the way you prefer to learn.

SELF-ASSESSMENT: HOW I PREFER TO LEARN

Before reading on, take the following self-assessment inventory. It will give you insights about how you prefer to gather and process information.

Each of us develops preferred ways of learning. These preferred ways of learning are more pleasurable, require less effort, and usually produce more

Learning Preference Inventory

In each group below, rank all four answers (A, B, C, D) from the least true of you to the most true of you. Give each possible answer a different score. There are no right or wrong answers; your opinion is all that matters. Remember, items that are MOST TRUE OF YOU get a 4.

Least true of you ▶ ① ② ③ ④ ◀ Most true of you

1. I would prefer to take a college course

_____ A. in science.	_____ B. in business management.	_____ C. in group dynamics.	_____ D. as an independent study that I design.

2. I solve problems by

_____ A. standing back, thinking, and analyzing what is wrong.	_____ B. doing something practical and seeing how it works.	_____ C. leaping in and doing what feels right at the time.	_____ D. trusting my intuition.

3. Career groups that appeal to me are

_____ A. engineer, researcher, financial planner.	_____ B. administrator, city manager, military officer.	_____ C. teacher, social worker, physical therapist.	_____ D. entrepreneur, artist, inventor.

4. Before I make a decision, I need to be sure that

_____ A. I understand all of the relevant ideas and facts.	_____ B. I'm confident my solution will work.	_____ C. I know how my decision will affect others.	_____ D. I haven't over-looked a more creative solution.

5. I believe that

_____ A. life today needs more logical thinking and less emotion.	_____ B. life rewards the practical, hard-working, down-to-earth person.	_____ C. life must be lived with enthusiasm and passion.	_____ D. life, like music, is best composed by creative inspiration, not by rules.

6. I would enjoy reading a book titled

_____ A. *Great Theories and Ideas of the Twentieth Century.*	_____ B. *How to Orga-nize Your Life and Accomplish More.*	_____ C. *The Keys to Developing Better Relationships.*	_____ D. *Tapping into Your Creative Genius.*

7. I believe the most valuable information for making decisions comes from

_____ A. logical analysis of facts.	_____ B. what has worked in the past.	_____ C. gut feelings.	_____ D. my imagination.

8. I am persuaded by an argument that

_____ A. offers statisti-cal or factual proof.	_____ B. presents the findings of recognized experts.	_____ C. is passionately presented by someone I admire.	_____ D. explores inno-vative possibilities for future change.

9. I prefer a teacher who

_____ A. lectures knowl-edgeably about the important facts and the-ories of the subject.	_____ B. provides practi-cal, step-by-step, hands-on activities with clear learning objectives.	_____ C. stimulates exciting class discus-sions and group projects.	_____ D. challenges me to think for myself and explore the subject in my own way.

10. People who know me would describe me as

| _____ A. logical. | _____ B. practical. | _____ C. emotional. | _____ D. creative. |

Total your 10 scores for each letter and record them below:

| _____ A. THINKING | _____ B. DOING | _____ C. FEELING | _____ D. INNOVATING |

Your scores suggest the following:

30–40	**You have a strong preference to learn this way.**
20–29	**You are capable of learning this way when necessary.**
10–19	**You avoid this way of learning.**

Note: These questions are for educational self-assessment purposes only and do not have any affiliation with the HBDI or any other tests or assessments.

successful learning than a less-preferred learning experience. For a quick understanding of learning preferences, recall the last time you learned a new video game or assembled something with a number of parts. Some people prefer to start playing or assembling immediately. They dive right in. Other people prefer to read the directions first. Only after they digest the written information do they start playing or assembling. Notice that you could approach these learning tasks either way, but you *prefer* one learning experience over the other.

Although there is no preferred way for everyone to learn, there is a preferred way or ways for *you* to learn. Your scores on the self-assessment indicate your order of preference for four different learning approaches: THINKING, DOING, FEELING, and INNOVATING. More specifically, your scores suggest what types of questions motivate you, how you prefer to gather relevant information, and how you prefer to process information to discover meaningful answers.

Traditional college teaching is characterized by lectures and textbook assignments. These learning experiences typically favor the learning preference of Thinkers, and, to a somewhat lesser degree, Doers. However, as more instructors discover the importance of learning preferences, many are adapting their teaching methods to help all learners maximize their academic potential.

As you might guess, you're bound to get instructors whose teaching methods don't match your learning preference(s). When you do, experiment with some of the suggestions that follow. Perhaps most important of all, develop flexibility in how you learn. The more choices you have, the richer your learning experience will be and the greater your success.

Knowledge of our brain dominance empowers us as individuals and groups to achieve more of our full potential.

Ned Herrmann

In the Table that follows, you'll discover how Thinkers, Doers, Feelers, and Innovators prefer to learn. You may want to start by reading the section about your own learning preference(s), based on your self-assessment score. There you'll find options to use when your instructors don't teach as you prefer to learn. By looking at the other learning preferences as well, you'll see additional ways to expand your menu of effective learning strategies. Your goal here is to find deep-processing strategies that are compatible with and supportive of your preferred way(s) of learning as well as to expand your ability to learn in many ways.

Highly effective learners realize that not all instructors will create the kind of learning experiences they prefer. They take responsibility for not only *what* they learn but also *how* they learn it. They are confident that, with smart studying and persistence, their brains are up to the task. They discover deep-processing methods that maximize their learning, regardless of the subject or the way the instructor teaches.

> Education is our passport to the future, for tomorrow belongs to the people who prepare for it today. . . . Give your brain as much attention as you do your hair and you'll be a thousand times better off.
>
> Malcolm X

> Young cat, if you keep your eyes open enough, oh, the stuff you would learn! The most wonderful stuff!
>
> Dr. Seuss

JOURNAL ENTRY 25

In this activity, you will apply what you have learned about your preferred ways of learning to improve your results in a challenging course.

❶ **Write about the most challenging course you are taking this semester.** Using what you just learned about how you prefer to learn, explain why the course may be difficult for you: Consider the subject matter, the teaching methods of the instructor, the textbook, and any other factors that may contribute to making this course difficult for someone with your preferred ways of learning. (If you are not taking a challenging course this semester, write about the most challenging course you have taken at any time in your education.)

❷ **Using what you now know about the way you prefer to learn, write about choices you can make that will help you learn this challenging subject more easily.** Refer to the table comparison of Thinking Learners, Doing Learners, Feeling Learners, and Innovating Learners for possible choices.

By choosing different ways of learning in a challenging course, you can avoid the excusing, blaming, and complaining of a Victim and apply the solution-oriented approach of a Creator.

	Thinking Learners	Doing Learners	Feeling Learners	Innovating Learners
Motivating questions that energize	**"What?" questions** *What theory supports that claim? What does a statistical analysis show? What is the logic here? What facts do you have? What have experts written about this?*	**"How?" questions** *How does this work? How can I use this? How will this help me or others? How did this work in the past? How can I do this more efficiently? How do experts do this?*	**"Why?" or "Who?" questions** *Why do I want or need to know this subject? Who is going to teach me? Who is going to learn this with me? Why do they want to know this information? Who here cares about me? Whom here do I care about?*	**"What if?" or "What else?" questions** *What if I tried doing this another way? What else could I do with this? What if the situation were different? What is this similar to?*
Preferred ways of gathering information	• enjoy pondering facts and theories • learn well from instructors who present information with lectures, visual aids, and PowerPoint slides; instructor-modeled problem solving; textbook readings; independent library research; and activities that call upon logical skills, such as debates • benefit from time to reflect on what they are learning	• enjoy taking action • learn well from instructors who present factual information and practical skills in a step-by-step, logical manner; who present models or examples from experts in the field; and who allow students to do hands-on work in guided labs or practice applications • benefit from the opportunity to dive right in and do the work	• enjoy personal connections and an emotionally supportive environment • learn well from instructors who are warm and caring; who value feelings as well as thoughts; and who create a safe, accepting classroom atmosphere with activities such as group work, role-playing, and sharing of individual experiences • benefit from an opportunity to relate personally with both their instructors and classmates	• enjoy imagining new possibilities and making unexpected connections • learn well from instructors who encourage students to discover new and innovative applications; who allow students to use their intuition to create something new; and who use approaches such as independent projects, flexible rules and deadlines, and a menu of optional assignments, metaphors, art projects, and visual aids • benefit from the freedom to work independently and let their imaginations run free
Preferred ways of processing information	• respect logical arguments supported by documented facts and data • are uncomfortable with answers that depend on tradition, emotion, personal considerations, or intuition • excel at analyzing, dissecting, figuring out, and using logic to arrive at reasoned answers	• honor objective testing of an idea or theory, whether their own or an expert's • are uncomfortable with answers based on abstract theories, emotion, personal considerations, or intuition • excel at being unbiased, taking action and observing outcomes, following procedures, and using confirmed facts to arrive at reasoned answers	• honor their emotions and seek answers that are personally meaningful • are uncomfortable with answers based on abstract theories or dispassionate facts and data • excel at responding to emotional currents in groups, empathizing with others, considering others' feelings in making decisions, and using empathy	• honor personal imagination and intuition • are uncomfortable with answers based on abstract theories, cold facts, hard data, emotion, or personal considerations • excel at trusting their inner vision, their intuitive sense of novel and exciting possibilities, and their imaginations

▶

	Thinking Learners	Doing Learners	Feeling Learners	Innovating Learners
	• like well-organized and well-documented information • benefit from deep-processing strategies that bring order to complex information, such as creating outlines or comparison charts	• appreciate well-organized and well-documented information • benefit from deep-processing strategies that bring order to complex information, such as creating flow charts or a model of the concepts to be learned	and gut feelings to arrive at personally relevant answers	
When your instructor doesn't teach to your preferred style *What you can do:*	• Construct important "What?" questions and search for their answers in class sessions and homework assignments. • Construct and answer other types of questions your instructor might ask: How? Who? Why? What if? • Read all of your textbook assignments carefully, creating well-organized notes that identify the key points. • Resist getting upset if your instructor asks you to work in groups or has students do some of the teaching. • Organize your lecture and reading notes in a logical fashion, using outlines and comparison charts wherever appropriate. • Study with classmates who have different preferred ways of learning from your own, as they may provide insights about how to learn best from your instructor's teaching style.	• Construct important "How?" questions and search for their answers. • Construct and answer other types of questions your instructor might ask: What? Who? Why? What if? • Practice using the course information or skills outside of class. • Find someone who uses the course information or skills in his or her work and shadow that person for a day or more. • Resist getting upset if your instructor seems more interested in theories than in application. • Organize your lecture and reading notes in a step-by-step fashion, using outlines and comparison charts wherever appropriate. • Study with classmates who have preferred ways of learning different from your own, as they may provide insights into how to learn best from your instructor's teaching style.	• Construct important "Who?" and "Why?" questions and search for their answers. • Construct and answer other types of questions your instructor might ask: What? How? What if? • Discover the value of this subject for you personally. • Organize your notes and study materials using concept maps. • Resist feeling upset if your instructor seems distant or aloof. • Practice using the course information or skill with people in your life. • Make friends with classmates and discuss the subject with them outside of class. • Record class sessions (with permission) and listen to the recordings during free time. • Study with classmates who have different preferred ways of learning from your own, as they may provide insights into how to learn best from your instructor's teaching style. • Teach what you are learning to someone else.	• Construct important "What if?" and "What else?" questions and search for their answers. • Construct and answer other types of questions your instructor might ask: What? How? Who? Why? • Resist feeling upset when your instructor or classmates don't immediately see something as you do. • Organize your notes and study materials using concept maps and personally meaningful symbols or pictures. • Think about the content creatively (how could I adapt this?) and metaphorically (what is this like?). • Study with classmates who have different preferred ways of learning from your own, as they may provide insights into how to learn best from your instructor's teaching style.

Ask your instructor to do the following:

Thinking Learners	Doing Learners	Feeling Learners	Innovating Learners
• Answer your important "What?" questions in class or in a conference. • List important points on the board or on handouts. • Provide handouts of PowerPoint presentations. • Allow students time to answer discussion questions in writing before answering them aloud. • Suggest additional readings, especially those written by recognized authorities in the subject. • Provide examples of past test questions. • Demonstrate the step-by-step solution of a math or science problem. • Provide data or other objective evidence that supports theories presented.	• Answer your important "How?" questions in class or in a conference. • Explain practical applications for theories taught in the course. • Provide a visual model of the concept (such as the Scripts Model in Chapter 6). • List important steps on the board or on handouts. • Demonstrate the information or skill in a step-by-step manner. • Invite guest speakers who can explain real-world application of the course information or skill in their daily work. • Observe and give corrective feedback as you demonstrate your hands-on understanding of the subject.	• Answer your important "Who?" and "Why?" questions in class or in a conference. • Explain how you might make a personal application of the course information. • Meet with your instructor outside of class, perhaps for tutoring, so you can get to know one another better and feel more comfortable in the class. • Provide occasional opportunities for small-group activities within the classroom. • Tell stories about how he or she (or someone else) has personally used the information or skills taught in the course. • Let you do some of the course assignments with a partner or in a group. • Allow students time to talk in pairs about discussion questions before answering them in front of the whole class.	• Answer your important "What if?" and "What else?" questions in class or in a conference. • Allow you to design some of your own assignments for the course. • Use visual aids to explain concepts in class. • Recommend a book for you to read by the most innovative or rebellious thinker in the field. • Evaluate your learning with essays and independent projects rather than with objective tests.

© Cengage Learning

MELISSA THOMPSON, *Madison Area Technical College, Wisconsin*

The challenge for me was chemistry. In lecture, the words were coming at me but the material wasn't sticking. The teacher was dry, standoffish, and intimidating, and he never joked around. I could read the book, reread it, and still wonder what I had just read. I was so frustrated because I needed to pass chemistry to get into my major. Realizing this, I was spending 10 to 12 hours a week studying, and I even started a study group and got a tutor. With all this help, I was doing fine on the homework, but the tests were killing me. I would take one look at them and my mind would go blank. I was stressed and so tempted to drop the course.

About that time I took the self-assessment in *On Course* about how I prefer to learn. I scored highest as a *feeling* learner, with *doing* learner second. I learned it's important for me to relate well personally with my instructors and classmates. Also, I want to see and touch what I'm learning, and I'm not comfortable with abstract theories and dispassionate facts. BINGO! The light went on. My favorite subjects in high school were classes like art and English where I could be creative and hands-on. My favorite teacher was my art teacher, a kind, caring person who told lots of stories that related art to lessons in life. Now I'm in chemistry, which is exactly the type of subject I'm uncomfortable with, and I have a professor who is distant and intimidating. I knew what I had to do, and I probably wouldn't have done it before taking my College Success class.

I asked my chemistry instructor if I could stay after class to talk with him. I explained what I had discovered about my learning preference and why I was so challenged by chemistry. He agreed to meet with me after every class. During lecture, I'd write questions in the margins of my notes or leave a space wherever I got lost. I'd also highlight things in my book that I didn't understand. Going over my questions with him after class was helpful because everything was fresh in my mind. He would take my questions and answer them in different ways than he had in class. Then I would tell him what I thought he was saying and he would coach me until I had it right. Once I got to know him, I realized he was actually very friendly and helpful. He's a quiet person, but I could tell how much he loves chemistry. Before, when I walked into class, I felt intimidated, but before long I felt more comfortable.

Soon after these meetings started, my grades began to come up. I was retaining the information and it showed. I worked hard, and in the end I did pass chemistry. If I hadn't found out about my learning preference and done something different, I don't think I would have passed. My professor is definitely a "thinker," and he handles things so differently than I do. Once I understood the situation, though, I knew I had to step up and be in control of my life, and I did.

Employing Critical Thinking

FOCUS QUESTIONS   How can you determine the truth in this complex and confusing world? How can you present your truths in a way that is logical and persuasive to others?

Imagine this: While deciding what classes to take next semester, you decide to register for Psychology 101. After checking the various times it will be offered, you're delighted to discover that one section of the course fits perfectly into your schedule. The instructor is Professor Skinner. Because two of your friends are taking the course with Professor Skinner this semester, you wisely ask for their opinions.

One friend says, "Dr. Skinner is terrible. Don't even think about taking his course!" But your second friend says, "Dr. Skinner is the best instructor I've ever had! You should definitely take his class." Darn. Now what do you do?

Before deciding, you'd be smart to apply some critical thinking. The term "critical" derives from the Greek word *kritikos,* which means having the ability to understand or decide by using sound judgment. Critical thinking helps us better understand our complex world, make wise choices, and create more of our desired outcomes and experiences. Because they know the importance of critical thinking in many realms of life, most college educators place it high on the list of skills they want their students to master.

Here's good news. You've already been using a powerful critical thinking skill—the Wise Choice Process. As you've experienced, thoughtfully answering the six questions of the Wise Choice Process guides you through the steps of identifying options, looking at likely outcomes, and choosing the best option(s) available at the time. Making wise choices, then, is a key use of critical thinking.

In addition, critical thinking helps in another important realm: constructing and analyzing persuasive arguments. Think of the countless times others have tried to persuade you to think or do something: *Mathematics is a fascinating subject* (think this), *Let me copy your chemistry notes* (do that), *Global warming is a huge threat* (think this), *Major in accounting* (do that), *My roommate is so inconsiderate* (think this), *Go to graduate school* (do that). And, of course, you're doing the same to them. Think this . . . do that.

Thus, much of life is a mental tug-of-war. Efforts to influence others' thoughts and actions lie at the heart of most human interaction, from conversations to wars. Think this . . . do that. It's no wonder the quality of your life is so greatly affected by your ability to construct and analyze persuasive arguments. You can even use these skills to decide whether or not to register for Professor Skinner's Psychology 101 class.

> Higher-order thinking, critical thinking abilities, are increasingly crucial to success in every domain of personal and professional life.
>
> Richard Paul

CONSTRUCTING LOGICAL ARGUMENTS

At many colleges, entire courses, even majors, are devoted to the study of argumentation. Here, we'll focus on two skills that are essential to the construction and analysis of persuasive arguments. The first skill is the ability to **construct a *logical* argument**. Three components of a logical argument are (1) reasons, (2) evidence, and (3) conclusions. As the building blocks of a logical argument, these ingredients may be offered in any order. Suppose, for example, someone wants to convince you to participate in your college's Sophomore Year Abroad Program. Here's how she might present her argument: *You should apply for our college's Sophomore Year Abroad Program. It'll change your life. I read an article in our college newspaper about the Sophomore Year Abroad Program. The author surveyed students who have completed the program, and 80 percent rated their experience as "life-changing."*

> Intelligence is something we are born with. Thinking is a skill that must be learned.
>
> Edward de Bono

Here's what this argument looks like when organized by its components:

1. **Reasons** (also called *premises, claims,* or *assumptions*) answer the question "Why?" Reasons explain why the audience should think or do something. Reasons are presented as true, but they may not be.	**Why?** *The Sophomore Year Abroad Program will change your life.*
2. **Evidence** (also called *support*) answers the question "How do you know?" Evidence provides support to explain how the persuader knows the reason(s) to be true. Evidence should be verifiable as true. Three common kinds of evidence are facts, data, and stories.	**How Do I Know?** *I read an article in our college newspaper about the Sophomore Year Abroad Program. The author surveyed students who have completed the program, and 80 percent rated their experience as "life-changing."*
3. **Conclusions** (also called *opinions, beliefs,* or *positions*) answer the question "What?" Conclusions state what the persuader wants the audience to think or do.	**What Should You Think Or Do?** *You should apply for our college's Sophomore Year Abroad Program.*

The problem with many youngsters today is not that they don't have opinions but that they don't have the facts on which to base their opinions.

Albert Shanker

© Cengage Learning

ASKING PROBING QUESTIONS

Essential to analyzing a logical argument is a second critical thinking skill: **asking probing questions**. A probing question exposes conclusions built on unsound reasons, flawed evidence, and faulty logic. Probing questions are the kind that a good lawyer, doctor, educator, parent, detective, lover, shopper, or friend asks to expose a hidden truth. The following chart lists some of the questions that critical thinkers might ask of any persuasive argument. Asking and answering these questions (and others) can help you both construct powerful arguments of your own and analyze the arguments of others.

Always the beautiful answer who asks a more beautiful question.

e.e. cummings

Questions About Reasons	Sample Probing Questions
• What reasons have been offered to support the conclusion? • Based on your experience and knowledge, do the reasons make sense? • Did the reasons derive from careful reflection and logical thinking, or are they misguided beliefs or prejudices? • Are there important exceptions to the reason? • Are the definitions of all key terms clear? • Are strong emotions being substituted for reasons?	• *When your brother studied for a year in Australia, was the experience life-changing for him?* • *What did the students mentioned in the newspaper article mean by "life-changing"?* • *Does it seem likely that such a program would change my life?* • *Do I even want to change my life?*

Questions About Evidence	Sample Probing Questions
• Is the source of the evidence reliable? • Is the evidence true? • Is the evidence objective and unbiased? • Is the evidence relevant? • Is the evidence current? • Is there enough evidence? • Does contradictory evidence exist? • Is the evidence complete?	• *Could the group of students polled have been specially selected to support the author's point of view about the Sophomore Year Abroad Program?* • *Does the person persuading me stand to gain if I choose to participate in the program?* • *Were enough students polled to make their results significant?* • *What percent of students from all previous Sophomore Year Abroad groups rated the experience as "life-changing"?*
Questions About Conclusions	**Sample Probing Questions**
• Why? • Is the conclusion logical, or are there errors in the reasoning? • Could a different conclusion be drawn from the same reasons and/or evidence?	• *Could there be another cause for the students' life-changing experiences besides the Sophomore Year Abroad Program?* • *Did the students who rated their experience as "life-changing" have anything else in common that might have been the cause of their life-changing outcome instead of the program?* • *Is the program today the same program that changed the lives of students in the survey?*

© Cengage Learning

> The real value of learning lies in answering questions and questioning answers.
>
> Marty Grothe

APPLYING CRITICAL THINKING

Let's observe these critical thinking skills in action. Listen in as two students debate their conclusions about the biology professor described in "A Fish Story" (the case study that opens this chapter). Note how they explain the reasons and evidence that lead them to their conclusions. And watch as each uses probing questions to challenge the argument of the other.

> Education must enable one to sift and weigh evidence, to discern the true from the false, the real from the unreal, and the facts from the fiction. The function of education, therefore, is to teach one to think intensively and to think critically.
>
> Martin Luther King

Emiko: I rated the biology professor as "terrible." I'd hate to have him as my instructor. **[Conclusion]**

Frank: Why? **[Probing question]**

Emiko: Are you kidding? College instructors are called "professors" for a reason. They're paid to "profess," and to profess means to *tell.* Professors are supposed to be the experts, so their job is to *tell* students what they need to know. **[Reason]**

Frank: Of course college instructors need to be experts in their subject. But is it really their job to tell students what they need to know? **[Probing question]** I think an instructor's job is to help students learn to think for themselves, not just memorize facts. **[Reason]** I'd love to have an instructor like that. I rated him as "excellent." **[Conclusion]**

Emiko: In the whole first week of the class, all he did was give his students a fish and then leave the room. **[Evidence]** Don't you think an instructor has a responsibility to at least be in the room? **[Probing question]**

Frank: The issue isn't whether the instructor was in the room. The issue is whether he was helping students learn. **[Reason]** The biology instructor did a lot more than give his students a fish and leave the room. He asked students to observe the fish and write down everything they observed. That request got them actively engaged in thinking like biologists on the first day of the course. **[Evidence]** In my opinion, that makes him an excellent instructor. **[Conclusion]**

Emiko: If a professor wants to get students actively engaged in their education, that's fine. But an instructor shouldn't frustrate and make students anxious on their very first day in college. Good instructors make their students feel comfortable. **[Reason]** Look at how anxious they were while waiting for the professor to return. They had no clue what was going on. **[Evidence]** That's why I think this instructor is terrible. **[Conclusion]**

Frank: Maybe the students were a bit anxious, but isn't that a good thing? **[Probing question]** Sometimes we need to be a little uncomfortable to learn something. **[Reason]** The best teacher I ever had in high school made everyone in the class uncomfortable by firing questions at us as fast as she could, especially at people who weren't paying attention or hadn't done the homework. I learned more in that class than in all my other high school classes combined. **[Evidence]** I would rather get a C from a professor who makes me think than get an A from a professor who simply feeds me answers to put on a test. **[Reason]**

Emiko: You wouldn't think that way if you wanted to be a doctor like I do. If I get a couple of Cs, I can pretty much forget about getting into a good medical school. **[Reason]** That's why I would avoid this professor like the plague. He's terrible! **[Conclusion]**

Although their arguments aren't airtight, these students deserve credit for using critical thinking skills. They are clearly making an effort to provide reasons and evidence to support their conclusions. Additionally, they're asking probing questions about each other's reasons, evidence, and conclusions. Like all critical thinkers, they are respectful skeptics.

To some, it may appear that the purpose of critical thinking is to win arguments. Although critical thinking can certainly do that, it actually has a loftier goal. Critical thinking helps us seek the truth. That's why, to be an effective critical thinker, you must be willing to abandon your position whenever you find another view that is a better explanation of reality. The ultimate goal of a critical thinker is not victory, then, but learning.

JOURNAL ENTRY / **26**

1 **Return to the beginning of this section where you were asked to imagine getting contradictory opinions about Dr. Skinner, the Psychology 101 instructor. Make a list of at least 10 probing questions you could ask your two friends to help you find the "truth" and make a wise choice about whether or not to take Dr. Skinner's class.** Your questions should probe their reasons, their evidence, and their conclusions. Among others, consider asking questions that use your knowledge of learning preferences.

2 **Write a logical argument that explains which character you think is most responsible for the group's grade of D in the case study "Professor Rogers's Trial" (found at the beginning of Chapter 5).** Be sure to state clearly your conclusion (who is most responsible), your reasons for this conclusion, and evidence from the case study to support your reasons. For example, your journal might begin, *I think the person most responsible for the group's grade of D is . . . The first reason I think this is . . . The evidence in the case study shows that . . . A second reason I think this person is most responsible is . . .* and so on.

Education's purpose is to replace an empty mind with an open one.

Malcolm S. Forbes

LIFELONG LEARNING / **at Work**

The intellectual equipment needed for the job of the future is an ability to define problems, quickly assimilate relevant data, conceptualize and reorganize the information, make deductive and inductive leaps with it, ask hard questions about it, discuss findings with colleagues, work collaboratively to find solutions and then convince others.

Robert B. Reich, former U.S. Secretary of Labor

Some students believe that once they graduate from college they'll finally be finished with studying and learning. In fact, a college diploma is merely a ticket into the huge University of Work. In one recent year, U.S. employers spent more than 55 billion dollars for employee training, according to the American Society for Training and Development.

Continuing education in the workplace includes instruction in hard skills, such as mastering a new product line, a computer system,

▶

SEEKING CREATORS

Candidates must demonstrate a commitment to lifelong learning, strong critical thinking skills, and the ability to adapt to new challenges.

or government regulations. Companies also offer their employees instruction in many of the same soft skills that you're learning in *On Course,* skills such as listening, setting goals, and managing your time and work projects. In fact, soft skills are in such demand in the workplace today that top training consultants charge many thousands of dollars *per day* to teach these skills to employees of American businesses.

Smart workers take full advantage of the formal classes provided by their employers. They also take full advantage of the informal classes provided by the University of Life. In this university, you have the opportunity to learn from every experience you have, especially those on the job. Lifelong learners aren't devastated by a setback, such as having a project crumble or even losing their job. They learn from their experiences and come back stronger and wiser than ever. A report by the Center for Creative Leadership compared executives whose careers got off course with those who did well. Although both groups had weaknesses, the critical difference was this: Executives who did *not* learn from their mistakes and shortcomings tended to fail at work. By contrast, those executives who *did* learn the valuable lessons taught by their mistakes and failures tended to rebound and resume successful careers.

Your work-world learning begins as soon as you get serious about finding your ideal job. Unless you're sure about your career path, you'll have much research to do. Even if you do feel sure about your career choice, further research might lead to something even better. More than 20,000 occupations and 40,000 job titles exist today, and you'll want to identify careers that match the personal talents and interests you identified in your self-assessment.

Your college's library or career center probably has a number of great resources to learn about careers. For example, computerized programs such as SIGI PLUS, CHOICES, and CIS may be available to explore thousands of career possibilities. Helpful books include the *Dictionary of Occupational Titles* (DOT), which offers brief descriptions of several thousand occupations; *The Guide for Occupational Exploration* (GOE), another source of occupational options; and the latest edition of the *Occupational Outlook Handbook* (OOH), which provides information about the demand for various occupations. With these resources, you can learn important facts about careers you may never have heard of, including the nature of the work, places of employment, training and qualifications required, earnings, working conditions, and employment outlook. Keep in mind that in today's fast-paced world, occupations will be available when you graduate that don't even exist today.

Ned Herrmann, creator of the Brain Dominance Inventory, wrote, "Experience has shown that alignment of a person's mental preferences with his or her work is predictive of success and satisfaction while nonalignment usually results in poor performance and dissatisfaction." So use your discoveries in this chapter about your learning preferences to help you choose a compatible career. See Figure 7.1 for some examples.

When you have narrowed your career choices, you may want to learn even more before committing yourself. To get the inside scoop on how a career may fit you, get some hands-on experience.

▶

A. Thinking Learner: biologist, stock broker, engineer, city manager, science teacher, computer designer/programmer, computer technician, detective, educational administrator, radiologist, electrical engineer, financial planner, lawyer, chemist, mathematician, medical researcher, physician, statistician, veterinarian

B. Doing Learner: reporter, accountant, librarian, bookkeeper, clinical psychologist, credit advisor, historian, environmental scientist, farmer, hotel/motel manager, marketing director, military personnel, police officer, realtor, school principal, technical writer

C. Feeling Learner: actor, social worker, clergy, sociologist, counseling psychologist, human resource manager, public relations specialist, journalist, musician, teacher, nurse, occupational therapist, organizational development consultant, recreational therapist, sales, writer

D. Innovating Learner: dancer, poet, advertising designer, florist, psychiatrist, artist, creative writer, entrepreneur, fashion artist, playwright, filmmaker, graphic designer, humorist, inventor, landscape architect, nutritionist, photographer, editor, program developer

FIGURE 7.1   Learning Preferences and Compatible Careers

Find part-time or temporary work in the field, apply for an internship, or even do volunteer work. At one time I thought I wanted to be a veterinarian, but one summer of working in a veterinary hospital quickly taught me that it was a poor career match for me. I'm sure glad I found out *before* I went through many years of veterinary school!

Now it's time for your job interviews. Keep in mind that most employers are looking for someone who can learn the new position and keep learning new skills for years to come. In fact, a recent U.S. Department of Labor study found that employers of entry-level workers considered specific technical skills less important than the ability to learn on the job. So, how can you present yourself in the interview as a lifelong learner? First, of course, have a transcript with good grades to demonstrate your ability to learn in college. Be ready for questions such as, "How do you keep up with advancements in your field? What workshops or seminars have you attended? What kind of reading do you do?" Go to the interview prepared to ask good questions of your own. And demonstrate

that one of the things you're looking for in a particular job is its ability to help you keep learning your profession.

Today's work world is marked by downsizing and rightsizing. Companies are operating with leaner staffs, and this means that every employee is critical to the success of the business. It also means that someone who can't keep up with inevitable changes is expendable. One powerful way to give yourself a competitive advantage is to continually learn new skills and knowledge, even before you need them on your job. When your supervisor says, "Does anyone here know how to use a desktop publishing program?" you'll be able to say, "Sure, I can do that." Another way to keep learning on the job is to seek out feedback. Superior performers want to hear what others think of their work, realizing that this is a great way to learn to do it even better.

According to Anthony J. D'Angelo, author of the *College Blue Book,* world knowledge doubles every 14 months. Suppose he's way off, and knowledge actually doubles only every five years, as others claim. That still means we'll have to keep

▶

"Even though you're exceptionally well qualified, Kate, I'd say that 'victim' is not a good career choice."

learning a little every day just to keep pace and a lot every day to get ahead. Educator Marshall McLuhan once said, "The future of work consists of *learning* a living (rather than *earning* a living)." His observation becomes truer with each passing day. Future success at work belongs to lifelong learners.

TECH TIPS: Lifelong Learning

Mindsetonline.com is the website of Carol Dweck, originator of the theory of Fixed and Growth Mindsets. Click on the link "Test Your Mindset." Then complete the 16-item online quiz and get immediate results. *(Web)*

Mindsetworks.com offers four assessments related to mindset. As a student, you'll be most interested in the first one: "What's My Mindset?" (for 12 to Adult). This quiz has only eight questions and can be completed in a few minutes. The site also has a couple of videos about fixed and growth mindsets. *(Web)*

VARK-learn.com is an online self-assessment that provides you with information about your "learning style." Is your preference Visual (seeing), Auditory (listening), Read/Write, or Kinesthetic (physically moving)? As with the learning inventory in this chapter, you would be best served by seeing your results on the VARK as indicating a preference for certain learning activities but not an inability to learn in other ways. *(Web)*

Develop Self-Respect

> **FOCUS QUESTIONS**   What is your present level of self-respect? How can you raise your self-respect, and therefore your self-esteem, even higher?

Self-respect is the core belief that I AM AN ADMIRABLE PERSON. If self-confidence is the result of **what** I do, then self-respect is the result of **how** I do it.

Two crucial choices that build up or tear down my self-respect are whether or not I live with integrity and whether or not I keep my commitments.

LIVE WITH INTEGRITY (I.E., NO CHEATING OR PLAGIARIZING)

The foundation of integrity is my personal value system. What is important to me? What experiences do I want to have? What experiences do I want others to have? Do I prize outer rewards such as cars, clothes, compliments, travel, fame, or money? Do I cherish inner experiences such as love, respect, excellence, security, honesty, wisdom, or compassion?

Integrity derives from the root word *integer,* meaning "one" or "whole." Thus we create integrity by choosing words and deeds that are one with our values. Many students say they value their education, but their actions indicate otherwise. They leave assignments undone; they do less than their best work; they miss classes; they come late. In short, their choices contradict what they say they value. Choices that lack integrity tear at an aware person's self-respect.

One of my greatest integrity tests occurred during my first year in college. First, a little background. In the public high school I'd attended, cheating was widespread. You could say it was part of the student culture. As for me, I prided myself that I never cheated . . . except in Latin. (Yes, at that time my high school actually offered three levels of Latin.) I knew cheating was wrong, but my Inner Defender was ever ready with excuses: *Everyone cheats. No one uses Latin anymore, so it's a huge waste of time. And if I don't cheat, everyone else will . . . and then my grade will suffer.* I became masterful at writing vocabulary words and verb conjugations on the tiniest pieces of paper imaginable. I got an A. *Mea culpa.*

Now fast-forward to the middle of my first semester in college. All of us were preparing for midterm exams. My Inner Critic, you may recall, had convinced me that I was in serious danger of failing out of college. Every one of my classmates, I believed, was smarter and better

Always aim at complete harmony of thought and word and deed.

Mohandas K. Gandhi

If you want to be respected by others, the great thing is to respect yourself. Only by that, only by self-respect will you compel others to respect you.

Fyodor Dostoyevsky

The willingness to accept responsibility for one's own life is the source from which self-respect springs.

Joan Didion

This above all; to thine own self be true

And it must follow, as the night the day

Thou canst not then be false to any man.

Polonius, in Shakespeare's Hamlet

prepared than I was. They had read books I hadn't even *heard* of. They had completed courses my high school didn't even *offer*. They could probably talk intelligently about ancient Rome ... in *Latin*. If I was going to survive in college, I decided, I would have to cheat. As I studied for midterms, I created some of the finest crib notes on planet Earth.

However, I was in for a jolt. When I arrived at my first college exam, the professor told us to write and sign the following statement on the front of our exam booklets: "I pledge my honor that I have neither given nor received assistance on this examination." And then he left the room!

Talk about a fork in the road! There I was with all of my cleverly miniaturized crib notes and (A) I had just signed a promise that I would not use them and (B) there was no instructor present to catch me if I did. Drat. What to do?

Academic integrity is another aspect of the deep culture of higher education. Chances are, your college has a written policy or honor code that upholds the value of academic honesty and condemns cheating. You'll find it in your college's catalog or on its website. Here's part of one from Amherst College: ... *the College considers it a violation of the requirements of intellectual responsibility to submit work that is not one's own or otherwise to subvert the conditions under which academic work is performed by oneself or by others.*

Academic dishonesty, the Amherst policy explains, *refers to any act that is intended to produce an academic assessment that is not commensurate with an individual's performance, or any act that is intended to unfairly assist or hinder an individual's academic efforts.* Because one of the purposes of higher education is to seek truth, stamping out cheating seems like a good idea.

So, you might wonder, how's the "stamping out" going? If you do a Google search for "academic integrity," you'll get more than 5,930,000 results. Clearly a hot topic. Donald McCabe, a professor at Rutgers University, has studied this topic for years. He surveyed 1,800 students from nine universities. Seventy percent of them admitted to cheating on exams, while 84 percent said they cheated on assignments. Educational Testing Service (ETS) reports that one website that sells term papers averages about 80,000 hits *per day*. Ironically, I found one such website that offers a choice of 60 term papers for sale on the topic of academic integrity. In other words, you can cheat by buying a paper that condemns cheating.

So, it would appear that many students cheat. Why not join them? Here are three, among many, reasons.

First, let's be practical. You might get caught. Because cheating is so widespread, educators are combating it in many ways. For example, just as there are websites for students to buy term papers, there are websites where instructors can check to see if a term paper has ever been turned in before. How about consequences? Better check your college's penalties for cheating. They can range from failing the test or assignment, to failing the course, or even to being expelled. Some colleges note the infraction on a student's transcript, a chilling message to all future employers.

Second, you'll learn more. If you're in college only to get a degree and what you learn doesn't matter, you might not care—that is, until you're in a job and need some of the skills you were supposed to learn in that course you cheated your way through. If you're a nursing student, I sure hope I never come under your care. If you're an engineering student, I sure hope I never drive over one of your bridges.

Finally, your self-respect will increase. At least that's what I experienced. You see, at my first college midterm exam many years ago, I decided not to cheat. My first thought was, *With the professor gone, it's too easy.* My second thought was, *If I cheat, I'll never know what I'm capable of . . . maybe it's a lot more than I think.* And then I thought, *It would be wrong. Even if no one else ever finds out, I'll know I cheated.* In that moment, at the ripe old age of 18, I decided that the cost of cheating is too high.

Here's what I learned. Each time we contradict our personal values, we make a withdrawal from our self-respect account. Each time we are true to our personal values, we make a deposit. When you find that your choices are out of alignment with your values, you need to make a change . . . for your own sake. You can't abandon what you hold sacred and still retain your self-respect.

KEEP COMMITMENTS

Now let's consider another choice that influences your self-respect. Imagine that someone has made a promise to you but doesn't keep it. Then he makes and breaks a second promise. And then another and another. Wouldn't you lose respect for this person? What do you suppose happens when the person making and breaking all of these promises is YOU?

True, your Inner Defender would quickly send out a smoke screen of excuses. But the truth would not be lost on your Inner Guide. The fact remains: You made commitments and broke them. This violation of your word makes a major withdrawal from your self-respect account.

To make a deposit in your self-respect account, keep commitments, especially to yourself. Here's how:

- **Make your agreements consciously.** Understand exactly what you're committing to. Say "no" to requests that will get you off course; don't commit to more than you can handle just to placate others.

- **Use Creator language.** Don't say, *I'll try to do it.* Say, *I **will** do it.* Or *I **won't** do it.*

- **Make your agreements important.** Write them down. Tell others about them.

- **Create a plan; then do everything in your power to carry out that plan.** Use your self-management tools to track your promises to yourself and others.

- **If a problem arises or you change your mind, renegotiate** (don't just abandon your promise).

> I would prefer even to fail with honor than to win by cheating.
>
> Sophocles

> Whenever I break an agreement, I pay the price first. It breaks down my self-esteem, my credibility with myself, my self-trust, my self-confidence. It causes me not to be able to trust myself. If I cannot trust myself, whom can I trust?
>
> Patricia J. Munson

The person we break commitments with the most is, ironically, ourself. How are you doing in this regard? Here's some evidence: How are you doing with the commitment you made to your goals and dream in Journal Entry 10? How are you doing with your 32-Day Commitment from Journal Entry 14?

If you haven't kept these commitments (or others), ask your Inner Guide, *What did I make more important than keeping my commitment to myself?* A part of you wanted to keep your agreement. But another, stronger part of you obviously resisted. Pursue your exploration of this inner conflict with total honesty and you may uncover a self-defeating pattern or limiting core belief that is crying out for a change. After all, our choices reveal what we *really* value.

Keeping commitments often requires overcoming enormous obstacles. That was the case with one of my students. Rosalie had postponed her dream of becoming a nurse for 18 years while raising her two children alone. Shortly after enrolling in college, her new husband asked her to drop out to take care of his two sons from a former marriage. Rosalie agreed, postponing her dream once more. Now back in college 10 years later, she made what she called a "sacred vow" to attend every class on time, to do her very best on all work, and to participate actively. This time she was committed to getting her nursing degree. Finally her time had come.

Then, one night she got a call from her son, who was now married and had a two-year-old baby girl. He had a serious problem: His wife was on drugs. Worse, that day she had bought $200 worth of drugs on credit, and the drug dealers were holding Rosalie's granddaughter until they got paid. Rosalie spent the early evening gathering cash from every source she could, finally delivering the money to her son. Then, all night she lay awake, waiting to hear if her grandchild would be returned safely.

At six in the morning, Rosalie got good news when her son brought the baby to her house. He asked Rosalie to watch the child while he and his wife had a serious talk. Hours passed, and still Rosalie cared for the baby. Closer and closer crept the hour when her college classes would begin. She started to get angrier and angrier as she realized that once again she was allowing others to pull her off course. And then she remembered that she had a choice. She could stay home and feel sorry for herself, or she could do something to get back on course.

At about nine o'clock, Rosalie called her sister who lived on the other side of town. She asked her sister to take a cab to Rosalie's house, promised to pay the cab fare, and even offered to pay her sister a bonus to watch the baby.

"I didn't get to class on time," Rosalie said. "But I got there. And when I did, I just wanted to walk into the middle of the room and yell, 'YEEAAH! I MADE IT!'"

If you could have seen her face when she told the class about her ordeal and her victory, you would have seen a woman who had just learned one of life's great lessons: When we break a commitment to ourselves, something inside

To me integrity is the bottom line in self-esteem. It begins with the keeping of one's word or doing what you say you will do, when you say you will do it, whether you feel like it or not.

Betty Hatch, president, National Council for Self-Esteem

You will always be in fashion if you are true to yourself, and only if you are true to yourself.

Maya Angelou

of us dies. When we keep a commitment to ourselves, something inside of us thrives. That something is self-respect.

JOURNAL ENTRY / 27

In this activity, you will explore strengthening your self-respect. People with self-respect honor and admire themselves not just for *what* they do but for *how* they do it.

Make a choice—write about one of the following:

(A) **Write about a time when you passed a personal integrity test.** Tell about an experience when you were greatly tempted to abandon one of your important values. Describe how you decided to "do the right thing" instead of giving in to the temptation.

(B) **Write about a time when you kept a commitment that was difficult to keep.** Fully explain the commitment you made to yourself or to someone else, and discuss the challenges—both inner and outer—that made it difficult for you to keep this promise. Explain how you were able to keep the commitment despite these challenges.

Asking probing questions leads to meaningful answers. Anticipate questions a curious reader might ask you about your stories . . . and answer them. For example, what effect did your choice have on your self-esteem?

Character, simply stated, is doing what you say you're going to do. A more formal definition is: Character is the ability to carry out a worthy decision after the emotion of making that decision has passed.

Hyrum W. Smith

Developing Emotional Intelligence

Successful Students . . .

▶ **demonstrate emotional intelligence,** using feelings as a compass for staying on course to their goals and dreams.

▶ **effectively reduce stress,** managing and soothing emotions of upset such as anger, fear, and sadness.

▶ **create happiness,** feeling fully and positively engaged in college and the rest of their lives.

Struggling Students . . .

▶ **allow themselves to be hijacked by emotions,** making unwise choices that get them off course.

▶ **take no responsibility for managing their emotions,** instead acting irrationally on impulses of the moment.

▶ **frequently experience negative emotions** such as boredom and unhappiness.

Creating worldly success is meaningless if I am unhappy. That means I must accept responsibility for creating the quality of not only my outcomes but also my inner experiences.

I create my own happiness and peace of mind.

CASE STUDY IN CRITICAL THINKING / After Math

When **Professor Bishop** returned midterm exams, he said, "In 20 years of teaching math, I've never seen such low scores. Can anyone tell me what the problem is?" He ran a hand through his graying hair and waited. No one spoke. "Don't you people even care how you do?" Students fiddled with their test papers. They looked out of the window. No one spoke.

Finally, Professor Bishop said, "Okay, Scott, we'll start with you. What's going on? You got a 35 on the test. Did you even *study?*"

Scott, age 18, mumbled, "Yeah, I studied. But I just don't understand math."

Other students in the class nodded their heads. One student muttered, "Amen, brother."

Professor Bishop looked around the classroom. "How about you, Elena? You didn't even show up for the test."

Elena, age 31, sighed. "I'm sorry, but I have a lot of other things besides this class to worry about. My job keeps changing my schedule, I broke a tooth last week, my roommate won't pay me the money she owes me, my car broke down, and I haven't been able to find my math book for three weeks. I think my boyfriend hid it. If one more thing goes wrong in my life, I'm going to scream!"

Professor Bishop shook his head slowly back and forth. "Well, that's quite a story. What about the rest of you?" Silence reigned for a full minute.

Suddenly **Michael**, age 23, stood up and snarled, "You're a damn joke, man. You can't teach, and you want to blame the problem on us. Well, I've had it. I'm dropping this stupid course. Then I'm filing a grievance. You better start looking for a new job!" He stormed out of the room, slamming the door behind him.

"Okay, I can see this isn't going anywhere productive," Professor Bishop said. "I want you all to go home and think about why you're doing so poorly. And don't come back until you're prepared to answer that question honestly." He picked up his books and left the room. Elena checked her watch and then dashed out of the room. She still had time to catch her favorite reality show in the student lounge.

An hour later, Michael was sitting alone in the cafeteria when his classmates Scott and **Kia**, age 20, joined him. Scott said, "Geez, Michael, you really

went off on Bishop! You're not really going to drop his class, are you?"

"Already did!" Michael snapped as his classmates sat down. "I went right from class to the registrar's office. I'm outta there!"

I might as well drop the class myself, Kia thought. Ever since she was denied entrance to the nursing program, she'd been too depressed to do her homework. Familiar tears blurred her vision.

Scott said, "I don't know what it is about math. I study for hours, but when I get to the test, I get so freaked it's like I never studied at all. My mind just goes blank." Thinking about math, Scott started craving something to eat.

"Where do you file a grievance against a professor around here, anyway?" Michael asked.

"I have no idea," Scott said.

"What?" Kia answered. She hadn't heard a word that Michael or Scott had said. All she could think about was how her whole life was ruined because she would never be a nurse.

Michael stood and stomped off to file a grievance. Scott went to buy some French fries. Kia put her head down on the cafeteria table and tried to swallow the burning sensation in her throat.

Listed below are the five characters in this story. Rank them in order of their emotional intelligence. Give a different score to each character. Be prepared to explain your choices.

Least emotionally intelligent ▶ ① ② ③ ④ ⑤ ◀ Most emotionally intelligent

___ **Professor Bishop**   ___ **Elena**   ___ **Kia**

___ **Scott**   ___ **Michael**

DIVING DEEPER

Imagine that you have been asked to mentor the person whom you scored a 1 (least emotionally intelligent). Other than recommending a counselor, how would you suggest that this person handle his or her upset in a more emotionally intelligent manner?

Understanding Emotional Intelligence

FOCUS QUESTIONS   What is emotional intelligence? How can you experience the full range of natural human emotions and still stay on course to a rich, fulfilling life?

I know it is hard to accept, but an upset in your life is beneficial, in that it tells you that you are off course in some way and you need to find your way back to your particular path of clarity once again.

Susan Jeffers

During final exam period one semester, I heard a shriek from the nursing education office. Seconds later, a student charged out of the office, screaming, scattering papers in the air, and stumbling down the hall. A cluster of concerned classmates caught up to her and desperately tried to offer comfort. "It's all right. You can take the exam again next semester. It's okay. Really." She leaned against the wall, eyes closed. She slid down the wall until she sat in a limp heap, surrounded by sympathetic voices. Later, I heard that she dropped out of school.

At the end of another semester, I had the unpleasant task of telling one of my hardest working students that she had failed the writing proficiency exams. Her mother had died during the semester, so I was particularly worried about how she would handle more bad news. We had a conference, and upon telling her the news, I began consoling her. For about a minute, she listened quietly and then said, "You're taking my failure pretty hard. Do you need a hug?" Before I could respond, she plucked me out of my chair and gave me a hug. "Don't worry," she said, patting my back "I'll pass next semester," and sure enough, she did.

For most of us, life presents a rough road now and then. We fail a college course. The job we want goes to someone else. The person we love doesn't return our affections. Our health gives way to sickness. How we handle these distressing experiences is critical to the outcomes and experiences of our lives.

Success depends on much more than a high IQ and academic success. Karen Arnold and Terry Denny at the University of Illinois studied 81 valedictorians and salutatorians. They found that 10 years after graduation, only 25 percent of these academic stars were at the highest level of their professions when compared with others their age. Actually, many were doing poorly. What seems to be missing for them is **emotional intelligence**.

In the realm of emotions, many people are functioning at a kindergarten level. There is no need for self-blame. After all, in your formal education, how many courses did you take in dealing with feelings?

Gay & Kathlyn Hendricks

An experiment during the 1960s shows just how important emotional control is to success. Four-year-old children at a preschool were told they could have one marshmallow immediately. Or if they could wait for about 20 minutes, they could have two. More than a dozen years later, experimenters examined the differences in the lives of the one-marshmallow (emotionally impulsive) children and the two-marshmallow (emotionally intelligent) children. The adolescents who as children were able to delay gratification scored an average of 210 points higher on their SATs (Scholastic Aptitude Tests). Additionally, the two-marshmallow teenagers had borne fewer children while unmarried and had experienced fewer problems with the law. Clearly, the ability to endure some emotional discomfort in the present in exchange for greater rewards in the future is a key to success.

FOUR COMPONENTS OF EMOTIONAL INTELLIGENCE

As a relatively new field of study, emotional intelligence is still being defined. However, Daniel Goleman, author of the book *Emotional Intelligence,* identifies four components that contribute to emotional effectiveness. The first two qualities are personal and have to do with recognizing and effectively managing one's own emotions. The second two are social and have to do with recognizing and effectively managing emotions in others.

1. **EMOTIONAL SELF-AWARENESS: Knowing your feelings in the moment.** Self-awareness of one's own feelings as they occur is the foundation of emotional intelligence and is fundamental to effective decision making. Thus, people who are keenly aware of their changing moods are better pilots of their lives. For example, emotional self-awareness helps you deal effectively with feeling overwhelmed instead of using television (or some other distraction) as a temporary escape.

2. **EMOTIONAL SELF-MANAGEMENT: Managing strong feelings.** Emotional self-management enables people to make wise choices despite the pull of powerful emotions. People who excel at this skill avoid making critical decisions during times of high drama. Instead they wait until their inner storm has calmed and then make considered choices that contribute to their desired outcomes and experiences. For example, emotional self-management helps you resist dropping an important class simply because you got angry at the teacher. It also helps you make a choice that offers delayed benefits (e.g., writing a term paper) in place of a choice that promises instant gratification (e.g., attending a party).

3. **SOCIAL AWARENESS: Empathizing accurately with other people's emotions.** Empathy is the fundamental "people skill." Those with empathy and compassion are more attuned to the subtle social signals that reveal what others need or want. For example, social awareness helps you notice and offer comfort when someone is consumed by anxiety or sadness.

4. **RELATIONSHIP MANAGEMENT: Handling emotions in relationships with skill and harmony.** The art of relationships depends, in large part, upon the skill of managing emotions in others. People who excel at skills such as listening, resolving conflicts, cooperating, and articulating the pulse of a group do well at anything that relies on interacting smoothly with others. For example, relationship management helps a person resist saying something that might publicly embarrass someone else.

> Every great, successful person I know shares the capacity to remain centered, clear and powerful in the midst of emotional "storms."
>
> Anthony Robbins

> Academic intelligence has little to do with emotional life. The brightest among us can founder on the shoals of unbridled passions and unruly impulses; people with high IQs can be stunningly poor pilots of their private lives.
>
> Daniel Goleman

Sally Forth. King Features Syndicate.

A common confusion generated by the English language is our use of the word "feel" without actually expressing a feeling. For example in the sentence, "I feel I didn't get a fair deal," the words "I feel" could be more accurately replaced with "I think."

Marshall B. Rosenberg

KNOWING YOUR OWN EMOTIONS

The foundation of emotional intelligence is a keen awareness of our own emotions as they rise and fall. None of the other abilities can exist without this one. Here are some steps toward becoming more attuned to your own emotions.

Build a Vocabulary of Feelings

Learn the names of emotions you might experience. There are hundreds. How many can you name beyond anger, fear, sadness, and happiness?

Be Mindful of Emotions As They Are Happening

Learn to identify and express emotions in the moment. Be aware of the subtleties of emotion, learning to make fine distinctions between feelings that are similar, such as sadness and depression.

Understand What Is Causing Your Emotion

Look behind the emotion. See when anger is caused by hurt feelings. Notice when anxiety is caused by irrational thoughts. Realize when sadness is caused by disappointments. Identify when happiness is caused by immediate gratification that gets you off course from your long-term goals.

Recognize the Difference Between a Feeling and Resulting Actions

In the midst of great joy do not promise to give a man anything; in the midst of great anger do not answer a man's letter.

Chinese proverb

Feeling an emotion is one thing; acting on the emotion is quite another. Emotions and behaviors are separate experiences—one internal, one external. Note when you tend to confuse the two, as a student did who said, "My teacher made me so angry I had to drop the class." You can be angry with a teacher and still remain enrolled in a class that is important to your goals and dreams. A fundamental principle of emotional intelligence is ***Never make an important decision while experiencing strong emotions.***

You will never reach your full potential without emotional intelligence. No matter how academically bright you may be, emotional illiteracy will limit your achievements. Developing emotional wisdom will fuel your motivation, help you successfully negotiate emotional storms (yours and others'), and enhance your chances of creating your greatest goals and dreams.

JOURNAL ENTRY / 28

In this activity, you will explore your ability to understand your own emotions and recognize them as they are occurring. This ability is the foundation for all other emotional intelligence skills.

1 **Write about an experience when you felt one of the following emotions: FRUSTRATION or ANGER, FEAR or ANXIETY, SADNESS or UNHAPPINESS.** Describe fully the cause (what happened) and your emotional reaction. Because emotions are difficult to describe, you may want to try a comparison like this: *Anger spread through me like fire in a pile of dry hay. . . .* or *I trembled in fear as though I was the next person to stand before a firing squad,* or *For two days, unhappiness wrapped me in a profound darkness.* Of course, create your own comparison. Your journal entry might begin, *Last week was one of the most frustrating times of my entire life. It all began when . . .* Most important, be aware of any emotions that you may feel *as* you are writing.

2 **Write about an experience when you felt HAPPINESS or JOY.** Once again, describe fully the cause (what happened) and your emotional reaction. A possible comparison: *Joy bubbled like champagne, and I laughed uncontrollably.* Most important, be aware of any emotions that you may feel *as* you are writing.

3 **Write about any emotional changes you experienced as you described each of these two emotions. What did you learn or relearn about how you can affect your emotions?** If you weren't aware of any changes in your present emotions as you described past emotions, see if you can explain why. Were you not experiencing any emotions at all? Or could you have been unaware of the emotions you were feeling?

It made me feel better sometimes to get something down on paper just like I felt it. It brought a kind of relief to be able to describe my pain. It was like, if I could describe it, it lost some of its power over me. I jotted down innermost thoughts I couldn't verbalize to anyone else, recorded what I saw around me, and expressed feelings inspired by things I read.

Nathan McCall

ONE STUDENT'S STORY

LINDSEY BECK, *Three Rivers Community College, Connecticut*

When I started college, I had been in an abusive relationship for almost three years. I was terrified to leave this man (I'll call him Henry) because we have a child together and he had convinced me that I had no worth as a human being without him. At 6'4", Henry is a foot taller and

Photo: Courtesy of Lindsey Beck

weighs twice as much as I do. He would punch or kick me until I was in so much pain I couldn't go to my classes. When I did go, I'd often leave early because he became convinced I was cheating on him and I didn't want to give him another reason to beat me. I have a fair amount of

academic ability and I did well in high school, but I started allowing my emotions to overrun my intelligence. It was like I had a bunch of emotions in a bowl and I'd just pull one out at random when something happened. One day when my mother expressed concern about my bruises, I got furious at her. But instead of getting angry at Henry for beating me, I'd feel afraid, confused, and depressed. Rather than stepping back and thinking logically about

▶

ONE STUDENT'S STORY *continued*

what was going on, I allowed my emotions to control me.

Studying became my escape. In my freshman year experience course, I loved expressing myself in my journals. In Chapter 8, I started writing about my emotions, and for the first time in years, I wasn't ashamed of my feelings. I decided to be totally honest, and I wrote down exactly what was going on and how I *really* felt about it (not how Henry told me I felt about it). Writing the journals really made me look at myself and ask, *What am I doing in this relationship?* When I read about

all of the positive ways I could manage my emotions, I started looking at things as though I wasn't going to take it anymore. I got stronger every day, and then one day I made the decision to leave Henry.

I've always done well at writing papers, studying, and taking tests, but I've never really taken responsibility for my emotions before. I learned that I need to get my emotional life under control if I want the rest of my life to work. I now realize that how I feel at one moment isn't necessarily how I'll feel 10 minutes later. Emotions change. Why let things

control me that are so temporary? By growing emotionally, I'm able to control my emotions instead of letting them control me. I am finally starting to picture a positive life for myself without Henry, and I am growing more confident every day. My dream is to earn a degree in microbiology and make a difference by working for the World Health Organization. Enrolling in this course was the best life decision I will probably ever make. If I hadn't, 10 years from now, I might not have wanted to change my life. However, I have been able to do that, and now I have my whole life ahead of me.

Photo: Courtesy of Lindsey Beck.

Reducing Stress

FOCUS QUESTIONS   How can you soothe stressful feelings that make life unpleasant and threaten to get you off course?

Changes and challenges are inevitable in our lives; thus, so is the potential for stress. Maybe you waited until the last minute to print your essay for English class and the printer was out of ink. Stress. Or you bounced a $6 check and the bank charged you a $25 penalty. Stress! Or you've got a test coming up in history and you're two chapters behind in your reading. STRESS!

Even life's pleasant events, like a new relationship or a weekend trip, can bring on a positive form of stress called *eustress*. If we're not careful, stress of one kind or another can bump us off course.

The process of living is the process of reacting to stress.

Stanley J. Sarnoff, M.D.

WHAT IS STRESS?

The American Medical Association defines stress as any interference that disturbs a person's mental or physical well-being. However, most of us know stress simply as the "wear and tear" that our minds and bodies experience as we attempt to cope with the challenges of life. The body's response to a stressor is much the same today as it was for our ancestors thousands of years ago. As soon as we perceive a threat, our brains release the stress hormones cortisol and epinephrine (also known as adrenaline), and instantly our bodies respond with an increase in heart rate, metabolism, breathing, muscle tension, and blood pressure. We're ready for "fight or flight."

To our ancestors, this stress response literally meant the difference between life and death. After they'd survived a threat (a saber-toothed tiger, perhaps), the stress hormones were gone from their bodies within minutes. In modern life, however, much of our stress comes from worrying about past events, agonizing about present challenges, and fretting about future changes. Instead of stress hormones being active in our bodies for only minutes, they may persist for months or even years. For many of us, then, stress is a constant and toxic companion.

WHAT HAPPENS WHEN STRESS PERSISTS?

Ongoing stress is bad news for our health, damaging almost every bodily system. It inhibits digestion, reproduction, growth, tissue repair, and the responses of our immune system. As just one example of the impact of long-term stress on our health, Carnegie Mellon University researchers exposed 400 volunteers to cold viruses and found that people with high stress in their lives were twice as likely to develop colds as those with low stress.

In fact, the National Institute for Mental Health estimates that 70 to 80 percent of all doctor visits are for stress-related illnesses. Physical symptoms of stress can be as varied as high blood pressure, muscle tension, headaches, backaches, indigestion, irritable bowel, ulcers, chronic constipation or diarrhea, muscle spasms, herpes sores, tics, tremors, sexual dysfunction, fatigue, insomnia, physical weakness, and emotional upsets.

Important to college students is the discovery that stress has a negative impact on memory. It also hinders other mental skills such as creativity, concentration, and attention to details. When you're feeling stressed, you can't do your best academic work, let alone enjoy doing it. So, when you feel stressed, what are your choices?

UNHEALTHY STRESS REDUCTION

When stressed, people in a Victim mindset seek to escape the discomfort as fast as possible. To do so, they often make unwise choices: drinking alcohol to excess, going numb for hours in front of a television or computer, working obsessively, fighting, taking anesthetizing drugs, going on shopping binges, eating too much or too little, smoking excessively, gulping caffeine, or gambling more than they can afford to lose. When confronted with the damage of their self-sabotaging behavior, they typically blame, complain, and make excuses. *Stress made me do it!*

Like the impulsive children in the marshmallow experiment, Victims seek instant gratification. They give little thought to the impact of these choices on their futures. By making one impulsive and ill-considered choice after another, Victims move further and further off course.

Every stress leaves an indelible scar, and the organism pays for its survival after a stressful situation by becoming a little older.

Hans Selye, M.D.

Of all the drugs and the compulsive behaviors that I have seen in the past twenty-five years, be it cocaine, heroin, alcohol, nicotine, gambling, sexual addiction, or food addiction, all have one common thread. That is the covering up, or the masking, or the unwillingness on the part of the human being to confront and be with his or her human feelings.

Richard Miller, M.D.

HEALTHY STRESS REDUCTION

People in a Creator mindset find better ways to reduce stress. They realize that managing emotions intelligently means making wise choices that release the grip of stress, not just mask it. Effective at identifying their distressing feelings early, Creators take positive actions to avoid being hijacked by emotional upset. Here's a menu of healthy and effective strategies for managing four of the most common symptoms of stress.

A special note to the highly stressed: Your Inner Defender may take one look at the list of strategies that follows and say something like, "I can't deal with this right now. It's just going to make me even *more* stressed out!" If that's really the case, consider making an appointment at your campus counseling office to get some caring, professional help for your stress.

Victim

Creator

To reduce your stress on your own, here's a simple, two-step plan. First, read the following section that addresses your most pressing symptoms of stress: feeling overwhelmed, angry, anxious, or sad. In that section, pick one stress reduction strategy and make a 32-Day Commitment (see the "Developing Self-Discipline" section of Chapter 4) to do it. In little more than a month, you'll likely feel less stressed. Better yet, you'll have proven that *you*, and not stress, are in charge of your life.

Feeling Overwhelmed

Feeling overwhelmed is probably the most common stressor for college students. Its message, if heeded, is valuable: Your life has gotten too complicated, your commitments too many. Feeling overwhelmed warns us that we've lost control of our lives. Creators may notice a tightness or pain in their jaws, shoulders, or lower backs. Or lack of sleep. Or they may notice themselves thinking, "If one more thing goes wrong, I'm going to scream!" Or, maybe they *do* scream! With this awareness, Creators understand it's time to take action. Many positive strategies exist for rescuing your life from the distress of feeling overwhelmed.

Choose New Behaviors. Here are some actions you can take when you feel that your life is stretched a mile wide and an inch thin. As you'll see, many of them are variations of self-management strategies you learned in **Chapter 4**:

- *Separate from an external stressor.* Perhaps the external stressor is a neighbor's loud music or a demanding job. You can choose to study in the library where it's quiet or find a new job with fewer demands.

- *List and prioritize everything you need to do.* Using a Next Actions List (see "Creating a Leak-Proof Self-Management System" section of **Chapter 4**), record all of your incomplete tasks according to life roles.

When you take full responsibility here and now for all of your feelings and for everything that happens to you, you never again blame the people and situations in the world outside of you for any unhappy feelings that you have.

Ken Keyes

Assign priorities to each task: A = Important & Urgent actions; B = Important & Not Urgent actions; C = All Unimportant actions.

- *Delete Cs.* Identify where you are wasting time and cross them off your list.

- *Delegate As and Bs.* Where possible, get another person to complete some of your important tasks. Ask a friend to pick up your dry cleaning. Pay someone to clean your apartment. This choice frees up time to do the tasks that only you can do, like your math homework.

- *Complete remaining As and Bs yourself.* Start with your A priorities, such as a looming term paper or a broken refrigerator. Handle them immediately: Visit the library and take out three books to begin researching your term paper topic. Call an appliance repair shop and schedule a service call. Spend time doing only A and B priorities and watch your overwhelm subside.

- *Discover time-savers.* Consciously make better use of your time. For example, keep an errand list so you can do them all in one trip. Or study flashcards during the hour between classes.

- *Eliminate time-wasters.* Identify and eliminate Quadrants III and IV activities. For example, reduce the time you spend on Facebook. Cut down on watching television. Stop playing video games.

- *Say "no."* Admit that your plate is full, and politely refuse requests that add to your commitments. If you do agree to take on something new, say "no" to something already on your plate. If saying "no" is difficult for you, do role-plays with a friend to practice. Or put it in writing. (Find more tips on this in the "Saying No" section of **Chapter 5**.)

- *Keep your finances organized.* A survey of 11,000 adults by *Prevention* magazine revealed that their number one source of stress is worry over personal finances. So curtail unnecessary spending, pay bills when due, balance your checkbook. Use the money-management strategies in **Chapter 1** for stress relief as well as debt relief.

- *Exercise.* Aerobic exercise increases the blood levels of endorphins, and these hormones block pain, create a feeling of euphoria (the exercise high), and reduce stress. One caution: Consult your doctor before dramatically changing your level of exercise.

- *Get enough sleep.* If sleep is a problem, don't eat after 7 p.m. and go to bed by 10 p.m. If thoughts keep running through your mind, write them down. Breathe deeply and relax. Clear your mind. If sleep eludes you, consider seeing a doctor. You can't learn effectively when deprived of sleep.

Choose New Thoughts. Because we create the inner experience of feeling overwhelmed in our mind, we can un-create it. Here's how:

- *Elevate.* See each problem in the bigger picture of your whole life. Notice how little importance it really has. From this new perspective, ask, "Will this problem really matter one year from now?" Often the answer is "no."

M uch of the stress that people feel doesn't come from having too much to do. It comes from not finishing what they've started.

David Allen

I like what exercise does for my mind. If I've had a bad day, if I'm feeling stressed out, if I'm feeling overwhelmed — it takes it all away.

Kelly Ripa

- *Trust a positive outcome.* How many times have you been upset by something that later turned out to be a blessing in disguise? Because it's possible, expect the blessing.
- *Take a mental vacation.* Picture a place you love (e.g., a white-sand beach, mountain retreat, or forest path) and spend a few minutes visiting it in your mind. Enjoy the peace and rejuvenation of this mini-vacation.

Feeling Angry

The sign of intelligent people is their ability to control emotions by the application of reason.

Marya Mannes

Healthy anger declares a threat or injustice against us or someone or something we care about. Perceiving this violation, the brain signals the body to release catecholamines (hormones) that fuel both our strength and our will to fight. Creators become conscious of oncoming anger through changes such as flushed skin, tensed muscles, and increased pulse rates.

With this awareness, Creators can pause and wisely choose what to do next, rather than lashing out impulsively. Emotions don't ask rational questions, so we must. For example, Creators ask, *Will I benefit from releasing my anger, or will it cost me dearly?*

When you perceive a true injustice, use the energy produced by your anger to right the wrong. However, to avoid being hijacked by anger and doing something you will regret later, here are some effective strategies:

Choose New Behaviors. Allow the tidal wave of anger-producing hormones about 20 minutes to recede. Here's how:

- *Separate.* Go off by yourself, allowing enough time to regain your ability to make rational, positive choices.
- *Exercise.* Moving vigorously assists in reducing anger-fueling hormones in your body.
- *Relax.* Slowing down also aids in calming your body, returning control of your decisions to you (as long as you don't spend this time obsessively thinking about the event that angered you).

I promised myself on the day of Cari's death that I would fight to make this needless homicide count for something positive in the years ahead.

Candy Lightner

- *Journal.* Write about your feelings in detail. Rant and rave to your journal. Explore the cause and effect of your anger. Take responsibility for any part you play in creating the anger. Honest expression of emotions can help the dark storm pass and rational thoughts return.
- *Channel your anger into positive actions.* That's what Candy Lightner did when a drunk driver—a repeat offender—killed her 13-year-old daughter, Cari, as she walked through their neighborhood. Lightner turned her anger into action and created Mothers Against Drunk Driving (MADD). Now a nationwide organization, MADD strives to end drunk driving and provide support for its victims. After your anger has subsided, the Wise Choice Process can help you decide on positive actions that you might take.

Choose New Thoughts. Because thoughts stir emotional responses, revising our anger-producing thoughts can calm us. Here's how:

- *Reframe.* Look at the problem from a different perspective. Search for a benign explanation for the anger-causing event. If you realize you were wronged unknowingly, unintentionally, or even necessarily, you can often see the other person's behavior in a less hostile way.

- *Distract yourself.* Consciously shift your attention to something pleasant, stopping the avalanche of angry thoughts. Involve yourself with uplift-ing conversations, movies, books, music, video games, puzzles, or similar diversions.

- *Forgive.* Take offending people off the hook for whatever they did, no matter how offensive. Don't concern yourself with whether *they* deserve forgiveness; the question is whether *you* deserve the emotional relief of forgiveness. The reason for forgiveness is primarily to improve *your* life, not theirs. We close the case to free ourselves of the daily self-infliction of poisonous judgments. Of course, forgiveness doesn't mean we forget and allow them to misuse us again.

- *Identify the hurt.* Anger is often built upon hurt: Someone doesn't meet me when she said she would. Below my anger, I'm hurt that she seems to care about me so little. Shift attention from anger to the deeper hurt. Consider expressing the hurt in writing.

> Living life as an art requires a readiness to forgive.
>
> Maya Angelou

Feeling Anxious

Healthy anxiety delivers a message that we may be in danger. Our brain then releases hormones that fuel our energy to flee. Many Victims, though, exagger-ate dangers, and their healthy concern is replaced by paralyzing anxiety or even terror about what could go wrong.

Creators become conscious of oncoming anxiety through their bodies' clear signals, including shallow breathing, increased pulse rate, and "butterflies" in the stomach. With this awareness, Creators can pause and wisely choose what to do next rather than fleeing impulsively from or worrying constantly about a nonthreatening person or situation.

One of the areas where emotions hinder academic performance is test anxiety. Unless you minimize this distress, you will be unable to demonstrate effectively what you know. Many colleges offer workshops or courses that offer instruction in anxiety-reducing strategies. Here are some wise choices to avoid being hijacked by anxiety, especially anxiety generated by a test.

> Anxiety … sabotages academic performance of all kinds: 126 different studies of more than 36,000 people found that the more prone to worries a person is, the poorer their academic performance, no matter how measured—grades on tests, grade-point average, or achievement tests.
>
> Daniel Goleman

Choose New Behaviors. As with anger, help the anxiety-producing chemi-cals to recede. Here's how:

- *Prepare thoroughly.* If your anxiety relates to an upcoming performance (e.g., test or job interview), prepare thoroughly and then prepare some more. Confidence gained through extensive preparation diminishes anxiety. Using your CORE Learning System—explained in the "Toolbox for Active Learners"—is a great way to increase your realistic expectations for success on any test.

- *Relax.* Slowing down helps you reclaim mastery of your thoughts and emotions (but don't spend this time obsessing about the cause of your anxiety).
- *Breathe deeply.* Anxiety and fear constrict. Keep oxygen flowing through your body to reverse their physiological impact. Find demonstrations of this kind of breathing by doing a search on YouTube.com for "Diaphragmatic Breathing" or "Belly Breathing."
- *Bring a piece of home to tests.* For example, bring a picture of your family.
- *Request accommodations.* Visit your college's disability services to see about making special arrangements, such as a longer time to take tests. Special arrangements usually require a note from a medical professional.

Choose New Thoughts. Changing our thoughts can soothe irrational anxieties. Here's how:

- *Detach.* Once you have prepared fully for an upcoming challenge (such as a test), there's no more you can do. Worrying won't help. So do everything you can to ready yourself for the challenge; then trust the outcome to take care of itself.
- *Reframe.* Ask yourself, "If the worst happens, can I live with it?" If you fail a test, for example, you won't like it, but could you live with it? Of course you could! (If not, consider seeking help to regain a healthy perspective.)
- *Visualize success.* Create a mental movie of yourself achieving your ideal outcomes. Play the movie over and over until the picture of success becomes stronger than your fear. For more on how to visualize effectively, see "Committing to Your Goals and Dreams" in **Chapter 3**.
- *Assume the best.* Victims often create anxiety through negative assumptions. Suppose your professor says, "I want to talk to you in my office." Resist assuming the conversation concerns something bad. In fact, if you're going to assume, why not assume it's something wonderful?
- *Face the fear.* Do what you fear, in spite of the fear. Most often you will learn that your fear was just a False Expectation Appearing Real.
- *Say your affirmation.* When anxiety-producing thoughts creep into your mind, replace them with the positive words of your affirmation.

> If your images are positive, they will support you and cheer you on when you get discouraged. Negative pictures rattle around inside of you, affecting you without your knowing it.
>
> Virginia Satir

Feeling Sad

Sadness is the natural response to the loss of someone or something dear. Fully grieving our loss is essential, for only in this way do we both honor and resolve our loss. Sadness and feeling "down" are also understandable reactions to the academic and social pressures that college students may experience, especially in their first year. Unhealthy sadness, however, becomes a lingering, helpless feeling that numbs us. If you feel gripped by such a depression, see a counselor at your college. Help is available!

For bouts with short-term sadness, however, there are numerous ways to bounce back on your own. First, recognize your body's clear signals: low energy, constant fatigue, and lack of a positive will to perform meaningful tasks. With this awareness, take steps to regain a positive experience of college and life. Here are some healthy options for doing so:

Choose New Behaviors. Help your body produce natural, mood-elevating hormones. Here's how:

- *Do something (anything!) toward your goals.* Get moving and produce a result, no matter how small. Accomplishment combats the blues.

- *Exercise.* Moving vigorously helps your body produce endorphins, causing a natural high that brightens your mood.

- *Listen to uplifting music.* Put on a song that picks up your spirits. Avoid sad songs about lost love and misery.

- *Laugh.* Like exercise, laughter is physiologically incompatible with melancholy. So rent a funny movie, go to a comedy club, read joke books or cartoons, or visit your funniest friend.

- *Breathe deeply.* Like fear, sadness constricts. Keep breathing deeply to offset the physiological impact of sadness.

- *Help others in need.* Assisting people less fortunate is uplifting. You experience both the joy of lightening their burden and the reminder that, despite your situation, you still have much to be grateful for.

- *Journal.* Writing about your feelings can help you come to terms with them more quickly and effectively. Often our emotions on paper seem much less distressing than those roaming unexamined in our minds and hearts.

- *Socialize with friends and loved ones.* Isolation usually intensifies gloominess. Socializing re-engages you with people who matter and helps you gain a healthier perspective on your situation.

Choose New Thoughts. As with other distressing emotions, changing our thoughts soothes sadness. Here's how:

- *Dispute pessimistic beliefs.* Dark thoughts thrive on pessimism. So challenge negative beliefs that make your present situation seem permanent, pervasive, or personal. Think, instead, how life will improve over time, how the problem is limited to only one part of your life, and how the cause is not a personal flaw in you, but something you can remedy with an action.

Bad things do happen; how I respond to them defines my character and the quality of my life. I can choose to sit in perpetual sadness, immobilized by the gravity of my loss, or I can choose to rise from the pain and treasure the most precious gift I have—life itself.

Walter Anderson

The greatest weapon against stress is our ability to choose one thought over another.

William James

- *Distract yourself.* As with anger, consciously replacing gloomy thoughts with pleasant ones will help stop the distress. So involve yourself with engaging activities that will take your thoughts on a pleasant diversion.
- *Focus on the positive.* Identify your blessings and successes. Think of all the things for which you are grateful, perhaps even making a list. Appreciate what you *do* have instead of regretting what you don't.
- *Find the opportunity in the problem.* At the very least, learn the lesson life has brought you and move on. At best, turn your loss into a gain.
- *Remind yourself, "This, too, shall pass."* A year from now, you'll be in an entirely different place in your life, and this emotional upset will be only a memory.
- *Identify others who have much more to be sad or depressed about.* Realize by this comparison how fortunate you actually are, changing your focus from your loss to all that you still have.

T he greater part of our happiness or misery depends on our dispositions and not our circumstances.

Martha Washington

CHOOSE YOUR ATTITUDE

When dealing with stress, the critical issue is, *Do you manage your emotions or do they manage you?* If you have made an honest effort to manage your emotions and they have defied you still, you may want to seek the help of a counselor or therapist. In some cases, persistent emotional distress is the result of a chemical imbalance that can be treated with prescription drugs. But if it's inspiration you seek, consider Viktor E. Frankl, a psychiatrist imprisoned in the Nazi concentration camps during World War II. In his book *Man's Search for Meaning,* Frankl relates how he and other prisoners rose above their dreadful conditions to create a positive inner experience.

In one example, Frankl tells of a particularly bleak day when he was falling into a deep despair. With terrible sores on his feet, he was forced to march many miles in bitter cold weather to a work site, and there, freezing and weak from starvation, he endured constant brutality from the guards. Frankl describes how he "forced" his thoughts to turn to another subject. In his mind he imagined himself "standing on the platform of a well-lit, warm and pleasant lecture room." Before him sat an audience enthralled to hear him lecture on the psychology of the concentration camp. "By this method," Frankl says, "I succeeded somehow in rising above the situation, above the sufferings of the moment, and I observed them as if they were already of the past."

T he greatest discovery of my generation is that human beings, by changing the inner attitudes of their minds, can change the outer aspects of their lives.

William James

From his experiences and his observations, Frankl concluded that everything can be taken from us but one thing: "the last of the human freedoms—to choose one's attitude in any given set of circumstances, to choose one's own way."

Creators claim the power to choose their outcomes whenever possible and to choose their inner experiences always. If Victor Frankl could overcome the stress of his inhumane imprisonment in a concentration camp, surely we can find the strength to overcome the stresses of our ordinary lives.

JOURNAL ENTRY | 29

In this activity, you will practice identifying positive methods for reducing the stress in your life.

1 **Write about a recent time when you felt overwhelmed, angry, sad, or anxious.** Choose an experience different from the one you described in Journal Entry 28. Fully describe the situation that caused your emotional response; then describe the distressing feelings you experienced; finally, explain what you did (if anything) to manage your emotions in a positive way.

2 **Identify two or more strategies that you could use in the future when you experience this emotion.** Explain each strategy in a separate paragraph, and remember the power of the 4Es—examples, experiences, explanation, and evidence—to improve the quality of your writing. When you're done, notice if simply writing about your stressors and ways to manage them may have reduced your level of stress. It did for students in a study at Southern Methodist University.

Emotion comes directly from what we think: Think "I am in danger" and you feel anxiety. Think "I am being trespassed against" and you feel anger. Think "Loss" and you feel sadness.

Martin Seligman

ONE STUDENT'S STORY

JAIME SANMIGUEL, *Miami Dade College, Florida*

I don't consider myself someone who lives in fear, and very few things in life intimidate me. However, the one fear that I could never overcome was my dread of public speaking. When I had to give a speech or read an essay aloud in junior high or high school, I would develop a shaky voice, get sweaty palms, and turn completely red. When I got to college, I took a fundamentals of speech class in which much of our grade depended on two speeches that we had to give using a PowerPoint presentation. My first speech didn't go very well. I hadn't really learned to use PowerPoint, and the slides didn't seem to fit what I was talking about. I began to feel insecure, and I started going all over the place. My teacher said the speech was okay, but I wasn't happy with it, especially because my goal is

to work in public relations, where I'll need to be able to speak to groups with confidence.

I was taking SLS 1125, Student Support Seminar, at the same time, and I discovered many helpful hints in *On Course* to overcome my fears. The first thing I did for my next speech was to make sure I was thoroughly prepared. This time I wrote out my whole speech first and then put my key points on index cards. I learned how to work PowerPoint and made sure all of the slides went with what I was talking about. I practiced giving my speech a number of times, with my dog as my audience. Another student in my class gave a great speech on the history of watches, and I visualized myself doing some of the things she had done, like using my hands effectively, looking relaxed, smiling, and

being more natural and friendly. I also did some relaxing and deep breathing, and that helped take my mind off my concerns. I used to worry that people would think I didn't know what I was talking about, but I changed these worries by picturing my audience as friends who want to know what I have to say. When I actually gave my speech, I picked out individual students and talked to each of them one at a time. These techniques helped me believe in myself more and not be so self-conscious in front of an audience, and in the end I passed the course with a B.

But just as important, in *On Course* I learned, "If you keep doing what you've been doing, you'll keep getting what you've been getting." I took ownership of the fact that if I want to be successful in a public relations career, I have to face and overcome my fears of giving presentations. I think I'm well on my way to achieving this goal.

Increasing Happiness

In 1999, scientific researchers started paying more attention to happiness.

For starters, the first positive psychology summit took place that year in Lincoln, Nebraska. Previously, most psychologists had viewed their role as helping people become less miserable. At the positive psychology summit, psychologists asked, "How can we apply science to help people become more happy?"

Since then, many millions of dollars have been spent on scientific research to answer this important question. In 2002, the first international conference on positive psychology was held to share what the research had found. Since then, dozens of similar conferences have been held around the world.

Meanwhile, happiness courses began popping up on college campuses. In 2006, Harvard University offered a course called "Positive Psychology 1504." An enrollment of 854 students made it Harvard's most popular course. Many other colleges now offer courses in positive psychology. Some offer master's or doctoral degrees in this emerging field as well. Recently a partnership of the Massachusetts Institute of Technology (M.I.T.) and Harvard University offered a free online course called "The Science of Happiness." Nearly 75,000 people worldwide enrolled, including your author.

The take-away from all of this attention on happiness seems obvious. People want to be happier. And we want to know how.

The reason to increase happiness may seem obvious: "Happy feels better than unhappy." But research has revealed many other benefits as well. When compared to unhappy people, happy people on average are more productive, likeable, active, friendly, helpful, resilient, and creative. Happy people tend to be healthier, have better relationships, earn higher salaries, and even live longer.

One study of happiness, for example, focused on autobiographical essays written by Catholic nuns in the 1930s and 1940s. Their average age at that time was 22. In 2001, scientists analyzed these essays for expressions of positive emotions. Then they looked to see what happened to the nuns in their study, many of whom have passed away. The findings? Happier nuns outlived less-happy nuns by an average of 10 years. Not only did they live longer, happier nuns were far less afflicted by Alzheimer's disease. So it appears that positive emotions contribute to both longevity and brain health.

LIMITS ON HAPPINESS

Research, sadly, has uncovered some bad news about efforts to increase happiness. It turns out we have limited control over our level of happiness. The major reason is heredity. It seems we're born with a happiness set point that's controlled by our genes. By studying identical twins—especially those raised apart—psychologists estimate that about 50 percent of our happiness is genetic. Just as we inherit height from our parents, we also inherit a happiness set point. And no one has figured out how to change the set point for happiness (or height, for that matter).

We hold these truths to be self-evident, that all men are created equal, that they are endowed by their Creator with certain unalienable Rights, that among these are Life, Liberty and the pursuit of Happiness.

from the United States Declaration of Independence

I am more concerned with the Gross National Happiness of my country, than with the Gross National Product.

Jigme Singye Wangchuck, King of Bhutan

What about the impact of life circumstances on happiness? you might ask. Surely happiness is raised or lowered by circumstances such as money, health, climate, physical appearance, ethnicity, gender, age, intelligence, and education. Actually, not so much. Research suggests that circumstances like these contribute only about 10 percent to our level of happiness. Sure, we get a burst of happiness when something good happens—like getting an A on a test or receiving a huge raise at work. But then something called **hedonic adaptation** takes over. Here's how it works: After something good happens, we quickly become used to it and slide back down to our happiness set point. In other words, when the *new* good thing becomes the *old* good thing, the thrill is gone. If you've ever had "too much of a good thing," you've experienced hedonic adaptation.

Here's an example of hedonic adaptation. Maybe you've thought, "If only I could win the lottery, then I'd be happy!" Psychologist Philip Brickman and his colleagues decided to find out if that's true. They asked winners of the Illinois State Lottery to rate their happiness. Then they asked non-winners to do the same. As you might expect, the happiness of lottery winners spiked right after their good fortune. About a year later, however, most of the winners were no happier than the non-winners. It turns out that once we can take care of basic needs, more money doesn't mean more happiness. That rascal hedonic adaptation tugs us back down to our set point. Think about all of the things you were once thrilled about…but now don't seem so great. That's the effect of hedonic adaptation.

Let's recap what we know so far. About 50 percent of our happiness is determined by a genetically fixed set point. And about 10 percent of our happiness is affected by our circumstances, but usually for only a short time. What about the other 40 percent? Here's where scientific research offers good news. It turns out there are many choices we can make to increase our happiness.

In fact, a number of the choices already discussed in *On Course* are strongly correlated with increasing happiness—for example, pursuing important goals, exercising, and developing positive relationships. Let's look at some other choices that increase happiness.

> [W]orking toward a meaningful life goal is one of the most important strategies for becoming lastingly happier.
>
> Sonia Lyubomirsky,
> psychologist

SAVORING PLEASURES

Pleasures increase happiness. You could experience pleasure by eating a delicious meal, dancing to great music, watching a child play with a kitten, receiving a full-body massage, or smelling cinnamon buns right from the oven. One of my pleasures is picking fresh, ripe tomatoes from my garden and adding them to a salad for dinner. Most pleasant experiences, however, fade quickly. Fortunately, there's a way to deepen and prolong pleasure. It's called **savoring**. When we savor an experience, our Inner Guide whispers, "Pay close attention to this…stay with it…stay with it… c'mon, stay with it a little longer." With savoring, we let a pleasant experience linger in our awareness, spreading like sweet cream poured into rich, dark coffee.

Pleasure not only results from a positive experience in the present. It also occurs when we revisit and savor positive events from the past. For example, a group of severely depressed people was asked to log onto a website each evening.

Leo Cullum/Conde Nast Collection

"But, remember, you're responsible for your own happiness."

By taking just a few extra seconds to stay with a positive experience—even the comfort of a single breath—you'll help turn a passing mental state into lasting neural structure.

Rick Hanson,
neuropsychologist

There they recorded three good things that had happened that day, no matter how small: "I went for a walk." Then, to dive a little deeper, they wrote why this good thing happened: "I decided the weather was too nice to stay inside all day." After 15 days of focusing their attention on and savoring the good things in their lives—no matter how small—94 percent reported improvement in their moods.

Neuropsychologist Rick Hanson reports that savoring pleasures actually changes our brains, making us more able to enjoy future pleasures. Positive experiences increase the release of the hormone dopamine. Dopamine makes you feel good. As you repeatedly create and savor positive experiences, your new neural networks become "stickier" for other positive experiences. The changes in your brain increase your ability to enjoy positive experiences, and enjoying positive experiences makes your brain more receptive to future pleasures.

Hanson suggests helpful strategies to keep hedonic adaptation from ruining this uplifting cycle. First, create a variety of pleasant experiences (not the same one over and over). Second, spread pleasant experience over time (not all at once). And, most of all, fully savor each pleasant experience. Focus your attention on it…and stay with it…and stay with it.

GRATITUDE

Psychologist Robert Emmons studies the relationship between gratitude and happiness. Gratitude, he says, is "a felt sense of wonder, thankfulness, and appreciation for life." His research, and the research of others, reveals that people who count their blessings on a regular basis experience a number of benefits. Not only are they happier than people who don't express gratitude, they also report greater vitality, optimism and satisfaction with life. Additionally, grateful people experience lower levels of stress and depression.

Scientists have experimented with many ways of expressing gratitude. One of the most obvious is to make a gratitude list: "I'm alive"; "I have food to eat"; "I have the opportunity to go to college." When I do this exercise, I find myself listing things I had never thought to appreciate before. For example, I'm grateful to the person who first picked beans off a coffee bush, roasted them, ground them, and poured hot water though them. Not to mention the person who thought of adding sugar and cream.

Another way to generate gratitude is to recall a painful experience from your past, then immediately contrast this past experience with what you are experiencing now. The key is noticing what you feel grateful for now that the pain is in the past: "I lived through it"; "I learned who my friends really are"; "I'm a much stronger person because of it"; "I'm much more willing to take on challenges."

You can also experience gratitude by writing a letter of thanks to someone who has been important in your life. This could be a parent, brother, sister, coach, teacher, employer or friend. In specific detail, tell this person why you are grateful to him or her. What did he or she say or do? How did it affect your life? How are you different because of him or her? If possible, deliver the letter in person and read the letter together. In one study, these gratitude visits led to large boosts in happiness that lasted anywhere from a week to a month.

> Let us rise up and be thankful, for if we didn't learn a lot today, at least we learned a little, and if we didn't learn a little, at least we didn't get sick, and if we got sick, at least we didn't die; so, let us all be thankful.
>
> **Buddha**

ENGAGEMENT

What these happiness strategies have in common is increasing our awareness of and savoring a positive experience. Ironically, another way to increase happiness is becoming so engaged in an activity that we *lose* awareness of anything beyond what we are doing. It isn't until later that we realize how enjoyable the experience was. Psychologist Mihaly Csikszentmihalyi (pronounced "*chick*-sent-me-hi") calls such times of complete engagement **flow states**. Flow results from total absorption in an activity. During flow, we have no thoughts or concerns about ourselves. Time is distorted, often passing very quickly. We are totally present in the moment.

What if you could experience flow in your college courses? Creators do all they can to maximize that possibility, and how you choose your courses and your instructors is a good first step. Victims typically create their

© Cengage Learning

course schedule based on convenience: *Give me a class at noon because I don't like to get up early.*

Creators have a very different approach. They realize that it's worth a sacrifice to get a course with an outstanding instructor, one who creates flow in the classroom. As you plan your schedule for next semester, ask other students to recommend instructors who . . .

- demonstrate a deep knowledge of their subject,

- show great enthusiasm for the value of their subject,

- set challenging but reasonable learning objectives for their students,

- offer engaging learning experiences that appeal to diverse learning preferences, and

- provide a combination of academic and emotional support that gives their students high expectations of success.

Imagine taking courses with instructors who are knowledgeable, enthusiastic, challenging, engaging, and supportive! These are the instructors who are going to create flow in their classrooms, help you achieve academic success, and inspire you to be a lifelong learner. And if you find a course in which you experience flow, you might very well have found your major...and maybe even your ideal career.

CONTRIBUTION

Let's consider one more way to increase your happiness. Start by imagining that scientists are monitoring your brain activity. They give you some money and a choice: You can keep the money or donate it to charity. Which choice do you think will create the greatest activity in your brain's reward center? If you said "donate the money to charity," you're right. Showing kindness to others increases positive emotions.

In a study at the University of California—Riverside, people were asked to perform acts of kindness. They chose such things as doing extra household chores, helping someone carry something, or making breakfast for a special friend. Not only did the participants' happiness go up immediately, the effects were still there a month later. As you might expect, participants who varied their acts of kindness and spread them out over time created even better results than those who did the same thing many times within a short period of time.

So, what kindness could you do today? It could be small (holding a door for someone). Or it could be big (offering to tutor someone who is struggling in a subject you've mastered). Or huge (taking actions to reduce world hunger). As many who help worthy causes will attest, they receive more than they give.

STRAWBERRY MOMENTS

Many of the scientific discoveries about happiness are illustrated by a parable I heard years ago. A man is walking on a narrow, rocky path on the side of a steep mountain when he encounters a hungry tiger. Terrified, the man grabs a vine and dangles over the edge of the cliff. He looks down and sees a second

B eing able to enter flow is emotional intelligence at its best; flow represents perhaps the ultimate in harnessing emotions in the services of performance and learning.

Daniel Goleman

N othing brings me more happiness than trying to help the most vulnerable people in society. It is a goal and an essential part of my life—a kind of destiny. Whoever is in distress can call on me. I will come running wherever they are.

Princess Diana

tiger waiting below. Then he feels a vibration in the vine, looks up, and sees a mouse chewing on the vine. As his distress increases, he notices a strawberry plant growing in a crevice on the side of the mountain. Holding the vine with one hand, the man reaches out and plucks a plump, red strawberry. He places it in his mouth and savors how delicious it tastes.

Life is full of difficulties, obstacles, challenges, and pain. At times, life seems to be one problem after another. We wonder, when will all of these problems end? And yet, among the problems is a strawberry—if we'll notice it. Maybe the strawberry is creating and savoring a momentary pleasure. Maybe the strawberry is feeling gratitude for what we have rather than distress for what we don't. Maybe the strawberry is engaging in flow. Maybe the strawberry is showing kindness to someone who is also facing one problem after another. The new science of positive psychology is discovering evidence that we can improve our happiness. To do so, we need to find our strawberries.

> The Constitution only gives people the right to pursue happiness. You have to catch it yourself.
>
> Benjamin Franklin

JOURNAL ENTRY / 30

In this activity, you'll experiment with one of two strategies intended to increase happiness. The first was briefly described in the preceding text; the second is new. Assignments similar to both of these have been employed with encouraging results in positive psychology classes at colleges such as the University of Michigan and the University of Pennsylvania.

1 **Complete one of the following:**

A. **Gratitude Letter:** Write a letter to someone who has been an important and positive influence in your life. Pick someone to whom you have never fully expressed your gratitude. In the letter, explain specifically and completely what this person did that you appreciate…and how the kindness has positively affected your life. (If you choose to share your letter with the person at a later time, consider getting together in a quiet setting and reading the letter aloud. If a face-to-face meeting isn't possible, you could mail the letter and call later to discuss it.)

B. **Me at My Best:** Describe in detail a time when you successfully faced a difficult situation, one about which you feel proud of the way you handled it. Be sure to discuss fully: 1) what the difficult situation was; 2) how you handled it; 3) what your handling of this situation shows about your inner strengths and character. While modesty can be a virtue, please don't let it distort the truth of what you did. Be honest about how you behaved and the inner qualities you demonstrated during a situation in which you were at your best.

2 **Read over what you wrote in Step 1, and take a few moments to savor what you did and what it says about your inner strengths and character. Then, honestly describe whether or not writing Step 1 of this journal entry lifted your spirits and improved your**

> Don't wait around for other people to be happy for you. Any happiness you get you've got to make yourself.
>
> Alice Walker

JOURNAL ENTRY / 30 *continued*

positive feelings. **Explain your reaction as best you can.** Remember, activities such as these work for some people but not for others, so you can be truthful about your own unique reaction.

Consider illustrating this journal entry with drawings, stickers, photos or other images.

EMOTIONAL INTELLIGENCE / at Work

SOFT SKILLS for CAREER SUCCESS

During nearly twenty years working as a consulting psychologist to dozens of companies and public agencies, I have seen how the lack of emotional intelligence undermines both an individual's and a company's growth and success, and conversely how the use of emotional intelligence leads to productive outcomes at both the individual and the organizational levels.

Hende Weisnger, Emotional Intelligence at Work

Imagine this: The local store manager of a large retail chain sends a one-line email to her department heads: "Quarterly sales figures on my desk by 9:00 a.m. tomorrow!" The head of the menswear department reads the email, feels insulted by the demanding tone, and fires back an angry email response: "I've been working here a hell of a lot longer than you have, and I don't appreciate your nasty reminders about when sales reports are due. You might try treating people more like colleagues and less like servants awaiting your every command." On an impulse, he copies his response to the company president and the five vice presidents at the store's national headquarters.

How much lost time and productivity do you think will result from this exchange of two emails? How much damage will be done to the employees' professional relationship and their ability to work well together in the future? How might their reputations and careers suffer when others hear rumors of this incident?

Now consider how different this event might have been if the head of the menswear department had followed a fundamental principle of emotional intelligence: ***Never make an important decision while in the grip of strong emotions***. Suppose he had read the store manager's email, taken a deep breath, and read it again. Feeling angry at what appeared to be the manager's dictatorial tone, what if he had waited about 30 minutes before responding? During that time, maybe he would have done some deep breathing. Maybe he would have recalled that the store manager has been very respectful of him since she took over the store six months before. Having calmed his initial upset, suppose he now went to the store manager's office and asked for a brief meeting. "You know," he says to her in this revised scene, "I just read your email about turning in the third-quarter sales figures, and I got that you're angry or upset. Is there something we need to talk about?" "What? Oh no," she responds, "there's no problem. I meant to send you a reminder last week, but I'm so far behind in my paperwork that I forgot. When I remembered this morning, I wrote the email while I was doing five other things. Sorry if it sounded like I was upset with you. On the contrary, I think you're doing a terrific job!"

Another name for emotional intelligence in the workplace is "professionalism." Professionals are aware of their own emotions, and they've developed methods for managing them. They're also good at perceiving emotions in others, and they know how to communicate effectively, building alliances rather than destroying them. Notice that in the

▶

revised scene just described, the department head doesn't reply to his manager with another email. He communicates with her in person. And he does so only after getting his emotions under control. Choices like these make all the difference when it comes to building a reputation as a business professional. And that reputation can be destroyed with one careless tantrum—or, in the digital age, with one reckless email, text message, tweet, or Facebook post.

Your emotional intelligence begins to impact your work life as soon as you consider a career path. If you choose work for which you have no passion or emotional commitment, you're starting your career with a huge handicap. Unmotivated by the outcomes or experiences of your work, you'll likely cut corners, doing less than is necessary to propel your career to success. By contrast, when you match your interests and talents to your career choice, you'll find work stimulating and success more likely. As Shoshana Zuboff, a psychiatrist and professor at Harvard Business School put it, "We only will know what to do by realizing what feels right to us."

Emotional intelligence continues to support your success during your job search. Chances are, every applicant invited for an interview has the training to do the job. So, what will distinguish you from the crowd? One answer lies in what employers are looking for beyond job skills. A 1997 survey of major corporations by the American Society for Training and Development discovered that four out of five companies seek emotional intelligence as one of the qualities they look for in new employees. Realizing this, you'll know to communicate not only your academic and job-related skills, but your emotional intelligence competencies as well.

Employers have good reason to seek employees with emotional intelligence. In his book *Working with Emotional Intelligence*, Daniel Goleman writes, "We now have twenty-five years' worth of empirical studies that tell us with a previously unknown precision just how much emotional intelligence matters for success." Goleman presents his analysis of what 121 companies reported as the necessary competencies for success in 181 different career positions. He found that two out of three of the abilities considered essential for effective job performance are emotional competencies. Put another way, according to employers themselves, emotional competence matters twice as much as other factors in job effectiveness.

You might think that the soft skills associated with emotional intelligence would be less important for those employed in highly technical and intellectual fields such as engineering, computer science, law, or medicine. Paradoxically, the exact opposite is true. Because academic success and high intelligence are required of all who enter these careers, virtually everyone in these careers is "book smart." However, not everyone is emotionally intelligent. In these professions, there is more variation in the "soft" domain than there is in education and IQ. Therefore, if you're at the top end of the emotional intelligence scale, you have a great advantage over your emotionally illiterate colleagues. As Goleman puts it, "'Soft' skills matter even more for success in 'hard' fields."

Although emotional intelligence is important in entry-level positions, as one moves up the ladder into leadership positions, it becomes essential. According to Goleman, employers report emotional intelligence as making up 80 to 100 percent of the skills necessary to be an outstanding leader. As just one example of its importance, leaders need to be able to spot and resolve conflicts that happen in their workforce. Otherwise such upsets can get an individual, group, division, or even the whole company off course.

Doug Lennick, executive vice president at American Express Financial Advisors, sums up the case for emotional intelligence in the workplace: "The aptitudes you need to succeed start with intellectual horsepower—but people need emotional competence, too, to get the full potential of their talents. The reason we don't get people's full potential is emotional incompetence."

TECH TIPS: Emotional Intelligence

MEIT (Mobile Emotional Intelligence Test) evaluates how effective you are at recognizing other people's emotions. The app presents you with a number of human faces, asking you to correctly label the emotion each is expressing. Other tests quiz you on the best ways to deal with different emotional situations. Your goal is to exceed 90 points (the average U.S. score is presently 89). *(Android, iOS)*

Awareness is an app designed by a psychotherapist that randomly "intercepts" your daily routine with a gentle gong sound. You're asked to record what you're doing and feeling at that moment. The app then guides you in a brief meditative exercise to bring your awareness to the present moment. The daily, weekly, and monthly reports help you discover patterns so you can change unwanted habits and lead a more peaceful life. *(Android, iOS)*

Gratitude Journal asks you to write down things for which you are grateful. You can set a timer that will remind you to add to your growing list of things for which you give thanks. For many people, reviewing such a list is uplifting. *(Android, iOS)*

Track Your Happiness begins with a one-time questionnaire. Then you decide when and how often you'd like to be contacted. On your chosen schedule, you'll receive an email or text and be asked to report what you are doing and how you are feeling. You'll receive periodic reports that identify the factors that increase your happiness. *(iOS)*

MindShift, created especially for teens and young adults, can help you deal with anxiety. The app helps you learn to relax, develop more supportive ways of thinking, and identify specific actions to reduce anxiety. The app offer strategies for dealing with test anxiety, social anxiety, and performance anxiety, among other distressing feelings. *(Android, iOS)*

Happify offers activities and games that are based on the scientific study of happiness. These activities help you strengthen five key happiness skills: Savoring, Gratitude, Aspirations, Giving, and Empathizing. The site says it tracks user data and finds that 86 percent of frequent users get happier within two months. *(Web, Android, iOS)*

Note: All of the above are free, but some may offer upgraded features for a fee.

BELIEVING IN YOURSELF

Develop Self-Acceptance

FOCUS QUESTION   Why is high self-esteem so important to success? What can you do to raise your self-esteem?

Roland was in his 40s when he enrolled in my English 101 class. He made insightful contributions to class discussions, so I was perplexed when the first two writing assignments passed without an essay from Roland. Both times, he apologized profusely, promising to complete them soon. He didn't want to make excuses, he said, but he was stretched to his limit: He worked at night, and during the day he took care of his two young sons while his wife worked. "Don't worry, though," he assured me, "I'll have an essay to you by Monday. I'm going to be the first person in my family to get a college degree. Nothing's going to stop me."

But Monday came, and Roland was absent. On a hunch, I looked up his academic record and found that he had taken English 101 twice before. I contacted his previous instructors. Both of them said that Roland had made many promises but had never turned in an assignment.

I called Roland, and we made an appointment to talk. He didn't show up. During the next class, I invited Roland into the hall while the class was working on a writing assignment.

"Sorry I missed our conference," Roland said. "I meant to call, but things have been piling up."

"Roland, I talked to your other instructors, and I know you never wrote anything for them. I'd love to help you, but you need to take an action. You need to write an essay." Roland nodded silently. "I believe you can do it. But I don't know if *you* believe you can do it. It's decision time. What do you say?"

"I'll have an essay to you by Friday."

I looked him in the eye.

"Promise," he said.

I knew that what Roland actually did, not what he promised, would reveal his deepest core beliefs about himself.

> The foundation of anyone's ability to cope successfully is high self-esteem. If you don't already have it, you can always develop it.
>
> Virginia Satir

SELF-ESTEEM AND CORE BELIEFS

So it is with us all. Our core beliefs—true or false, real or imagined—form the inner compass that guides our choices.

At the heart of our core beliefs is the statement *I AM ___*. How we complete that sentence in the quiet of our souls has a profound effect on the quality of our lives.

High self-esteem is the fuel that can propel us into the cycle of success. Do we approve of ourselves as we are, accepting our personal weaknesses along with our strengths? Do we believe ourselves capable, admirable, lovable, and fully worthy of the best life has to offer? If so, our beliefs will make it possible for us to choose wisely and stay on course to a rich, full life.

> Self-esteem is the reputation we have with ourselves.
>
> Nathaniel Branden

For example, imagine two students: one with high self-esteem, the other with low self-esteem. Picture them just after they get very disappointing test scores. What do they do next? The student with low self-esteem will likely choose options that protect his fragile self-image, options such as dropping the course rather than chancing failure. The student with high self-esteem, on the other hand, will likely choose options that move her toward success, options such as persisting in the course and getting additional help to be successful. Two students, same situation. One focuses on weaknesses. One focuses on

AS SMART AS HE WAS, ALBERT EINSTEIN COULD NOT FIGURE OUT HOW TO HANDLE THOSE TRICKY BOUNCES AT THIRD BASE.

Sidney Harris/ScienceCartoonsPlus.com

Self-esteem is more than merely recognizing one's positive qualities. It is an attitude of acceptance and non-judgment toward self and others.

Matthew McKay &
Patrick Fanning

strengths. The result: two different choices and two very different outcomes.

The good news is that self-esteem is learned, so anyone can learn to raise his or her self-esteem.

KNOW AND ACCEPT YOURSELF

People with high self-esteem know that no one is perfect, and they accept themselves with both their strengths and weaknesses. To paraphrase philosopher Reinhold Niebuhr, successful people accept the things they cannot change, have the courage to change the things they can change, and possess the wisdom to know the difference.

Successful people have the courage to take an honest self-inventory, as you began doing with the self-assessment in Chapter 1. They acknowledge their strengths without false humility, and they admit their weaknesses without stubborn denial. They tell the truth about themselves and take action to improve what they can.

Fortunately for Roland, he decided to do just that. On the Friday after our talk, he turned in his English 101 essay. His writing showed great promise, and I told him so. I also told him I appreciated that he had let go of the excuse that he was too busy to do his assignments. From then on, Roland handed in his essays on time. He met with me in conferences. He visited the writing lab, and he did grammar exercises to improve his editing skills. He easily passed the course.

A few years later, Roland called me. He had transferred to a four-year university and was graduating with a 3.8 average. He was continuing on to graduate school to study urban planning. What he most wanted me to know was that one of his instructors had asked permission to use one of his essays as a model of excellent writing. "You know," Roland said, "I'd still be avoiding writing if I hadn't accepted two things about myself: I was a little bit lazy and I was a whole lot scared. Once I admitted those things about myself, I started changing."

Each of us has a unique combination of strengths and weaknesses. When struggling people become aware of a weakness, they typically blame the problem on others or they beat themselves up for not being perfect. Successful people, however, usually make a different choice: They acknowledge the weakness, accept it without self-judgment, and, when possible, take action to create positive changes. As always, the choices we make determine both where we are headed and the quality of the journey. Developing self-acceptance helps us to make those choices wisely.

JOURNAL ENTRY | 31

In this activity, you will explore your strengths and weaknesses and the reputation you have with yourself. This exploration of your self-esteem will allow you to continue revising any limiting beliefs you may hold about yourself. By doing so, you will take an important step toward your success.

1 **In your journal, write a list of 10 or more of your personal strengths.** For example, mentally: *I'm good at math;* physically: *I'm very athletic;* emotionally: *I seldom let anger control me;* socially: *I'm a good friend;* and others: *I'm almost always on time.*

2 **Write a list of 10 or more of your personal weaknesses.** For example, mentally: *I'm a slow reader;* physically: *I'm out of shape;* emotionally: *I'm easily hurt by criticism;* socially: *I don't listen very well;* and others: *I'm a terrible procrastinator.*

3 **Using the information in Steps 1 and 2, write about the present state of your self-esteem.** What was your self-esteem score when you took the self-assessment in Chapter 1? What do you think your score will be when you take it again in Chapter 9? If you think your two scores will be different, to what do you attribute the difference? Are you satisfied with where you think your self-esteem is today? If not, what can you do to improve it?

To create an outstanding journal, remember to use the five suggestions in the section 'Write a Great Life' in Chapter 1. Especially remember to dive deep!

> We cannot change anything unless we accept it.
>
> Carl Jung

ONE STUDENT'S STORY

WYNDA ALLISON PAULETTE, *National Park Community College, Arkansas*

When I started back to college, I was 41 years old. I was on a "wing and a prayer." I didn't know if I had it in me to be successful in school, with all the responsibilities I had in my life. I didn't know if I was smart enough or even had the abilities to work on a college level after so many years. But what I did know was that I wanted to succeed. I would do my best. I had managed well in every other facet of my life, and I wanted to prove to myself that I could get a good education and set a good example for my children.

So, there I was in Success Seminar class, reading *On Course.* I read the "One Student's Stories" and began taking a personal inventory of my own life. Some of the journal entries I wrote left me mentally exhausted, because our instructor was always asking us to "dig deeper," and deeper I would go. I would write about subjects that I had left firmly in my past, re-open them, and give myself the opportunity to see them in a whole new light. Eventually, I was able to look at the "horrible" mistakes I had made in my life as lessons instead of failures. I could lay down negative thoughts that I harbored about myself and begin to see the ways I had grown as a human being. I began taking steps unknowingly to practice self-love and acceptance. I learned so much about myself and got

Photo: Courtesy of Wynda Allison Paulette

▶

ONE STUDENT'S STORY   *continued*

so much out of the class that when the end of the semester came, and we were required to turn in our notebooks, I wrote this poem/story to include for my instructor. It only took a few minutes to write but summed up my journey quite well.

The Friend

I once had a person in my life who I professed to care about; but the truth is, I didn't like Her much at all.

My friends would say how pretty and smart She was; I would silently disagree.

I made decisions that would hurt Her . . . choices that would inconvenience Her and take Her off track.

I never worried about Her wellbeing. In my eyes, She didn't deserve my love.

I single handedly set that poor girl back 20 years, with all the unnecessary problems I put in Her path.

I silently watched Her go through bad relationships, unproductive friendships, and unnecessary hardships without bothering to intercede.

I saw Her sink farther and farther from Her dreams, and thought She got what She deserved.

I judged Her so harshly, disrespected Her, and felt no remorse. . . .

UNTIL-

One day I looked at that person, REALLY took the time to see Her and started to see the good in Her. . . .

I began to respect Her for the grace with which She handled even the hardest of times . . . and for the optimistic way She viewed the world.

I began to see Her worth shine from within brighter than a whole vault full of gold.

I saw a beauty within Her so great that it made me weep.

I began to encourage Her every day, and assure Her that Her dreams could be realized and that She could accomplish anything She set Her brilliant mind to do.

I fell in love with Her for the first time. I began to admire and respect Her.

I regretted the horrible times I had put Her through: the setbacks, the wrongs. . . .

But now, looking back, I realize that woman I now love would not be the person She is

If She had not traveled the dark paths I led Her through. . . .

. . . Nor would She appreciate the sunshine nearly as much.

For within Her is a well-seasoned, understanding, empathetic, responsible, caring human being.

That woman is ME.

My story is still ongoing. There will always be struggles; nothing will ever be "laid at my feet." But I also learned through all the hard work I put into Success Seminar, and all of the valuable lessons and information that I was able to reap from the text and the exercises, that life is full of possibility. There are no dead-end roads, only new routes to forge through and lessons to learn. Most of all, we have to learn to love and believe in ourselves.

Photo: Courtesy of Wynda Allison Paulette.

Staying On Course to Your Success

Successful Students . . .

- ▶ **gain self-awareness,** consciously employing behaviors, beliefs, and attitudes that keep them on course.
- ▶ **adopt lifelong learning,** finding valuable lessons and wisdom in nearly every experience they have.
- ▶ **develop emotional intelligence,** effectively managing their emotions in support of their goals and dreams.
- ▶ **believe in themselves,** seeing themselves as capable, lovable, and unconditionally worthy human beings.

Struggling Students . . .

- ▶ **make important choices unconsciously,** being directed by self-sabotaging habits and outdated life scripts.
- ▶ **resist learning new ideas and skills,** viewing learning as fearful or boring rather than as mental play.
- ▶ **live at the mercy of strong emotions** such as anger, sadness, anxiety, or a need for instant gratification.
- ▶ **doubt their competence and personal value,** feeling inadequate to create their desired outcomes and experiences.

Planning Your Next Steps

Although our travels together are coming to an end, your journey has really just begun. Look out there to your future. What do you want to have, do, or be? What actions do you need to take to achieve your desired outcomes and experiences? Make a plan and go for it!

Sure, you'll get off course at times. But now you have strategies—both outer and inner—to get back on course. Before heading out toward your goals and dreams, take a moment to review those strategies. Any time you want, you can look over the table of contents of this book for an overview of what you've learned. Scan the chapter-opening charts to review the choices of successful and struggling people. Reread a strategy as a reminder. Perhaps most important of all, reread your journal. At any time, you can return to *On Course* and to your journal to remind yourself of anything you forget. And, believe me, you *will* forget. You *will* get off course. But you have the power to remember . . . to make wise choices . . . to get back on course…and to create the life of your dreams.

Destiny is not a matter of chance; it is a matter of choice. It is not a thing to be waited for; it is a thing to be achieved.

William Jennings Bryan

ASSESS YOURSELF, AGAIN

On the next page is a duplicate of the self-assessment you took in **Chapter 1**. Take it again. (Don't look back at your previous answers yet.) In Journal Entry 32, you will compare your first scores with your scores today, and you will consider the changes you have made. Acknowledge yourself for your courage to grow. Look, also, at the changes you still need to make to become your best self.

You now have much of what you need to stay on course to the life of your dreams. The rest you can learn on your journey. Be bold! Begin today!

Onward!

It isn't where you came from; it's where you're going that counts.

Ella Fitzgerald

© Cengage Learning

Self-Assessment

Read the following statements and score each one according to how true or false you believe it now is about you. To get an accurate picture of yourself, consider what IS true about you (not what you want to be true). Remember, there are no right or wrong answers. Assign each statement a number from 0 to 10, as follows:

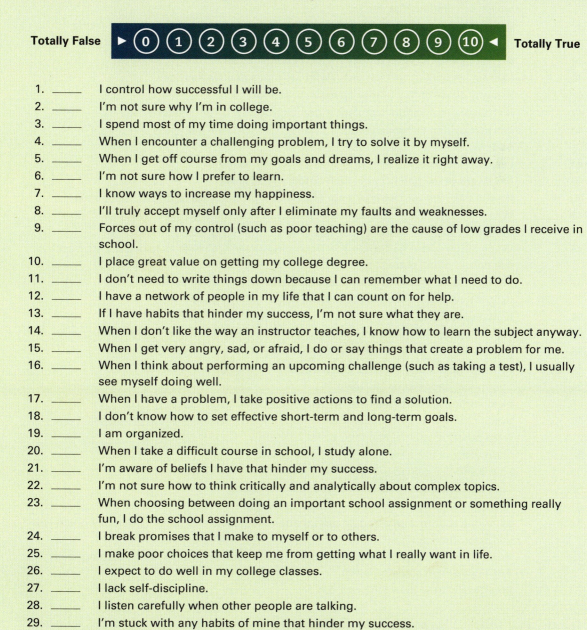

Totally False ▶ ⓪ ① ② ③ ④ ⑤ ⑥ ⑦ ⑧ ⑨ ⑩ ◀ **Totally True**

1. _____ I control how successful I will be.
2. _____ I'm not sure why I'm in college.
3. _____ I spend most of my time doing important things.
4. _____ When I encounter a challenging problem, I try to solve it by myself.
5. _____ When I get off course from my goals and dreams, I realize it right away.
6. _____ I'm not sure how I prefer to learn.
7. _____ I know ways to increase my happiness.
8. _____ I'll truly accept myself only after I eliminate my faults and weaknesses.
9. _____ Forces out of my control (such as poor teaching) are the cause of low grades I receive in school.
10. _____ I place great value on getting my college degree.
11. _____ I don't need to write things down because I can remember what I need to do.
12. _____ I have a network of people in my life that I can count on for help.
13. _____ If I have habits that hinder my success, I'm not sure what they are.
14. _____ When I don't like the way an instructor teaches, I know how to learn the subject anyway.
15. _____ When I get very angry, sad, or afraid, I do or say things that create a problem for me.
16. _____ When I think about performing an upcoming challenge (such as taking a test), I usually see myself doing well.
17. _____ When I have a problem, I take positive actions to find a solution.
18. _____ I don't know how to set effective short-term and long-term goals.
19. _____ I am organized.
20. _____ When I take a difficult course in school, I study alone.
21. _____ I'm aware of beliefs I have that hinder my success.
22. _____ I'm not sure how to think critically and analytically about complex topics.
23. _____ When choosing between doing an important school assignment or something really fun, I do the school assignment.
24. _____ I break promises that I make to myself or to others.
25. _____ I make poor choices that keep me from getting what I really want in life.
26. _____ I expect to do well in my college classes.
27. _____ I lack self-discipline.
28. _____ I listen carefully when other people are talking.
29. _____ I'm stuck with any habits of mine that hinder my success.
30. _____ My intelligence is something about myself that I can improve.

31. _____ I often feel bored, anxious, or depressed.
32. _____ I feel just as worthwhile as any other person.
33. _____ Forces outside of me (such as luck or other people) control how successful I will be.
34. _____ College is an important step on the way to accomplishing my goals and dreams.
35. _____ I spend most of my time doing unimportant things.
36. _____ I am aware of how to show respect to people who are different from me (race, religion, sexual orientation, age, etc.).
37. _____ I can be off course from my goals and dreams for quite a while without realizing it.
38. _____ I know how I prefer to learn.
39. _____ My happiness depends mostly on my circumstances.
40. _____ I accept myself just as I am, even with my faults and weaknesses.
41. _____ I am the cause of low grades I receive in school.
42. _____ If I lose my motivation in college, I don't know how I'll get it back.
43. _____ I have a written self-management system that helps me get important things done on time.
44. _____ I seldom interact with people who are different from me.
45. _____ I'm aware of the habits I have that hinder my success.
46. _____ If I don't like the way an instructor teaches, I'll probably do poorly in the course.
47. _____ When I'm very angry, sad, or afraid, I know how to manage my emotions so I don't do anything I'll regret later.
48. _____ When I think about performing an upcoming challenge (such as taking a test), I usually see myself doing poorly.
49. _____ When I have a problem, I complain, blame others, or make excuses.
50. _____ I know how to set effective short-term and long-term goals.
51. _____ I am disorganized.
52. _____ When I take a difficult course in school, I find a study partner or join a study group.
53. _____ I'm unaware of beliefs I have that hinder my success.
54. _____ I know how to think critically and analytically about complex topics.
55. _____ I often feel happy and fully alive.
56. _____ I keep promises that I make to myself or to others.
57. _____ When I have an important choice to make, I use a decision-making process that analyzes possible options and their likely outcomes.
58. _____ I don't expect to do well in my college classes.
59. _____ I am a self-disciplined person.
60. _____ I get distracted easily when other people are talking.
61. _____ I know how to change habits of mine that hinder my success.
62. _____ Everyone is born with a certain amount of intelligence, and there's not really much you can do to change that.
63. _____ When choosing between doing an important school assignment or something really fun, I usually do something fun.
64. _____ I feel less worthy than other people.

Transfer your scores to the scoring sheet on the next page. For each of the eight areas, total your scores in columns A and B. Then total your final scores as shown in the sample on the next page.

Self-Assessment Scoring Sheet

	SAMPLE		SCORE #1: Accepting Personal Responsibility		SCORE #2: Discovering Self-Motivation

SAMPLE

A	B
6. _8_	29. _3_
14. _5_	35. _3_
21. _6_	50. _6_
73. _9_	56. _2_
_28_ + 40 −	_14_ = 54

SCORE #1: Accepting Personal Responsibility

A	B
1. ___	9. ___
17. ___	25. ___
41. ___	33. ___
57. ___	49. ___
___ + 40 −	___ = ___

SCORE #2: Discovering Self-Motivation

A	B
10. ___	2. ___
26. ___	18. ___
34. ___	42. ___
50. ___	58. ___
___ + 40 −	___ = ___

SCORE #3: Mastering Self-Management

A	B
3. ___	11. ___
19. ___	27. ___
43. ___	35. ___
59. ___	51. ___
___ + 40 −	___ = ___

SCORE #4: Employing Interdependence

A	B
12. ___	4. ___
28. ___	20. ___
36. ___	44. ___
52. ___	60. ___
___ + 40 −	___ = ___

SCORE #5: Gaining Self-Awareness

A	B
5. ___	13. ___
21. ___	29. ___
45. ___	37. ___
61. ___	53. ___
___ + 40 −	___ = ___

SCORE #6: Adopting Lifelong Learning

A	B
14. ___	6. ___
30. ___	22. ___
38. ___	46. ___
54. ___	62. ___
___ + 40 −	___ = ___

SCORE #7: Developing Emotional Intelligence

A	B
7. ___	15. ___
23. ___	31. ___
47. ___	39. ___
55. ___	63. ___
___ + 40 −	___ = ___

SCORE #8: Believing in Myself

A	B
16. ___	8. ___
32. ___	24. ___
40. ___	48. ___
56. ___	64. ___
___ + 40 −	___ = ___

Interpreting Your Scores

A score of . . .

0–39   Indicates an area where your choices will **seldom** keep you on course.

40–63   Indicates an area where your choices will **sometimes** keep you on course.

64–80   Indicates an area where your choices will **usually** keep you on course.

Choices of Successful Students

Successful Students . . .

▶ **accept personal responsibility,** seeing themselves as the primary cause of their outcomes and experiences.

▶ **discover self-motivation,** finding purpose in their lives by discovering personally meaningful goals and dreams.

▶ **master self-management,** consistently planning and taking purposeful actions in pursuit of their goals and dreams.

▶ **employ interdependence,** building mutually supportive relationships that help them achieve their goals and dreams (while helping others do the same).

▶ **gain self-awareness,** consciously employing behaviors, beliefs, and attitudes that keep them on course.

▶ **adopt lifelong learning,** finding valuable lessons and wisdom in nearly every experience they have.

▶ **develop emotional intelligence,** effectively managing their emotions and the emotions of others in support of their goals and dreams.

▶ **believe in themselves,** seeing themselves as capable, lovable, and unconditionally worthy human beings.

Struggling Students . . .

▶ **see themselves as victims,** believing that what happens to them is determined primarily by external forces such as fate, luck, and powerful others.

▶ **have difficulty sustaining motivation,** often feeling depressed, frustrated, and/or resentful about a lack of direction in their lives.

▶ **seldom identify specific actions needed to accomplish a desired outcome,** and when they do, they tend to procrastinate.

▶ **are solitary,** seldom requesting, even rejecting, offers of assistance from those who could help.

▶ **make important choices unconsciously,** being directed by self-sabotaging habits and outdated life scripts.

▶ **resist learning new ideas and skills,** viewing learning as fearful or boring rather than as mental play.

▶ **live at the mercy of strong emotions, such as anger,** sadness, anxiety, or a need for instant gratification.

▶ **doubt their competence and personal value,** feeling inadequate to create their desired outcomes and experiences.

JOURNAL ENTRY / **32**

In this activity, you'll examine the changes you have made since the beginning of this course, and you'll plan your next steps toward success in college and in life.

1 In your journal, write the eight areas of the self-assessment and transfer your score from the assessment you took in "Assess Yourself" in Chapter 1 (first score) and your score from the scoring chart above (second score), as follows:

First Score	Second Score	
_____	_____	I. Accepting personal responsibility
_____	_____	2. Discovering self-motivation
_____	_____	3. Mastering self-management
_____	_____	4. Employing interdependence
_____	_____	5. Gaining self-awareness
_____	_____	6. Adopting lifelong learning
_____	_____	7. Developing emotional intelligence
_____	_____	8. Believing in myself

2 Comparing the results from the two self-assessments, write in depth about the area(s) in which you have raised your score. Remember to answer questions that a thoughtful reader would have about what you are writing, diving deep by using the 4Es (examples, explanations, experiences, and evidence)!

3 Further comparing the results from the two self-assessments, write in depth about the area(s) in which you most want to continue improving. Remember the saying "If you keep doing what you've been doing, you'll keep getting what you've been getting." With this idea in mind, identify the specific changes you'd like to make in your behaviors, thoughts, emotions, and beliefs in the months and years to come.

By the way, if one of your scores went down over the semester, consider that this result may not indicate that you became less effective; rather, it may indicate that you are now more honest with yourself or more aware of what's necessary to excel in this area.

4 Write one last entry in which you sum up the most important discoveries you've made in this course and plans for a great future. Dive deep!

In 2002, I hit rock bottom when I moved into a homeless shelter. For the next four years, I cycled in and out of one shelter after another. There, I saw how people can become passive and numb, with no life or hope left in their eyes. They smell bad, walk with their heads down, and are filled with negativity. Their only goal in life is getting a handout. I knew I couldn't allow a sheltered life to become my life.

I was a Detroit police officer from 1985 to 1998. In 1996 I lost my mother and not long after that my 17-year-old son died of an asthma attack. In my mind, crying on someone's shoulder was a sign of weakness, so I kept it all inside. I had been drinking before, but now I started drinking even more. I left the police force in 1998 and started a limo service. Four years later, I was arrested for drunk driving and lost my license. When I couldn't pay rent, the woman I was living with put me out, and I lived in my car for two months. That's when I turned to a homeless shelter for help.

My first concern was to become self-supporting, but I wasn't sure where to start. I went to a state employment service and told a counselor, "I want a college degree, not one of those low-paying jobs listed in the job bank." She told me about scholarships at the local community college, and with her help, I registered for classes in 2007. I hadn't been a student for 30-plus years, and the thought of attending college scared me. But I had a goal. I wanted to become a computer systems security analyst, a career that starts at about $48,000. The money sure sounded good.

In my English Fundamentals class I encountered *On Course.* The book gave me insights into my past failures and successes and provided specific strategies for achieving success in college and in my life. I realized that many of my past problems were rooted in Victim language. When I was on the police force, I felt that some of the supervisors picked on me. I'd say they didn't like me because I wasn't in the right group. The truth was, I was missing a lot of work, but I always shifted the blame. After reading about Victim/Creator, I told myself, *You have to rebuild yourself. No one else is going to do it for you.* I even started telling people back at the shelter about what I was learning in this class.

My greatest concern about attending college was how to organize my time. The newly discovered Creator in me used the Four-Quadrant Chart to prioritize my daily tasks. As I used the self-management tools in the book, I developed self-confidence that I would do well in college. I showed the next actions list to others and told them how important it is to have a list to keep you focused. If someone tells you they have tickets to the Detroit Pistons game, you have to say no and do what is important for your goals.

Along with how to organize my time, I discovered the beauty of interdependence. Two of my English classmates and I decided to meet in the writing center after each class and work on our assignments together. We encouraged each other and became teachers as well as students. Our new-found interdependence made us feel valuable and gave us increased confidence and feelings of self-worth. This confidence translated into academic success as well. I earned a 3.88 GPA, high honors, for my first semester.

In the next semester, I got a part-time job in the writing center. I love to see a twinkle in students' eyes when I help them do well on a paper. I also started volunteering at the Washtenaw Literacy program. I continue to use *On Course* principles in my daily life, and I share them at the tutoring center, in my volunteer work, and at the shelter. These principles provide the best hope for people to lead successful, happy, and unsheltered lives. Two of the men from the shelter are now enrolled at the college, and they come to me when they have a problem. One guy still has a Victim mentality. I tell him, "Why do you blame your woe-is-me on everyone else and not look in the mirror and see yourself as the cause? If I can help you, I will. But you have to help yourself first."

People have to learn to stand on their own two feet, and I now have the skills to help others do that. I've even changed my career goal. I plan to teach elementary school. For me it's no longer about the money. It's about sharing myself. After experiencing the lessons in *On Course*, I feel I have something to share. My fear of failure is gone. Being a Creator, I believe in myself and feel confident that I can solve any problems I face. Now I want to share that feeling with others.

Photo: Courtesy of Stephan J. Montgomery.

STUDY SKILLS
A Toolbox for Active Learners

Becoming an Active Learner

FOCUS QUESTIONS How does the human brain learn? How can you use this knowledge to become a highly effective learner?

Earlier chapters in *On Course* present essential *soft* **skills** for success in college and beyond. This section presents a toolbox of *hard* **skills** for becoming an active and highly effective learner.

As mentioned in Chapter 1, both soft skills and hard skills are learnable. Soft skills, however, are invisible and more difficult to measure than hard skills. Some people refer to soft skills as inner strengths, personal qualities, or non-cognitive factors. Your grandmother may have simply called these qualities "character." Examples of soft skills explored in *On Course* are personal responsibility, self-motivation, self-discipline, interdependence, self-awareness, emotional intelligence, and believing in yourself.

Hard skills are more visible and measureable than soft skills. The processes for learning and assessing them are more apparent. Since your main job as a student is learning, you'll need hard skills that will make you an effective learner. Also called study skills, these hard skills will improve your learning (and grades) in college. But that's not all.

After college, these skills will help you in your career and whenever you are facing the 21st-century challenge of lifelong learning. You'd be hard-pressed to find a job in today's economy that doesn't require the ability to learn quickly and effectively. Every time you download a new app to your smartphone, create a will, take out a mortgage, start a new hobby, or vacation in a foreign country, you'll need to employ effective learning skills. And that's just the beginning of all you'll need to learn to create a great life.

> We now accept the fact that learning is a lifelong process of keeping abreast of change. And the most pressing task is to teach people how to learn.
>
> Peter Drucker

ASSESS YOUR STUDY SKILLS FOR COLLEGE SUCCESS

Before we begin an exploration of effective learning skills, take a few minutes to complete the self-assessment questionnaire on the following pages. At the end of this Toolbox of learning skills, you'll have an opportunity to repeat this self-assessment and compare your two scores. I think you're going to be impressed by what you've learned about learning!

As you take this self-assessment, be absolutely honest so you can learn the truth about your present learning skills. This valuable information can pave the way to making significant improvements in your future learning efforts.

Study Skills Self-Assessment

Read the following statements and score each one according to how true or false you believe it is about you. To get an accurate picture of yourself, consider what IS true about you (not what you *want* to be true). Remember, there are no right or wrong answers. Assign each statement a number from 0 to 10, as follows:

Totally False ▶ ⓪ ① ② ③ ④ ⑤ ⑥ ⑦ ⑧ ⑨ ⑩ ◀ **Totally True**

1. _____ I understand how the human brain learns, and I use that knowledge to study effectively.
2. _____ When I read an assignment in my textbooks, I have trouble identifying the most important information.
3. _____ I know effective strategies for memorizing important things such as facts, details, and formulas.
4. _____ I don't know how to create graphic or linear organizers.
5. _____ I'm good at figuring out what's important during a class discussion or lecture.
6. _____ After I get a test back, I check my grade to see how I did and then throw it away.
7. _____ When writing a paper, I know how to add supporting details that make my main ideas clear.
8. _____ After I finish taking a test, I have no idea what kind of grade I will get.
9. _____ While reading an assignment, I have an effective system for marking or writing down important ideas.
10. _____ When I review my notes after class, they are complete and easy to understand.
11. _____ Before studying for a test, I condense all of my class notes, homework, reading assignments, and course handouts into one document, and then I study from this new document.
12. _____ I do most (sometimes all) of my studying on the day before or the day of a test.
13. _____ When I take a test, I feel calm and confident.
14. _____ When I write the answer to an essay question, I find it difficult to organize my ideas.
15. _____ When I study for a test, I use a number of different learning strategies.
16. _____ After reading, I don't recall much of what I just read.
17. _____ My class and homework notes include most of the information that later appears on a test.
18. _____ I know at least three different ways to organize my study materials so the information makes the most sense to me.
19. _____ I study for math tests by looking over the problems I solved for homework and/or the ones the instructor solved in class.

20. _____ When I take a test, I have a plan to get the most possible points.
21. _____ I usually write one draft of a paper and that's what I turn in.
22. _____ A few days after I take a test, I don't remember much of what I studied.
23. _____ After reading a homework assignment, I take time to think, write, or talk with others about the main points of what I just read.
24. _____ I've never learned how to take good notes during a class.
25. _____ I study in a quiet place where I'm not disturbed.
26. _____ I feel unprepared when I take a test because I don't really know how to study effectively.
27. _____ I don't understand how to write a good paper in college.
28. _____ I know how to do well on a test no matter what kind of questions the instructor asks: multiple-choice, true/false, fill-in-the-blank, matching, problems, or essays.
29. _____ How learning happens is a mystery to me.
30. _____ I'm good at identifying the important information in a reading assignment.
31. _____ While studying, I make a list of questions that I think will be on a test.
32. _____ During a lecture or class discussion, I have trouble staying focused.
33. _____ I'm bad at memorizing important formulas, details, and facts.
34. _____ After I get a test back, I analyze and correct all of the errors I made.
35. _____ My papers are pretty short because I have difficulty adding supporting details that make my main ideas clear.
36. _____ I know how to tell how well I have learned a subject even before I take a test.
37. _____ When I read, I don't write in my book or take separate notes.
38. _____ My class notes are difficult to understand when I look at them a few days later.
39. _____ I study for tests by re-reading my textbooks, class notes, and course handouts.
40. _____ I study each subject frequently, and I spread my study sessions over the whole course.
41. _____ I lose points on tests because of things like spending too much time on one question or taking too much time to answer a question that's worth only a few points.
42. _____ The papers I write are well organized.
43. _____ I don't participate in class discussions or activities.
44. _____ When I finish a reading assignment, I remember most of what I read.
45. _____ When I take a test, there are questions about things that weren't in my notes.
46. _____ When I study, there are often distractions and I can't concentrate.
47. _____ When I study for a math test, I solve many problems of the same kinds that will be on the test.
48. _____ Certain kinds of test questions are difficult for me and I don't do well on them.
49. _____ I understand and use all four steps of the writing process: Prewriting, Writing, Revising, and Editing.
50. _____ I ask questions in class whenever I'm confused.
51. _____ After reading a textbook, I don't think much about what I read until right before the test.
52. _____ I take good notes during a lecture or class discussion.
53. _____ When I take a test, I find questions I didn't study for.
54. _____ I use an effective learning system when I study, so I feel well prepared when I take a test.
55. _____ I know how to write a good paper in college.
56. _____ I feel nervous and my mind goes blank when I take a test.

Transfer your scores to the scoring sheets on the next page. For each of the seven areas, total your scores in columns A and B. Then total your final scores as shown in the sample.

Self-Assessment Scoring Sheet

SAMPLE

A		B	
6. _8_		29. _3_	
14. _5_		35. _3_	
21. _6_		50. _6_	
73. _9_		56. _2_	
_28_ + 40 −		_14_ = 54	

SCORE #1: Learning Actively

A		B	
1. ___		8. ___	
15. ___		22. ___	
36. ___		29. ___	
50. ___		43. ___	
___ + 40 −		___ = ___	

SCORE #2: Reading

A		B	
9. ___		2. ___	
23. ___		16. ___	
30. ___		37. ___	
44. ___		51. ___	
___ + 40 −		___ = 40 ___	

SCORE #3: Taking Notes

A		B	
5. ___		24. ___	
10. ___		32. ___	
17. ___		38. ___	
52. ___		45. ___	
___ + 40 −		___ = ___	

SCORE #4: Organizing Study Materials

A		B	
11. ___		4. ___	
18. ___		39. ___	
25. ___		46. ___	
31. ___		53. ___	
___ + 40 −		___ = ___	

SCORE #5: Rehearsing and Memorizing Study Materials

A		B	
3. ___		12. ___	
40. ___		19. ___	
47. ___		26. ___	
54. ___		33. ___	
___ + 40 −		___ = ___	

SCORE #6: Taking Tests

A		B	
13. ___		6. ___	
20. ___		41. ___	
28. ___		48. ___	
34. ___		56. ___	
___ + 40 −		___ = ___	

SCORE #7: Writing

A		B	
7. ___		14. ___	
42. ___		21. ___	
49. ___		27. ___	
55. ___		35. ___	
___ + 40 −		___ = ___	

Interpreting Your Scores

A score of . . .

0–39   Indicates an area where your study skills will **seldom** support deep learning.

40–63   Indicates an area where your study skills will **sometimes** support deep learning.

64–80   Indicates an area where your study skills will **usually** support deep learning.

HOW THE HUMAN BRAIN LEARNS

Much has been discovered, especially in the last few decades, about how human beings learn. To benefit from these discoveries, let's take a quick peek into our brains. The human brain weighs about three pounds and is composed of trillions of cells. About 100 billion of them are neurons, and here's where much of our learning takes place. When a potential learning experience occurs (such as reading this sentence), some neurons send out spikes of electrical activity. This activity causes nearby neurons to do the same. When neurons fire together, they form what is called a "neural network."

The human brain has the largest area of uncommitted cortex (no particular required function) of any species on earth. This gives humans extraordinary flexibility and capacity for learning.

Eric Jensen

I like to picture a bunch of neurons joining hands in my brain, jumping up and down, and having a learning party. If this party happens only once, learning is weak (as when you see your instructor solve a math problem one day and you can't recall how to do it the next). However, if you cause the same collection of neurons to fire repeatedly (as when you solve 10 similar math problems yourself), the result is likely to be a long-term memory. According to David Sousa, author of *How the Brain Learns,* "Eventually, repeated firing of the pattern binds the neurons together so that if one fires, they all fire, ultimately forming a new memory trace."

Here's the takeaway: If you want learning to stick, you need to create strong neural networks. In this way, learning literally changes the structure of your

Neurons before learning.

© Cengage Learning

Neurons after learning.

© Cengage Learning

brain. Through autopsies, neuroscientist Robert Jacobs and his colleagues determined that graduate students actually had 40 percent more neural connections than those of high school dropouts. Jacobs's research joins many other brain studies to reveal an important fact: **To excel as a learner, you need to create as many neural connections in your brain as possible.**

THREE PRINCIPLES OF DEEP AND LASTING LEARNING

With this brief introduction to what goes on in our brains, let's explore how highly effective learners maximize their learning. Whether they know it or not, they have figured out how to create many strong neural connections in their brains. And you can, too.

How? The short answer is: **Become an active learner**. Learning isn't a spectator sport. You don't create deep and lasting learning by passively listening to a lecture, casually skimming a textbook, or having a tutor solve your math problems. In order to create strong neural networks, you've got to participate actively in the learning process.

Now, here's the longer answer. Good learners, consciously or unconsciously, implement three principles for creating deep and lasting learning:

1. **Prior Learning.** Brain research reveals that when you connect what you are learning now to previously stored information (i.e., already-formed neural networks), you learn the new information or skill faster and more deeply. For example, the first word-processing program I learned was Word Perfect. It took me a long time to learn because I had no prior knowledge about word processing; thus, my brain contained few, if any, neural networks relevant to what I was learning. First, I needed to learn what word processing can do (such as delete whole paragraphs). Then I needed to learn how to perform that function with Word Perfect. Years later, I needed to learn another word-processing program, Microsoft Word. Since I already knew what word processing can do, I was able to learn this new program much faster. Put another way, I already had neural networks in my brain related to word processing, and learning Microsoft Word got those neurons partying.

   The contribution of past learning to new learning helps explain why some learners have difficulty in college with academic skills such as math, reading, and writing. If their earlier learning was shaky, they're going to have difficulty with new learning. They don't have strong neural networks on which to attach the new learning. It's like trying to construct a house on a weak foundation. In such a situation, the best option is to go back and strengthen the foundation, which is exactly the purpose of developmental (basic skills) courses. However, there's no point trying to learn these foundational skills the same way you learned them before. After all, how you learned them before didn't make the information or skills stick. So this time you'll want to employ more effective learning strategies, ones that will create the necessary neural networks. If that's your situation, this time you'll have

We're on the edge of an explosion in knowledge about how to learn most effectively.

Jeffrey D. Karpicke, psychology instructor, Purdue University

When information goes "in one ear and out the other," it's often because it doesn't have anything to stick to.

Joshua Foer

the advantage of employing the more effective strategies described here in *On Course*. And if you're a learner with a strong foundation, you'll find strategies here that will increase your effectiveness as a learner even more.

2. **Quality of Processing.** How you exercise affects your physical strength. Likewise, how you study affects the strength of your neural networks and therefore the quality of your learning. Some information (such as math formulas or anatomy terms) must be recalled exactly as presented. For such learning tasks, effective memorization strategies work best. However, much of what you'll be asked to learn in college is too complex for mere memorization (though many struggling students try). For mastering complex information and skills, you'll want to use what learning experts call **deep processing**. These are the strategies that successful learners use to maximize their learning and make it stick. You'll learn both effective memorization and deep-processing strategies in this Toolbox.

Don't use just one deep-processing strategy, however. Successful athletes know the value of cross training, so they use a variety of training strategies. Similarly, successful learners know the value of employing a variety of deep-processing strategies. That's because the more ways you deep-process new learning, the stronger your neural networks become.

When you actively study any information or skill, use *many different and effective deep-processing strategies.* By doing so, you create and strengthen related neural networks and your learning soars.

3. **Quantity of Processing.** The quality of your learning is also affected by how often and how long you study. This factor is often called "time on task," and the most effective approach is **distributed practice**. The human brain learns best when learning efforts are distributed over time. No successful athlete waits until the night before a competition to begin training. Why, then, do struggling students think they can start studying the night before a test? An all-night cram session may make a deposit in their short-term memories. It might even allow them to pass a test the next day. However, even students who got good grades have experienced the ineffectiveness of cramming. This effect is sometimes called "learning amnesia." It's the frustrating experience of not being able to remember what was learned in a previous course when you need it. Forgetting happens when we don't create strong neural networks that make learning last. To create strong neural networks, you need to process the target information or skill with *many different* deep-processing strategies and do it *frequently.*

In addition to how frequently you use deep-processing strategies to study, also important is the *amount of time* you spend learning each time. Obviously, deep processing for 60 minutes generates more learning than deep processing for only 5 minutes. So, highly effective learners put in **sufficient time on task**. The traditional guideline for a week's studying is 2 hours for each hour of class time. Thus, if you have 15 hours of classes per week, the estimate for your "sufficient time on task" is about 30 hours per week. Many struggling students neither study very often nor very long. However, some fool themselves by

M athematics teachers . . . see students using a certain formula to solve problems correctly one day, but they cannot remember how to do it the next day. If the process was not stored, the information is treated as brand new again!

David A. Sousa

A lmost everyone has had occasion to look back upon his school days and wonder what has become of the knowledge he was supposed to have amassed during his days of schooling.

John Dewey

putting in "sufficient time," but spend little of it engaged in effective learning strategies (such as the ones you are about to learn). Instead, they skim complex information in their textbooks. They attempt to memorize information they don't understand. Their minds wander to a conversation they had at lunch. They rummage through their book bags and dresser drawers and closets looking for their class notes. They surf the Internet. They play a video game…or five. They phone a classmate. They send a couple of text messages, and the next thing they know, it's time to go to bed. When they fail the test the next day, they complain, "But I studied *so long!*"

Some students have a chemical imbalance that prevents them from focusing for long periods of time, and their learning suffers. If you think this may be true for you, make an appointment with your college's disability counselor to get help. But the reason most students struggle with learning is fully within their control. You don't need a genius IQ to be a good learner and do well in college. What you do need is a learning system that employs what science has discovered about how the human brain learns. Billions of neurons between your ears are ready to party. Let the learning festival begin!

G ood learners, like everyone else, are living, squirming, questioning, perceiving, fearing, loving, and languaging nervous systems, but they are good learners precisely because they believe and do certain things that less effective learners do not believe and do. And therein lies the key.

Neil Postman & Charles Weingartner

The CORE Learning System

Four general strategies are common to good learners. To remember these strategies, think of the word CORE (see **Figure T.1**). CORE stands for **Collect**, **Organize**, **Rehearse**, and **Evaluate**. The CORE learning system is effective because it automatically guides you to employ all three of the active learning principles discussed earlier. Thus, by applying what is known about how the human brain learns, the CORE learning system helps you create deep and lasting learning. Here's how it works:

Collect: In every waking moment, we're constantly collecting perceptions through our five senses. Without conscious effort, the brain takes in a multitude of sights, sounds, smells, tastes, and physical sensations. Most perceptions disappear within moments. Some, such as our first language, may stick for a lifetime. Thus, much of what we learn in life we do without intention. In college, however, learning needs to be more conscious. That's because instructors expect you to learn specific information and skills. Then, of course, they want you to demonstrate that knowledge on quizzes, tests, exams, term papers, and other forms of evaluation. In college, two of the most important ways you'll collect information and skills are through reading textbooks and attending classes and labs.

Organize: Once we collect information, we need to make sense of it. When learning in everyday life, we tend to organize collected information

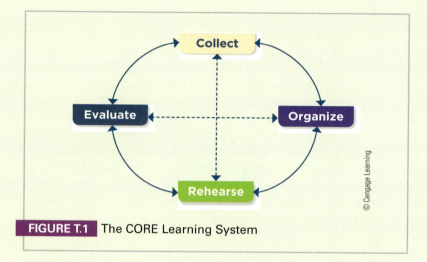

© Cengage Learning

FIGURE T.1   The CORE Learning System

> When something is meaningful it is organized; when it is organized, it is simplified in the mind.
>
> **Robert Ornstein**

in unconscious ways. We don't even realize that we're doing it. However, in a college course, you need to organize information systematically so it makes sense to you. In fact, making meaning from collected information is one of the most important outcomes of studying.

Rehearse: Once we collect and organize our target knowledge, we need to remember it for future use. Rehearsing (also called "practicing") strengthens neural networks and makes learning stick. When you solve 10 challenging math problems, you're rehearsing. Over time, the process of solving becomes easier and more natural. Good learners know how to rehearse information and skills so they can use them, whether on a test, in their career, or in their personal life.

Evaluate: Life is great at giving us informal feedback about the quality of our learning. Maybe you tell a joke and forget the punch line. You know immediately you have more learning to do. Higher education, however, provides us with more formal feedback. Yup, those pesky tests, term papers, quizzes, lab reports, essays, classroom questions, and final exams. Evaluations—whether informal and formal—are an essential component of all learning. That's because without feedback, we can never be sure if our learning is accurate or complete.

> Research has shown that students learn best when they themselves are actively engaged in the subject instead of simply listening to someone else speak.
>
> **Barbara Oakley,**
> *A Mind for Numbers*

In this "Toolbox for Active Learners," you'll learn proven strategies for

- **Collecting** key information,
- **Organizing** that information into effective study materials,
- **Rehearsing** information and skills for future use, and
- **Evaluating** how well you have learned.

But learning doesn't occur in a tidy, step-by-step fashion. At any moment while learning, you may need to jump to a different component in the CORE system. For example, while **Rehearsing**, you might realize that some information doesn't make sense to you. So you stop and **Organize** it in a different way. At other times you may engage two or more components at once. For instance, when **Rehearsing** study materials, you're probably **Evaluating** your mastery of that knowledge at the same time. Thus, you can expect to use the four components of the CORE Learning System in any order and in any combination.

Although the CORE system is an effective blueprint for creating deep and lasting learning, not all learners prefer to **Collect**, **Organize**, **Rehearse**, and **Evaluate** in the same way. That's why you'll encounter many different strategies in this Toolbox. Your task is to experiment with and find the ones that work best for you. What you'll ultimately construct is a personalized learning system, one you can use for the rest of your life. In this way, you can be confident of your ability to learn anything you need to know on the path to achieving your goals and dreams in college and beyond.

R emember, it's not the size of the brain that matters; it's the number of connections between neurons.

David A. Sousa

EXERCISE: ACTIVE LEARNING

Identify one thing you have learned simply because you enjoyed learning it. **Then write or discuss answers to each of the following questions.**

A. How did you gather the information or skills you needed to learn this? (**Collect**)

B. What did you do to learn the information or skills needed to learn this? (**Organize**)

C. What else did you do to learn this? (**Rehearse**—Variety)

D. How often did you engage in learning this? (**Rehearse**—Frequency)

E. When you engaged in learning this, how long did you usually spend? (**Rehearse**—Duration)

F. What feedback did you use to determine how well you had learned this? (**Evaluate**)

ONE STUDENT'S STORY

KASE CORMIER, *Asheville-Buncombe Technical Community College, North Carolina*

At the beginning of my first semester in college, I was overwhelmed. I had been out of school for more than 10 years and wasn't sure how to make the adjustment to being back in school after all that time. In previous attempts at school I had felt dumb; I had an awful memory and a learning disability that made writing and spelling difficult. While looking over the syllabi for my five classes, I had no idea how I was going to fit all that knowledge into my brain. The information for Anatomy and Physiology was enough by itself; adding in essays, computer projects, and reading assignments from other classes made my head spin. On top of all that, I was required to take a study skills class. A friend who had taken the class before told me it was worth it. Skeptical, I responded, "Are you kidding me? There is no way I'll get anything out of that class, and I have no more time."

The week before classes began, I decided to get a head start on the dizzying amount of reading I had to do. I picked up the *On Course* textbook and skimmed the pages lazily until I got to the section on "Becoming an Active Learner." The information on creating "neural networks" piqued my interest, and I read about the three principles of deep learning: connect new information to things you already know, use a lot of different study techniques, and study often. Although it was interesting at the time, I had too much to do to let it sink in; yet as the semester progressed, those three principles began popping into my head. I could practically feel my neurons firing off faster and faster as I learned new material, trying to find ways to process and retain everything I was being taught. Every class moved quickly, and I found that I only had a short amount of time to learn something. I kept applying those techniques, and as long as I connected new information back to what I already knew, found new and creative ways to learn it, and repeated those activities often, I could fit so much more information into my head. Better than simply cramming for a test, those principles enabled me to do more than just learn new information. They helped me retain it as well.

These three learning principles were extremely important for Anatomy and Physiology because of how much information we were responsible for. Cramming for the next test wouldn't work; every section was laying groundwork for the future, and I needed to retain that information. To create varied learning experiences, I tried out several different study groups, each with a different style of learning, until I finally found a group that I connected with; afterward, I supplemented my primary study group with other groups to have some variety. I worked hard with each group, even making up silly games to explore different ways of learning the material. One game was "flashcard races." We put the names of the cranial nerves on flashcards, shuffled them, and then raced to see who could put them in order first. The more different ways I studied the information, the stronger my neural connections became. I took every opportunity to study in open lab, and in class, I asked lots of questions. My classmates joked with me, saying that I asked "Why?" too much, but I explained that it helped me relate the information to things I already knew. After our final lecture exam (which happened to be on neurons), my study buddies all gave me a hug and thanked me for improving the study sessions with my silly games and constant questioning. We all got As!

The *On Course* principles may seem worthless at first, but don't be fooled. They stay with you and change the way you learn. I am grateful that I took the initiative to read the section on learning before my classes started. In high school I was a C student, but this semester I earned a 4.0! Connecting information to what I already knew, using a variety of study techniques, and studying often definitely helped make my first semester back in college a success.

Photo: Courtesy of Kase Cormier.

Reading

The first step in the CORE Learning System is **Collecting** knowledge, and one of the most important ways you'll **Collect** knowledge in college is by reading. During your studies you can expect to read many thousands of pages. You'll read textbooks, reference books, journals, novels, articles, handouts, websites, and more. Most of the tests you'll take will be based on your reading. And so will the essays and research papers you'll write. Obviously, then, reading is one of the most important skills you can have for success in college.

Sadly, according to American College Testing (ACT), many college-bound students lack this skill. Nearly half of the 1.2 million students who recently took the ACT college entrance test scored low in reading. This is bad news. According to ACT, the ability to read and understand complex texts is essential for college success. In fact, this skill separates students who are ready for college from those who are not. And because of all of the reading that is required in college, even students with good reading skills will benefit from becoming more accomplished.

The learning strategies you'll encounter in this section have one thing in common: they cure **mindless reading.** Mindless reading occurs when you run your eyes over a page only to realize later that you recall little of what you read. The opposite of mindless reading is **active reading**. Active reading is characterized by intense mental engagement in what you are reading. This highly focused involvement leads to significant neural activity in your brain, assists deep and lasting learning, and (good news for students) leads to high grades.

READING: THE BIG PICTURE

When reading mindfully, you are actively **Collecting** key concepts, ideas (main and secondary),

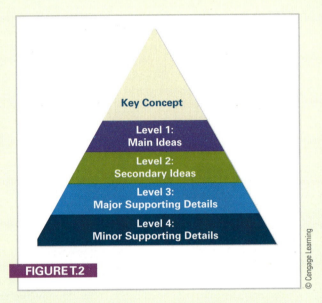

FIGURE T.2

© Cengage Learning

and supporting details (major and minor). When placed by levels of significance, information you read looks like **Figure T.2**.

A **key concept** is the main topic you are reading about. Examples of key concepts include *inflation*, *mitosis*, *World War II*, or *symbolic interactionism*.

Ideas that expand on concepts are divided into main and secondary ideas. A **main idea** (sometimes called a "thesis") is the most important idea the author wants to convey about a key concept. Two authors may write about the same key concept but present different main ideas. For example, they may both write about *inflation* but disagree about its cause. One might say, "The primary cause of inflation is war." The other may say, "The rising cost of production is the main cause of inflation."

A **secondary idea** (sometimes called a "topic sentence") elaborates on a main idea by answering questions that readers may have about it. For example, one question about inflation might be, "What effect do taxes have on rising costs?" Another might be "How do labor unions affect the cost of production?"

Each idea—main or secondary—is typically followed by **supporting details** such as examples, evidence, explanation, and experiences.

To illustrate the relationship of levels, imagine that your instructor asks your class the following. "In Chapter 2 of *On Course*, a key concept is personal responsibility. What is the main idea about it?" (If you have read the chapter, pause for a moment and decide how you would answer, because how well you answer provides feedback about your present reading abilities.)

Imagine one of your classmates replying, "The main idea in the second chapter of *On Course* is that personal responsibility is an important inner quality for creating academic, professional, and personal success."

"Well done," your instructor says, "and what are some of the secondary ideas?"

Another student answers, "When we are being responsible we respond to life's challenges as Creators not as Victims. Another secondary idea is that our inner conversations affect whether or not we make responsible choices. And a third idea is that using a decision-making model called the Wise Choice Process helps us make responsible choices."

"Excellent," your instructor enthuses. "You've demonstrated you understand some of the important ideas of the chapter. Now, someone please elaborate on the Wise Choice Process." In response, a third student *explains* the six steps of the Wise Choice Process and then gives an *example* of how she used it to make a recent decision. By elaborating, she offers supporting details that answer the questions a thoughtful reader would have about the Wise Choice Process, such as "What is it and how can it be used?"

So as you look at the following learning strategies, keep in mind the big picture of reading: **Your goal is to Collect key concepts, important ideas, and supporting details.**

CHALLENGES WITH READING

Following are common challenges with reading in higher education. Circle the numbers next to the challenges you are having (or can foresee having) in reading for your present courses. Even if you consider yourself a good reader, circle the numbers next to at least two areas in which you could improve. If you have a challenge not on the list, use one or both blank spaces at the bottom of the list to add your own challenge(s).

1. I have no idea how to read effectively.
2. I feel overwhelmed by the amount of reading I have.
3. I don't complete all of my reading assignments because I get distracted.
4. I usually do my reading assignments at times when I'm not at my best mentally.
5. I think I understand what I read, but when I take a test on it, I don't do well.
6. I don't like one of my courses, so I can't get motivated to read.
7. I complete all of my reading assignments, but I don't do well on tests about the reading.
8. I'm not interested in many of the things I have to read about.
9. I don't know how to tell the difference between a main idea and supporting details.
10. I highlight almost everything in a reading assignment because it all seems important.
11. I don't remember much of what I read.
12. One of my textbooks is too difficult to understand.
13. I get confused because there are so many new words that I don't understand.
14. I read my math assignments but when I take a test, I don't do well.

15. When I read, the slightest noises distract me.

16. I'm a slow reader, and I can't keep up with the amount of reading assigned.

17. When I read, I can't figure out what parts are important.

18. My textbook is boring, and I don't enjoy reading it.

19. I lose concentration, and my mind wanders while I'm trying to read.

20. English is my second language, and sometimes I just don't understand.

21. I don't do well on tests that are based on reading assignments.

22. When I read online assignments such as journal articles, I don't want to waste paper and money by printing all of the pages; still I need a way to make sure I understand the information.

23. I read and reread some of my assignments and still don't understand the material.

24. _____
_____

25. _____
_____

STRATEGIES TO IMPROVE READING

Following you'll find many of the very best strategies for mastering the skill of reading. After reading each strategy, pause and decide if it would help you overcome any of the challenges you circled. If so, mark it in some way (e.g., underline, circle, highlight, star). Later on, you can decide which of these strategies to experiment with to improve your reading.

Before Reading

1. Approach reading with a positive attitude. Attitude is a foundation of your success because it influences the choices you make. Nowhere is this truer than in reading. Do you have negative attitudes about reading in general or reading specific subjects? Or do you harbor doubts about your ability to understand what you read? Do you think of any reading assignments as beyond your understanding, boring, worthless, or stupid? If so, replace negative attitudes with positive ones. Realize that reading offers you access to the entire recorded knowledge of the human race. With effective reading skills, you can learn virtually any information or skill you need in order to improve your life, but only if you approach each reading assignment with a positive attitude.

2. Create a distributed reading schedule. A marathon reading session before an exam is seldom helpful. Instead, spread many shorter sessions over an entire course. For example, plan to finish your 450-page history text by reading 30 to 40 pages each week. You can easily reach that goal by reading just 5 or 6 pages a day. A distributed schedule like this keeps you current with your assignments, helps you concentrate for your entire reading session, and increases how much you recall from what you read.

3. Read when you're most alert. Are you a morning person or a night person? Or do you hit your mental peak in the middle of the day? Whenever you experience your greatest mental alertness, that's the time of day to read, especially your most challenging subjects.

4. Read where you can concentrate. Focus is essential to active reading. Here are some keys to achieving that focus:

- read in a quiet room,
- at a desk,
- with an ergonomic chair,
- good lighting,
- a cool temperature, and
- a do-not-disturb sign on the door.

Short of this ideal, consider a quiet corner in the library or even an empty classroom. Choose a place that eliminates (or at least minimizes) distractions. Turn off your cell phone, open your book, and dive in.

5. Review past readings. As a warm-up before you read, glance at pages you have previously read. Look at past chapter titles and text headings to jog your memory. Review any marks and annotations you added on the first read-through (see Strategies 15–16 for how to do this). Look over any separate notes you took (Strategy 17). Reviewing like this takes advantage of one of the three principles of deep and lasting learning: prior learning. When you connect what you are reading now to previously stored information (i.e., already-formed neural networks), you learn the new information or skill faster and more deeply.

6. Preview before reading. Like observing a valley from a high mountain, previewing a reading assignment provides the big picture of what's to come. You'll see the important ideas and their organization, which increases understanding when you read. At the beginning of a course, it's wise to preview the entire textbook. Most of the time, however, you'll be previewing a single chapter. Thumb through the pages, taking in chapter titles, chapter objectives, focus questions, text headings, charts, graphs, illustrations, previews, and summaries. Note any words that are specially formatted, such as with CAPITALS, **bold**, *italics*, and so on. In just a few minutes, you will have a helpful overview of what you are about to read. A chapter preview should take no longer than five minutes and include a quick look at some or all of the following features:

- **Table of Contents:** The fastest way to preview is to look at the table of contents. It provides an outline of your reading. For an example, see the table of contexts of this book.

- **Chapter Objectives or Focus Questions:** Usually placed at the beginning of a chapter, these features identify what you can expect to learn from the chapter. Each section in *On Course* starts with one or more Focus Questions.

- **Chapter Titles and Headings:** Thumb through the pages you're about to read, and note the titles and headings. They provide a helpful

overview of the topics you'll be reading about. For example, here are three levels of information presented in Chapter 2 of *On Course*:

Accepting Personal Responsibility

Adopting a Creator Mindset

Victim and Creator Mindsets

Responsibility and Culture

Responsibility and Choice

- **Special Formatting:** Words in CAPITALS, **bold**, *italics*, or **color** put a spotlight on key concepts and ideas. When you see special formatting, the author is saying, *This is important information!* A common use of specially formatted text is to call attention to key words. That is why **Creator mindset** and **Victim mindset** are bolded in Chapter 2.

- **Visual Elements:** Charts, graphs, illustrations, cartoons, photographs, and diagrams are included to reinforce concepts in the text and improve readers' understanding. For example, the two drawings in the section called "How the Human Brain Learns" illustrate how learning changes neurons in the brain. Captions for visual elements usually explain their significance.

- **Chapter Summaries:** Many college texts provide a summary at the end of a chapter. This summary typically identifies the important ideas in the chapter.

While it's taken quite a few words to describe these six options for previewing a reading assignment, once you get skilled, previewing will take you only a few minutes to do.

7. Do a quick read. With a "quick read," you skim an entire assignment, reading as fast as you can. Insufficient by itself, a quick read lays a foundation so you can later reread more thoroughly. The second time you have familiar information to build on. A quick read is a particularly helpful pre-reading strategy when learning unfamiliar subjects. It's also a good option when you have only a few minutes. Just remember to come back later and do a more thorough reading.

8. Identify the purpose of what you're reading. To keep the big picture in mind, ask yourself, "What's the point of what I'm about to read?" For example, the "point" of every section of *On Course* is to present empowering beliefs and behaviors. Then you can decide which ones to add to your toolbox for success in college and in life. By keeping this purpose in mind, you program yourself to **Collect** the most important ideas as you read. The purpose of what you are reading right now is to identify strategies that may help you improve your reading comprehension and speed.

9. Create a list of questions. If the author provides focus questions, use them to start this list. Next, turn chapter titles or section headings into questions. For example, if the heading in a computer book reads "HTML Tags," turn this heading into one or more questions: *What is an HTML tag? How are HTML tags created?* If you see questions within the text, add them to your list. The process of reading for answers to questions, especially those you're really curious about, heightens your concentration, increases your active involvement, and improves your understanding.

While Reading

10. Read in chunks. Poor readers read one word at a time. Good readers don't read words; they read ideas, and ideas are found in groups of words, or chunks. For example, in the following sentence, try reading all of the words between the diamonds at once:

◆ If you read ◆ in chunks ◆ you will increase ◆ your speed ◆ and your comprehension. ◆

Like any new habit, this method will initially feel awkward. However, as you practice you'll find you can take in bigger chunks of information at increasingly faster rates of speed, like this:

◆ If you read in chunks ◆ you will increase your speed ◆ and your comprehension. ◆

Since much of your reading time occurs while you pause to take in words (called a "fixation"), the fewer times you pause, the faster you can read. In addition to taking in larger chunks of information, you can nudge yourself even faster by moving your fingers along the line of text as a speed regulator. As you get practiced at taking in more words in one fixation, you can increase the speed of your fingers and read even faster.

11. Concentrate on reading faster. In one experiment, students increased their reading speed up to 50 percent simply by concentrating on reading as fast as they could while still understanding what they were reading. You, too, can probably read faster by just *deciding* to. Time yourself to see how long it takes you to read five pages of a book. Then see if you can improve your reading time for the next five pages. And so on. However, dismiss the idea that you're ever going to read an entire book in 30 minutes, as some speed reading programs promise. There is little evidence that the average person can achieve anywhere near that reading speed with enough comprehension to make the effort worthwhile. Be happy if you can improve your reading speed by 50 percent without losing comprehension. After all, the goal of reading is not to finish fast but to **Collect** key concepts, main ideas, and supporting details.

12. Pause to recite. Have you ever finished reading an assignment only to realize you have no idea what you just read? Here's a remedy. Stop at the end of each section and summarize aloud what you

SPEED READING COURSE
7·00 — 7·05

Mike Flanagan/Cartoon Stock

understand to be the main ideas and supporting details. The more difficult the reading, the more often you'll want to pause to recite. Each recitation will give you instant feedback about how well you understand the author's ideas. When you can't smoothly recite the essence of what you have read, go back and read the passage again. Try reading aloud the words you have underlined or highlighted. Keep working actively with the ideas until you understand them completely. Pause and experiment with this strategy right now. What are the 12 reading strategies you have just encountered? How many can you recall? How much do you remember about them?

13. Read for answers to questions on your list. If you've created a list of questions (Strategy 9), now is the time to cash in on that effort. For example, suppose you're about to read a chapter in your accounting book titled "The Double-Entry Accounting System." On your list of questions, you've written "What is a double-entry accounting system?" As you read the chapter, look for and underline the answer. Then write the question in the margin alongside. If you finish your reading assignment and still have unanswered questions on your list, ask your instructor for answers during class or office hours.

14. Write new questions and their answers. As you read, you may realize the author is answering a question you don't have on your list. For example, the author may answer your question: "*What is a double-entry accounting system?*" Then she may go on to answer another question: "*Why is a double-entry accounting system better than a single-entry system?*" In fact, authors will often present you with a question and then immediately go on to answer it. Underline the answer and write the question in the margin alongside.

15. Mark your text. As you read, keep asking yourself: What's the key concept . . . what are the main ideas about the concept . . . and what support is offered? Identifying main and supporting ideas is usually easier after you've read a whole paragraph, or even a whole section. Once you decide what's important, mark these ideas in your book.

As a guideline, mark only 10 to 15 percent of your text. That limitation will help you select what is truly important. How you mark is limited only by your imagination, but here are some options:

- Underline with a pen or pencil.
- Highlight with a colored accent marker (main ideas can be highlighted in one color and supporting ideas in another).
- Circle specialized terms and underline their definitions.
- Place a symbol in the margin to draw attention to an important idea (e.g., a star).
- Place a question mark next to a puzzling idea you want to ask about in class.

Later you'll be **Collecting** these ideas to create effective study materials, and your markings will make that process much easier.

16. Annotate your text. To annotate means to add comments. Writing your own comments in the blank spaces on each page helps you stay focused, minimize mindless reading and maximize understanding. Like marking your text, annotating helps you **Collect** main ideas and supporting details from which you'll later create study materials. Here are some ways to annotate:

- Summarize an important idea in your own words.
- Draw a diagram or picture to represent information in the text.
- As mentioned in Strategies 13 and 14, underline the answer to a question (either yours or the author's) and write the question in the margin alongside.
- Write questions you want to ask in class.
- Create a written conversation with the author: "*What's your evidence for this claim?*" or "*This seems to contradict what my instructor said in class!*"

Of course, you can also take notes in a separate notebook or computer file, and later you'll learn a number of strategies for doing just that. **Figure T.3** offers an example of how you might mark and annotate a passage from a biology text.

What is science?

Biology is a science. The word *science* comes from a Latin word meaning "to know." <u>Science is a way of thinking and a method of investigating the natural world in a systematic manner.</u> We test ideas, and based on our findings, we modify or reject these ideas. The process of science is investigative, dynamic, and often controversial. The observations made, the range of questions asked, and the design of experiments depend on the creativity of the individual scientist. However, science is influenced by cultural, social, historical, and technological contexts, so the process changes over time.

What are the steps of the scientific method?

Steps:
- *Observe*
- *Question*
- *Develop hypothesis*
- *Predict results*
- *Experiment*
- *Analyze data*
- *Draw conclusions*

The scientific method has similarities to the Wise Choice Process!

The **scientific method** <u>involves a series of ordered steps.</u> Using the scientific method, scientists make <u>careful observations</u>, ask <u>critical questions</u>, and <u>develop hypotheses</u>, which are tentative explanations. Using their hypotheses, scientists <u>make predictions</u> that can be tested by making further observations or by <u>performing experiments.</u> They gather **data**, information that they can analyze, often using computers and sophisticated statistical methods. They interpret the results of their experiments and <u>draw conclusions</u> from them. As we will discuss, scientists pose many hypotheses that cannot be tested by using all of the steps of the scientific method in a rigid way. Scientists use the scientific method as a generalize framework or guide.

FIGURE T.3 Text Marked and Annotated

Source: From Eldra P. Solomon, Linda R. Berg, Diana W. Martin, *Biology*, 8th Edition, p. 15.
© Cengage Learning, 2008.

ACTIVITY 2A: MARKING AND ANNOTATING TEXT

As you read the following text, mark key concepts, important ideas, and supporting details. Then write questions or comments in the margin. Afterward, compare your results with one or more classmates.

Cultural Diversity

It is rare for a society to be culturally uniform. As societies develop and become more complex, different cultural traditions appear. The more complex the society, the more likely its culture will be internally varied and diverse. The United States, for example, hosts enormous cultural diversity stemming from religious, ethnic, and racial differences, as well as regional, age, gender, and class differences. Currently, more than 12 percent of people in the United States are foreign born. In a single year, immigrants from more than 100 countries come to the United States (U.S. Census Bureau 2007). Whereas earlier immigrants were predominantly from Europe, now Latin America and Asia are the greatest sources of new immigrants. One result is a large increase in the number of U.S. residents for whom English is the second language. Cultural diversity is clearly a characteristic of contemporary American society.

The richness of American culture stems from the many traditions that different groups have brought with them to this society, as well as from the cultural forms that have emerged through their experience within the United States. Jazz, for example, is one of the few musical forms indigenous to the United States. An indigenous art form refers to something that originated in a particular region or culture. However, jazz also has roots in the musical traditions of slave communities and African cultures. Since the birth of jazz, cultural greats such as Ella Fitzgerald, Count Basie, Duke Ellington, Billie Holiday, and numerous others have not only enriched the jazz tradition, but have also influenced other forms of music, including rock and roll.

Native American cultures have likewise enriched the culture of our society, as have the cultures that various immigrant groups have brought with them to the United States. With such great variety, how can the United States be called one culture? The culture of the United States, including its langrage, arts, food customs, religious practices, and dress, can be seen as the sum of the diverse cultures that constitute this society.

Source: From Margaret L. Andersen and Howard F. Taylor, *Sociology: The Essentials.* 5th Edition, pp. 46–47. © Cengage Learning, 2009.

17. Take notes. Many strategies exist for **Collecting** ideas from textbooks. Some strategies suggest taking notes in a separate binder or computer file. Later on you'll learn a number of nifty strategies for doing just that. However, there is one option that is ideally suited for taking notes while reading a text, so we'll look at it here. Start by writing the chapter title at the top of your note page or computer file (this is usually the key concept). Beneath the chapter title, copy the first main heading (Level 1 Main Idea). Below the first Main Idea, any subheadings (Level 2 Secondary Ideas), indenting a few spaces to the right. Here's what this would look like for Chapter 2 of *On Course*:

Structure	Example
Key Concept	Accepting Personal Responsibility
— Level 1 Main Idea	— Adopting a Creator Mindset
— Level 2 Secondary Idea	— Victim and Creator Mindsets
— Level 2 Secondary Idea	— Responsibility and Culture
— Level 2 Secondary Idea	— Responsibility and Choice
— Level 1 Main Idea	— Mastering Creator Language
— Level 2 Secondary Idea	— Self-Talk
— Level 2 Secondary Idea	— The Language of Responsibility
— Level 1 Main Idea	— Making Wise Decisions
— Level 2 Secondary Idea	— The Wise Choice Process

© Cengage Learning

As you read the chapter, add additional information to clarify these ideas. Include major and minor supporting details, indenting them additional spaces to the right. **Figure T.4** shows what the expanded notes might look like after reading the sections about "Adopting a Creator Mindset."

18. Read for IOUs. Eventually you'll have to read something you don't want to. Maybe you're only taking a course because it's required. Or maybe the author of your textbook has a writing style that puts you to sleep (hopefully not this one!). Excuses aside, you still need to pass the course. That's when the IOU strategy can help. IOU stands for **"Interesting or Usable."** The goal is to increase concentration (and decrease mindless reading). As you read the assignment, intentionally look for anything you think is *interesting* or *usable*.

"Interesting" could be a fact that might interest a friend, a beautifully crafted sentence, or even one perfectly chosen word. In the midst of reading an article that I found boring, I was fascinated to discover that the wonder drug penicillin was created from ordinary blue bread mold. I found that fact very interesting, and my level of concentration shot up as I read on for other interesting details. Also look for something practical or "usable." Maybe it's a way you can reduce pollutants where you live. Or how to write an effective cover letter when applying for a job. Or ways to help your children (present or future) develop their creativity. As you read a "boring" assignment, take on the role of a miner panning for gold in a stream of ideas. You may handle a lot of boring rocks, but keep your mind alert knowing that at any moment you may discover a gold nugget— something personally *interesting* or *usable*! And in the process, you'll also **Collect** key concepts, main ideas, and supporting details that will help you pass the course.

19. Look up the definition of key words. Use a dictionary when you don't know the meaning of a key word. Consider starting a vocabulary list in your journal. Or create a deck of index cards with new words on one side and definitions on the other. Writing the word in a sentence is a good idea, too. (**Figure T.5** shows a sample vocabulary flashcard.) Online dictionaries, like Merriam-Webster's (m-w.com), offer an option that lets you hear the correct pronunciation of a word. To lock them in your memory, slip new words into your conversations and writings. Developing an extensive and eloquent vocabulary is a great success strategy. Wondering how many words you ought to know? Linguist David Crystal estimates that the

Accepting Personal Responsibility

Adopting a Creator Mindset

"Personal *response-ability* is the ability to respond wisely at each fork in the road, your choices moving you ever closer to your desired outcomes and experiences. The opposite is waiting passively for your life to be determined by luck or powerful others." P. 43

Example: Deborah—English 101 student who blames her writing problems on teachers and keeps failing the course (Victim mindset).

Victim and Creator Mindsets

—Victim mindset: Keeps people from seeing and acting on choices that could help them achieve the life they want

—Creator mindset: Causes people to see multiple options, choose wisely among them, and take effective actions to achieve the life they want

—Benefits of Creator mindset: More often achieve goals and dreams

    —Example of Creator mindset: Rosa Parks ("Mother of modern-day civil rights movement")

    —Study by Vallerand and Bissonette—"Significantly more of the Creator-like students were still enrolled in college [a year later] than the Victim-like students" P. 45

Responsibility and Culture

—Psychologist Julian Rotter studied "locus of control" (belief about where the power over our lives is located)

—North Americans tend to have "inner locus of control"

—Some other cultures (e.g., Latino/a) tend to have "outer locus of control"

Responsibility and Choice

—The key ingredient of personal responsibility is choice (the moment between stimulus and response)

—Victim choices: Blaming, complaining, excusing, repeating behavior

    —Energy is used to judge themselves or others

    —Results: Seldom achieves goals

—Creator choices: Seeking solutions, taking actions, trying something new

    —Energy is used to seek solutions to problems

    —Results: Often achieves goals

    —No one makes Creator choices all the time. Goal is to do it more often

—Creator Belief: I am responsible for creating my life as I want it

    —Not always true, but causes a Creator to look for solutions

—"Ultimately each of us creates the quality of our life with the wisdom or folly of our choices" P. 48

FIGURE T.4 Expanded Notes

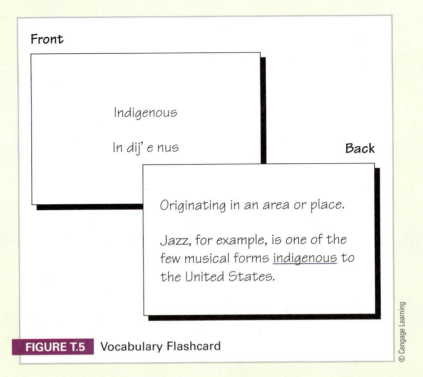

Front

Indigenous

In dij' e nus

Back

Originating in an area or place.

Jazz, for example, is one of the few musical forms <u>indigenous</u> to the United States.

© Cengage Learning

FIGURE T.5   Vocabulary Flashcard

average college graduate has an active vocabulary of 60,000 words and the ability to recognize an additional 75,000.

20. Use context clues to determine the meaning of key words. Context clues are hints that help you make educated guesses about the definitions of challenging words. Context clues most often appear in the same sentence as the challenging word, though sometimes they are in a nearby sentence. Four common kinds of context clues include:

- **Synonyms:** A word with the same meaning as the challenging word.

  Illustration: After learning about Victim and Creator language, he modified his vocabulary with great **celerity** and haste. (*Celerity* means "haste" or "speed.")

- **Antonyms:** A word with the opposite meaning of the challenging word.

  Illustration: In the past, he was criticized for his poor judgment. Since learning the Wise Choice Process, he is now praised for his **sagacity**. (*Sagacity* means "good judgment.")

- **Examples:** An example provided of the challenging word.

  Illustration: **Injunctions** such as "don't be successful" or "don't believe in yourself" can cause someone to make unwise choices. (*Injunction* means an "order, usually one prohibiting something.")

- **Explanations:** A clarification of the challenging word.

  Illustration: His classmate is so *insouciant* that it seems she cares little about anything. (*Insouciant* means "marked by unconcern or lack of caring.")

21. Read critically. Not all ideas in print are true. Learn to read critically by being a healthy skeptic. Look for red flags that may suggest a credibility problem. Who is the author? What are the author's credentials? What assumptions does the author hold? Does the author stand to gain (e.g., money, status, revenge, reputation) by your acceptance of his or her opinion? Are the facts accurate and relevant? Is the evidence sufficient? Are the author's positions developed with logic or only strong emotions? Are sources of information identified?

ACTIVITY 2B: USING CONTEXT CLUES

Make an educated guess, based on context clues, about the meaning of the underlined words below. Then look the words up in a dictionary to see how accurate your guesses were.

1. She was <u>prostrate</u>, lying face down on the cold earth.

2. He lived an <u>insular</u> life, isolated from problems that others face.

3. The <u>protagonist</u>, as the main character in a story, often has a difficult and life-changing decision to make.

4. <u>Churlish</u> as a child, she has grown into a well-mannered young woman.

5. His <u>terpsichorean</u> skills made him a popular partner at the dance.

6. Despite his age and sophistication, he had the face of a <u>gamin</u>, one of those homeless boys who roam the streets of London.

7. In the past he would <u>perseverate</u> about his complaints. Now he merely states his complaint once and moves on.

8. He had an <u>avuncular</u> smile, though certainly no one would ever claim him as an uncle.

9. Surprisingly, the minister's argument was <u>secular</u> rather than spiritual in nature.

10. Colleges, universities, and other institutions that engage in <u>andragogy</u> must be concerned with educating the whole adult, not just the intellect.

Are they believable? Are they current? Are various sides of an issue presented, or only one? Given that anyone can post information on the Internet, reading critically is especially important when assessing information that you encounter online. Chapter 7 provides more on how to be a critical thinker.

22. Apply special strategies for reading mathematics. When you read a math book, you are not only reading to identify important information, you are also reading to learn a skill: how to solve math problems. Learning both information and a skill at the same time requires a high level of mental engagement. Pause after reading each new method and consider how you can use it to solve problems. Mark and annotate the key steps for using the method to solve a problem. Also mark any helpful tips for solving problems of the type you are reading about. When a sample problem is solved, actively engage your mind, making sure you understand exactly what is occurring in each step. Use the margin to write the process in your own words, and, where possible, translate mathematical steps into plain English. Most important, when you come upon practice problems, don't just read them, solve them. The fact that you understand the solution of a problem in your book doesn't mean you can do it yourself. Solving problems needs to be part of your reading effort.

23. Apply special strategies for reading science. The *scientific method* is the foundation for writing in science.

- The scientific method begins with a **question** about the physical world. (*Why is the human brain about seven times larger than might be predicted for a mammal of our size?*)

- Scientists then offer a possible answer, called a **hypothesis**. (*Humans developed larger brains to deal successfully with complicated social networks.*)

- Next, scientists **experiment** to find evidence proving or disproving the hypothesis. (*One experiment compared the brain sizes of various kinds of hyenas— some that live in groups and some that live alone.*)

- Finally, scientists draw a **conclusion** based on the evidence. (*Indeed, the evidence shows a correlation between brain size and the complexity of social networks in hyenas, suggesting that the hypothesis is true.*)

So, when you read a science text, mark and annotate the elements of the scientific method: questions, hypotheses, experimental evidence, and conclusions.

24. Apply special strategies for reading literature. As with reading math and science, reading fiction poses unique challenges. When reading short stories, plays, or novels, it helps to understand how fiction differs from nonfiction. For narrative fiction, your first goal is to understand what happens in the story (the plot). Who is the main character? What challenges does this person face? What choices does he or she make? And how are the challenges resolved? For most popular fiction, that's about it. However, for the kind of literature you'll read in college, instructors will want you to understand the "theme" and appreciate artistic elements used by the author. The theme in fiction is similar to the main idea in nonfiction. However, there's a significant difference in presentation. Whereas the main idea in nonfiction is usually stated, the theme in fiction is usually implied. Thus, the need for interpreting fiction. For example, both nonfiction and fiction can convey the idea that "Beliefs are stronger than reality." In nonfiction, the author would write that statement (a main idea) and then elaborate with supporting details such as examples, experiences, or even scientific studies. In fiction, authors don't *tell* the main idea, they *show* it. To do so, an author of fiction might write a story about a person whose beliefs conflict with "reality" and show how those beliefs cause that character to make unwise choices. As with life, fiction requires interpretation to extract meaning. Unlike life, however, fiction provides artistic elements that guide effective readers to the theme the author intends. For example, an author may suggest the theme of a story or novel through imagery and symbolism. If you take

a literature course, you will learn more about these and many other artistic elements available to writers of fiction.

25. Understand graphic information. Many textbook authors present information not only in words but also in picture forms such as…

- pie charts
- tables
- bar graphs
- line graphs
- flow charts
- diagrams
- time lines

In the margin or other white space, write an explanation of each graphic item. Or copy the graphic item into your notes and write your explanation there. For example, the graphic in the section "Victim and Creator Mindsets" (Chapter 2) visually depicts the different choices of Victim mindsets and Creator mindsets. How would you explain the model in your own words?

After Reading

26. Reflect on what you read. Upon finishing a reading assignment, lean back, close your eyes, and ask and answer questions that will help you see the big picture. For example…

- What are the key concepts?
- What are the main ideas about those concepts?
- What are the supporting details?
- What do I personally think and feel about the author's main ideas and supporting details?

Recalling key ideas from what you have just read is one of the most powerful learning strategies you can apply to your reading assignments. This is a learning strategy you can use any time and place. For example, just before going to sleep or as you wake up, recall what you read for homework.

27. Reread difficult passages. On occasion, every reader needs to revisit difficult passages to understand them fully. I recall one author whose writing made me feel like a dunce. However, somewhere around my fifth or sixth reading (and using strategies in this section), a light went on in my brain and I thought, "Oh . . . so that's what he means! That's not nearly as complicated as I thought!" Trust that by using the strategies presented here, you can comprehend any reading assignment if you stick with it long enough. Having a growth mindset (explained in Chapter 7) can help greatly in developing this trust.

28. Recite the marked text. Read aloud the parts of the text you have underlined or highlighted. Attempt to blend the ideas into a flowing statement by adding connecting words between the words in your text. In effect, you'll be summarizing the key points of the material you just read. You may even want to write the summary because writing is another way to solidify learning.

29. Talk about what you read. Explain the main ideas and supporting details. Especially helpful is having this conversation with another student in your class who has read the same assignment. This study partner can give you feedback on where you may have misunderstood or left out something important.

30. Read another book on the same subject. Sometimes another author will express the same ideas more clearly. Ask your instructor or a librarian to suggest other readings. For very difficult material, try to find a book on the same topic written for children. A book for younger learners may provide just the information or explanation you need to make sense of your college textbook.

31. Seek assistance. Still having problems understanding what you read? Ask your instructor to explain muddy points. Or see if your college has a reading lab or a tutoring center. For some subjects—such as math, science, and foreign languages—there may be dedicated personnel to help. If all else fails, see if your college has a diagnostician who can test you for a possible learning disability. Such a specialist may be able to help you improve your reading skills.

Reading: Do One Different Thing This Week

In this section of your Toolbox for Active Learners, you've been introduced to 31 strategies for becoming an active and effective reader. Here's an opportunity to experiment with one of them. First, review the strategies. Identify those you marked because they could help with one of your learning challenges. Now pick the one strategy you think would best help you improve your reading skills.

In the "My Commitment for Reading" box in the following chart, write the strategy with which you will experiment. Write just the number of the strategy and the one-sentence description of it that is in bold print. (For example, "**20. Use context clues to determine the meaning of key words.**") Then track yourself for one week, putting a check in the appropriate box each day that you practice this strategy. Your goal is to do it every day. After seven days, evaluate your results. If your reading skills improve, you'll have a learning tool you can use for the rest of your life.

My Commitment for Reading:

_____

_____

_____

☐ Day 1   ☐ Day 2   ☐ Day 3   ☐ Day 4   ☐ Day 5   ☐ Day 6   ☐ Day 7

During my seven-day experiment, what happened?

As a result of what happened, what did I learn or relearn?

As a result of what I learned or relearned, I will….

In the previous section, we discussed the many hours you will spend in college **Collecting** information and skills from your reading assignments. In this section, we will examine the second most time-consuming way you will **Collect** information while in college: attending classes. In pursuing a four-year degree, students spend nearly 400 hours in a formal classroom. Students seeking a two-year degree spend about half that time in class.

Your instructors, of course, expect you to learn what they cover in these classes. Unless you're motivated and able to take effective notes, however, most of what you hear in class will zip through your short-term memory and be quickly forgotten. More than one hundred years ago, Hermann Ebbinghaus conducted the first studies of memory. He discovered that we lose about 75 percent of what we learn within 24 hours. That's why effective note-taking is an essential skill for achieving academic success in college.

Taking notes while attending a class is similar to taking notes while reading a textbook. However, taking notes during a class offers additional challenges. For one thing, as you mark or annotate a textbook, you stop reading. Thus, while reading you are in total control of how fast you receive new information. By contrast, when you take notes during a class, the speaker keeps talking. You have little or no control over the speed of information delivery. This situation places greater demands on your ability to identify key concepts, main ideas, and supporting details. Then you need to write them down accurately and completely.

And that's not all. You're likely to encounter instructors who will provide unique obstacles to note-taking: They may speed talk until your head spins.

Or . . . drone . . . on . . . so . . . sloooowly . . . you . . . have . . . trouble . . . staying . . . awake. They may be poorly organized. Or have accents that you have difficulty understanding. Some instructors may wander maddeningly from the topic. Or distract you with irritating mannerisms. Or all of the above.

A summary of research on note-taking compiled by Kenneth Kiewra reports sobering news. Lecture notes taken by first-year students contain, on average, only 11 percent of the important ideas presented during a class. The result should be obvious. No matter how well you study, you can't pass tests by studying only 11 percent of the important ideas in a course.

You can choose to complain, blame, and make excuses for why it's impossible to take good notes in a class. Or, you can take full responsibility for your learning outcomes and experiences. Regardless of how many obstacles the instructor or the subject presents, it's your job to take effective notes. In this section, you'll learn how.

TAKING NOTES: THE BIG PICTURE

To take effective class notes, you need to answer two key questions: *What* should I write in my notes and *how* should I write that information?

First, consider *what* to write in your notes. Despite a popular misconception, the answer is not "everything the instructor says." Even if you could write that fast, having a word-for-word transcript of a class is not the goal of note-taking. As with reading, the goal of note-taking is **Collecting** key concepts, main ideas, and supporting details. Thus, much of what you learned earlier about taking notes while reading also applies to taking notes in class. But you'll need some new strategies to compensate for the challenges of writing notes while someone is speaking.

As for *how* to write your notes, a number of note-taking systems have been invented, but essentially they all fit into one of two categories: linear or graphic. Examples of these methods will be explained shortly.

Many students worry about taking perfect class notes because they use their notes to study for tests. If that's you, stop worrying. In the CORE Learning System you don't study from either your class notes or your textbooks. Instead, as you'll learn later, after **Collecting** key concepts, main ideas, and supporting details from all sources, you'll **Organize** this information into effective study materials (sometimes called "study guides"). It is these study materials that will help you create deep and lasting learning.

For now, simply examine the note-taking strategies that follow and choose the ones that you think will best help you **Collect** important knowledge during each class. No single method of note-taking works best for everyone, so experiment and personalize a note-taking system that works best for you.

As you examine the following strategies, keep in mind that the big picture of note-taking is essentially the same as for reading: **You are Collecting key concepts, main ideas, and supporting details.**

CHALLENGES WITH TAKING NOTES

Following are common challenges with taking notes in higher education. Circle the numbers next to the challenges you are having (or can foresee having) in taking notes for your present courses. Even if you consider yourself a good note taker, circle the numbers next to at least two areas in which you could improve. If you have a challenge not on the list, use one or both blank spaces at the bottom of the list to add your own challenge(s).

1. I really have no clue how to take good notes in a college class.

2. I can't figure out what's important, so I try to write down everything the instructor says.

3. I have a class that is mostly discussion, and I have no idea what to write in my notes.

4. I leave important information out of my notes, and that information often shows up on tests.

5. One of my instructors jumps all over the place, and I can't follow what he's saying.

6. Instructors use a lot of words I've never heard before, and I get confused.

7. One of my instructors has a strong accent that's really difficult to understand.

8. I tried recording lectures, but when it comes time to study, there's too much to listen to.

9. I have a huge lecture class, and I find it difficult to stay focused.

10. The instructor solves math problems on the board so fast that I can't get them all written down.

11. When students answer questions in class, I can't tell if what they're saying is important.

12. I get distracted by students who are whispering to each other, and that messes up my notes.

13. My teacher never takes questions, so I've got some wrong information in my notes.

14. Sometimes an instructor says something that just doesn't seem to fit anywhere in my notes.

15. While I'm writing notes, I miss what the instructor says next.

16. I take so many notes that later I can't make much sense out of them.

17. Most of my classes are boring lectures that put me to sleep.

18. I take notes, but I often have gaps where I fell behind or wasn't paying attention.

19. I copy notes from the instructor's PowerPoint slides, but later it seems like I'm missing important information.

20. During classes, my mind wanders and I don't hear some of what the instructor says.

21. I understand the words my instructors use in class, but on exams they use different words and I get confused.

22. I like math, but my class notes are worthless when it comes time to study for a test.

23. When a PowerPoint slide just has a chart or graph, I don't know what to write in my notes.

24. My instructor talks too fast and there's no way I can keep up with my notes.

25. The instructor mostly reads or repeats what's in the text, so why take notes at all?

26. _____

27. _____

STRATEGIES TO IMPROVE TAKING NOTES

Following, you'll find many of the very best strategies for mastering the skill of taking good notes. After reading each strategy, pause and decide if it would help you overcome any of the challenges you circled. If so, mark it in some way (e.g., underline, circle, highlight, star). Later on, you can decide which of these strategies to experiment with to improve your reading.

Before Taking Notes

1. Create a positive affirmation about taking notes. Some students hold negative beliefs about their ability to take good notes or the value of doing so. Create an affirming statement about taking notes. For example, *I take notes that record all of the main ideas and supporting details, making learning easy and fun.* Repeat this note-taking affirmation to motivate new learning attitudes and behaviors. (See "Believing in Yourself: Write a Personal Affirmation" in Chapter 3 for more information about creating affirmations.)

2. Assemble appropriate supplies. Experiment and decide on the best note-taking supplies for you. Find a pen you like writing with. Keep your notes in ring binders, composition books, spiral binders, or a laptop computer. Ring binders are handy because you can add and remove pages easily. This option is helpful when an instructor provides handouts or you revise your notes. If you use one binder for all of your classes, use tabs to separate the notes for each class. If you take class notes on a laptop computer, be sure to back up your files often to avoid the disaster of losing notes because of a hard-drive crash.

3. Complete homework assignments before attending class. Remember, neural networks created by past learning make present learning easier. That's why you'll benefit from completing assignments *before* class. This effort increases your ability to understand lectures and discussions. Also, you'll know better what belongs in your notes. For example, you'll know if the instructor is repeating what was in the reading or adding new information. And, suppose the instructor's presentation style presents a challenge (such as speed talking). Because the information is already familiar, you'll more easily spot key concepts, main ideas, and supporting details. If your homework includes solving problems, complete them before class as well.

4. Go over notes from previous class sessions. You can review or recite your notes, or both. *Reviewing* means reading over your notes silently. *Reciting* means speaking them aloud. As with completing homework before class, going over your notes activates prior learning and helps you understand new information presented in the next class.

5. Prepare a list of questions. After completing homework assignments, write questions you have about the information. If you write them on binder paper, leave a space after each question for the answer. If you write questions on index cards, you can put answers on the other side. If you place questions in a computer file, it's easy to add the answers. Bring these questions to class, study group meetings, tutoring sessions, or a conference with your instructor. Make sure you get an answer to all of your questions. Also, note which of your questions show up on a test. As you improve your ability to predict test questions, your grades will improve as well.

6. Eliminate distractions. Before entering the classroom, address any physical, mental, or emotional distractions. Visit the restroom, eat a nutritious snack, get a drink of water (or bring some with you if permitted). If a problem is distracting you, write it down. Make yourself a promise to address the problem later (maybe with the Wise Choice Process presented in Chapter 2). Then focus your full attention on the class. There's no point in attending a class physically if you aren't there mentally.

7. Attend every class. As obvious as this suggestion may seem, some students don't create good notes simply because they aren't in class. Sure, you can borrow notes from another student. But is it smart to bet your academic success on someone else's note-taking skill? Remember, research reveals that first-year students' notes contain only 11 percent of the important ideas presented during a class. Your notes, after applying the strategies in this section, will be far more effective than that!

8. Arrive early and choose a good seat. A "good" seat is one that allows you to concentrate on the source of information. For a lecture class, sitting up front is wise (why do you suppose theaters charge the most for front-row seats?). For a discussion class, consider sitting near a side wall halfway back so you can see and hear everyone in the class. If the chairs are arranged in a circle, sitting opposite the instructor gives you a great vantage point for **Collecting** information from everyone. There's no "right" seat in a classroom, but there is definitely a "good" seat for you.

9. Be organized. At the end of each term, you'll have note pages galore for each course. To keep them organized, write on one side of the page only and place some or all of the following information at the top of each note page:

- Course name
- Date of the class

- Topic of the class (usually listed in the course syllabus)
- Any associated reading assignments (also usually listed in the course syllabus)
- Page number (in case your notes get mixed up later)

While Taking Notes

First, let's consider WHAT to write in your notes.

10. Listen actively. Good notes contain key concepts, main ideas, and supporting details. **Collecting** this information *accurately* and *completely* takes active listening. When you listen actively, you're able to reflect back what a speaker says. In a conversation with a friend, you might reflect: *Sounds like you had an exciting time white water rafting last weekend.* Or in a music class, you might reflect, *So, you're saying a divertimento is a short musical piece that was popular during the Classical period.* When taking notes, you'd simply write an abbreviated version of this reflection: *Divertimento—a short musical piece popular during the Classical period.* Inner chatter competes with active listening, so quiet your Inner Critic and Inner Defender during class. Don't judge yourself: *I have no clue what he's talking about; I am such a dunce.* And don't judge others: *This jerk is the worst teacher on the planet.* (For more information about avoiding Victim language, see "Mastering Creator Language" in Chapter 2.) Replace judgments with an active effort to hear all of the speaker's key concepts, main ideas, and supporting details. After all, if you don't **Collect** the course information completely and accurately, then your entire learning effort is sabotaged from the start. See "Strengthening Relationships with Active Listening" in Chapter 5 for more suggestions to improve active listening.

11. Ask and answer questions. When you bring questions to class, raise your hand and ask. When your instructor asks a question, raise your hand and answer. When you don't understand an idea, raise your hand and ask: *Excuse me, Professor, what holds atoms together in a molecule?* Or, if you're too confused to formulate a question, simply request more information: *Would you please say more about Kant's idea that metaphysics can be reformed through epistemology?* If asking a question isn't an option, leave a space in your notes and write a question in the margin. Many choices exist for later filling in the answer: Listen for the instructor to answer your question during the class. Visit the instructor during his or her office hours. Look for the missing information in your textbook. Ask a classmate or study group member for help. Seek assistance at your college's tutoring center.

12. Listen for verbal cues. Instructors often provide verbal cues to introduce a main idea or supporting detail. These cues help you decide *what* to write in your notes. When you hear any of the following, get ready to record an important idea:

- *The point is . . .*
- *The following is very important . . .*
- *Be sure to write this next idea in your notes . . .*
- *On page 135 underline the following . . .*
- *Let me repeat that. . .*
- *The key here is . . .*
- *That's a great answer to my question . . .*
- *A third component is . . .*
- *The main symptom of this problem is . . .*

- *The next step for solving this problem is . . .*
- *If you remember only one thing from today's class, remember that . . .*
- *The key point here is . . .*
- *(and the granddaddy of them all) This will be on the test.*

Also, instructors often give verbal cues before presenting supporting details. When you hear any of the following, get ready to record one or more supporting details:

- *To illustrate this point . . .*
- *Evidence for this includes . . .*
- *A good example is . . .*
- *To explain that idea further . . .*
- *This was proven in a study that showed . . .*

Listen for additional kinds of supporting details such as personal experiences, experiments, dates, anecdotes, definitions, lists, names, facts, and data.

13. Watch for visual cues. Record in your notes anything your instructors write on the board or project on a PowerPoint slide. You can be confident they think the information is important if they go to that trouble. Another visual cue occurs when instructors pause to look at their notes. What they say next is likely to be an important

A NOTE TO "LISTENERS" | Perhaps you've noticed that in most class discussions, only a few "talkers" participate. The majority of students choose the role of "listeners." Sure it can be intimidating to speak up in class, especially a large one. However, if you don't occasionally ask or answer questions, you're either being a passive learner or acting as a Victim. Either way, you're missing out on the benefits of being an active learner. Benefits include

- deeper and longer-lasting learning,
- better grades, and
- making a positive impression on the instructor (which can benefit you in many ways, such as a strong recommendation for a scholarship, job, or graduate school).

If you always choose to be a listener, what's your excuse? Your Inner Critic may tell you that everyone else already understands or that you'll look stupid if you say the "wrong" thing. Instead, heed your Inner Guide who knows that you're responsible for **Collecting** *accurate* and *complete* information. How else can you learn the target knowledge and earn a good grade? You may not be a natural "talker," but you can always choose to act like one when it's to your benefit. Consider an experiment: Set a goal to ask or answer at least one question in every class for one week. But watch out . . . you might learn so much you get hooked!

idea. And watch for instructors getting excited about an idea. That's another cue they think an idea is important.

14. Take notes on discussions. In a class discussion, your goal for note-taking is the same as for a lecture. You need to **Collect** key concepts, main ideas, and supporting details *accurately* and *completely*. However, discussions can make note-taking a challenge. You need to distinguish between classmates' ideas that are on target and those that are irrelevant, superficial, or simply wrong. In most cases, you can count on your instructor to sort the diamonds from the debris.

Look for two kinds of questions. One kind is closed-ended and has a "right" answer. For example, *What is the atomic weight of carbon?* After asking a question of this kind, instructors will typically keep taking answers until the correct one is offered. Or they will give it themselves.

The second kind is an open-ended question. These questions call for a more complex answer and there may be various possible answers. For example, *Why do you suppose the poet Robert Frost chose the color "yellow" in the line "Two roads diverged in a yellow wood"?* Instructors may praise a good answer, elaborate on an incomplete answer, or restate a confusing answer so that it is now helpful. Listen carefully for what instructors say at the end of a discussion. This is when they often state the "correct" idea they have been seeking to draw out during the discussion.

15. Stay focused. Focus is essential for learning. If the subject interests you, staying focused is easy. However, when the subject or instructor's style bores you, staying focused is a challenge. Struggling students allow wandering thoughts to sabotage their learning. By contrast, successful students stay focused on **Collecting** key concepts, main ideas, and supporting details *even when they don't feel like it*.

To stay focused, keep asking and answering, "What's the main point here?" Another

concentration trick is the IOU technique described in the Reading section (Strategy 18). Listen for what you find personally *interesting* or *useable*, even when much of the information is neither. If your mind continually wanders during a class, set a goal to reduce this self-defeating habit. Each time you lose focus, put a check mark in the margin of your notes. At the end of class, total your check marks. Then set a goal to reduce that number in the next class. Soon you'll be filling pages of notes with key concepts, main ideas, and supporting details even in subjects for which you have little interest (but want a passing grade).

Now, we'll consider HOW to write your notes.

16. Take notes with an outline. Now that we've looked at ways to determine *what* to put in your notes, let's consider the second critical choice: *how* to write your notes. As mentioned earlier, the two general methods of note-taking are linear and graphic. First, we'll consider linear notes, which are the more common of the two. "Linear" means in a line. When you take notes in a linear fashion, you record ideas as much as possible in the order they are presented. Outlines are good for this. They record ideas and supporting details on separate lines, using indentations to indicate levels of importance. You can view an example of an informal outline in **Figure T.6** and an example of an informal outline with content in **Figure T.7**. Note the use of short phrases instead of full sentences to greatly condense what the speaker says. Here's how to take notes with an outline:

- Write a *key concept* at the top of a page. This information is usually expressed in a word or phrase. This might be the title of a chapter or a key word in the instructor's course outline. For example, the key concept in a history class might be "Causes of World War II," in a biology class it might be "Cell Communication," and in a psychology class it could be "Abraham Maslow."

- Record *main ideas (level 1)* beginning at the left margin. For a formal outline, start each level 1 line with a Roman numeral (e.g., I, II, III, IV).

Levels of Information	Structure of Informal Outline Notes	Structure of Formal Outline Notes
Key Concept	Key Concept	Key Concept

Level 1
  Level 2
    Level 3
    Level 3
	Main Idea
	  Secondary Idea
	    Major Supporting Idea
	    Major Supporting Idea
		I. Main Idea
		  A. Secondary Idea
		    1. Major Supporting Idea
		    2. Major Supporting Idea

Level 2
    Level 3
      Level 4
      Level 4
	Secondary Idea
	    Major Supporting Idea
	      Minor Supporting Idea
	      Minor Supporting Idea
		B. Secondary Idea
		    1. Major Supporting Idea
		      a. Minor Supporting Idea
		      b. Minor Supporting Idea

Level 1
  Level 2
    Level 3
    Level 3
      Level 4
      Level 4
	Main Idea
	  Secondary Idea
	    Major Supporting Idea
	    Major Supporting Idea
	      Minor Supporting Idea
	      Minor Supporting Idea
		II. Main Idea
		  A. Secondary Idea
		    1. Major Supporting Idea
		    2. Major Supporting Idea
		      a. Minor Supporting Idea
		      b. Minor Supporting Idea

Level 2
    Level 3
    Level 3
	Secondary Idea
	    Major Supporting Idea
	    Major Supporting Idea
		B. Secondary Idea
		    1. Major Supporting Idea
		    2. Major Supporting Idea

© Cengage Learning

FIGURE T.6 Structure of an Outline

- Under each main idea, indent a few spaces and record related *secondary ideas (level 2)*. For a formal outline, start each level 2 line with a capital letter (e.g., A, B, C, D).

- Under each secondary idea, indent a few more spaces and record any related *major supporting details (level 3)*. For a formal outline, begin each level 3 line with an Arabic numeral (e.g., 1, 2, 3, 4).

- If you need to add *minor supporting details (level 4)*, indent those lines a few more spaces and, for a formal outline, begin those lines with small letters (e.g., a, b, c, d).

Outlines are most helpful when instructors present well-organized lectures. If your instructor provides printed lecture notes or uses PowerPoint slides, you've probably got an organized instructor. If, however, your instructor jumps from topic to topic and back again, all is not lost. That's when a concept map can ride to the rescue.

17. Take notes with a concept map. In this graphic note-taking method, *where* you place information (key concepts, main ideas, and supporting details) is the key. Placement shows both their level of importance and their relationship to one another. In general, the closer an idea is to the middle of a page, the more important it is. **Figure T.8** shows the structure of a concept map and **Figure T.9** shows an example of a concept map with content. Here's how to take notes with a concept map:

- Write the *key concept* in the middle of a page. Then underline or circle it. This information is usually just a word or phrase. For example, if the topic of a class session is "Photosynthesis" or "Logical Fallacies" or "Abraham Maslow," that is what you would write in the middle of the page.

- Write *main ideas (level 1)* near the key concept, underline or circle them. Then draw lines connecting them to the key concept.

- Write *secondary ideas (level 2)* near their related main idea, underline or circle them. Then draw lines connecting them to the related main ideas.

Course: Psychology 101
Date: October 5
Topic: Abraham Maslow

Abraham Maslow (1908–1970)
— Family immigrated to Brooklyn
    — One of seven children
    — Unhappy, neurotic child
— Taught at Teachers College, Brooklyn College, Brandeis
— Sought to understand human motivations
— Became leader of humanistic psychology movement of the
    1950's and 1960's

Maslow's Hierarchy: Theory of Human Motivation (like a pyramid)
— Physiological needs (the foundation)
    — Food, rest, shelter, etc.
— Safety needs
    — Security, stability, freedom from fear
— Psychological needs
    — Belonging, love, affiliation, acceptance, esteem, approval,
        recognition
— Self-actualization (top of the pyramid)
    — Need to fulfill oneself
        — Maslow: "to become everything that one is capable of
            becoming."

Humanistic psychology
— Maslow led the "Third Force" in psychology
    — Alternative to...
        — Freudian psychoanalysis
        — Behaviorist psychology
— Stressed the power of a person to choose how to behave
    — As opposed to...
        — Freudians: Choices controlled by childhood influences
        — Behaviorists: Choices controlled by conditioning
— Appealed to the individualistic, rebellious college students of the
    1960's

FIGURE T.7   Informal Outline Example

Source: From Kanar, *The Confident Student,* 3e, p. 353, © 1998.

- Write *major supporting details (level 3)* near their related secondary idea, underline or circle them. Then draw lines connecting them to the related secondary idea.

- Write *minor supporting details (level 4)* near their related major supporting idea, underline or circle them. Then draw lines connecting them to the related major supporting idea.

Concept maps are helpful when lecturers leap from idea to idea. They are also good for taking notes on class discussions that move back and forth between topics. As a speaker returns to an

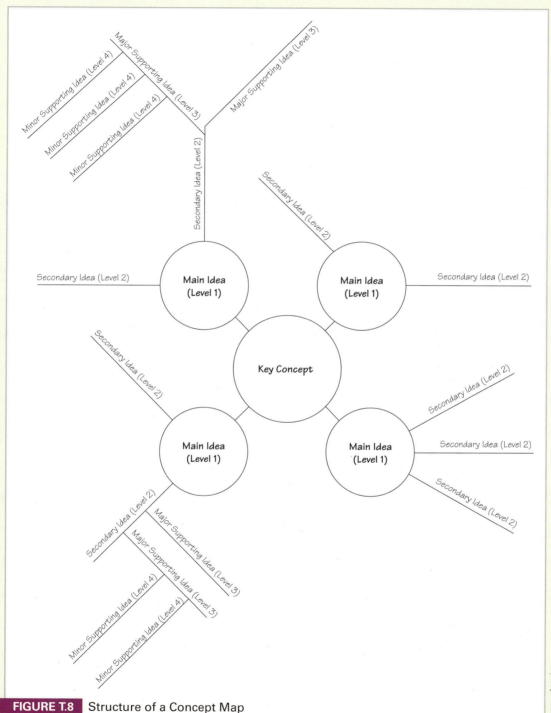

FIGURE T.8 Structure of a Concept Map

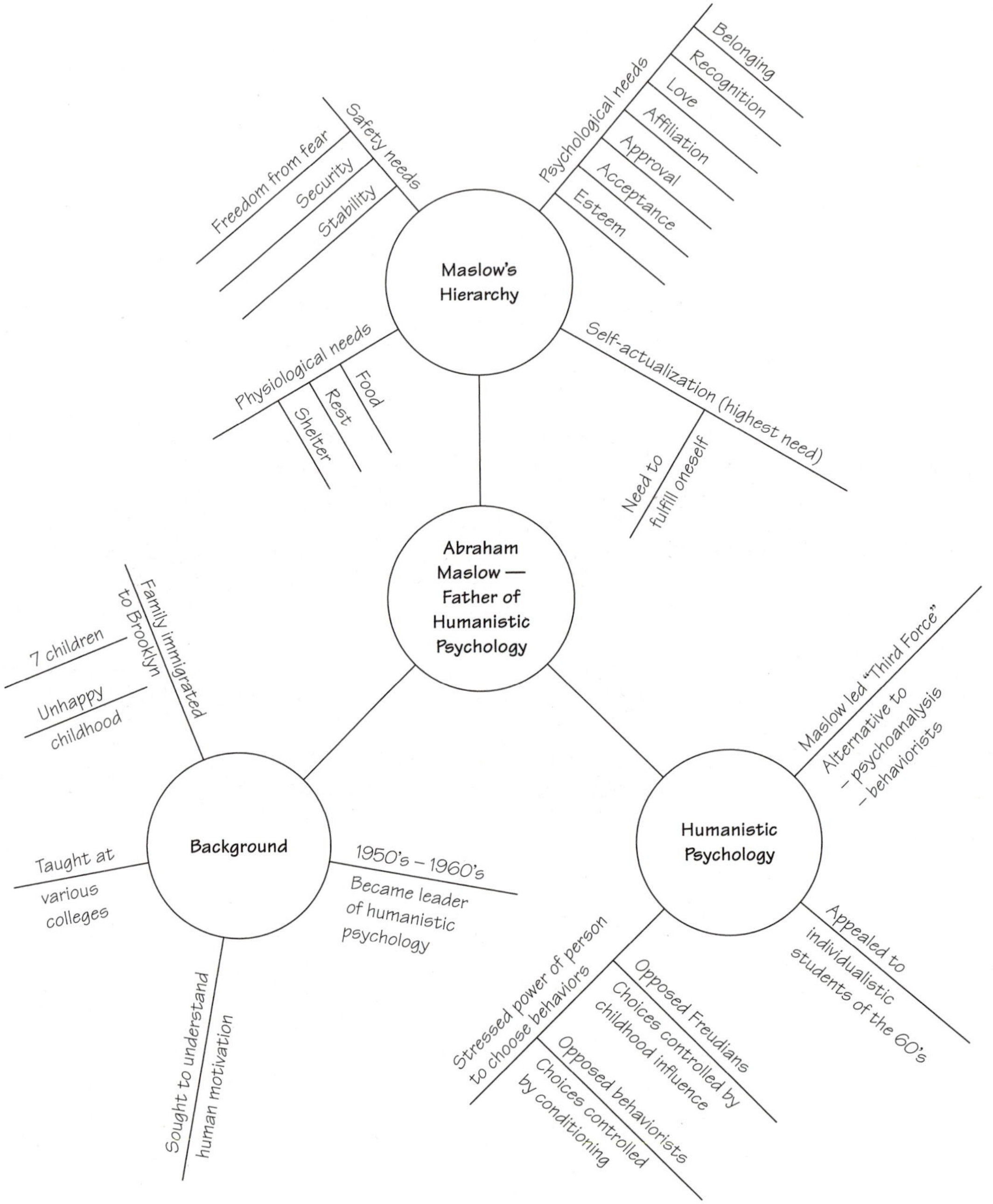

FIGURE T.9   Concept Map Example

Maslow's Hierarchy

- Safety needs
  - Freedom from fear
  - Security
  - Stability
- Psychological needs
  - Belonging
  - Recognition
  - Love
  - Affiliation
  - Approval
  - Acceptance
  - Esteem
- Self-actualization (highest need)
  - Need to fulfill oneself
- Physiological needs
  - Food
  - Rest
  - Shelter

Abraham Maslow — Father of Humanistic Psychology

Background

- Family immigrated to Brooklyn
- 7 children
- Unhappy childhood
- Taught at various colleges
- 1950's – 1960's Became leader of humanistic psychology
- Sought to understand human motivation

Humanistic Psychology

- Maslow led "Third Force" — Alternative to – psychoanalysis – behaviorists
- Appealed to individualistic students of the 60's
- Opposed Freudians Choices controlled by childhood influence
- Opposed behaviorists Choices controlled by conditioning
- Stressed power of person to choose behaviors

© Cengage Learning

earlier idea, simply go to that part of the concept map, add the new information, circle or underline it, and draw a line connecting it to related information. The visual nature of a concept map makes it especially appealing to students who like a picture of what they are learning.

18. Use three-column notes for mathematics.

Math instructors spend much class time demonstrating how to solve problems. A three-column approach is extremely helpful for **Collecting** their methods. First, divide your note page into three columns. Title the left-hand column "Problem," the middle column "Solution," and the right-hand column "Explanation." When the instructor presents a problem, write it in the left column. As the instructor demonstrates how to solve the problem, write all steps in the middle column, making sure you understand each one. In the right-hand column, add any explanation that will help you understand how to solve similar problems. For example, you might add an explanation of each step or convert unfamiliar symbols into words.

Structure of Three-Column Math Notes

Problem	Solution	Explanation
The math problem as presented by the instructor	Step 1 Step 2 Step 3 Step 4 Step 5 Etc.	Elaboration to explain steps of the solution

© Cengage Learning

You'll find an example of three-column math notes in the "Organizing Study Materials" section of this Toolbox. See Strategy 17.

19. Speed up note-taking. Most speakers talk much faster than you can write (or even type, if using a computer), so here are three strategies for speeding up your note-taking:

- *Condense*: Don't attempt to write everything. Listen for a couple of minutes and identify the key concept, a main idea, and one or two secondary ideas. Then paraphrase them in your own words.

- *Leave a blank space:* When you miss something, skip ahead leaving a few blank lines in your notes. Pick up writing what is being said now. As with unanswered questions, you can return later to fill in the blank space. Options include asking the instructor (in class, if appropriate, or during office hours), a classmate, or a tutor. Or you can review your reading assignment for the missing information.

- *Use abbreviations:* Create your own personal shorthand. The following are some possible abbreviations:

Ex	example	&	and
con't	continued	dept	department
imp	important	→	leads to
#	number	=	equals
1st	first	vs	versus
w/	with	w/o	without
nec	necessary	etc	and other things

20. Record the class. Suppose you try the previous suggestions and still aren't happy with the quality of your notes. Consider asking your instructor for permission to record the class. You can listen to the recording as many times as needed to fill in gaps in your notes or review difficult concepts. *Caution*: Don't procrastinate until you have 45 hours of recorded class sessions and only 24 hours before the final exam. Instead, listen often to short segments. Each time, practice different note-taking strategies until you perfect your own personalized system. Like any skill, the more you practice the better you'll get.

A BIT OF HERESY | In many study skills books, another method of note-taking is usually presented. Named for the university where it originated, the Cornell Method calls for note paper to be divided into three sections (see the "While Organizing Study Materials" section of this Toolbox for the structure). Section A is used for recording notes from a reading assignment or class session. However, the Cornell Method offers no unique suggestions about *how* to record notes in that section. Sections B and C are employed later for adding key words, questions, and summaries, so they also offer no guidance about *how* to take notes. Thus, although the Cornell Method is usually presented as a note-taking system, it actually offers no strategies for *how* to take notes while reading or attending class (only *where* to record them). So, in the CORE Learning System, the Cornell Method is not considered a note-taking method. It is, however, a very powerful method for **Organizing**, **Rehearsing**, and **Evaluating** learning, so we will examine the use of this valuable strategy in upcoming sections.

After Taking Notes

21. Polish your notes within 24 hours. As soon as possible after each class, make sure your notes are *accurate*, *complete*, and *understandable*. Do some or all of the following:

- Finish partial sentences.
- Expand on key words.
- Fill in blank spaces with missing information.
- Correct misspellings.
- Clarify unreadable words and confusing sentences.
- Delete unnecessary information.
- Revise drawings or charts.
- Correct steps in problem solving.

Afterward, if you still have gaps or confusion in your notes, meet with classmates, a tutor, or your instructor to address the problems. Not only does this action provide you with polished notes, it continues the active process of creating deep and lasting learning.

22. Compare notes. Compare your class notes with those of your study group members or other motivated classmates. See if others have **Collected** any important information that you missed. See where their notes may have different information and decide whose version is more accurate. This effort will help you all **Collect** additional information and further polish your notes.

ACTIVITY 3A: PRACTICING NOTE-TAKING

Form pairs and decide who will be Person A and Person B. Have a third person read aloud the following information as if delivering a lecture in a psychology class. Person A takes notes on the lecture using an outline. Person B takes notes using a concept map. Afterward. . . .

- Compare notes with the original for *accuracy* and *completeness*.
- Discuss any challenges you had **Collecting** all of the key concepts, main ideas, and supporting details.
- Discuss which note-taking method (outline or concept map) you prefer and why.
- If you have read information in Chapter 3 about achievement motivation (V × E = M), discuss if that previous knowledge helped you take better notes as you listened to this lecture.

THE LECTURE

Many psychologists believe each of us, to varying degrees, has an internally driven need for achievement. The achievement motive pushes us to seek success and significant accomplishment in our lives. Studies have shown that people who rate high in achievement motivation tend to work harder and more persistently on tasks, and they tend to achieve more than those who rate low in achievement motivation.

However, whether you'll work hard on any particular task depends on your expectations of success and how much you value the task. You can have a high internal need for achievement but choose not to persist on a task either because you place no value on it or because you lack confidence in your ability to succeed. For example, young children who experience failure on mathematics problems early in life can develop a helpless attitude that prevents them from persisting and succeeding on mathematical tasks later on. Conversely, children who perform well on such tasks gain confidence in their ability and appear motivated to take on similar tasks in the future.

How can the achievement motive be measured? According to experts, you can't get a very accurate measure by asking. Instead, it's better to examine a person's fantasies, wishes, and dreams. Over time you'll find common themes that clearly illustrate how much the person values and needs achievement. One technique is to present an ambiguous picture and instruct the individual to make up a story about its content. David McClelland and others have found that people tend to reflect their need for achievement in the repeating themes of their stories. This kind of technique for assessing psychological characteristics—called a *projective test*—is often used to study personality.

Parents and teachers play an important part in determining achievement motivation. If parents value a task, it's likely their child will value it too and be more motivated to succeed. What children are told about their performance on a task is also important. For example, if children are praised for their effort, they tend to work harder, report more enjoyment, and show more interest. On the other hand, if they're told that performance is tied to an ability such as natural intelligence, children show less achievement motivation—especially if they fail or perform poorly on the task.

Every society in the world establishes standards for achievement—the skills and tasks deemed important and unimportant—and these standards influence what the members of the society seek to achieve and perhaps the level of productivity of the society as a whole. For example, whether a society values individual success or collective success seems to affect individual levels of achievement motivation. Middle-school athletes in the United States report more self-confidence than comparable students in Korea, and they are more easily motivated, presumably because a great emphasis is placed on individual success in the United States.

Many researchers believe gender differences in achievement—such as the tendency for men to outperform women in mathematics—may be partly tied to such cultural factors. In the United States, for instance, the parents of sons place greater value on success in mathematics than do the parents of daughters; at the same time, boys often receive the message that they should study less, which helps explain why girls outperform boys in other subjects. Consequently, the expectations and values of the parents help to determine the achievement motivation of the children.

Source: From *Psychology* by James S. Nairne, © Cengage Learning.

Taking Notes: Do One Different Thing This Week

In this section of your Toolbox for Active Learners, you've been introduced to 22 strategies for taking effective notes. Here's an opportunity to experiment with one of them. First, review the strategies. Identify those you marked because they could help with one of your learning challenges. Now pick the one strategy you think would best help you improve your note-taking skills.

In the "My Commitment for Taking Notes" box in the following chart, write the strategy with which you will experiment. Write just the number of the strategy and the one-sentence description of it that is in bold print. (For example, "**18. Use three-column notes for mathematics.**") Then track yourself for seven days of classes in a row, putting a check in the appropriate box each day that you practice this strategy. Your goal is to do it in each class for all seven days. After seven days of taking class notes, evaluate your results. If your note-taking skills improve, you'll have a learning tool you can use for the rest of your life.

My Commitment for Taking Notes:

_____

_____

_____

☐ Day 1   ☐ Day 2   ☐ Day 3   ☐ Day 4   ☐ Day 5   ☐ Day 6   ☐ Day 7

During my seven-day experiment, what happened?

As a result of what happened, what did I learn or relearn?

As a result of what I learned or relearned, I will….

Organizing Study Materials

To pass the many quizzes, tests, and exams they will take in college, students obviously need to know how to study. But, many do not.

In fact, the study methods of many students—even those who were "good" students in high school—are only marginally effective in college. Even when they pass tests, many students understand and remember only a fraction of what they studied. Imagine the problems this missing knowledge causes when it's needed later in the same course. Or later in a more advanced course. Or even later in a career. Relying on ineffective study skills leads to shallow and short-lived learning. Such ineffective learning is a sure way to undermine academic, professional, and even personal success.

You're about to explore a number of strategies that will help you *learn in a deep and lasting way.* Mastering these strategies will provide you with the ability to improve your learning outcomes and experiences for the rest of your life. And, yes, your grades in college will almost surely go up as well.

ORGANIZING STUDY MATERIALS: THE BIG PICTURE

Effective learners, you'll recall, take advantage of three principles that contribute to deep and lasting learning. First is **prior learning**. This means relating new information to what you already know. Second is the **quality of processing.** This means using many different kinds of deep-processing strategies. And third is the **quantity of processing**. This means using frequent practice sessions of sufficient length distributed over time.

In this section we're going to explore study strategies that address the *quality of processing*. To do

so, read about and experiment with the many deep-processing strategies that follow. As you do, keep in mind the big picture of this second step of the CORE Learning System: **Having Collected knowledge from reading assignments and taking class notes (Step 1), you're now going to Organize it all in ways that are meaningful to you (Step 2). Your goal is the creation of many different kinds of effective *study materials*. Engaging actively in the process of Organizing study materials will greatly enhance your understanding of what you are learning.**

CHALLENGES WITH ORGANIZING STUDY MATERIALS

Following are common challenges with **Organizing** study materials in higher education. Circle the numbers next to the challenges that you are having (or can foresee having) in **Organizing** study materials for your present courses. Even if you consider yourself good at studying, circle the numbers next to at least two areas in which you could improve. If you have a challenge not on the list, use one or both blank spaces at the bottom of the list to add your own challenge(s).

1. I have no idea how to organize my study materials.

2. I don't understand how to make a linear organizer from my notes.

3. I study by reading my textbook a second time; I don't really know another way.

4. No matter how long I study for a test, instructors always ask questions I didn't anticipate and/or can't answer.

5. I don't know what supplies I need to organize my study materials in an effective way.

6. To prepare for a test, I read what I've under-lined or highlighted in my textbooks.

7. Even if something makes sense when I study it, I often get confused when I see it on a test.

8. No matter how much I read and reread my math book, it doesn't make sense to me.

9. I memorize all the key terms that are in bold, but when I take a test, I don't know how to use the information.

10. I have trouble concentrating when I study be-cause I don't like most of my courses.

11. I don't understand how to make a graphic or-ganizer from my notes.

12. I'm lousy in some subjects, so there's really no reason why I should study hard for them.

13. When I study for a test, the slightest noises distract me.

14. My grades aren't nearly as good as they were in high school, so I guess how I studied then doesn't work for me now.

15. I prepare for math tests by reading over my class notes and the problems I solved for homework.

16. I don't really have a good place to study.

17. I am often surprised by a test question that I didn't study for.

18. I only know one way to get ready for a test.

19. I study for tests by going over my homework and rereading my class notes.

20. I like learning by listening, but my instructor won't let me record the class.

21. I usually study with the television on.

22. The only time I have for studying is about midnight when I get home from work.

23. The words the instructors use in class are not exactly the words that show up on a test.

24. I got good grades in high school without studying; in college I read over my class notes the night before a test.

25. I study for hours, but my grades don't show it.

26. _____

27. _____

STRATEGIES TO IMPROVE ORGANIZING STUDY MATERIALS

Following you'll find many of the very best strategies for **Organizing** your study materials. After reading each strategy, pause and decide if it would help you overcome any of the challenges you circled. If so, mark it in some way (e.g., underline, circle, highlight, star). Later on, you can decide which of these strategies to experi-ment with to improve your ability to **Organize** study materials.

General Study Guidelines

1. Employ peak learning times. Some people are most alert in the morning, whereas others learn best at night. Still others think best in the middle of the day. At what time of day are you at your best? One hour of studying in your peak times is probably worth two (or more) hours in your off times. Schedule each day to use your peak learning times for studying.

2. Tackle challenging subjects first. Take on difficult subjects when your mind is alert and most receptive to new information. Save your easier subjects for later. As Mark Twain once said, "If it's your job to eat a frog, it's best to do it first thing in the morning. And if it's your job to eat two frogs, it's best to eat the biggest one first."

3. Take regular breaks. Your brain functions best when fueled with oxygen, water, and glu-cose. Every 30 to 60 minutes, get up and stretch. Drink water. If hungry, snack on fruit, which contains glucose. Stretch and walk around for a few minutes. When you resume studying, not only will your muscles be more relaxed, but your brain will have more oxygen as well, up to 15 percent more, according to some studies.

Caution: Avoid getting sidetracked while taking a break.

4. Change subjects periodically. Research about learning reveals that we remember the most from the beginning of a learning session and the next most from the end of a session. We learn the least during the middle of a session. This finding is called the *primacy-recency* effect. Changing tasks periodically provides more beginnings and endings. That's why you'll usually learn more from three one-hour sessions on different subjects than you will from one three-hour session on the same subject.

5. Adopt a growth mindset. Having positive beliefs about the value of effective studying improves your learning outcomes. According to psychologist Carol Dweck, one important belief is that *the ability to learn can be improved.* Dweck calls this belief a "**growth mindset.**" The opposite mindset is that you're stuck with the learning ability you were born with. The reality? Working hard and using effective learning strategies improves your ability to learn. To begin developing a growth mindset about learning, create an affirming statement about the value of using high-quality study strategies. For example, *My CORE Learning System makes learning more effective and fun.* Along with your personal affirmation, repeat this learning affirmation in order to make new choices about studying.   (In Chapter 7, you'll learn more about developing a growth mindset.)

Before Organizing Study Materials

6. Create an ideal study space. Having comfortable places to study has many advantages. Your learning resources are always close at hand. You aren't distracted by unfamiliar sights or sounds. And your mind becomes accustomed to shifting into learning gear whenever you enter your study area. Design your study area so you enjoy being there. Minimum requirements include a comfortable chair, plenty of light, room to spread out your course materials, and space to store your books and supplies. Personalize your study area to make it even more inviting. For example, display pictures of loved ones or add plants. Do whatever it takes to create a space you look forward to entering. Some studies have shown that we learn at a deeper level when we study in different places. So, you may want to have a variety of places to study. Just make sure they all provide an opportunity for deep concentration.

7. Arrange to be undisturbed. Do whatever is necessary to minimize interruptions while you study. Schedule regular study times and ask friends and relatives not to contact you during those times. Put a Do-Not-Disturb sign on your door. Let voice mail take telephone calls. Resist checking emails or text messages. If necessary, study where no one can easily disturb you, such as at your campus library. Protect the sanctity of your study time. One way to decide is ask yourself, "Would a basketball coach allow players to ____ during practice?" Fill in the blank with what you're considering doing while studying. If the answer is no, then you probably shouldn't be doing it either.

8. Create a distributed study schedule. As you know, active learners engage in numerous study sessions spread over time. So refer to your calendar where you have recorded all of the announced tests for your classes (you *have* done this, right?). Then choose a date before each test when you will begin serious studying. As a guideline, start seven days before a regular test and up to fourteen days before a major exam. Plan to use one quarter to one third of the days for creating study materials (as you will learn to do in this section). Use the remaining days to **Rehearse** these materials using the strategies you'll learn in the next section.

See **Figure T.10** for a sample seven-day distributed study schedule for a test held on Friday. After exploring the strategies in this section and the next, you'll be able to decide which specific **Organizing** and **Rehearsing** strategies work best for you.

Day	Task	Time
Friday	Organize Study Materials	1 hour
Saturday	Organize Study Materials	2.5 hours
Sunday	Organize Study Materials	1 hour
	Rehearse & Memorize Study Materials	1.5 hours
Monday	Rehearse & Memorize Study Materials	1 hour
Tuesday	Rehearse & Memorize Study Materials	1 hour
Wednesday	Rehearse & Memorize Study Materials	2 hours
Thursday	Rehearse & Memorize Study Materials	1 hour
Friday	Take the Test	

© Cengage Learning

FIGURE T.10 Sample Seven-Day Distributed Study Schedule

9. Gather all course materials. Start with your textbooks (marked and annotated) and your class notes. Add to them all other course documents, such as handouts, study guides, graded tests and essays, and study group notes.

While Organizing Study Materials

10. Condense course materials. Since you have already marked and annotated all of your reading assignments and taken detailed notes in class, you will have a large **Collection** of information and skills. As a result, you may think you have all you need for studying. Not true. Learning from these raw materials is seldom effective. Instead, good learners condense all of these materials into the key concepts, main ideas, and supporting details of the course. Then they **Organize** this condensed knowledge into effective *study materials.* But one thing at a time. Here's an effective way to condense:

- Read through the markings, annotations, and notes you added to your course materials. As you do, place a star beside key concepts, main ideas, and supporting details.

- Now, reread only the information you marked with a star, find the most important ideas within those, and put a second star beside them.

- Finally, reread just the ideas you have marked with two stars, identify the most important of these, and put a third star beside them.

- Read through all starred information one more time and circle the key concepts.

By doing this process, you should have condensed your course materials by at least half (preferably more) and identified various levels of information:

- Key concepts (circled)
- Level 1: main ideas (three stars)
- Level 2: secondary ideas (two stars)
- Levels 3 and 4: supporting details—major and minor (one star)

Now your goal is to **Organize** this condensed information in ways that will help you understand it thoroughly. The **Organizing** options described next fall into one of two broad categories: *linear* or *graphic* (just as with note taking). Experiment to find which options work best for you. Keep in mind that while a particular **Organizational** approach may work well for one subject (e.g., sociology), a different approach may be better for another subject (e.g., mathematics).

11. Create outlines (linear organizer). Now you're ready to use the key concepts, ideas, and supporting details you have just identified with circles and stars. Use them to create an outline using the process described in the "Taking Notes" section of this Toolbox. However, there's a simpler way to craft an outline for study purposes. Simply copy your textbook's table of contents onto a blank page. Even easier, sometimes you can find the book's table of contents on the publisher's or author's website. Then you can just copy and paste it into your own study materials. Add to it starred information from *all* of your course materials. It's likely that you will have some starred information (e.g., material from lecture notes) that does not fit into the outline created from the textbook. In that case, create a new section in the outline and add the new information. Outlines make particularly valuable study materials when preparing for essay tests or writing a paper (composition) to demonstrate your learning. See Activity 4A to practice creating an outline from a table of contents.

12. Create concept blocks (linear organizer).

Concept blocks organize information from all course materials (textbook, class notes, etc.) into tightly focused paragraphs. Each paragraph explains one key concept from the course. Here's how to create concept blocks:

- Write each key concept (circled in your notes) on a separate index card or type them into a computer file. A computer file has the obvious advantage of allowing you to move information easily from one location to another. This is a valuable option when writing and revising concept blocks, as you will see.

- Search your course materials for starred main ideas, secondary ideas, and supporting details. Copy this information onto index cards and place them in piles with the related key concept. If working on a computer, simply copy/paste related material together with the key concept.

- Now **Organize** the information (main ideas and supporting details) for each key concept. If using index cards, physically place each pile on a flat surface and move them around until you achieve a logical order. If using a computer, copy and paste ideas where they belong.

- Finally, write a paragraph for each key concept, linking together the relevant main ideas and supporting details.

Concept blocks make particularly helpful study materials when preparing for essay questions. **Figure T.11** illustrates four concept blocks for the CORE Learning System.

---

1) COLLECT: Gather target knowledge that is accurate and complete. The most common way that students encounter new knowledge is by reading assignments and attending classes. This knowledge goes into short-term memory, and if not quickly recorded in some more permanent way, much is quickly forgotten. Thus, good learners become skilled at marking and annotating their textbooks and taking effective class notes. In these ways, they collect knowledge and begin the process of creating deep and lasting learning.

2) ORGANIZE: Use collected knowledge to create many different kinds of effective study materials. A collection of information and skills is meaningless until the learner understands it. Understanding is improved when learners organize collected knowledge so that it makes sense to them. Two broad categories of organizers are linear (e.g., outline) and graphic (e.g., concept map). Neural networks grow stronger when learners organize their knowledge in many different ways.

3) REHEARSE: Devote enough distributed time to work with study materials. Rehearsal strategies include reviewing, reciting, visualizing, and memorizing by rote. To aid learning, spend sufficient "time on task." Also distribute rehearsal efforts over time (rather than cramming). Remembering is enhanced by rehearsing in the same way that the learning will be tested. For example, if you will be tested with essay questions, rehearse by answering essay questions.

4) EVALUATE: Seek feedback to assess learning. Feedback provides information about how well a learner has mastered the target knowledge. One way to evaluate mastery of information is to quiz yourself (as when you write the definition of a key term from memory). One way to evaluate your mastery of a skill is to solve a problem (as when you work a math problem). You can also seek feedback from others (as when study group members ask each other questions). Ultimately, quiz and test grades provide feedback about how well the instructor thinks you are mastering the knowledge of a course.

© Cengage Learning

FIGURE T.11   Concept Blocks for the CORE Learning System

ACTIVITY 4A: CONVERTING A TABLE OF CONTENTS INTO A FORMAL OUTLINE

The box on the left contains the table of contents from a European history textbook. The box on the right contains the start of a conversion of the book's table of contents into a formal outline. Complete the conversion. You will not necessarily have information for all of the rows in the box on the right.

© Cengage Learning

Chapter 30 Europe in a Globalizing World 1991 to the Present	Key Concept
I. Eastern Europe After Communism	Level 1
A. Russia from Foe to Partner	
B. The Dismemberment of Yugoslavia	Level 2
C.	
D.	
E.	
II. European Integration	Level 1
A.	
B.	
C. Nation-States in a New Context	Level 2
D.	
E.	
F.	
III. Europe and Globalization	Level 1
A.	
B. International Security and Terrorism	Level 2
C.	
D.	
IV.	Level 1
A.	
B.	Level 2
C.	

© Cengage Learning

Source: From *Making Europe: People, Politics, and Culture* by Frank L. Kidner, Maria Bucur, Ralph Mathiesen, Sally McKee, and Theodore Weeks.

13. Create test questions (linear organizer). Put yourself in the mind of the instructor preparing a test. What information or skill does she expect you to learn? Write questions that will reveal your understanding of that target knowledge. Although any questions about the key concepts and main ideas of the course make helpful study materials, they are most effective when you know the kinds of questions that will be on the test. The best way to find out is to ask. "*Professor, what kinds of questions will be on the midterm exam? True/false? Multiple-choice? Matching? Short answer? Essay? Word problems? Translations?*" Some instructors will tell you exactly what to expect. Others won't answer your question directly but may offer hints, provide sample questions, or even give you copies of past tests. Here are additional ways to generate test questions:

- Turn headings from your textbook into questions.
- Turn chapter learning objectives and/or summaries into questions.
- Find questions in your class notes that the instructor asked during class.
- Find concepts (circled) and main ideas (starred) in your textbook or class notes and turn them into questions.
- Make a list of key terms and turn them into questions.
- See if your textbook has practice problems either in the book or on a related website.
- Exchange possible test questions with study group members.

It's a great feeling to begin a test and find that you have practiced answering nearly every question on it.

14. Create flashcards (linear organizer). On one side of an index card, write a question that your instructor might ask on a test. On the back of the card, write the answer. Examples include a . . .

- date and what happened on that date
- word and its definition

- graph and its meaning
- person's name and what he or she is noted for
- math problem and its solution
- quotation and who said it

Show your flashcards to your instructor or a tutor. Ask them to verify the appropriateness of the questions and the accuracy of the answers. Carry flashcards with you everywhere. Pull them out for a quick review whenever you have a few extra minutes. If you study them only 20 minutes per day, that's more than two extra hours of studying each week. A number of free websites allow you to create flashcards and even play games with the content. To find such a site, simply type "flashcards" into an Internet search engine. (Be cautious about using flashcards created by other students, as their answers may be incorrect.) Flashcards make valuable study materials in courses where you expect objective tests such as true/false, definitions, matching, multiple-choice, fill-in-the-blank, and some kinds of math problems. A few examples of flashcards are shown on page 304.

15. Create concept maps (graphic organizer). Earlier, you learned how to take class notes using a concept map. Whether or not you choose to take class notes with concept maps, strongly consider them for creating study materials. You'll see an example of a concept map and the steps for creating one in the "Taking Notes" section of this Toolbox. Concept maps have a number of benefits when used as study materials. First, they clearly show the relationship among levels of information (i.e., key concepts, main ideas, and supporting details). They aid learning by combining the left brain's verbal and analytical skills with the right brain's spatial and creative abilities. Concept maps are simple to expand, so you can easily add new information from various sources. And they are especially useful when preparing for an essay test or term paper.

16. Create hierarchies (graphic organizer). Like a concept map, a hierarchy visually depicts the

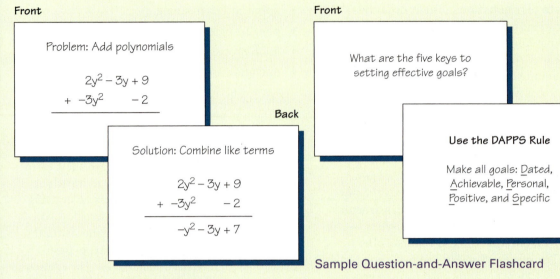

Sample Problem-Solution Flashcards
Source: From Kanar, *The Confident Student*, 3e, p. 353, © 1998.

relationships among levels of information. How-ever, with a hierarchy, you place the key concept at the top (instead of in the middle) of a page. Then you place each additional level of information be-low that. With this arrangement of information, a hierarchy is especially helpful for understanding a subject that requires classifications (e.g., biology) or organizational charts (e.g., political science). Here's how to create a hierarchy:

- Write the *key concept* at the top of a page.
- Write *level 1—main ideas* (three stars) in the space below the key concept. Enclose or under-line the main ideas and draw lines that connect them to the key concept above.
- Write *level 2—secondary ideas* (two stars) in the space below the main ideas. Enclose or underline the secondary ideas and draw lines that connect them to the main ideas above.
- Write *level 3—major supporting details* (one star) in the space below the secondary ideas. Enclose or underline the major supporting details and draw lines that connect them to the secondary ideas above.

- If you have *level 4—minor supporting details,* add them in the space below and connect them to the major supporting ideas above.

Figure T.12 shows the structure of one kind of hierarchy.

17. Create three-column study charts for math (graphic organizer). In the previous section, you learned to take math notes using three-column charts. If you're doing that, you are well on your way toward **Organizing** helpful study materials for that course. If not, simply begin now by dividing blank pages into three columns and titling them: Problem, Solution, and Explanation. Now add one problem at the top of the left-hand column of each page; include problems representing different levels of difficulty:

- **Easy problems:** These could be problems your instructor solved in class that you im-mediately "got." These might be problems you correctly solved on a test or homework assign-ment. Or they could even be problems you initially did wrong but have since learned how to solve.

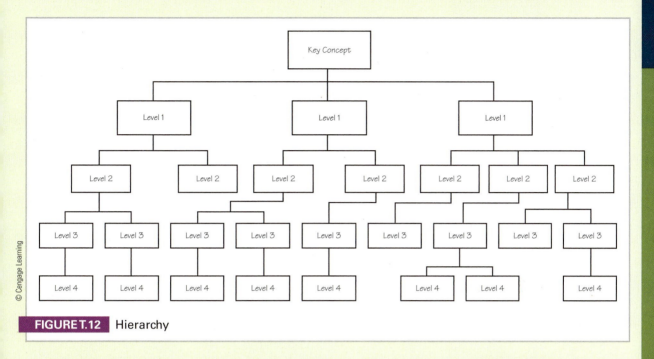

FIGURE T.12   Hierarchy

- **Challenging problems:** These might be problems that you got wrong on a test or homework assignment and still don't understand how to solve. Or they might be problems your instructor solved in class but continue to baffle you. Or, they could be sample problems you haven't tried to solve, but just looking at them, you doubt whether you can. These challenging practice problems could come from sources such as class notes, homework, tests, the tutoring center, or the website for your textbook.

Now do your best to solve each problem in the middle column, while writing explanations (e.g., directions, key terms, and rules) in the right-hand column. Because you are creating study materials, it is essential that you understand each step in the solution as well as its explanation. If you get stuck on a problem, set it aside and save it. You'll learn how to deal with these challenging problems in the next section of this Toolbox. For now, include as many solved problems as you can. **Figure T.13**

shows an example of a three-column study chart for math.

18. Create comparison charts (graphic organizer). A comparison chart is a table that compares two or more related items (e.g., people, theories, facts, events, novels). These study materials help you develop a deep understanding about how these items are alike and unalike. **Figure T.14** shows a comparison chart for examining inner voices. Here are the directions for creating such a chart:

- Make a table with one row for each item you are learning and one column for each aspect you plan to compare/contrast.

- In Column 1 (left side of table), write the items to be examined (e.g., Inner Voices: Inner Critic, Inner Defender, Inner Guide).

- In Row 1 (top of table), write the aspects you plan to compare/contrast (e.g., Use of Life Energy, Language Used, Typical Results). Any

Problem	Solution	Explanation
Find an equation of the line with slope 4 that contains the point (2, −1).	Step 1: $y = 4x + b$	Substitute 4 for the "m" in $y = mx + b$; "m" is the slope.
	Step 2: $-1 = 4(2) + b$	Replace x with 2 and y with −1 in the equation.
	Step 3: $-1 = 8 + b$	In ordered pairs, the first value is for x, the second is for y.
	Step 4: $-9 = b$	Multiply to simplify.
	Step 5: Equation: $y = 4x - 9$	Solve for b by subtracting 8 from both sides.
	Step 6: $-1 = 4(2) -9$ Is this true?	Replace the "b" with −9 in the equation $y = 4x + b$.
	Step 7: $-1 = 8 - 9$ YES	Check the answer by substituting the x and y values in the answer.

© Cengage Learning

FIGURE T.13   Three-Column Study Chart for Math

Inner Voices	Use of Life Energy	Language Used	Typical Results
Inner Critic (Victim Voice)	Judging oneself	Self-Criticizing	Seldom achieves desired outcomes and experiences
Inner Defender (Victim Voice)	Judging others	Blaming others, complaining, and excusing self of personal responsibility	Seldom achieves desired outcomes and experiences
Inner Guide (Creator Voice)	Taking positive action to improve a situation	Taking personal responsibility ("I language") and implementing a positive plan for action	Often achieves desired outcomes and experiences

© Cengage Learning

FIGURE T.14   Comparison Chart

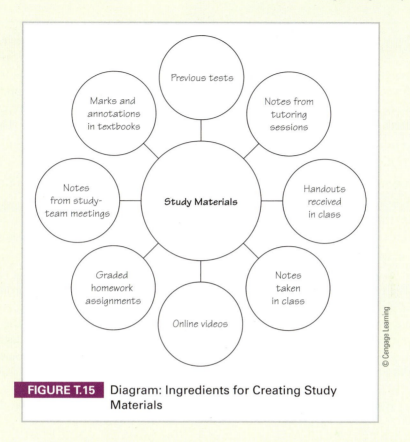

© Cengage Learning

FIGURE T.15   Diagram: Ingredients for Creating Study Materials

aspect related to all (or even most) items is appropriate to include in a comparison chart.

- Complete the chart by filling in the remaining boxes with the appropriate information.

The simplest kind of comparison chart is a T-chart, which compares just two items. Each chapter in *On Course* begins with a T-chart comparing successful students with struggling students.

19. Create diagrams and drawings (graphic organizer). For visual learners, a picture can be worth a thousand words. When you convert words into visual information, you give your brain an additional way to encode it. This process helps you both understand and remember the information better. In a biology class, for example, a picture can help you learn the parts of a cell. **Figure T.15** offers a diagram showing how **Collected** information from course materials (the outer circles) can be combined to create effective study materials (the inner circle). Numerous Internet sites explain how to create other graphic organizers. To find them, use an Internet search engine with terms such as *graphic organizers, concept maps,* and *mind maps.* You'll be amazed at how many different ways you can depict information graphically!

20. Create Cornell study sheets. Walter Pauk, an educator at Cornell University, devised a simple and helpful way to organize study materials. Cornell study sheets are very useful when you **Rehearse** and **Evaluate** the target knowledge, as you'll learn to do in the next section. Here's how to construct one:

- Create a blank Cornell study sheet by drawing lines on notebook paper to create the three

A NOTE ABOUT CORNELL STUDY SHEETS

As mentioned earlier, many study skills books suggest writing your notes from reading assignments and class sessions directly on Cornell-formatted pages. This approach is usually called the "Cornell note-taking system." By contrast, I recommend that you take your reading and class notes on regular paper or a computer. Then, do three things to deep process the information you have **C**ollected:

1. Polish your notes, making sure they are complete and accurate. (Strategy 21 in the "After Taking Notes" section of this Toolbox)

2. Condense your notes, identifying key concepts, ideas, and supporting details. (Strategy 10 in the "While Organizing Study Materials" section)

3. **O**rganize the condensed notes, creating effective study materials (e.g., outlines, concept maps) that include information from *all* course materials. (Any of the strategies in this section.)

Now, if you wish, copy your polished, condensed, and organized study materials onto a Cornell study sheet.

Here's why I urge you to wait to create Cornell study sheets until you have thoroughly processed your original notes. Let's say you write your original notes on Cornell study sheets. Now you will be tempted to study from them without polishing, condensing, or **O**rganizing the information. This means you're skipping essential steps necessary for creating deep and lasting learning. But suppose you do polish, condense, and **O**rganize the notes you took on Cornell-formatted pages. Now you need to write them on other pages anyway. So there was no real purpose for taking them on Cornell-formatted pages to begin with. Here's the bottom line: The best use for Cornell-formatted pages is for **O**rganizing, **R**ehearsing, and **E**valuating (not **C**ollecting) what you are learning.

sections depicted in **Figure T.16**. If working on a computer, use the table feature in your word processing program. Simply create a table with two rows and two columns. Drag the middle vertical line to the left to widen Section A and narrow Section B. Drag the middle horizontal line toward the bottom to lengthen Section A. Then merge the bottom two columns to create Section C.

- In Section A, copy study materials you have already created, such as outlines and concept maps.
- Compose questions about the information found in Section A. Write each question in Section B alongside its answer in Section A.
- Circle or underline key concepts in Section A. Write each key concept in Section B alongside its definition or explanation in Section A.
- In Section C, write a summary of the key concepts, main ideas, and supporting details that appear in Section A.

See **Figure T.17** for an example of a completed Cornell study sheet. Note that Section A (the largest section) contains an informal outline that was created (as described in Strategy 6), polished, and then copied onto the study sheet.

21. Create audio recordings. You can make a recording of most of the study materials discussed here. For example, you can record the text of concept blocks. Or you record questions, leave a 10- to 15-second silence, and then record the answer. The pause gives you time to fill in the answer. For example: "Seven tools for improved self-management are . . . *15-second pause* . . . a weekly calendar, monthly calendar, next actions list, tracking form, waiting-for list, project folder, and 32-day commitment." Recordings are especially helpful study materials for auditory learners who remember best what they hear. Recorded study materials also help you make use of time that might

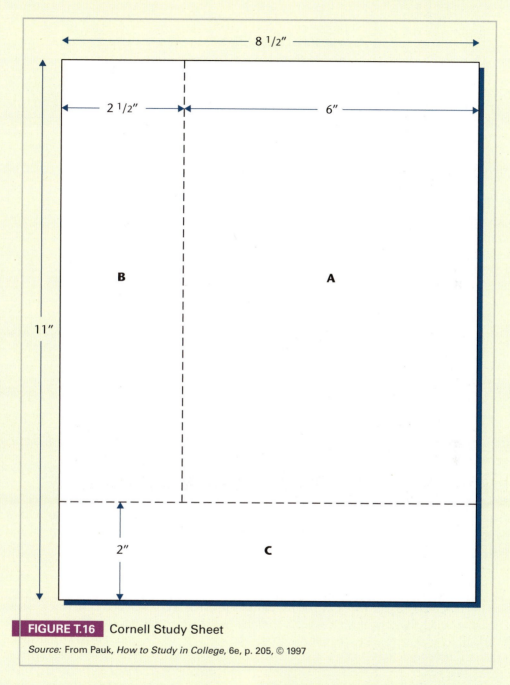

8 1/2"

2 1/2"   6"

B   A

11"

2"   C

FIGURE T.16   Cornell Study Sheet

Source: From Pauk, *How to Study in College,* 6e, p. 205, © 1997

otherwise be wasted. Simply listen when you are doing other tasks that don't require as much attention. For example, commuting or waiting for appointments.

After Organizing Study Materials

22. Read more on the same subject. Are you having difficulty understanding the information in your notes? Consider **Collecting** more. Ask your

	Course: Psychology 101
	Topic: Abraham Maslow
	Abraham Maslow (1908–1970)
	– Family immigrated to Brooklyn from Russia
	– One of seven children
	– Unhappy, neurotic child
What was the psychological	– Taught at Teachers College, Brooklyn College, Brandeis
movement that Maslow led?	– Sought to understand human motivations
When did he become leader	– Became leader of humanistic psychology movement of
of this movement?	the 1950s and 1960s.
What are the five levels of	Maslow's hierarch: theory of Human Motivation (like a pyramid)
motivation, according to	– Physical (the foundation)
Maslow's Hierarchy?	– Food, water, air, rest, health, exercise, etc.
What are examples of	– Safety needs
each level?	– Security, stability, shelter, freedom from fear
	– Social needs
	Love, belonging, connection, affiliation
	– Psychological needs
	– self-esteem, power, approval, recognition, confidence
Self-actualization	– Self-actualization (top of the pyramid)
	– Need to fulfill oneself, creation
	– Maslow: "To become everything that one is capable
	of becoming."
	Humanistic psychology
	– Maslow led the "Third Force" in psychology
	– Third Force—alternative to other approaches of psychology
How does humanistic	– Freudian psychoanalysis
psychology differ from	– Behaviorist psychology
Freudian and behavioral	– Stressed the power of a person to choose how to behave
psychology regarding	– Other approaches minimized the importance of conscious choice
"choice" in human behavior?	– Freudians: Choices controlled by childhood influences
	– Behaviorists: Choices controlled by conditioning
	– Appealed to the individualistic, rebellious college students
	of the 1960s

Abraham Maslow became the leader of the humanistic psychology movement in the 1950's and 60's. Unlike Freudian and behavioral psychologists, humanists believe people have the power to choose their own behaviors. Maslow is most noted for his efforts to identify forces that motivate human beings. His "hierarchy" proposes that some needs must be addressed before others. The most primary needs are physical (air, water, food). Next comes safety (freedom from fear, shelter from cold). Then social needs such as love and belonging. Next, psychological needs such as self-esteem, power, approval, recognition and confidence. Self-Actualization sits a top Mazlow's pyramid of motivation.

FIGURE T.17 Cornell Study Sheet Completed Example

instructor, tutor, or a librarian to suggest additional reading materials. Sometimes another author will express the same idea in a way that will flip a switch in your head and get your neurons firing. This extra information may clarify muddy areas. Or it may fill gaps in your study materials. If you have difficulty understanding your textbook, look for a book on the same subject written for younger students. It may present the same information in a way that is easier to comprehend. After reading this simpler version, return to your study materials with an improved understanding.

23. Get feedback on your study materials. Show them to classmates and study group members. Show them to a tutor. Show them to your instructor. Ask for their suggestions to improve the accuracy, completeness, and organization of your study materials.

24. Seek help. If you don't understand something you're studying or need more one-on-one explanations, make an appointment with your instructor. You can also go to the tutoring center on your campus to get assistance. If the first tutor you see isn't much help, ask for a different tutor the next time. Keep seeking help until you understand the information or skill well enough to create well-**Organized** study materials.

Organizing Study Materials: Do One Different Thing This Week

In this section of your Toolbox for Active Learners, you've been introduced to 24 strategies for **Organizing** study materials. Here's an opportunity to experiment with one of them. First, review the strategies. Identify those you marked because they could help with one of your learning challenges. Now pick the one strategy you think would best help you improve your ability to **Organize** study materials.

In the "My Commitment for Organizing Study Materials" box in the following chart, write the strategy with which you will experiment. Write just the number of the strategy and the one-sentence description of it that is in bold print. (For example, "**20. Create Cornell study sheets.**") Then track yourself for one week, putting a check in the appropriate box each day that you practice this strategy. Your goal is to do it every day. After seven days, evaluate your results. If your skills for organizing study materials improve, you'll have a learning tool you can use for the rest of your life.

My Commitment for Organizing Study Materials:

_____

_____

_____

☐ Day 1   ☐ Day 2   ☐ Day 3   ☐ Day 4   ☐ Day 5   ☐ Day 6   ☐ Day 7

During my seven-day experiment, what happened?

As a result of what happened, what did I learn or relearn?

As a result of what I learned or relearned, I will . . .

Rehearsing and Memorizing Study Materials

No matter how good your study materials are, if you can't remember what's in them, you're going to fail. This outcome is likely whether the test is given by an instructor, an employer, or by life itself. That's why the ability to understand *and* remember what you learn is essential to success.

In the previous section, we explored strategies for developing a deep and lasting *understanding* of what we want to learn. To do so, we gathered all of the knowledge we had **Collected** from reading assignments and class sessions. Then we **Organized** that knowledge to create a variety of helpful study materials. In this way we continued to build the neural networks that store our knowledge for future use.

In this section, we'll take these efforts another step toward creating deep and lasting learning. We'll look at strategies to *remember* what we are learning. To do so, we'll explore effective ways to **Rehearse** study materials. Here is the learning principle that guides our efforts: *To strengthen neural networks, use many different kinds of* **Rehearsal** *strategies and distribute these efforts over time.*

As may be obvious, *understanding* and *remembering* reinforce one another. Thus, efforts to remember also help you understand, just as efforts to understand help you remember. That's why it's so important to include in your CORE Learning System both **Organizing** for understanding and **Rehearsing** for remembering. In fact, I hope you're experiencing confidence that you can learn virtually any information or skill. The key is choosing effective study strategies and spending sufficient time on task. You're not only fully responsible for your learning; you're also completely up to the challenge!

REHEARSING AND MEMORIZING STUDY MATERIALS: THE BIG PICTURE

Rehearsal is what learning researchers call efforts to remember something. **Rehearsal** strategies generally fall into one of two kinds—elaborative and rote. In this section, we will look at both.

In most cases, **elaborative rehearsal** will better serve your learning goals in college. These strategies use deep processing that strengthens both understanding *and* remembering. They do so by focusing on meaning, by showing relationships between ideas, and by connecting new knowledge with old. As such, elaborative rehearsal enhances deep and lasting learning.

By contrast, **rote rehearsal** is more about remembering than understanding. As such, it employs surface processing such as memorizing by sheer repetition. There is both good and bad news about rote rehearsal. The good news is that memorized facts and details can be valuable. For example, rote rehearsal is probably how you learned both the alphabet and multiplication tables, and this information has certainly come in handy over the years. But there's bad news as well. Mindlessly memorizing information can fool you into thinking you understand something when you don't. Then you stroll into a test feeling prepared . . . only to discover how wrong you were. Memorizing a math formula doesn't mean you know how to apply it. And even if you do pass the test, the knowledge you memorized without understanding will probably be gone when you need it later on.

So, experiment with the many **Rehearsal** strategies in this section. As you do, continue personalizing a CORE Learning System. It will help you create deep and, in particular, *lasting* learning.

As a bonus, most **Rehearsal** strategies perform double duty. As you **Rehearse**, you also get feedback that allows you to **Evaluate** your learning. For example, when you **Rehearse** by quizzing yourself and get a wrong answer, that's valuable feedback. It prompts you to **Collect** more information, **Organize** it differently, and/or keep **Rehearsing**.

While examining the following strategies, keep in mind the big picture of **Rehearsing** study materials. **Rehearsing, when effective, make learning stick. First, use *elaborative* Rehearsal strategies to learn and remember complex ideas; use *rote* Rehearsal strategies to memorize facts and details. Second, employ frequent Rehearsal sessions of sufficient length distributed over time. Third, use feedback about how well you are learning to Evaluate and, if needed, revise your approach.**

CHALLENGES WITH REHEARSING AND MEMORIZING STUDY MATERIALS

Following are common challenges with **Rehearsing** and memorizing study materials in higher education. Circle the numbers next to the challenges that you are having (or can foresee having) in **Rehearsing** and memorizing study materials for your present courses. Even if you consider yourself good at studying, circle the numbers next to at least two areas in which you could improve. If you have a challenge not on the list, use one or both blank spaces at the bottom of the list to add your own challenge(s).

1. I have no idea how to rehearse and memorize my study materials.

2. Most of the time I don't feel like studying, so I don't study very long.

3. I do okay the first time I'm tested on something, but if it comes up on a later test, I don't do as well.

4. I have trouble when instructors expect us to know something thoroughly, like the similarities and differences between four theories of psychology.

5. When I study, I think I understand the information, but when I take a test, I can't remember it.

6. In high school I could cram the night before a test and get good grades, but that isn't working in college.

7. When I look over the problems that my math instructor solved in class, I understand them; but on a test, I can't remember how to solve them.

8. I do okay on essay tests, but I have trouble remembering information for short-answer, objective tests.

9. I make a lot of errors in my writing class because I can't remember the grammar rules.

10. I have a poor memory.

11. No matter how long I study for a test, there are always questions I can't answer.

12. I don't know how to memorize things like dates or formulas.

13. I have no idea how to use Cornell study sheets.

14. I always studied by myself in high school; now that my grades are dropping, I wish I knew good ways to study with a group.

15. Reviewing my math homework doesn't seem to help when I take tests.

16. I wish I knew ways to remember more of what I study.

17. I don't know how to study for an open-book exam.

18. I do okay on short-answer, objective tests, but I have trouble with essay questions.

19. The way I studied in high school doesn't work for me in college, but I don't know what else to do.

20. I'm good at remembering facts, but my instructor says I don't get the big picture of the course.

21. I basically study every subject the same way.

22. I read my notes over and over, but I still don't do well on the test.

23. I use flashcards to memorize all of the information for a test, but I still don't do well on tests.

24. _____
_____

25. _____
_____

STRATEGIES TO IMPROVE REHEARSING AND MEMORIZING STUDY MATERIALS

Following you'll find many of the very best strategies for **Rehearsing** and memorizing your study materials. After reading each strategy, pause and decide if it would help you overcome any of the challenges you circled. If so, mark it in some way (e.g., underline, circle, highlight, star). Later on, you can decide which of these strategies to experiment with to improve your ability to **Rehearse** and memorize study materials.

Before Rehearsing and Memorizing Study Materials

1. Form a study team. Many of the following learning strategies are enhanced by doing them with others. That's why teaming up with fellow Creators can increase the effectiveness of your study time. Follow the suggestions in "Start a Study Group" (Chapter 5) to ensure that your study team functions at top form.

2. Create a distributed study schedule. Remember: *Learning is enhanced by frequent practice sessions of sufficient length distributed over time.* Here's an example. Suppose two classmates each study 20 hours for a final exam. One classmate crams all 20 hours of his studying into the 24 hours before the test. The other distributes her effort by studying two hours each day for 10 days before the test. Both study for the same amount of time. However, the second student will likely experience deeper and longer lasting learning. Her advantage is distributing her study time over 10 sessions.

Review suggestions in the earlier section "Before Organizing Study Materials" for creating a distributed study schedule. Notice that the first 25 to 33 percent of time goes to **Organizing** a variety of effective study materials. The remaining time is used to deep-process the study materials using the **Rehearsal** strategies that follow. Your payoff will be improved learning, not to mention better grades.

3. Assemble all study materials. In the previous section, you learned how to create a great variety of study materials. Have all of your study materials handy as you begin this stage of your learning. You'll understand and remember more of what you study if you **Rehearse** different kinds of study materials. For example, you might **Rehearse** with an outline one day, a concept map the next, and flashcards the next.

While Rehearsing and Memorizing Study Materials

4. Review your study materials. *Reviewing* means reading over your study materials silently and with great concentration on the meaning. To avoid mindless reviewing, do the following three steps:

- Review a section of your study materials.
- Look away and ask yourself, *What are the key concepts, main ideas, and supporting details of what I just read?* Think through complete answers.
- Look back at your study materials to confirm the accuracy of your answers.

Repeat these three steps with additional sections of your study materials. Reviewing in this way causes you to make sense of and remember what you have just read. This process also **Evaluates** on how well you understand the content of your study materials.

5. Recite your study materials. *Reciting* is similar to reviewing but is done *aloud*. You may have used reciting when you met someone for the first time. Perhaps you said the person's name aloud to help you remember it. "It's nice to meet you, *Clarissa*. I've never met anyone named *Clarissa*. Is *Clarissa* a family name?"

As you read your study materials aloud, add any related information that comes to mind. Now look away from your study materials and do your best to say the same information again. Pretend you're explaining the information to someone who isn't in the course but is interested in the information. Look back at your study materials and compare the information there with what you have been saying. Repeat the process with each section of your study materials. Continue doing this look-away technique until what you recite captures the essence of what is in your notes. By reciting aloud, you engage multiple senses (sight and sound), thus creating stronger neural networks.

6. Visualize your study materials. Visualizing means creating a picture in your mind. Although visualizing works with any study materials, it is particularly helpful when studying graphic organizers (e.g., concept maps, hierarchies, comparison charts, pictures, or diagrams). Here's how to do it: Look at your study materials carefully, noticing as many details as possible. Look away (or close your eyes) and do your best to visualize an exact copy of your study materials. Look again at your study materials, and notice what's missing in your mental picture. Keep doing this process until you can visualize an exact duplicate of your study materials. If your study materials are detailed, you can work on one section at a time. For example, suppose you're trying to remember the 27 bones in a human hand. Look at a picture of a hand; then close your eyes and visualize just one finger in your mind, including the name of each bone. Go back and forth between the picture in your mind and your study materials until they are identical. Now move on to another finger, and then another, and finally the whole hand. A few hours after your session, close

your eyes and see if you can visualize the hand and all 27 bones. Do it again before going to sleep, then daily for a week, and once a week thereafter. This repeated visualization takes little effort, creates lasting learning, and you can do it anytime, anywhere.

7. Rewrite your study materials — without looking. First, visualize your study materials (as in the previous strategy). Then record on paper the image in your mind. Finally, compare your written copy to the original and make any needed corrections or additions. Repeat this process until you can accurately produce a copy of your study materials. The physical activity of writing or drawing engages your brain in a new way. Thus, the process helps to strengthen the neural networks related to the information.

8. Use Cornell study sheets. (See the "While Organizing Study Materials" section of this Toolbox for how to create them.) Remember that Section A of a Cornell study sheet contains information you have **Organized** in your preferred way (e.g., outlines or concept maps). Section B contains key words and questions about the information in Section A. Section C contains a summary of the key concepts and main ideas in Section A. To **Rehearse** information on Cornell study sheets, do the following:

- Study the content of Section A using either reviewing or reciting. Keep rehearsing the content in Section A until you feel confident that you understand it fully.

- Now hide Section A with a blank sheet of paper and look at Section B. There you will see the key words and questions you have written. Explain the key words and answer the questions as thoroughly as you can. Afterward, uncover the information in Section A and check the accuracy of your responses.

- Finally, cover the whole page and write a summary of the information in Section A. Then, uncover Section C on your Cornell study sheet and compare summaries. As your learning deepens, you may find that your latest summary is even better than the one you wrote earlier.

Note how this process offers both an excellent learning technique and an instant **Evaluation** of your learning. If you can't explain the key concepts or answer the questions in Section B, you know you have more studying to do. The same is true if you can't create a summary as good as—or better than—the one you originally wrote in Section C.

9. Test yourself. Get out the list of possible test questions you prepared (see the "While Organizing Study Materials" section of this Toolbox for how to prepare questions). Taking a practice test is a great way to both **Rehearse** and **Evaluate** your knowledge. Think of a self-test as a dress **Rehearsal** for the real thing. To that end, do your best to duplicate the actual test situation. For example, practice answering the kinds of questions that will be on the real test (e.g., multiple-choice, short answer, true/false, essay, problems). If the test will be timed, time your own practice test. If possible, test yourself in the room where the real test will be given. If you expect distractions during the test, reproduce them as well. As a bonus, when you excel in a practice test, confidence will replace self-doubts. After taking the practice test, get feedback on your answers. The best person to provide this feedback is your instructor. Others to ask include tutors in the learning center, friends who already took the class and did well, and classmates.

10. Hold a study team quiz. Here's a variation on a self-test. Ask study team members to bring questions to a meeting and quiz each other. Don't move on until everyone agrees on an answer. If needed, find the correct answer in your course materials (e.g., textbook or class notes). Or set the question aside to ask your instructor. To add fun to your efforts, search the Internet for sites that allow you to create learning games such as Jeopardy (the television quiz show). For those motivated by friendly competition, make a game out of the quiz by awarding points for correct answers. Perhaps the person with the highest score gets treated to lunch by the others. This competition is one in which everyone wins by enhancing their learning.

11. Study three-column charts for math. (See "While Organizing Study Materials" for an example.) The key to studying mathematics is solving problems, solving problems, and solving more problems. Here's where the three-column math charts you created are so helpful. Take a blank sheet of paper and hide Column 2 (Solution) and Column 3 (Explanation). Now all you can see is the problem in Column 1. Solve the problem on the blank sheet of paper (which is covering the Solution and Explanation columns). If you have difficulty solving the problem, give yourself hints by uncovering part of the solution or explanation. After solving the problem, uncover Columns 2 and 3. Then check both your solution and your understanding of the process. If a problem continues to stump you, seek help from your instructor, a tutor, or classmates who excel in math. Trust that with enough practice and enough help, you'll be able to solve even the most difficult problems. Remember, you don't learn to solve math problems by only watching your instructor solve them. You don't even learn to solve math problems by only reading how. You learn to solve math problems by *solving* math problems.

12. Practice academic skills. Mathematics is one of many courses you may take in college that teach a skill. Others include writing, speech, studio art, theater, dance, counseling, instrumental music, reading, and foreign languages, to name a few. As with mathematics, the key to developing a skill is **Rehearsal**. Take advantage of every practice opportunity provided by your instructor or the college. For example, if you're studying German, visit the language lab and listen to recordings in German. But . . . don't stop there . . . be a Creator and invent other ways to practice your new language skill. When my college roommate took German, he found a German-born barber who gave him both a haircut and practice in speaking German. Every two weeks for four semesters, my roommate got a haircut and talked German with a native speaker. He earned straight As in the course (and looked mighty well-groomed as well). Don't fool yourself into thinking you have mastered a skill because you understand it when you read or hear someone else talk about it. To master a skill, you need to do it. And do it. And do it.

13. Study with flashcards. (See "While Organizing Study Materials" for suggestions on creating flashcards.) Carry a deck of rubber-banded flashcards with you at all times. Pull them out for a quick review whenever you have a few extra minutes that you'd otherwise waste. If you study your flashcards just 15 minutes per day (say in three sessions of 5 minutes each), that's nearly two extra hours of studying each week!

The process is simple. Look at the front side of a flashcard and decide on an answer. Turn the card over. If you got the answer correct, put a dot in the upper right hand corner of the answer side. Now place the card on the bottom of your deck and keep repeating the process, perhaps shuffling the deck now and then. When you place the third dot on a card (meaning you got it correct three times), transfer that card to a second deck. Keep studying Deck 1 until all cards are moved to Deck 2. Review Deck 2 occasionally to keep your learning fresh. Flashcards are great study tools when preparing for short-answer tests, such as true/false, multiple-choice, matching, and fill in the blank.

14. Listen to self-made audio recordings. (See Strategy 21 in "While Organizing Study Materials" for an explanation.) When I was in graduate school, I had a long commute to the campus. I turned these boring drive times into valuable study times by listening to recordings I had made of my study materials. Think of unproductive time you could use for studying. For example, walking between classes, eating lunch alone, shopping, or waiting for a friend. Not only does listening to recordings squeeze more study time into each day, you're also adding variety to your **R**ehearsal methods, which strengthens your learning even more.

15. Prepare for open-book tests. Perhaps you wonder: What's to prepare? After all, the answers are right there in the book. Don't get suckered into thinking an open-book test is easy and you

don't need to study. If you do, you'll spend much of the test frantically flipping through your book looking for answers. Instead, ask your instructor if the test is "open notes" as well as open book. If so, **O**rganize your study materials as usual, **R**ehearse them as usual, and bring them to the test along with your book. (If your study materials are good, you may not even need your book.) If you're allowed to bring only your book to the test, transfer as many of your study materials into your book as allowed. Then, study your book just as you would your study materials. Remember, during the test, every student will have access to the information in the book. Your big advantage is that you have mastered the information by **O**rganizing and **R**ehearsing your study materials. Plus, you know where all of the key concepts, main ideas, and supporting details are in your book or (better yet) study materials. While others are desperately flipping the pages of their books, you'll be confidently answering test questions.

16. Memorize by chunks. Occasionally you may find it desirable—or even required—to memorize something for a course (e.g., a poem, a formula, or a summary from your Cornell study sheets). An important thing to know about memorizing is that *reading* information and *recalling* information strengthen different neural connections. Since you need to *recall* the information on a test, you want to strengthen the neural networks that manage recall (not reading). That's why simply reading something over and over is an ineffective way to memorize it. Here is one way to create strong neural networks for recalling information. If you memorize the words with a full understanding of their meaning, you'll be engaged in *elaborative* **R**ehearsal. However, if all you do is memorize the words like a parrot, you're using *rote* **R**ehearsal.

- Recite the entire text you want to memorize (e.g., poem, formula, summary, etc.)

- Now recite only the first chunk of information (e.g., line, string of symbols, sentence, etc.) from the text.

- Look away from the text and recite the first chunk.
- Look back at the text and recite the first *and* second chunks.
- Look away and recite this longer chunk aloud without looking at the text.
- Keep adding chunks until you can correctly recite the entire text aloud five times without looking at it.
- Take a 10-minute break and again recite the entire text aloud from memory until you do it correctly five times in a row.
- Thereafter, recite daily the entire text from memory; give extra practice to sections that are a challenge for you to recall.

If you wish, you can substitute writing for reciting in any of the steps. In fact, you'll probably find it helpful to alternate back and forth between reciting and writing.

17. Memorize with letter cues. Here's another way to memorize information word for word. As in the previous strategy, the key is strengthening the neural networks for *recalling* (not *reading*) information. For example, suppose you wanted to memorize the beginning of a famous soliloquy from Shakespeare's *Hamlet*:

> To be, or not to be: that is the question:
> Whether 'tis nobler in the mind to suffer
> The slings and arrows of outrageous fortune,
> Or to take arms against a sea of troubles,
> And by opposing end them?

First, become familiar with the meaning of the text by reading it over a couple of times, or by having someone explain it to you. Writing it out by hand is another way to become familiar with the words and ideas. Now record just the first letter of each word and the punctuation. The five lines from *Hamlet* would look like this:

> T b, o n t b: t i t q:
> W 't n i t m t s
> T s a a o o f,
> O t t a a a s o t,
> A b o e t?

Now use only these letters as cues to recite the five lines. If you get stuck, look at the original, and then return to using only the letter cues. After a while, begin reciting lines without looking at the letter cues. Remember to think about the meaning of the words to help you recall them. By the way, if you understand what Hamlet is saying here, you'll realize that he is engaged in a poetic variation of the Wise Choice Process (see Chapter 2).

18. Memorize with acronyms. An acronym is a word made from the first letters of other words that you want to remember. For example, the DAPPS Rule is presented in Chapter 3. DAPPS is an acronym that helps you remember the qualities of an effective goal: **Dated**, **Achievable**, **Personal**, **Positive**, **Specific**. If you want to remember the names of the Great Lakes, use the acronym HOMES: **Huron**, **Ontario**, **Michigan**, **Erie**, **Superior**. In this way, remembering one word (the acronym) cues you to recall the words you want to remember. Acronyms can be real words (HOMES) or made-up words (DAPPS).

19. Memorize with acrostics. Acrostics are sometimes called sentence acronyms. Like acronyms, acrostics are made from the first letters of other words. However, you don't create a new word from the initial letters. Instead, you create a sentence. For example, biology students may be required to know the taxonomic classifications: kingdom, phylum, class, order, family, genus, species. Taking the first letter of each word in this list, you can create the sentence "**King Peter came over for grape soda.**" Music students can recall the notes on the lines of a musical staff (E-G-B-D-F) by the sentence "**Every good boy does fine.**" Suppose you want to remember the order of operations for math (parentheses, exponents, multiply, divide, add, and subtract). The acrostic "**Please excuse my dear Aunt Sally**" will help. Notice that an acrostic is an especially helpful tool when you need to remember items in a particular order.

20. Memorize with associations. When you associate something new with something you already know, the new information is easier to recall. Suppose you want to remember the name of your new mathematics teacher, Professor Getty. You could associate his name with the Battle of Gettysburg that you studied in American history. You might even visualize him wearing a uniform and carrying a musket. Now you'll remember his name. Have you ever thought of something important in the middle of the night but you can't recall it in the morning? If you have paper and pen available, a note is the obvious solution. Otherwise, try tossing a pillow (or some other item) into the middle of your room and consciously associate the pillow with the important thought. When you see the pillow in the morning, you'll usually remember.

21. Memorize with the loci technique. The loci (pronounced *low-sigh*) technique is a variation of association. *Loci* is Latin for "places," so with this strategy, you associate items you want to memorize with familiar places. Suppose you're studying parts of the brain and you want to remember the *amygdala*, which plays an important role in processing and remembering emotional reactions. Think of a familiar place, such as your living room. Picture your television turned to your favorite talk show and the host introducing an angry woman wearing a bright red dress. The host is saying, "Please welcome Amy G. Dala." Review this mental image several times a day for two or three days. When you need to recall the *amygdala*, mentally visit your living room, turn on the television, and there's angry ol' Amy G. Dala waiting to be introduced. You can now associate other parts of the brain with additional places in your living room. Say, isn't that a neo-cortex sitting on your couch?

After Rehearsing and Memorizing Study Materials

22. Review, Review, Review. Repetition strengthens memory. Shortly after a study period, spend a few minutes reviewing your outlines, graphic organizers, flashcards, Cornell study sheets, or whatever study materials you prefer. Two hours later review again. For the next three days, review your study materials daily. Next, review them weekly.

I've found that reviewing before going to sleep and just as I wake up helps me to remember. But the ideal time to review is any time you can. Repeated reviews take little effort but creates much learning.

23. Teach what you learn. If you ask your instructors when they achieved a deep and lasting understanding of their subject, most will say it was when they started teaching it. Explaining a complex idea requires a thorough understanding. And stumbling over an explanation is clear evidence of incomplete learning. So find people to teach. Say, "Let me tell you something fascinating that I learned in one of my classes." Teaching is also a great activity to do in a study group. Suppose each time your group met, each member gave a five-minute lecture on something important they had learned in the course that week. Other teaching possibilities are only limited by your imagination. One student I knew put her children to bed each night in a most ingenious way. Using hand puppets, she delivered animated lectures to her children about what she had learned in college that day. Every night her kids couldn't wait for Professor Hand to tuck them in. Now that is a Creator!

24. Post memory cards. Create cards with words, diagrams, formulas, or concepts you want to memorize. Post these cards where you'll see them often (on your mirror, refrigerator, and so on). Then go about your daily life. Over the next week or two, you will unconsciously absorb some or all of the posted information.

25. Use a postage stamp review. Here's one of my favorite strategies for test preparation. About seven days before a test, condense all of your study materials to one side of a sheet of paper (8.5" by 11"). Every couple of hours, **Rehearse** the summarized information. Every day thereafter, copy your notes onto a sheet of paper one half as large—condensing ideas as necessary. Then **Rehearse** the condensed information several times that day. As your page of notes gets smaller by half each day, you'll need to use abbreviations, acronyms, and symbols to get all of the information to fit.

Eventually your notes will be on a piece of paper about the size of a postage stamp. Study these tiny notes right up to the exam. On the way to the exam, roll your postage stamp into a tiny ball and toss it in the trash. You're ready for the test.

ONE STUDENT'S STORY

MICHAEL CHAPASKO, *Blinn College, Texas*

When I was a kid, I didn't learn as fast as my classmates. My mom suggested that I go to the public school where she taught because they had a content mastery program that helped kids one-on-one when they needed it. I wasn't happy about it, but I made the move and got prescribed Adderall to help me stay focused. Come to find out I was a very smart kid when I could focus. Being one of the few kids with dyslexia, I felt embarrassed when I had to take my tests in different rooms or needed one-on-one help. When I got to high school, classes were getting harder, and I started to think I couldn't learn at the pace of everyone else, even with the Adderall. I got down on myself and didn't study much. I blamed my problems on my ADHD and dyslexia. Then in the middle of high school, I moved to a new school. Everything about this new school was intimidating. It was one of the top 10 academic high schools in the nation! Even though I didn't study while at my previous high school, my class rank had been 56 in a class of 808. In my new high school, however, I dropped to number 203 in a class of 480. Then I really got down on my ability to learn, but I still didn't study.

After high school, I decided to go to Blinn College, and in my first semester I took an *On Course* class. I didn't expect it to help me the way it did, but it really changed my whole outlook on studying. I got really interested when I read how the human brain learns. I played football, basketball, and baseball in high school. Now I'm into body building, and I work out every day. I understand how muscles work, and I found it interesting to think of the brain as a muscle. Instead of thinking about the brain as a muscle, I just figured you were either born smart or you weren't. I know the harder you work a muscle, the bigger and stronger it gets, but you can't do it all in one day. I also know the more you practice a certain movement or pattern, the better you get at it. When I got a 52 on my first exam in business law, I knew something had to change in the way I studied. So I decided to apply my new knowledge about how the brain works and use some of the learning strategies in *On Course*.

Just like working out, I started spreading my studying over more time and using different ways to learn. Eventually, I came up with a way of studying that works for me. When I was studying for my first business law test, I had quit reading the book when I didn't understand it. With my new approach, I read each assignment completely and got as much out of it as I could. I even tried to stay a couple of weeks ahead in assignments. My professor posted video lectures on our eCampus site, so after reading, I'd watch a related lecture online. The professor cut the information in the book down to what I really needed to know. When I attended the next class, his lecture would be a review of what I had read and what was on the video. That repetition deepened my understanding of the material because I had already heard it before. When he asked questions in class, I was ready to participate. I also found flashcards to be helpful, especially for introductory courses like business law where you have to learn a lot of new terms. I usually prefer to study alone, but if it's something I don't understand, then I like being in a group with students who understand the course. I often get their explanations better than the instructor's. Another strategy I've found helpful is to look over my past tests. Even glancing at them for a few minutes helps me remember things I need to know for the next test.

By the time I took the second exam in my business law course, I had a whole new way of studying. Using my new strategies, I ended up making a 96! I no longer thought about dropping the class because at that point I knew I could do it! One of my coaches used to say, "Hard work beats talent when talent refuses to work hard." Now I'm not only working hard, I'm working smart.

Photo: Courtesy of Michael Chapasko.

Rehearsing and Memorizing Study Materials: Do One Different Thing This Week

In this section of your Toolbox for Active Learners, you've been introduced to 25 strategies for **Rehearsing** and memorizing study materials. Here's an opportunity to experiment with one of them. First, review the strategies. Identify those you marked because they could help with one of your learning challenges. Now pick the one strategy you think would best help you improve your ability to **Rehearse** and memorize study materials.

In the "My Commitment for Rehearsing and Memorizing Study Materials" box in the following chart, write the strategy with which you will experiment. Write just the number of the strategy and the one-sentence description of it that is in bold print. For example, **"9. Test yourself."** Then track yourself for one week, putting a check in the appropriate box each day that you practice this strategy. Your goal is to do it every day. After seven days, evaluate your results. If your skills for **Rehearsing** and memorizing study materials improve, you'll have a learning tool you can use for the rest of your life.

My Commitment for Rehearsing and Memorizing Study Materials:

_____

_____

_____

☐ Day 1   ☐ Day 2   ☐ Day 3   ☐ Day 4   ☐ Day 5   ☐ Day 6   ☐ Day 7

During my seven-day experiment, what happened?

As a result of what happened, what did I learn or relearn?

As a result of what I learned or relearned, I will . . .

A test is a game . . . an important game, but a game nonetheless.

First, let's review why tests in college are important (as if you didn't know). Tests contribute to your course grade, and that grade becomes a part of your permanent record. If your grades are consistently low, you will be put on probation or even expelled. Low grades may cause you to lose financial aid. If you're an athlete, low grades can cost you eligibility for intercollegiate sports.

However, if your grades are consistently high enough, you'll eventually earn a degree. Then your grades will be of interest to future employers, graduate schools, and car insurance companies, to name a few. One of my students told me that even the parents of his fiancé asked to see a copy of his transcript. Perhaps they thought his grades would reveal what kind of husband he would make for their daughter.

So tests are important. But they *are* just a game, and you win the test game by scoring the maximum number of points possible. Three factors determine how well you score on tests:

- **Factor 1: How well have you prepared?** If you have diligently completed each step of the CORE Learning System, you are extremely well prepared! Look around the room at the other students taking the test. Remind yourself that you are as well prepared as all of them and more prepared than most of them. You have worked hard, used a powerful learning system, and the result is deep and lasting learning. You have every reason to be confident!
- **Factor 2: How well do you take tests?** Most people assume that tests reveal how much you know and maybe even how intelligent you are.

In an ideal world, perhaps this would be true. Here on planet Earth, however, another critical factor influences your grades: Your skill at taking tests. Without this skill, your grades may only vaguely represent how much you know or how intelligent you are. Every game requires special skills for scoring points. In this section, you'll learn some of the very best skills for maximizing the number of points you earn on every test. Get ready to learn how to be "test smart."

- **Factor 3: How much have you learned from previous tests?** Every test provides feedback. Self-aware Creators pay attention to feedback and use it to their advantage. If a test score reveals that you're on course, you can confidently keep doing whatever you've been doing. However, if a test score reveals that you are off course, it's time to change tactics.

TAKING TESTS: THE BIG PICTURE

In previous sections you discovered how to be a good learner. Now you'll learn how to be a good "test taker." Here's good news: There are only so many ways an instructor can ask you to demonstrate your knowledge and skills. Your challenge is to determine the most likely ways and prepare accordingly. So, experiment with the many following strategies and, as you do, keep in mind the big picture of test taking: **Your goal for each test is to score the maximum number of points possible. Just as there is an art to learning, so is there an art to taking tests. It's called being *test smart*.**

CHALLENGES WITH TAKING TESTS

Following are common challenges with taking tests in higher education. Circle the numbers

Genevieve Shapiro/Cartoon Stock

next to the challenges that you are having (or can foresee having) in taking tests for your present courses. Even if you consider yourself good at taking tests, circle the numbers next to at least two areas in which you could improve. If you have a challenge not on the list, use one or both blank spaces at the bottom of the list to add your own challenge(s).

1. I have no idea how to be test-smart.

2. I get so nervous while taking tests that my mind goes blank.

3. I usually do pretty well on essay questions, but I mess up on short-answer, factual questions.

4. I often spend a lot of time on one question and don't finish the test.

5. I don't do well on tests that are based on lectures.

6. I do fine on quizzes that cover only a small part of the course, but I mess up on big tests like midterm or final exams.

7. I always lose points on multiple-choice questions.

8. I almost never have enough time to finish a test.

9. When I study, I feel like I know the material, but I just don't test well.

10. Sometimes I lose points because I don't read the directions carefully.

11. On factual questions I get fooled by the tricks that instructors play, like making false statements sound true.

12. A friend told me she has a plan for getting the most points possible on a test. I don't understand how she does it.

13. I go into tests with a lot of negative thoughts about failing.

14. I usually do pretty well on factual questions, but I mess up on essay tests.

15. I can't concentrate during a test. The slightest noise distracts me.

16. I don't do well on fill-in-the-blank tests.

17. On essay tests, I'm never really sure what the instructor is asking for.

18. One of my instructors says I should learn from the mistakes I make on tests, but I don't know how.

19. I usually think I did really well on a test, but when I get it back, I seldom do as well as I thought.

20. I don't do well on true/false questions.

21. I have a tendency to rush through a test and then I end up making silly mistakes.

22. I don't do well on tests that are based on reading assignments.

23. I second guess myself by thinking the easy questions are harder than they really are.

24. Some of my tests are on Scantron bubble sheets, so I get a score but don't know which questions I missed.

25. I can never remember the formulas to solve math problems.

26. Open-books tests seem like they would be easy, but I never do well on them.

27. _____
    _____

28. _____
    _____

STRATEGIES TO IMPROVE TAKING TESTS

Following, you'll find many of the very best strategies for taking tests. These strategies assume you have prepared well using the CORE Learning System. After reading each strategy, pause and decide if it would help you overcome any of the challenges you circled. If so, mark it in some way (e.g., underline, circle, highlight, star). Later on, you can decide which of these strategies to experiment with to improve your ability to take tests.

Before Taking Tests

1. Actively use the CORE Learning System. This means when you walk into the test room, you have already. . .

> **C**ollected complete and accurate information from all reading assignments, course materials, and class sessions,
>
> **O**rganized many different kinds of effective study materials,
>
> **R**ehearsed these study materials with a distributed study schedule, and
>
> **E**valuated to confirm your understanding of all study materials.

2. Create a positive affirmation about taking tests. Create an affirming statement, such as *I am fully prepared, test-smart, and confident of earning a high score*. Along with your personal affirmation repeat this test-taking affirmation to revise your beliefs about your ability to do well on tests. (See "Believing in Yourself: Write a Personal Affirmation" in Chapter 3 for more information about creating affirmations.)

3. Visualize success. Create a mental movie of yourself taking the exam with great success. In your mind, picture yourself...

- understanding every question
- answering each one quickly and correctly
- finishing on time, and, later,
- getting your test back with the grade you want (or even higher)

Play this positive movie in your mind often. Let it build your confidence and prepare you to think, feel, and act positively during the real test. (Read "How to Visualize" in Chapter 3 for information on how to create a visualization.)

4. Arrive early and get comfortable. Avoid the stress of running late. Get to the test location in plenty of time, and choose your preferred place to sit. If seeing other people leave early gets you nervous, sit up front where you can't see what's going on behind you. Set up your supplies (pens, pencils, paper, white-out, allowed books, calculator with fresh batteries, and so on). Have a watch or clock so you can keep track of time. Consider bringing a picture that inspires you, like a photo of your family or a picture of yourself in a graduation gown. If it's a long exam, bring water and snacks, if allowed.

5. Prepare yourself physically and emotionally. Be sure to get a good night's sleep and eat well before a test. You don't want to be distracted by tiredness or hunger. As your instructor hands out the test, breathe deeply and relax. Your studying is done. Now it's game time and your goal is simple: Earn the most points possible. You're ready. Repeat your affirmation. Visualize your success. Take another deep breath and get ready to score! You can do this!

While Taking Tests

6. Write memory cues on the test. As soon as you receive the test, write any information on the test that will help you earn points. If there's not enough white space on the test pages, use the back of a page. (Confirm with your instructor that it's okay to write on the test. If it isn't, ask if you can write notes on a blank piece of paper.) Possible cues to write on the test include an acronym, a date, a formula, or a quotation you plan to use in answering an essay question—anything you might forget when you need it later.

7. Preview the test. Just as previewing a reading assignment is valuable, so is previewing a test. Note the kinds of questions. Note the point value of various questions. Read the directions carefully so you understand the rules of the game. For example, on a multiple-choice test, if the directions ask you to mark *two or more* answers and you mark only one, you'll lose points. Also, be alert for directions that change the rules. In one part of the test a wrong answer may be penalized, whereas in another part of the test it may not be. This knowledge will determine whether or not you guess at an answer. Be sure you understand exactly what you are being asked to do. If unsure, ask the instructor to clarify.

8. Make a test-smart plan. Remember, your goal is to earn as many points as possible. The first rule of a test-smart plan is *Answer easy questions first*. Skim the test and answer any questions you can answer quickly and correctly. Answering easy questions first has three advantages: It makes sure you earn these points. It builds confidence that calms test anxiety. And, while answering the easy questions, you may come across answers to other questions on the test.

The second rule of a test-smart plan is *Spend time in proportion to points available*. Having answered the easy questions, now answer the remaining questions that are worth the most points. Suppose you're taking a 50-minute test with 50 true/false questions worth two points each. Your plan is obvious. Assign one minute to answer each question. If you spend 5 minutes answering one question and 5 minutes answering another, now you have only 40 minutes to answer the remaining 48 questions. Or consider a different situation: You're taking a 50-minute test with ten true/false questions worth two points each and two short-answer essay questions worth 40 points each. Make sure you get as many of those 80 essay points as possible. Since each essay is worth 40 percent of the total points available, you assign 40 percent of the time available (20 minutes) to each . . . which leaves

10 minutes to answer the true/false questions. Without this plan, you might spend 20 minutes answering the true/false questions, leaving yourself less time to gobble up all those essay points.

9. Answer true/false questions. Obviously, the best situation is when you know whether the statement is true or false. However, all is not lost if you are unsure. Even by guessing, you'll likely get half of them correct, and here are six test-smart strategies for improving those odds:

A. If any part of a statement is false, the answer is false.

B. If the question contains an **unconditional** word (100% with no exception), such as *all, every, only, never,* or *always,* the answer is probably false.

C. If the question contains a **conditional** word (less than 100% with some exceptions), such as *generally, some, a few, occasionally, seldom, usually, sometimes,* or *often,* the answer is probably true.

D. If the statement has two negatives, cross them both out and see if the statement is true or false.

E. If the sentence contains words you've never heard of, guess false. (This suggestion assumes you've studied thoroughly and will recognize key terms in the course.)

F. If you are reduced to taking a pure guess, choose "True." It is easier for instructors to write a true statement; plus, most would prefer that you think about the correct answer.

10. Answer multiple-choice questions. Multiple-choice questions offer a statement or question, and then present alternative ways to complete the statement or answer the question. A multiple-choice question is actually a group of true/false questions. Your task, then, is to read each statement and choose the correct (true) answer. When you are stumped, here are ways to be test-smart. The following options won't always get you the correct answer, but when you are reduced to making pure guesses, they can improve your odds of choosing the correct answer.

A. In the directions, see whether you can choose only one answer or more than one answer for each question.

ACTIVITY 6A: MAKING A TEST-SMART PLAN

Imagine that you have just received the test for a 1-hour-and-40-minute final exam. Determine the number of minutes you will assign to each section and the order in which you will complete them. Be prepared to explain your choices.

Section 1. Forty multiple-choice questions

        Possible points: 20

        Level of difficulty: Medium

        ___ (Amount of time in minutes)

        ___ (Order: 1st, 2nd, 3rd, 4th, or 5th)

Section 2. Five true/false questions.

        Possible points: 20

        Level of difficulty: High

        ___ (Amount of time in minutes)

        ___ (Order: 1st, 2nd, 3rd, 4th, or 5th)

Section 3. Ten fill-in-the blank questions

        Possible points: 10

        Level of difficulty: Low

        ___ (Amount of time in minutes)

        ___ (Order: 1st, 2nd, 3rd, 4th, or 5th)

Section 4. One essay question

        Possible points: 40

        Level of difficulty: Low

        ___ (Amount of time in minutes)

        ___ (Order: 1st, 2nd, 3rd, 4th, or 5th)

Section 5. One essay question

        Possible points: 10

        Level of difficulty: High

        ___ (Amount of time in minutes)

        ___ (Order: 1st, 2nd, 3rd, 4th, or 5th)

B. Be sure to read all answers before making a choice. Answer A may be partly true and tempting, but Answer D may be truer and therefore is the answer you should choose.

C. Cross out all obviously incorrect answers, such as those that are intended to be humorous.

D. Cross out answers with unconditional (100%) words like *all, always, never, must,* or *every.*

E. Look for grammatical clues to cross out an answer (e.g., the subject in the question doesn't agree with the verb in one of the answers).

F. When the answers are numbers, cross out the highest and lowest.

G. If two answers are similar (e.g., such as *independent* and *interdependent*), choose one of them as the correct answer.

H. If you know two or more answers are correct, choose "All of the above" as the correct answer. An exception is when the directions allow you to choose more than one correct answer.

I. If one answer has a more thorough answer than the others, choose that answer as correct.

J. If the question is based on a reading passage, read the question and possible answers *before* reading the passage. Then read the passage with the specific purpose of finding the answer.

Example: The 1964 Republican nominee for president of the United States was

A. Barry Goldfarb

B. Barry Goldwater

C. Bugs Bunny

D. Hubert Humphrey

E. All of the above

Answer: Cross out "Bugs Bunny," which is obviously intended as a joke. Cross out "All of the above" because Bugs Bunny is incorrect. Choose either "Barry Goldfarb" or "Barry Goldwater" since they are two similar answers. (In fact, the answer is Barry Goldwater, a senator from Arizona, who was defeated in the election by Lyndon B. Johnson.)

11. Answer matching questions. Matching questions provide you with two columns of items and ask you to "match" them by something they have in common (e.g., authors matched with their books, words matched with their definitions, or discoveries matched with their discoverers). The greater the number of items to be matched, the lower your probability of guessing the correct answer. However, the more correct answers you can identify, the more you increase your odds of getting the remaining ones correct.

A. Read the directions to see if an answer can be used only once or more than once.

B. Note whether each column has the same number of items. If one column has more items, then some items will not be used, or some items will be used more than once.

C. Match all of the pairs you are sure of, and cross them out as you go (unless an item can be used more than once).

D. Look over the remaining questions, looking for clues that reveal the kind of word(s) required to make a match (e.g., the match requires a person, book title, date, or place). If there is only one of that kind, you have a match.

E. Go through the lists once more, matching all remaining pairs as best you can. You may see matches this time through that you didn't see earlier.

Example: Match the following items. Each item may be used only once.

____ 1 *1984*	A. Mark Twain
____ 2. Samuel Clemens	B. *Wrote Great Expectations*
____ 3. Birth date of Nathaniel Hawthorne	C. Hauberk
____ 4. Charles Dickens	D. 1804
____ 5. A long tunic made of chain mail	E. Book written by George Orwell

Answer: We're going to assume that the only answer you know is that Samuel Clemens's pen name was "Mark Twain." Thus, you would answer Number 2 first and cross out Mark Twain in the answer column. Now use test-smart strategies to get the remaining four questions correct. Be sure to cross out answers as you use them.

Question 2: Answer A—This is the answer you knew and did first.

Question 3: Answer D—1804 is the only date so it has to be the answer for a birth date.

Question 1: Answer E—Because *1984* is italicized, it is almost certainly a book title.

Question 4: Answer B—Of the remaining two answers, Charles Dickens is the only person, and must therefore be the author of *Great Expectations*.

Question 5: Answer C—"Hauberk" is the only answer left, so by elimination, it must be the answer.

RECOGNITION VERSUS RECALL

For true/false, multiple-choice, and matching questions, the test provides the correct answer, and you simply need to *recognize* it. In preparing for recognition questions, rote **Rehearsal** methods usually work fine. To answer fill-in-the-blank, lists, short-answer, essay, and problems, you need to *recall* information and problem-solving processes from memory. In preparing for recall questions, elaborative **Rehearsal** methods are typically more effective.

12. Answer fill-in-the-blank questions. Fill-in-the-blank questions present a sentence with one or more words (or phrases) left out. Your task is to insert the correct word or phrase. Despite the increased level of challenge, being test-smart can improve your chances of earning points on fill-in-the-blank questions.

A. Unless the directions say you will be penalized for a wrong answer, always write something in the blank.

B. Make sure your answer fits grammatically into the sentence (e.g., don't insert a noun if the space in the sentence requires a verb).

C. Use the length of the blank to indicate whether the correct answer is one or more words.

D. If you see two or more blanks, realize you need to have a different word or phrase in each blank.

E. Because fill-in-the-blank questions usually ask about key concepts, these concepts are often mentioned elsewhere in the test. Keep alert for them as you do other parts of the test.

F. After inserting the answer, read the sentence to make sure it makes sense.

Example: To excel as a learner, create as many _____ in your brain as possible.

Answer: To excel as a learner, create as many <u>neural networks</u> in your brain as possible.

Note: If you don't know the answer, this is going to be a difficult question to answer. The one clue you do have to be test-smart is that the blank seems too long for just one word (though be alert for instructors who will play with the line length just

to keep you guessing). If you thought the answer might be "deep processing," you would realize that this answer doesn't make sense in the sentence. If you wrote "brain connections," your instructor may give you points even though it is not the preferred answer.

13. Answer questions that ask for a list. Lists require the recall of a number of separate items, similar to a shopping list. Sometimes you are told how many items you are expected to include in the list; sometimes the number is not mentioned. Here's how to be test-smart when providing a list.

A. If the number of requested items is provided, circle that number in the question so you know exactly how many items need to be in your answer list.

B. Underline key term(s) so you are sure what items to include in your list.

C. If you studied the terms with an acronym, jot it down on the page as a memory jogger (e.g., DAPPS rule = **Dated**, **Achievable**, **Personal**, **Positive**, **and Specific**).

D. If the question tells you how many items to list, provide that many answers even if you have to guess at some.

Example: List four preferred ways of learning identified by Ned Herrmann.

Answer: 1. Thinking 2. Doing 3. Feeling 4. Diving Deep

Note: While the first three answers in the list above are correct, the fourth is wrong. The correct answer is "Innovating." However, it was test-smart of this student to take a guess because, in the rush of grading, the instructor might be distracted by the first three correct answers and give full credit for this question. (See Chapter 7 for more information about Ned Herrmann's theory of learning preferences.)

14. Answer short-answer questions. Short-answer questions are mini-essays, usually one paragraph in length. The best approach, then, is to state a main idea. Then offer specific supporting details to demonstrate your thorough understanding of the idea. It's difficult to fake knowledge on a short-answer question, but there are some test-smart strategies that can maximize the number of points you earn.

A. Always write something. Your instructor can't give you points for a blank space.

B. Circle the *guide word* in the writing prompt (e.g., Describe the advantages of using a tracking form). Guide words reveal the way in which the instructor expects you to develop the topic. See **Figure T.18** for a description of 12 common guide words.

C. Underline the topic in the writing prompt (e.g., Describe the advantages of using a tracking form). Referring to the underlined words helps you stay focused on the topic.

D. On a blank sheet of paper or the back of a test page, jot down any related ideas and supporting details you can think of. If you have time, write a rough draft of your answer and copy it onto the test.

E. Begin writing your answer by turning the question or writing prompt into your main idea. Again, imagine that the prompt is "Describe the advantages of using a tracking form." Begin your answer, "Using a tracking form has a number of advantages." This beginning helps you stay focused on the topic as you write your paragraph.

F. Develop your paragraph with supporting details such as examples, evidence, explanations, and experiences. If you're at a loss for supporting details, see if you can find some within other questions on the test.

G. The space provided usually indicates how much writing your instructor expects, so plan your answer to fit in that space (unless there's a note such as "Continue your answer on the back of this page").

H. End your paragraph with a wrap-up sentence (e.g., "There are other advantages to using a tracking form, but these are three of the most valuable").

I. Proofread your paragraph. Even if instructors don't consciously take off points for errors, such distractions can undermine an otherwise positive impression of your answer.

Example: Describe the advantages of using a tracking form.

Answer: Using a tracking form has a number of advantages. First, a tracking form helps users focus their efforts on accomplishing goals in one area of their lives, such as a math course. Further, a tracking form encourages users to choose specific outer and inner behaviors that will help accomplish their goals. For example, a math student might choose an outer behavior of working on math homework for at least 20 minutes a day. As an inner behavior, the student might choose to say his math affirmation daily. A third advantage of using a tracking form is that after two weeks of tracking, users can see exactly what they did and did not do to accomplish their goals. This self-generated feedback helps them make course corrections, increasing their chances of achieving their goals. There are other advantages to using a tracking form, but these are three of the most valuable.

15. Answer definition questions. A definition is a specific kind of short-answer question. Definition questions are common on tests in introductory courses where learning new terminology is essential. As before, circle the guide word and underline the term to be defined. An effective definition includes three components: category, unique characteristics, and elaboration. For elaboration, an example is often ideal.

Guide Words	What to Do	Example Questions
1. **Analyze**	Identify the parts of something and explain how those parts contribute to the whole.	*Analyze* the skills of a test-smart student. *Analyze* the symbolism of the white whale in Herman Melville's *Moby Dick*.
2. **Compare**	Show similarities of two or more things. (Note: some instructors also want you to show differences as well.)	*Compare* linear and graphic organizers. *Compare* democracy and socialism.
3. **Contrast**	Show differences between two or more things.	*Contrast* Creators and Victims. *Contrast* Flemish and Italian painters during the Renaissance.
4. **Define**	State the meaning of something.	*Define* a self-sabotaging script. *Define* standard deviation.
5. **Describe**	Tell about in some detail.	*Describe* an effective self-management system. *Describe* the efforts of England's King Henry VII to consolidate royal power.
6. **Discuss (or Explain) Why**	Provide a detailed account showing cause.	*Discuss why* it is important to be an active learner. *Explain why* Chebyshev's theorem is important.
7. **Discuss (or Explain) Effect**	Give the results of something.	*Discuss* the long-term *effects* of stress on physical health. *Explain* the *effect* of global warming.
8. **Discuss (or Explain) How**	Provide the details of a process.	*Discuss how* students can maintain or increase their academic motivation. *Explain how* hydrogen and oxygen combine to make water.
9. **Evaluate**	Assess strengths and weaknesses, providing reasons.	*Evaluate* the quality of writing in your first *On Course* journal entry. *Evaluate* a vegetarian diet.
10. **Explain**	Make clear or comprehensible.	*Explain* the three components of a logical argument. *Explain* the health risks of binge drinking.
11. **Illustrate**	Offer an example.	*Illustrate* the use of the Wise Choice Process. *Illustrate* the benefits of using cascading style sheets in the creation of a website.
12. **Summarize**	Provide a condensed version, highlighting main points only.	*Summarize* the reasons that interdependence is important in the workplace. *Summarize* the plot of *Huckleberry Finn* by Mark Twain.

© Cengage Learning

FIGURE T.18 One Dozen Common Guide Words

Example: Define a 32-Day Commitment.

Answer: [**Category** →] A 32-Day Commitment is a self-management tool. [**Unique characteristics** →] It is used to develop or eliminate a habit. First, you identify a behavior you will or will not do for 32 days. Then, you check off each day that you keep the commitment. [**Elaboration** →] I made a 32-Day Commitment to study biology for at least 30 minutes every day. I found the commitment very challenging, but also rewarding. By about day 15, I actually started to understand what I was reading in the textbook, and I raised my grade from a low C to a high B. (Learn more about 32-Day Commitments in "Developing Self-Discipline" in Chapter 4.)

16. Answer essay questions. Essay questions require an in-depth discussion of a topic. In the next section of this Toolbox, you will learn many writing skills that will help you excel at answering essay questions. Here we will address two writing challenges that are unique to taking an essay test. First, you usually need to write your essay from information stored in your memory (not in your notes). Second, you have a time limit in which to write (unless it is a take-home exam). Thus, essay questions not only test your knowledge of the course content, they also test your writing ability. Here are some test-smart strategies for answering essay questions:

A. Read the directions carefully. As with short-answer questions, circle guide words in the essay prompt. Words such as *define, compare, contrast, describe, evaluate, summarize,* and *explain the cause* require different sorts of responses. Be sure you understand what you are being asked to write. (See **Figure T.18:** One Dozen Common Guide Words.)

B. Underline all key terms in the writing prompt. Suppose the topic says "Describe the following economic theories: Classical, Marxist, and Keynesian." If you do a great job on Classical and Keynesian theories but don't mention Marxist theory, you'll lose many possible points.

C. If the question gives you a choice of topics to write about, be sure to write the correct number of essays. If you write more essays than asked for, you're wasting precious time on questions you didn't need to answer (and probably won't get points for). And if you answer fewer, you'll certainly lose points.

D. Don't start writing immediately. Instead, brainstorm by jotting down ideas related to the topic. If you need more ideas, glance over the rest of the test to see if other questions or answers suggest additional ideas or supporting details to add to your brainstorm.

E. Revise the question or topic and use it as the first sentence of your essay. (See Strategy 14E for how to do this.)

F. Organize your ideas with your preferred method (e.g., outline or concept map). Creating a clear organization helps you maximize points earned. If you have more main ideas in your plan than you have time to write about, cross out the ones for which you have the fewest supporting details. You're likely to earn more points for four to six well-developed paragraphs than you will for seven to ten poorly developed paragraphs.

G. Develop each main idea in a separate paragraph, offering specific support such as examples, evidence, explanations, and experiences. Don't leave information out of your essay because you think the instructor already knows it. Remember, this is not a test to see if your *instructor* can answer the question; the test is to determine if *you* can. You'll be wise to write to a general audience: a group of intelligent, interested readers who know very little about your topic. This approach will assure that you include all relevant information that could earn you points. (Strategy 18 in the next section of this Toolbox offers more information on how to develop a paragraph effectively.)

H. Write a satisfying conclusion, perhaps summarizing the main points you have made. (Strategy

20 in the next section provides suggestions for concluding your essay.)

I. Save time for revising. As you read over what you have written, identify and answer questions your reader may have about your ideas. For example, readers often want to know "Why?" and "How do you know?" Add additional supporting details (examples, evidence, explanations, and experiences) to undeveloped paragraphs.

J. Proofread carefully for grammar, spelling, and punctuation errors.

K. If your handwriting is difficult to read, recopy for legibility. For further neatness, consider printing, writing on every other line, and writing on one side of the paper only.

Example: Describe one of the obstacles that challenged your success in college. Then explain how you applied one or more specific *On Course* strategies to overcome the challenge. Finally, end by describing what happened after using the *On Course* strategy.

Answer: Read any of the "One Student's Story" essays in *On Course* for excellent responses to this essay prompt.

Here are some final tips for maximizing essay points:

- Always write something. Your instructor can't give you points for a blank page.

- Leave three or four blank lines after each answer in case you think of something later that you can add at the end.

- If you can't finish, provide an outline or concept map for what you would have written with more time. You may get some points for your plan.

- If you can type, consider asking if you can bring a laptop computer to the test. You'll be able to write faster and make corrections more easily. Of course, you'll need some way to print your test before handing it in.

17. Solve math problems. Mathematics tests usually ask you to solve problems of the type you have been studying. If you have been solving practice problems successfully throughout the course, you are well prepared. Here are some test-smart strategies to apply during a math test:

A. As soon as you get the test, write notes and formulas on the test. If you freeze up later, you'll have access to this essential information.

For Better or For Worse®   by Lynn Johnston

B. Do a first pass through the test and solve all of the problems you can do easily. You never want to lose points by leaving a problem undone that you could have solved, but ran out of time.

C. Make a second pass through the test to work on the more challenging problems. Begin to solve each problem by estimating the answer.

D. As you do a problem, write out every step of your solution. Even if you get the answer wrong, the instructor may give you some points.

E. When finished with each problem, compare your answer with the estimate you made in Step C.

F. As time allows, revisit each problem and double-check all calculations.

18. If you get stuck, move on. Don't sit there wasting time on a question you can't answer. Not only will you lose time that you need for earning points, you'll also undermine your confidence by focusing on what you *don't* know instead of what you *do* know. If you doubt an answer that you've given or you've given no answer at all, put a light check mark next to the question. If time allows, return later and review your answer with fresh eyes.

19. If you feel anxious, refocus. Turn over your test and squeeze your eyes closed. Take a deep breath, tighten and release your muscles, roll your head slowly in a circle, and then roll it back the other way. Say your affirmation. Remind yourself how well prepared you are. Remind yourself that a test is just a game to see how many points you can earn. Refocusing should take no more than a minute or two, just enough time to reboot your mind. Now turn over your test and get some points!

20. Review your answers. Start with the sections that offer the most points. Then, check answers in other parts of the test in descending order of points available. For math problems, look for possible errors in each line of your solution.

21. Provide an answer for every question. When you have reviewed all of your answered questions, revisit unanswered questions. Run your finger along the words and read the question aloud (whisper). Highlight key words. Close your eyes and see if you can picture the answer in your study materials. Glance through the test to see if the answer may be included in another question. As a final resort, guess. You might just get some points if your guess is close.

22. Proofread. Don't even think of handing in your test yet. Read over all of your answers, looking for misspellings, grammar errors, goofs, blanks—anything that could lower your point total. Use white-out for making corrections neatly. Use every second to squeeze out a few more points!

After Taking Tests

23. Reward yourself. No matter how you think you did on the test, give yourself a treat for your efforts before and during the test—go out to dinner, call an old friend, take a bubble bath, rent a movie.

24. Study the instructor's feedback. When you get the test back, don't just look at the grade. Read the instructor's comments. For recognition questions (e.g., true/false, multiple-choice, or matching), all you may see are Xs to indicate errors. For recall questions (e.g., essay or math problems), your instructor may provide commentary to explain why you earned or lost points. Whatever feedback the instructor provides, its purpose is to get you on course. Gobble it up. If there's an error or comment you don't understand, make an appointment with your instructor to discuss your confusion.

25. Correct answers you missed. Creators learn from their mistakes and seldom make them twice. Ask the instructor or classmates for the correct answers. Rehearse correct answers to short-answer and essay tests by writing them out. Afterward, show your revised work to your instructor. Ask if the new answers express what the instructor was looking for. If not, what is missing? .Finally, ask what grade the new answer would get. Not only will this process help you provide better answers on your next test, you will also be demonstrating to your instructor how motivated you are to learn. Mastering correct answers is important in any course, but is absolutely essential in courses that build directly on previous knowledge, such as mathematics and foreign languages. Once you fall behind in those courses, you're lost.

26. Analyze your errors. By analyzing your errors, you can determine how to score more points on the next test. There are seven problems that typically cost students points on a test. For example, you might have lost points because you studied the wrong material or because you didn't have a test-smart plan. Use the Test Debrief (**Figure T.19**) to identify where you lost points, and make a plan for earning more points on your next test.

27. Get help. Before the next test, seek help from your instructor, tutors, or classmates. Go to the learning center on your campus. If you haven't already created a study group, start one. If they are offered, attend workshops on test preparation and test anxiety. By seeking help, you can learn the information you got wrong on the previous test and improve your preparation for the next one.

28. Seek accommodations. If you have a documented learning disability, you may request special arrangements that will help you demonstrate on a test what you have learned. For example, you may qualify for additional time to take a test. The place to make such a request is through your college's disability services.

TEST DEBRIEF

Directions: Consider the seven test-taking problems below, and estimate the number of points you lost on the test for each problem. Circle the problem(s) that cost you the most points, and implement the solution(s) as you prepare for the next test.

Problem 1: I didn't study some of the information or skills covered on the test.
Points lost: _____
Solution: Be more assertive about discovering what content will be covered on the test. Check the course syllabus; ask classmates, tutors, and especially the instructor. Add this material to your CORE Learning System.

Problem 2: I did study the information or skills covered on the test, but I got questions wrong anyway.
Points lost: _____
Solution: Experiment with **Organizing** new kinds of study materials. Try different ways of **Rehearsing** your study materials. Distribute your studying over longer periods of time and increase your time on task. Implement more **Evaluations** to assess your understanding (e.g., have study team members and/or tutors test your knowledge).

Problem 3: I wasn't good at answering the kind of questions the instructor asked.
Points lost: _____
Solution: Do all you can to determine what kind of questions will be on the test. Construct and take practice tests that use those kinds of questions. Have study team members also construct questions of this kind. Show the questions you create and your answers to a tutor or your instructor for feedback. Keep creating and answering these kinds of questions until you become skilled at answering them.

Problem 4: I didn't follow the directions.
Points lost: _____
Solution: Take time to read all of the directions carefully, circle guide words, and underline key terms. When you proofread, confirm that you have done what was asked.

Problem 5: I lost points for questions I could have answered but didn't get to.
Points lost: _____
Solution: Make a test-smart plan that focuses on accumulating the greatest number of points possible. Determine where the easy, point-rich questions are and make a plan to answer those questions first. Set time limits for each section so you don't get stuck and lose points by not answering questions in other parts of the test.

Problem 6: I knew the answers but made careless mistakes.
Points lost: _____
Solution: Move steadily through the test, but don't rush. Think carefully about what each question is asking and about the best way to answer it. Allow time at the end to check all answers and proofread carefully before handing in the test.

Problem 7: I panicked and was too stressed to answer questions, even those for which I knew the answer.
Points lost: _____
Solution: Overlearn the content and take numerous practice tests under "game" conditions to build test-taking skills and confidence. Visualize your success and create a positive affirmation about your test-taking ability. Make and follow a test-smart plan. If you get stuck during the test, don't waste time on a tough question; move on. If you feel anxious, refocus. Keep reminding yourself that taking tests is a game and that your job is simply to earn the most points possible. If test anxiety continues to plague you, consider seeing a counselor for further suggestions and help.

Points lost for the Seven Problems should total the number of points you lost on the test.

FIGURE T.19 Test Debrief

ONE STUDENT'S STORY

ASHLEY E. BENNET, *Heartland Community College, Illinois*

Not long ago, I took my first step onto the Heartland Community College campus as a legitimate college student. Having gone through the placement testing, piles of enrollment paper work, supply shopping, and various other preparations, I felt ready and eager to begin what I "thought" college would be. However, what I experienced was nowhere near what I expected. Beginning college is a challenging experience for anyone; however for me, adjusting from home schooling to a college campus of roughly 15,000 students was a blind free fall. You see, attending Heartland was the first time I had ever been in a formal classroom. Previously, all of my learning had been done at home. I took my tests on a computer program, and if I got an answer wrong, I used it as feedback. Then I'd study what I got wrong, learn it more thoroughly, and retake the test.

In my first semester in college, I took two courses: algebra and a success course. In math, I had one major difficulty: the terrors of testing. I took tests every Monday, and they were so different from what I was used to. Just thinking about the tests beforehand caused me emotional distress in my day-to-day life. When I studied, I struggled to retain information

due my anxiety. Actually, anxiety doesn't even begin to describe what I felt. I would breach the threshold of a full on panic attack before I even left for class. At the test, I would sit down, fiddle, get distracted, fiddle some more, and then slip into complete hysteria simply thinking about the time as it continued ticking away, with my test nowhere near finished. For the first couple of weeks, I went through the same panic before and during every test. I thought there was no escaping it…fortunately, I was wrong!

When I look back today and consider all that I went through back then, I am amazed and proud of the accomplishments that I have made since. Armed with the *On Course* textbook from my success course, I came across helpful strategies for taking tests. As I began to use the strategies, I gained a great deal of confidence and improved my ability to study and take exams.

First, I began to prepare for tests differently. One thing I did was organize thorough study materials. One was a variation of the 3-column approach for studying math. I would solve problems and alongside I'd put down key terms so I could remember the formulas. That helped take a pretty major weight of worry off my shoulders. I'm a big tea drinker,

and I'd relax while studying by treating myself to my favorite tea. I also created an affirmation to help me feel more confident: *I am prepared to do my best on this test.* I would review almost anywhere. For example, sometimes I'd stop when I was leaving the house and see if I could remember a formula or a way to solve a particular problem.

I also used new strategies during tests. I started arriving at the test about 20 minutes early. This gave me time to find a good seat, do some breathing exercises, say my affirmation, and clear my head. When the test began, I worked on the easier problems first and saved the more challenging ones until later. This got my confidence up and set me up for doing my best. The final test in my math class gave me an opportunity to see how helpful these strategies are. I made it through all the questions I knew without looking at the clock. Then I went back to do the harder ones. The strategies I used obviously worked for me because I got an A in math.

My anxiety level on the first math tests I took was about a seven or eight on a scale of ten. After I started using my new strategies, my test anxiety went down to a three. As my first semester is coming to a close, I can say with confidence that I am and will continue to be prepared to do my best on any and every test.

Photo: Courtesy of Ashley E. Bennet.

Taking Tests: Do One Different Thing This Week

In this section of your Toolbox for Active Learners, you've been introduced to 28 strategies for taking tests. Here's an opportunity to experiment with one of them. First, review the strategies. Identify those you marked because they could help with one of your challenges. Now pick the one strategy you think would best help you improve your ability to take tests.

In the "My Commitment for Taking Tests" box in the following chart, write the strategy with which you will experiment. Write just the number of the strategy and the one-sentence description of it that is in bold print. (For example, **"26. Analyze your errors."**) To build a habit, it's best to take the action every day. This will work fine if you choose an action that can be done *Before* or *After* a test. However, if the strategy you choose is done *While* you are taking a test, you are unlikely to have seven tests in seven days. If this is the case, practice your chosen strategy for seven *tests* (or quizzes) in a row. After your experiment (seven days or seven tests), assess your results. If your understanding of how to be an effective test taker improves, you'll have a learning tool that will maximize your grades in higher education.

My Commitment for Taking Tests:

_____

_____

_____

☐ Day 1   ☐ Day 2   ☐ Day 3   ☐ Day 4   ☐ Day 5   ☐ Day 6   ☐ Day 7

During my seven-day experiment, what happened?

As a result of what happened, what did I learn or relearn?

As a result of what I learned or relearned, I will . . .

Along with reading, few academic skills support your success in college more than effective writing. In most college courses, you'll be asked to do at least some—and perhaps much—writing. You'll write compositions, lab reports, term papers, journal entries, and research papers. Additionally, you'll take many tests and exams that contain essay questions. Obviously, then, writing well increases your ability to earn good grades in college. But this is only one of writing's many benefits.

After you graduate, writing well can help you acquire and advance in the career of your choice. In fact, you'll likely write more in your career than you ever expected. With the growth of the Internet and a global economy, more and more business is transacted through e-mail and websites. The popularity of social networking sites and the explosion of blogging create additional needs for good writing. In both your professional and personal life, writing gives you a means to inform, persuade, or even entertain people. And writing helps you maintain relationships, especially with people who are far away. While these benefits may be evident, here is one that may be less obvious: **Writing well enhances learning.**

- *We do not write in order to be understood; we write in order to understand.*
  –Robert Cecil Day-Lewis

- *Writing became such a process of discovery that I couldn't wait to get to work in the morning. . . .*
  –Sharon O'Brien

- *The best way to become acquainted with a subject is to write a book about it.*
  –Benjamin Disraeli

- *Writing is making sense of life.*
  –Nadine Gordimer

- *Learn as much by writing as by reading.*
  –Lord Acton

Among other reasons, writing enhances learning because the process raises questions that require answers. For instance, if you were writing a personal essay about self-awareness, you might anticipate your readers wondering: *How did you become aware of your self-sabotaging scripts?* Or, in writing a more academic paper about self-awareness, you might find yourself asking, *How does the activity of neurons contribute to self-awareness?* Your effort to **Collect**, **Organize**, and write answers to these (and other) questions expands your understanding of yourself, other people, and the world. And that is the essence of learning!

Here's another reason why writing enhances learning: Like learning, writing is a process. Most experts recognize four components in the writing process: prewriting, writing, revising, and editing. As you'll see, these four have much in common with the four components of the CORE Learning System. In fact, knowing the CORE Learning System gives you a real advantage when it comes to writing.

- **Prewriting** (also called *invention*) includes any preparation you do before actually writing. Guiding this process is an awareness of your audience and your purpose for writing. Prewriting activities include **Collecting** ideas and supporting details. Next comes **Organizing** these raw materials into a possible structure. Prewriting is a step that many novice writers unwisely skip.

- **Writing** (also called *drafting*) is the act of creation—turning your raw materials into a document that achieves your defined purpose. As you write, your mind both **Rehearses** the ideas you want to express and **Evaluates** your understanding of them. Thus, while writing you may realize that you need to **Collect** more information, re-**Organize** the information you already have, or both. When the first draft is complete, novice writers often pat themselves on the back and declare themselves done. Experienced writers know they have only just begun.

- **Revising** (also called *rewriting*) means "seeing again." When revising, you "re-see" in order to **Evaluate** your present draft. Does it say what you mean? Will it achieve your purpose for writing? If you have a poor understanding of your subject, your writing will likely be muddy and unclear. Revising, which is a kind of **Rehearsing**, helps identify what you don't understand and encourages you to think more critically about the subject. With this effort come both a deeper understanding and the ability to express that understanding more effectively in writing. That's why experienced writers often spend as much (or even more) time revising as they took planning and writing the first draft.

- **Editing** (also called *proofreading*) eliminates surface problems such as errors in grammar, sentence structure, and spelling. When writing is littered with errors, your readers may wonder if your thinking is as careless as your proofreading. Worse, they may not understand what you mean. Either way, surface errors undermine the achievement of your purpose. Editing is your final **Evaluation** of how well you think your writing will achieve its purpose.

Perhaps now you understand why so many instructors require writing. To write well requires you to be the most active of learners, developing deep and lasting learning. And that, after all, is the goal of all good teaching.

WRITING: THE BIG PICTURE

So, experiment with the many writing strategies that follow. As you do, keep in mind the big picture of writing: **The goal of writing is to inform, persuade, or entertain your intended audience. Thus, writing requires that you anticipate and answer the questions that engaged readers will have about your subject. Importantly, writing is not only an important means of communication with others. It is also one of the most powerful ways to create deep and lasting learning for ourselves.**

CHALLENGES WITH WRITING

Following are common challenges with writing in higher education. Circle the numbers next to the challenges that you are having (or can foresee having) in writing for your present courses. Even if you consider yourself good at writing, circle the numbers next to at least two areas in which you could improve. If you have a challenge not on the list, use one or both blank spaces at the bottom of the list to add your own challenge(s).

1. I have no idea how to write a good paper in college.

2. The thing that gives me the most difficulty is coming up with topics to write about.

3. I don't know how to write a good beginning.

4. I have too many ideas, and they get jumbled up when I write.

5. I've been told that my writing is "choppy." I wish I knew how to correct that.

6. My English instructors say I have good ideas, but my grammar errors detract from my writing.

7. Instructors tell me I don't write in my own voice; they say my writing sounds "stilted."

8. I can't write about subjects I'm not interested in, and very few of my courses interest me.

9. Instructors tell me that my writing is too vague and general.

10. One criticism I often get on my essays is "wordy."

11. I hate writing so I usually put off an assignment until the night before it's due.

12. When I try to write, my mind usually goes blank.

13. I've been told my problem is poor organization.

14. My essays are never as long as they are supposed to be. I run out of things to say.

15. I sit for hours trying to write, but it's really difficult for me to get started.

16. When I write, the slightest noises distract me.

17. I've been told that my biggest writing problem is lack of development.

18. A comment I often get on my essays is that my main point is unclear.

19. My instructor assigned a persuasive paper, but I don't know how to write one.

20. We're supposed to do research and document our sources, but I never learned how.

21. My instructor says I need better transitions, but I'm not sure how to do that.

22. I don't know how to write an effective conclusion.

23. _____

24. _____

"Write about dogs!"

George Booth/Conde Nast Photos/Illustrations

STRATEGIES TO IMPROVE WRITING

Following you'll find many of the very best strategies for writing. After reading each strategy, pause and decide if it would help you overcome any of the challenges you circled. If so, mark it in some way (e.g., underline, circle, highlight, star). Later on, you can decide which of these strategies to experiment with to improve your ability to write college compositions and essay tests.

Before Writing

1. Create a positive affirmation about writing. Create an affirming statement such as, *I use all four steps of the writing process to express my ideas clearly and effectively.* Use this affirmation to develop a "growth mindset" about writing. As explained in Chapter 7, a "growth mindset" includes a core belief that you can improve your academic outcomes by employing effective strategies and hard work. (The opposite belief is that there is nothing you can do to improve your academic results, which is a Victim mindset.)

2. If you get to choose the topic for your writing, select one that truly interests you. You'll enjoy researching and writing about something meaningful to you, and your grades will probably improve as well. Even if your instructor assigns the topic, look for an approach to the topic that appeals to you.

3. Begin immediately. As soon as you can, write something, anything about the topic—even a few brief notes. This effort engages your unconscious mind, which will continue mulling over the topic even while you're involved in other activities. Later when you're writing, these unconscious ideas may bubble into awareness and help you write with more depth. Also, start immediately to allow time to employ each of the four steps of the writing process. For example, your writing schedule should include time to set your writing aside for at least a day before making final revisions (Step 3) and edits (Step 4).

4. Carry index cards for <u>C</u>ollecting ideas.
Once you begin thinking about a subject, ideas will sometimes pop into your mind at the strangest times. You might be ordering French fries in the cafeteria when a great idea hits you. Don't think you'll remember the idea later. Pull out an index card and write yourself a note. Keep the cards rubber-banded together for **<u>O</u>rganizing** later.

5. Create focus questions. Make a list of questions to guide your **<u>C</u>ollection** of information. Choose questions that arouse your curiosity. If you want to know the answers yourself, you'll be more motivated to find answers that you can shape into a successful writing assignment. For example, suppose you're going to write about financial aid. You might be very interested to know:

- What are the secrets for getting the most scholarship money?
- What mistakes keep students from getting all of the financial aid available to them?
- Is there a legal way to avoid repaying student loans?

Write each question on a separate index card or type a list of questions into a computer file.

6. Discuss your topic with others. Engage as many people as possible in a conversation about your topic. Start by asking your focus questions and follow where they lead. If possible, interview experts. For example, think how much you could learn about financial aid by talking with the head of your college's financial aid office. Having a conversation about your topic will get your neurons firing and your creative juices flowing. **<u>C</u>ollect** the best ideas and supporting details by writing them on index cards.

7. Seek ideas and supporting details in your campus library. If your topic calls for research, go to your campus library. Employ interdependence and ask a librarian for help. Librarians can show you how to find information in books, periodicals, journals, CD-ROMs, and other reference material. Record the source of your information so you can include it in your list of references. Index cards are perfect for **<u>C</u>ollecting** both the information and the sources.

ACTIVITY 7A: WRITING FOCUS QUESTIONS

Write two focus questions about each of the following topics. Make them questions that arouse your curiosity to know the answers.

Sleep

1.

2.

Relationships

1.

2.

Happiness

1.

2.

8. Search the Internet for more ideas and supporting details. As you may know, two popular search engines are Google and Yahoo; Wikipedia is a free online encyclopedia with about three million entries. Keep in mind, however, that anyone can post information on the Internet—it may or may not be accurate and correct. You need to use critical thinking to select reliable information. Better yet, ask a librarian to suggest trusted online sources for your topic. Many colleges subscribe to Internet resources that can only be accessed with a password that a librarian can provide to you.

9. Group your notes. Once you've **Collected** a stack of note cards on your topic, it's almost time to write . . . but not quite yet. First, group your notes by sorting them into piles, with one pile for each main idea or focus question. Better yet, type your notes into a computer; then, cut and paste them into clusters of related ideas. In our example of writing about financial aid, three of these clusters would contain ideas related to your focus questions:

- What are the secrets for getting the most scholarship money?
- What mistakes keep students from getting all of the financial aid available to them?
- Is there a legal way to avoid repaying student loans?

It's likely that you'll have gathered additional information as well. Find logical categories for these extra ideas as well. For example, you might group ideas together related to:

- The differences between grants, scholarships, and loans
- Government sources of financial aid
- Private sources of financial aid
- Ways to qualify for low-interest loans
- The consequences of not paying back student loans

10. Identify your audience. Every piece of writing has one or more intended readers. After all, there's no point in writing to no one. In most college writing, you will be informing your instructors about what you have learned. Perhaps you see the challenge: You'll be telling instructors about subjects that they know more about than you do. Usually the best approach is to write to a general audience. Picture a *general audience* as a group of interested, well-educated readers who know little or nothing about your topic. In this way, you will be more likely to provide all of the ideas and supporting details needed to show your instructors that you have mastered their course content. Sometimes instructors will specify your audience (e.g., readers of your college newspaper). If so, use this information to make choices as you write such as:

- *What tone (formal or informal) to adopt?*
- *What information to include or exclude?*
- *How much evidence is needed to overcome resistance?*

11. Define your thesis. A thesis states the most important idea you want to convey to your audience. Everything else you write merely supports this idea by answering questions that an engaged reader might have about your thesis. A thesis is made up of two elements: (1) the **topic** you're writing about and (2) the **claim** you make about the topic. Thus, a thesis statement is usually one sentence and has the following structure:

[Topic] + [Claim].

The two most common kinds of writing in college are informative and persuasive. The thesis of **informative** writing tells your readers something they presumably don't already know. For example:

[Subprime mortgage loans] + [are those made to borrowers with questionable ability to pay back the money they borrow].

The thesis of **persuasive** writing asks your readers to think or do something that presumably they are not inclined to think or do:

Think: [*Franklin Pierce*] + [*was one of the finest American presidents*].

Do: [*The student government*] + [*is an organization you should join*].

ACTIVITY 7B: WRITING THESIS STATEMENTS

Write four thesis statements in the following spaces about the topic of self-management, two each for informing and persuading. Note that the informing and persuading topics have different audiences.

Inform a general audience something about self-management:

1.

2.

Persuade a group of high-school seniors to think or do something related to self-management:

1.

2.

Sometimes you'll know immediately what your thesis is. Other times you may need to think and write for a while before a thesis emerges. Even after you've settled on your thesis, it may very well change as the process of writing causes you to learn more about your topic. Eventually, though, you'll need to settle on a clearly stated thesis, because an essay without a thesis is like a body without a spine—nothing holds it together.

12. <u>O</u>rganize your ideas and supporting details. Earlier in this Toolbox, we looked at linear and graphic ways to **<u>O</u>rganize** information. These methods also work well for **<u>O</u>rganizing** information during prewriting. Let's revisit two of these strategies and introduce a third.

Outline. (For a review of how to create an outline, along with an example, see the "While Taking Notes" section of this Toolbox.) When creating an outline for a writing assignment, place your thesis statement at the top of a page (realizing that it may change as you write). Below it and flush to the left margin, add each topic group you determined in Strategy 9. These are now your main ideas (Level 1). Next, indent a few spaces and add secondary ideas (Level 2) beneath each main idea. Finally, indent a few more spaces and add supporting ideas (Levels 3 and 4). Most word processing

programs have a feature to help you create an outline. In Microsoft Word, for example, you'll find it in the View menu.

Concept Map. (For a review of how to create a concept map, along with an example, see the "While Taking Notes" section of this Toolbox.) To create a concept map for a writing assignment, write your thesis statement at the top of a page. Then write the key concept in the middle of the page and either underline or circle it. Now draw lines out from the key concept and write the topic of each of the topic groups you determined in Strategy 9; these will be your main ideas (Level 1). Next, draw lines out from your main ideas, and write secondary ideas (Level 2). Farther out from the center of the concept map, write your supporting details (Levels 3 and 4). If you like organizing with concept maps, you may want to experiment with computer software designed for creating them. To find such software, search for "concept map software" using an Internet search engine.

Question Outline. Here's a variation of an outline that's easy, quick, and effective. After determining your thesis, choose the most interesting questions from the list you created in Strategy 5. Make sure you have enough information to answer each question thoroughly

... or **Collect** more. Use one question as the topic of each body paragraph. Thus, if you choose four questions, you'll probably be writing a six-paragraph essay (after adding your introduction and conclusion). It is possible, of course, that you could write two or more paragraphs to answer a question, making your essay longer than six paragraphs. Here's what a Question Outline about scripts might look like:

– Introduction (including the thesis)
– What are scripts?
– How do we write our scripts?
– Why do some scripts sabotage our success?
– How can we revise self-sabotaging scripts?
– Conclusion

While Writing

13. Use an essay blueprint. When you want to assemble something with many parts, a picture can help. For beginning writers, a blueprint showing a good way to assemble the parts of an essay is also a big help. Just as there are many blueprints for building a house, so are there many blueprints for writing an essay. But the one in **Figure T.20** is both effective and easy to understand. When one of my students saw this essay blueprint, she exclaimed, "So *that's* what the structure of an essay looks like? I can do *that*!"

Each part in the blueprint is explained in the strategies that follow. As you add these parts to the essay blueprint, realize that the structure is flexible and can be modified. For example, the essay blueprint shows a six-paragraph essay; if you have a different number of main ideas, simply add or delete body paragraphs. Also, Paragraph 5 in the essay blueprint presents a feature (refutation) that is useful in a persuasive essay but usually unnecessary in an informative essay. As you become a more skilled writer, you will begin to take more and more liberties with this blueprint. Ultimately you'll be creating your own original ways to organize your main ideas and supporting details.

14. Write a hook. The beginning of your essay should hook your readers' interest. To do so, start with an engaging strategy such as a question, quotation, humor, surprising data, shocking statement, or fascinating story. Even though a *hook* is the first thing your audience reads, you don't have to write it first. In fact, you may think of a good hook only after writing the entire first draft of

ACTIVITY 7C: CREATING A QUESTION OUTLINE

Imagine that you have been assigned to write an essay about self-management and your audience is high school seniors. Write a thesis statement for that essay (you may use one of the thesis statements you defined in Activity 7B). Below the thesis, write a question outline containing at least four questions. Don't forget to include an introduction and conclusion.

Thesis Statement:

Question Outline:

Paragraph 1: Introduction

   Hook
   Thesis
   Agenda

Paragraph 2: Body Paragraph #1

   Transition (presenting Main Idea #1)
   Secondary Ideas and Supporting Details (4E's)

Paragraph 3: Body Paragraph #2

   Transition (presenting Main Idea #2)
   Secondary Ideas and Supporting Details (4E's)

Paragraph 4: Body Paragraph #3

   Transition (presenting Main Idea #3)
   Secondary Ideas and Supporting Details (4E's)

Paragraph 5: Refutation (included in a persuasive essay)

   Transition (presenting opponents' argument)
   Refutation (presenting reasons and evidence to weaken opponent's argument)

Paragraph 6: Conclusion

   Summary or Echo
   Restatement of Thesis

© Cengage Learning

FIGURE T.20   Essay Blueprint

your essay. If you read the beginning of any section in this book, you will see my efforts to "hook" your interest. For example, I began the section on "Rewriting Your Outdated Scripts" in Chapter 6 with the story of my student Diana screaming at me in class. My hope was that Diana's dramatic and unexpected anger would hook your attention and motivate you to read on to find out more.

15. Add your thesis statement. After hooking your reader's attention, present your thesis—the key concept about which you are writing. Your thesis statement may be exactly as you wrote it in Strategy 11, or you may now decide that it needs revision. In fact, it's possible (even probable) that you will revise your thesis statement a number of times. That's because the writing process helps you learn even more deeply about your topic.

16. Write an agenda. An agenda for a meeting lists the main ideas that will be discussed. Similarly, an agenda for an essay states the main ideas that readers can expect the author to discuss. Agendas appear more commonly in long essays, articles, or even books. However, even in a short essay, they can be a great help to keep both your readers and you (the author) focused. For example, suppose your thesis is *Students should get involved in campus activities.* Your agenda might give a list of the reasons: *First, getting involved in campus activities will increase your chances of earning a degree. Second, you'll meet people who may become lifelong friends. And finally, involvement in campus activities offers valuable learning experiences that are unavailable in an academic classroom.* This three-part agenda lets your readers know exactly the points you intend to present. Even if you choose not to include an agenda in your essay, having one in your mind helps keep your essay organized.

17. Use transitions. A transition is a bridge between ideas. Well-chosen words, phrases, or sentences help your readers follow the flow of your ideas. One important place to use a transition is at the beginning of a paragraph. You want to make sure you don't lose your readers as you shift to a new thought. A good transition connects the idea just discussed with a new idea . . . and maybe even includes a reminder of the thesis. For example, suppose your thesis intends to persuade your readers to get involved with campus activities. Further, suppose that you have just completed a paragraph about how involvement in campus activities increases a student's chances of earning a degree. The first sentence of your next paragraph might be: *Not only will getting involved with campus activities increase your chances of earning a degree, you'll also meet people who may very well become lifelong friends.* Notice how the transition does three things:

- It reminds readers of the thesis: *Get involved with campus activities.*

- It reminds readers about the main idea made in the previous paragraph: *Getting involved in campus activities increases your chances of earning a degree.*

- It creates a bridge to the main point of the new paragraph: *By getting involved in campus activities, you'll meet people who may very well become lifelong friends.*

The beginning of paragraphs is only one place in your essay where transitions are helpful. When you offer concrete support for main ideas, you can signal with transitional words such as *for example, as an illustration,* or *for instance.* When you point out similarities, signal with *likewise* or *similarly.* When you point out differences, signal with *by contrast, but, however,* or *on the contrary.* When you summarize or conclude, signal with *in other words, in summary, in conclusion,* or *finally.* Treat your readers like tourists in a strange land. As their guide, you don't want to lose or confuse them.

18. Add support. To generate specific and sufficient support, expand each body paragraph with

---

ACTIVITY 7D: WRITING AN AGENDA

Imagine that you're writing an article for your college newspaper on the topic of "Improving Self-Management." Following is the hook and thesis statement (underlined) that you've written. Complete this introductory paragraph by adding an agenda.

Do you feel as though you're falling further and further behind in your assignments? Do you wish you could use your time more efficiently and effectively? Do you wish you could get all of your course work done and still have time to play? Well, you can. <u>The key is learning how to use effective self-management tools.</u>

secondary ideas and supporting details. This is easy to do when you remember to use the 4E's. The 4E's represent four questions that almost always need answering as you develop a paragraph:

- Can you give an EXAMPLE of that?
- Can you give an EXPERIENCE to illustrate that?
- Can you EXPLAIN that further?
- Can you give EVIDENCE to support that?

Answering one or more of the 4E's causes you to dive deeper and makes your writing more complete and fully developed.

19. Offer a refutation in a persuasive essay.
When you write to persuade, assume your readers resist what you want them to think or do. (After all, if they already agree with you, there's no need to persuade them.) Put yourself in their place and see if you can empathize with their reasons for resisting. Then dispute those reasons. For example, why might fellow students resist your efforts to persuade them to get involved in campus activities? Maybe they think they are too busy with their classes, assignments, and possibly a job. How could you refute their belief that they are too busy? As another example, in the section "A Few Words of Encouragement" in Chapter 1, I used refutation in my efforts to persuade you to give the strategies in *On Course* a fair chance. Take a look and see if . . .

A. I empathized with a reason that you may have resisted this course (if you did) and

B. I offered a refutation that reduced or even eliminated your resistance.

20. Write a satisfying conclusion. One common way to conclude is to summarize the main points you have made. For example, *So, if you want to become an effective learner, become a master of the C.O.R.E Learning System.*

A more sophisticated conclusion is called an **echo**. An echo restates all or part of an idea presented earlier in your essay. For example, suppose your hook asked, *Do you realize that college*

graduates earn nearly a million dollars more in their lives than non-grads? You might echo this thought in your conclusion by ending with: *So, if you want to raise your lifetime earnings by nearly a million dollars, make getting your college degree a high priority.*

After Writing

21. Incubate. Set your writing aside and do something else . . . in fact, anything else. That's right—don't even think about what you wrote for at least a couple of hours. Better yet, for a couple of days. When you return to your writing later, you'll see your writing with new eyes. You'll notice problems and possibilities that previously were invisible to you. Obviously you can use this strategy only if you make the wise choice to start your writing long before it's due.

22. Revise. As mentioned earlier, "re-vision" means to "see again." After incubation, you'll be ready to see your writing with new eyes. Look for major changes to improve the quality of your communication. Consider a revised thesis statement, better organization, additional support (4E's: examples, experience, explanation, evidence), improved transitions, a catchier hook, a stronger conclusion. Perhaps most important, make sure that you have answered all important reader questions. Remember, good writing anticipates and answers questions that interested readers might ask. Even if you created questions before writing and answered them as you wrote, be alert for new questions that emerge as you revise. Two questions that almost always need answering are "*Why?*" and "*How do you know?*" Other important questions begin with *What? When? Who? Where? How?* and *What if?*

23. Cite sources. If you include an idea that you **Collected** during your research, credit the source. You can give credit as you paraphrase the idea in your own words. For example, *According to author Dorothy Canfield Fisher, beginning writers seldom revise. But she believes that writers, to* *excel, must master the art of revision.* Or you can simply quote the original and give appropriate credit. For example, *Mary Heaton Vorse, author of 18 books, offers this practical advice for writers, "The art of writing is the art of applying the seat of the pants to the seat of the chair."* Not to credit the source of an idea or words is **plagiarism**, which is intellectual theft.

In a research paper, add a bibliography of any works cited. This information tells your readers how to find the original sources for your information. There are two major formats for bibliographies and citations.

- MLA (Modern Language Association) format is widely used in the humanities, especially for writing about language and literature.

- APA (American Psychological Association) format is commonly required for writing in the social and behavioral sciences.

For research papers, instructors will usually indicate which style to use. Writing centers often have handouts explaining the formats, along with helpful examples. For a sample bibliography, refer to the one at the end of *On Course.*

24. Read aloud. By reading aloud, you'll hear sentences that don't flow smoothly and need revision. After all, if you stumble over your own words, you can be sure your reader will, too. It's not unusual for good writers to revise some sentences many times. It's amazing how many ways you can say almost the same thing. But what you are looking for is the *best* way.

25. Edit carefully. Writing filled with errors is distracting to readers. At best, errors will cause them to think less of what you have to say (especially college instructors). At worst, your readers may misunderstand. The challenge with proofreading your own writing is that you know what is *supposed* to be there . . . and that is what you will often see instead of what is *actually* there. Here's a proofreading trick that can help: Start proofreading with the last sentence. Then proofread the second-to-last sentence. And continue proofreading

backward from the end of your writing to the beginning. In this way, you can focus on the surface details of grammar, spelling, and punctuation without being distracted by the flow of ideas. If writing on a computer, remember that a computer's spell check will not pick up words used incorrectly but spelled correctly (such as using *there* for *their*). Your computer may also help you identify possible grammar errors that need to be corrected. But be careful, because sometimes it will point out "errors" that aren't errors at all.

26. Seek help. Ask your instructor if it's okay to get help before turning in your writing for a grade. If so, take advantage of various options. Some instructors provide class time for peer review. If not, you can create your own peer review by exchanging essays with one or more classmates. A simple but powerful peer-review strategy is simply asking each other questions: *Which sentence is your thesis statement? Why do you believe this? Can you give an example of that? Is there a more effective conclusion than this?*

Another option is seeking help at your campus tutoring center. Understand that a tutor's job is not to write or even rewrite your paper. A good tutor will help you organize your thoughts, identify areas for revision, and provide study materials for your grammar or punctuation problems. Finally, a great option is to take a rough draft to an appointment with your instructor and ask for feedback before you write your final draft.

27. Keep an error log. Some instructors, especially for a writing class, will point out your grammar and punctuation errors. When you get a writing assignment back with errors noted, enter them in an error log. An error log is a record of every sentence in which you had a grammar or punctuation problem. Below the error sentence, rewrite the sentence correctly. Then, write the relevant grammar or punctuation rule(s) so you can learn to correct all errors of the same kind. You'll find this information in the grammar section of a writing handbook, or you can ask a writing tutor to help you identify the rule. Everyone makes errors, but Creators seldom make the same mistake twice. Here's an example:

Error Sentence: I went to the tutoring center, the tutor I was supposed to see wasn't there.

Corrected Sentence: I went to the tutoring center, but the tutor I was supposed to see wasn't there.

Rule: When two complete sentences are joined with only a comma, this error is called a comma splice. There are three ways to correct a comma splice: (1) Replace the comma with a period, capitalize the next word, and create two complete sentences. (2) Replace the comma with a semicolon. (3) Add a coordinating conjunction (i.e., *and, but, or, nor, for, so,* or *yet*) after the comma.

Keeping an error log is time-consuming at first, but seeing your errors disappear from future papers is a great reward.

28. Rewrite graded papers. Most instructors provide feedback on major problems with your writing (e.g., unclear purpose, poor organization, lack of support). Use this feedback to rewrite and improve your assignment. Such a revision is the ultimate **Rehearsal** of your writing skills and can help you immensely. Impressed with your initiative, most instructors will be glad to meet with you to discuss your revision. Some will even raise your grade if your revision shows improvement. Regardless of how your instructor responds to your rewrites, realize that there is as much, if not more, learning available to you in revising as there was in writing the original.

Writing: Do One Different Thing This Week

In this section of your Toolbox for Active Learners, you've been introduced to 28 strategies for becoming an effective writer. Here's an opportunity to experiment with one of them. First, review the strategies. Identify those you marked because they could help with one of your writing challenges. Now pick the one strategy you think would best help you improve your writing skills.

In the "My Commitment for Writing" box in the following chart, write the strategy with which you will experiment. Write just the number of the strategy and the one-sentence description of it that is in bold print. (For example, "**27. Keep an error log.**") Then track yourself for one week, putting a check in the appropriate box each day that you practice this strategy. Your goal is to do it every day. After seven days, evaluate your results. If your writing skills improve, you'll have a learning tool you can use for the rest of your life.

My Commitment for Writing:

_____

_____

_____

☐ Day 1   ☐ Day 2   ☐ Day 3   ☐ Day 4   ☐ Day 5   ☐ Day 6   ☐ Day 7

During my seven-day experiment, what happened?

As a result of what happened, what did I learn or relearn?

As a result of what I learned or relearned, I wil . . .

TECH TIPS: Active Learning

Evernote is an electronic notebook that makes it easy to collect and organize notes. Type notes using your keyboard, record audio notes, and even take pictures. You can create to-do lists, record voice reminders, and organize your daily schedule. You can even add websites to your notes. *(Web, Android, and iOS)*

Google Docs (another helpful Google offering) allows you to create and share documents online. Google Docs is especially helpful when you need to collaborate on a group project, research paper, or study materials. Instead of emailing documents back and forth, everyone can work on the same document from separate locations. *(Web)*

My Study Life helps you manage your classes, tasks, and assignments. If you didn't already find a productivity website or app that you like, this might be the one. You can track tasks, add exam dates, manage classes, and receive reminders of upcoming events. The dashboard shows an overview of your entire day plus tasks completed and unfinished. *(Web, Android, and iOS)*

Koofers.com offers more than two million practice tests and flashcards to help you prepare for exams. An additional feature in Koofers offers student-created ratings of more than 600,000 instructors, which could help you make wise choices in selecting future courses. *(Web)*

Quizlet provides an opportunity to study with digital flashcards, either those you make or the many already on the site. You can choose to click a flashcard to reveal the answer. Or you can choose among three engaging study tools (Speller, Learn, and Test) or two interactive games (Scatter and Space Race). You can track your study progress and even compete with others. Heads up, though, when using flashcards created by others; the answers could be wrong! *(Web, Android, and iOS)*

StudyBlue, like Quizlet, lets you make digital flashcards or use ones already created by others. Flashcards can contain pictures as well as text. As you study the flashcards, the program tracks what you have learned and suggests areas in which you need more studying. You can set reminders for upcoming tests so you provide enough time for distributed study. You can also create a StudyBlue community of fellow students by adding them to your contacts. *(Web, Android, and iOS)*

Audacity is a downloadable audio recorder and editor. If you have permission to record a lecture or class discussion, Audacity could be the means. Remember, though, that every hour of recordings will necessitate another hour of listening to get the full value. A good use is listening to recordings while commuting or working at a mindless task. *(Windows and Mac)*

PowerPoint, Prezi, and HaikuDeck offer different approaches to creating visually appealing presentations. Use in a speech class or any course that requires you to give a speech or verbal report. (*Web*) (PowerPoint is part of the Microsoft Office Suite, which is not available for free.)

Note: All of the above (except as noted) are free, but some may offer upgraded features for a fee.

Assess Your Study Skills
For College Success—Again

You're now familiar with the CORE Learning System as well as many strategies for implementing it. Following is a duplicate of the learning skills self-assessment you took at the beginning of this Study Skills Toolbox. Now take it again. (Don't look back at your previous answers yet.) By comparing your two scores, you'll be able to see your present understanding of how to learn your way to success in college and beyond.

As you take this self-assessment, be absolutely honest so you can learn the truth about where your learning skills are at this time. This valuable information can pave the way to making significant improvements in your future learning efforts.

Study Skills Self-Assessment

Read the following statements and score each one according to how true or false you believe it is about you. To get an accurate picture of yourself, consider what IS true about you (not what you *want* to be true). Remember, there are no right or wrong answers. Assign each statement a number from 0 to 10, as follows:

Totally False ◀ (0) (1) (2) (3) (4) (5) (6) (7) (8) (9) (10) ▶ **Totally True**

1. _____ I understand how the human brain learns, and I use that knowledge to study effectively.
2. _____ When I read an assignment in my textbooks, I have trouble identifying the most important information.
3. _____ I know effective strategies for memorizing important things such as facts, details, and formulas.
4. _____ I don't know how to create graphic or linear organizers.
5. _____ I'm good at figuring out what's important during a class discussion or lecture.
6. _____ After I get a test back, I check my grade to see how I did and then throw it away.
7. _____ When writing a paper, I know how to add supporting details that make my main ideas clear.
8. _____ After I finish taking a test, I have no idea what kind of grade I will get.
9. _____ While reading an assignment, I have an effective system for marking or writing down important ideas.
10. _____ When I review my notes after class, they are complete and easy to understand.
11. _____ Before studying for a test, I condense all of my class notes, homework, reading assignments, and course handouts into one document, and then I study from this new document.
12. _____ I do most (and sometimes all) of my studying on the day before or the day of a test.

13. _____ When I take a test, I feel calm and confident.

14. _____ When I write the answer to an essay question, I find it difficult to organize my ideas.

15. _____ When I study for a test, I use a number of different learning strategies.

16. _____ After reading, I don't recall much of what I just read.

17. _____ My class and homework notes include most of the information that later appears on a test.

18. _____ I know at least three different ways to organize my study materials so the information makes the most sense to me.

19. _____ I study for math tests by looking over the problems I solved for homework and/or the ones the instructor solved in class.

20. _____ When I take a test, I have a plan to get the most possible points.

21. _____ I usually write one draft of a paper and that's what I turn in.

22. _____ A few days after I take a test, I don't remember much of what I studied.

23. _____ After reading a homework assignment, I take time to think, write, or talk with others about the main points of what I just read.

24. _____ I've never learned how to take good notes during a class.

25. _____ I study in a quiet place where I'm not disturbed.

26. _____ I feel unprepared when I take a test because I don't really know how to study effectively.

27. _____ I don't understand how to write a good paper in college.

28. _____ I know how to do well on a test no matter what kind of questions the instructor asks: multiple-choice, true/false, fill-in-the-blank, matching, problems, or essays.

29. _____ How learning happens is a mystery to me.

30. _____ I'm good at identifying what is important information in a reading assignment.

31. _____ While studying, I make a list of questions that I think will be on a test.

32. _____ During a lecture or class discussion, I have trouble staying focused.

33. _____ I'm bad at memorizing important formulas, details, and facts.

34. _____ After I get a test back, I analyze and correct all of the errors I made.

35. _____ My papers are pretty short because I have difficulty adding supporting details that make my main ideas clear.

36. _____ I know how to tell how well I have learned a subject even before I take a test.

37. _____ When I read, I don't write in my book or take separate notes.

38. _____ My class notes are difficult to understand when I look at them a few days later.

39. _____ I study for tests by re-reading my textbooks, class notes, and course handouts.

40. _____ I study each subject frequently, and I spread my study sessions over the whole course.

41. _____ I lose points on tests because of things like spending too much time on one question or taking too much time answering a question that was worth only a few points.

42. _____ The papers I write are well organized.

43. _____ I don't participate in class discussions or activities.

44. _____ When I finish a reading assignment, I remember most of what I read.

45. _____ When I take a test, there are questions about things that weren't in my notes.

46. _____ When I study, there are often distractions and I can't concentrate.

47. _____ When I study for a math test, I solve many problems of the same kinds that will be on the test.

48. _____ Certain kinds of test questions are difficult for me and I don't do well on them.

49. _____   I understand and use all four steps of the writing process: Prewriting, Writing, Revising, and Editing.

50. _____   I ask questions in class whenever I'm confused.

51. _____   After reading a textbook, I don't think much about what I read until right before the test.

52. _____   I take good notes during a lecture or class discussion.

53. _____   When I take a test, I find questions I didn't study for.

54. _____   I use an effective learning system when I study, so I feel well prepared when I take a test.

55. _____   I know how to write a good paper in college.

56. _____   I feel nervous and my mind goes blank when I take a test.

Transfer your scores to the scoring sheets on the next page. For each of the seven areas, total your scores in columns A and B. Then total your final scores as shown in the sample.

Self-Assessment Scoring Sheet

SAMPLE

A	B
6. _8_	29. _3_
14. _5_	35. _3_
21. _6_	50. _6_
73. _9_	56. _2_

_28_ + 40 − _14_ = 54

SCORE #1: Learning Actively

A	B
1. ___	8. ___
15. ___	22. ___
36. ___	29. ___
50. ___	43. ___

___ + 40 − ___ = ___

SCORE #2: Reading

A	B
9. ___	2. ___
23. ___	16. ___
30. ___	37. ___
44. ___	51. ___

___ + 40 − ___ = 40 ___

SCORE #3: Taking Notes

A	B
5. ___	24. ___
10. ___	32. ___
17. ___	38. ___
52. ___	45. ___

___ + 40 − ___ = ___

SCORE #4: Organizing Study Materials

A	B
11. ___	4. ___
18. ___	39. ___
25. ___	46. ___
31. ___	53. ___

___ + 40 − ___ = ___

SCORE #5: Rehearsing and Memorizing Study Materials

A	B
3. ___	12. ___
40. ___	19. ___
47. ___	26. ___
54. ___	33. ___

___ + 40 − ___ = ___

SCORE #6: Taking Tests

A	B
13. ___	6. ___
20. ___	41. ___
28. ___	48. ___
34. ___	56. ___

___ + 40 − ___ = ___

SCORE #7: Writing

A	B
7. ___	14. ___
42. ___	21. ___
49. ___	27. ___
55. ___	35. ___

___ + 40 − ___ = ___

Interpreting Your Scores

A score of . . .

0–39 Indicates an area where your study skills will **seldom** support deep learning.

40–63 Indicates an area where your study skills will **sometimes** support deep learning.

64–80 Indicates an area where your study skills will **usually** support deep learning.

EXERCISE: ACTIVE LEARNING

In the chart below, transfer your scores from the scoring chart in the "Becoming an Active Learner" section of this Toolbox (first score) and the scoring chart from above (second score):

First Score	Second Score	
_____	_____	1. Becoming an Active Learner
_____	_____	2. Reading
_____	_____	3. Taking Notes
_____	_____	4. Organizing Study Materials
_____	_____	5. Rehearsing and Memorizing Study Materials
_____	_____	6. Taking Tests
_____	_____	7. Writing

In which study skill(s) have you improved the most? Please explain.

In which study skill(s) do you want to improve even more? Please explain.

What is your plan for making that improvement? Please explain.

Conversation with the Author

Since the first edition of *On Course* more than two decades ago, a number of students have contacted the author with thoughtful questions. Following are some of those questions and Skip Downing's answers:

Q. What inspired you to write this book?

A. The short answer is I was tired of seeing my students—most of whom had everything necessary to be a success in college (and in life)—sabotage their success. I decided to stop complaining and see what I could do about it. The longer answer, which addresses how I was also in need of help in getting my own life on course, is explained in the "Travel with Me" section early in the *On Course* book.

Q. Of all the strategies in *On Course*, which one helped you the most when you were in college?

A. I'll say self-management, particularly persistence. In my first semester in college, I quickly learned that most of my classmates had better academic preparation than I did. My roommate, for example, had read many books I had never even heard of. Additionally, in my first semester I received discouraging feedback from some of my instructors. I recall one instructor whose only comment on my first assignment was, "This is not a very good way to start your college career." However, experiences like that made me grit my teeth and work even harder. I guess I believed that with hard work I could overcome my obstacles, and that turned out to be a self-fulfilling prophesy.

Q. What inner quality do you wish you had had more of when you were in college?

A. All of them. But if I had to choose one, I would say a passion for lifelong learning. In college I only studied what was assigned and all I cared about was the grade. My regret today is that I didn't squeeze more value from my college experience. I now "study" harder than I ever did in college because I love learning new ideas, particularly in the realm of "what makes us tick." In college, I went to the library to study but hardly noticed the miles of shelved books. Today I go to a library and feel a sense of awe that human beings have learned so much and that through books (and now the Internet), that wealth of knowledge is available any time I want it.

Q. Did you struggle in college and, if so, is that how you created such great tips?

A. I guess my answer depends on what you mean by "struggle." If you mean did I have a difficult time getting passing grades, the answer is no. Even though I had a rough first semester, soon after I figured out how the game of school is played. While I was never a threat to be valedictorian, I got decent grades. However, if by "struggle" you mean having difficulty learning at a deep level and using what I was learning to improve my life, the answer is yes, I struggled. If I could do college over, I would focus on learning instead of grades. Fortunately, I had an opportunity to do just that when I returned to graduate school for the second time when I was in my 40s.

That's when I learned to love learning. What a great experience! It was like the universe gave me a do-over. If I had only one wish for my students, it would be that they would fall in love with learning.

Q. Using the first person in a textbook is unusual. What is your reason for using this approach throughout the entire book?

A. I thought long and hard before deciding to use the first person in *On Course*. When I was writing the first draft, I don't believe there were any student success texts that employed the first person. As with all of the textbooks I had read in college, the authors were hidden behind a curtain (like the Wizard of Oz). So, it was going to be a risk. However, I ultimately decided that putting myself in the book was the best way to convey that when it comes to making the most of our lives, all of us—students, instructors…all of us—face similar challenges. I am not a third-person observer of how to create a rich, full life…I am fully engaged as a participant in that quest. I want what you want. We're all in this university of life together; we're all creating our outcomes and experiences by the choices we make every day. Like life, creating success in college isn't easy, but there are ways to make it easier.

Q. In your book, the success skills make sense and seem so easy, but sometimes I can't do it. I wonder what it takes for a person to actually apply these skills.

A. I understand your frustration. I've felt that way at times myself. However, as is so often the case, the answer is found right there in our excuses. Here's your excuse: "Sometimes I *can't* do it." Is that really true? Of course you *can* do it because if sometimes you *can't* do it, then logically sometimes you *can* do it. So, "Sometimes I can't do it" is the kind of subtle excuse

we tell ourselves when we're in a Victim mindset. We justify our behaviors and outcomes by telling ourselves an untruth. More bluntly, we lie to ourselves. There is no strategy in *On Course* that you can't do. That's why when you are in a Creator mindset you tell yourself the truth, which is: "Sometimes I *choose* not to do it." And in that moment of clarity and awareness, you have the option to draw on inner strengths, to choose thoughts and actions that will keep you on course to your desired outcomes and experiences. If you choose anything else (say, missing class or not seeking help on difficult math problems or reading your textbooks mindlessly), you would likely benefit from developing the inner qualities and strategies in *On Course* to help you make wiser choices. What inner quality is needed to go to class even when you don't feel like it? What inner strength is needed to ask for help even though asking for help embarrasses you? What strategy is needed to read actively, even when the subject doesn't interest you? I'm not saying it's easy. Goodness knows, I struggle too…and I'm tempted to justify my lack of success in some endeavor by saying "I can't." But in most cases, my Inner Guide knows, "I'm choosing not to…." And if I'm choosing *not to do* something that advances my life, I can also choose *to do* something that does. And that is more often than not the truth.

Q. What is the purpose of including journal entries in each of the chapters?

A. Reflection deepens learning, and the journals in *On Course* apply this powerful learning strategy. They guide you to take what you have just read about—a success principle or practice—and apply it to your own life. When you dive deep in your journal entries, you begin making the strategies your own. When you use the strategies in your life, you improve your outcomes and experiences. By improving your outcomes and experiences, you begin an upward spiral of success and personal development. Reading the success strategies in *On Course* and not writing the journals would be like only reading about exercising and then wondering why you aren't getting in shape.

Q. How did you come up with all of these strategies?

A. My first exposure to success strategies was in a three-day personal effectiveness seminar that I took because I was struggling in both my personal and professional life. Some of the strategies I learned in the seminar helped me, so I shared them with my students. When I saw the strategies helping my students, too, I went on a quest to learn more of them. I already had my doctoral degree in English, but my new quest motivated me to complete a master's degree in counseling. I was blessed to have awesome instructors in that program, and I learned many more strategies. If it worked for me, I offered it to my students and observed their responses. I kept teaching the strategies that helped them improve their outcomes and experiences in college. Today, *On Course* contains the very best strategies I've come across in a search that spans more than two decades. What makes them "best" is that each strategy works for many students, helping them to achieve more of their potential in college…and in life.

Q. Why do you put quotations in the margins?

A. Here are four reasons: 1) I love to learn what people who have given a great deal of thought to an important issue have to say about it, and I hope my readers do, too. 2) Because the quotations express ideas in a different way than I do, they may

help clarify a point in the book. 3) I have included quotations from diverse thinkers and cultures to convey the universality of these ideas. 4) As with quotations embedded in an article ("The noted expert Farley Studebaker says, "…."), I hope the quotations demonstrate that the ideas and strategies in the book are not just a whim of mine. Rather the ideas and strategies are the product of thinkers and researchers who have come up with powerful answers to the key question addressed in *On Course*: "How can each of us live up to our potential and create a rich, personally fulfilling life?"

Q. Are the case studies in *On Course* true stories?

A. The case studies are not "true" in the sense that the events happened to real people exactly as they are described. But in another sense they are truer than a narrative of actual events. When case studies in *On Course* work as they intended, they show you students dealing with the kinds of complex challenges that anyone might encounter on the path to a college degree. There are no simple answers to the questions posed by the case studies; there are no right answers in the back of the book. Instead each of us must apply our present beliefs—derived from our own unique experiences—to make sense of each case study. Then, during a discussion with classmates and instructors, we get the opportunity to test our answers against those of others. Thus, by applying critical thinking to the situations faced by characters in the case studies, we have the opportunity to develop new insights that can help us successfully confront similar problems in our own lives.

Q. I did an Internet search for "Goal Setting" and came across dozens of sites that use the acronym S.M.A.R.T. to represent the qualities of an effective goal. Why did you come up with your own acronym (D.A.P.P.S.) instead of using S.M.A.R.T.?

A. I very much wanted to use S.M.A.R.T. because who doesn't want to have a SMART goal? However, the more I looked at the acronym, the more problems I found. First, the acronym has been around a long time and users have begun taking liberties with what the five letters stand for. "S" sometimes stands for "specific" and at other times "simple." "M" is used for both "measureable" and "manageable." "A" is used for both "attainable" and "action-oriented." In various versions, "R" stands for "relevant," "relative," and "realistic." And "T" shows up as "time-bound," "timely," or "tangible." So the first problem is: What do the letters in S.M.A.R.T. stand for? A second problem is that the most common words for the letters "S" and "M" are "specific" and "measureable." In my mind, these are essentially the same quality. If something is *specific* (achieve a 3.5 GPA, for example), it is also *measureable*; that means that these two letters actually represent only one quality. And finally, SMART leaves out two qualities that I believe are essential components of an effective goal: Personal and Positive. If a goal isn't Personal (that is, if it's someone else's goal for you, not your own), you're unlikely to persist when the going gets tough. And if a goal isn't Positive, your best choices can be confusing. For example, if my goal is "not to fail math" (a negative goal), I can simply drop the course…but is that what I really want? If my goal is "to pass math with an A" (a positive goal), then withdrawing is no longer an option. So, while I would have preferred to go with the established acronym, creating D.A.P.P.S. seemed like a smart choice.

Q. One of my classmates said she thought that self-motivation should be the first inner quality presented in the book. She said that without self-motivation, no one would do anything. That started a class discussion in which different students made a case for every one of the eight qualities coming first. Why did you put the eight choices of successful students in the order you did?

A. Over the years, I've heard compelling arguments that each of the eight "Choices of Successful Students" is the most important and, therefore, should come first. I haven't been able to figure out how to present them all first, so here's my rationale for the present order. For me, **responsibility** is the foundation of our success because until I see myself as shaping my own life by my choices, all of the other inner qualities are likely to be unhelpful. Once I realize that (as one of my students put it), I am driving my own car, the next step is determining my destination. This choice generates **motivation** to move my life in a particular direction. With a destination in mind, now I need **self-management** to keep taking the purposeful actions that propel me toward my goals and dreams. Once I realize that big goals and dreams are difficult (maybe impossible) to achieve alone, I understand the importance of **interdependence**. At this point, I may think I'm doing everything "right," but somehow I'm off course. How did that happen? That's when I need to become more **self-aware** so I can spot the habitual thoughts, behaviors, emotions and beliefs (scripts) that are sabotaging my success. At this point (if not before) I begin to realize how much more I need to learn to achieve my goals, and I become a **lifelong learner**. I also see that I need **emotional intelligence** in order to regulate my emotions as well as deal effectively with the emotions of others or I'm likely to be dragged off course. Because I need to **believe in myself** throughout the journey, I distributed strategies to develop this quality throughout the book. I'm tempted to do that with all eight of the inner qualities, but that seems to create other, more serious problems of organization. So, that's my reasoning. And I'm fine when I hear of instructors who choose to present the chapters in a different order that makes sense to them. Ultimately, it doesn't matter what order you put the tires on a car; what matters is that the car has all of its tires so it can get on the road to success.

Adams, Kathleen. *Journal to the Self: Twenty-Two Paths to Personal Growth.* Warner Books, 1990.

Allen, David. *Getting Things Done.* Viking, 2001.

———. *Making It All Work.* Viking. 2009.

Branden, Nathaniel. *The Psychology of Self-Esteem.* Jossey-Bass, 2001.

Bucher, Richard D. *Diversity Consciousness.* Prentice Hall, 2014.

Burka, Jane B., and Lenora M. Yuen. *Procrastination.* DeCapo, 2008.

Burns, David, M.D. *Feeling Good.* Harper, 2008.

Ciarrochi, Joseph, and John H. Beck. *Emotional Intelligence in Everyday Life.* Psychology Press, 2013.

Covey, Stephen R. *7 Habits of Highly Effective People.* Simon and Schuster, 2013.

Csikszentmihalyi, Mihaly. *Flow: The Psychology of Optimal Experience.* Harper & Row, 2008.

Davis, Martha, Elizabeth Robbins Eshelman, and Matthew McKay. *The Relaxation and Stress Reduction Workbook.* New Harbinger, 2008.

Dweck, Carol. *Mindset: The New Psychology of Success.* Ballantine Books, 2007.

Fieori, Neil. *The Now Habit.* Tarcher, 2007.

Firestone, Robert W., Lisa Firestone, Joyce Catlett, and Pat Love. *Conquer Your Critical Inner Voice.* New Harbinger, 2002.

Frankl, Viktor E., M.D. *Man's Search for Meaning.* Washington Square Press, 1959.

Gladwell, Malcolm. *Outliers: The Story of Success.* Back Bay Books, 2011.

Glasser, William. *Reality Therapy.* Harper & Row, 1978.

Goleman, Daniel. *Emotional Intelligence.* Bantam Books, 1995.

———. *Working with Emotional Intelligence.* Bantam Books, 2000.

Haidt, Jonathan. *The Happiness Hypothesis.* Basic Books, 2006.

Hanson, Rick. *Hardwiring Happiness.* Harmony Books, 2013.

Herrmann, Ned. *The Creative Brain.* Brain Books, 1989.

Holden, Robert. *Authentic Success.* Hay House, 2011.

Howard, Pierce J. *The Owner's Manual for the Brain.* William Morrow, 2014.

Iyengar, Sheena. *The Art of Choosing.* Twelve Publishers, 2011.

Jensen, Eric. *Brain-Based Learning.* Corwin, 2008.

Kahneman, Daniel. *Thinking, Fast and Slow.* Macmillan, 2011.

Kernis, Michael. *Self-Esteem: Issues and Answers.* Psychology Press, 2006.

Lehrer, Jonah. *How We Decide.* Houghton Mifflin Harcourt, 2009.

Lyubomirsky, Sonja. *The How of Happiness.* Penguin Books, 2007.

Matsumoto, David, and Linda Juang. *Culture & Psychology.* Wadsworth, 2008.

McKay, Matthew, Patrick Fanning, Carole Honeychurch, and Catherine Sutker. *The Self-Esteem Companion.* MJF Books, 2001.

Merlevede, Patrick E., Denis Bridoux, and Rudy Vandamme. *7 Steps to Emotional Intelligence.* Crown House, 2001.

Merrill, A. Roger. *Connections: Quadrant II Time Management.* Publishers Press, 1987.

Moule, Jean. *Cultural Competence: A Primer for Educators.* Wadsworth/ Cengage, 2012.

Oakley, Barbara. *A Mind for Numbers.* Tarcher, 2014.

Olpin, Michael, and Margie Hesson. *Stress Management for Life.* Cengage Learning, 2015.

Orman, Doc. *The Test Anxiety Cure.* Stress Management Group, 2014.

Peck, M. Scott, M.D. *The Road Less Traveled.* Simon and Schuster, 1978.

Peterson, Brooks. *Cultural Intelligence: A Guide to Working with People from Other Cultures.* Intercultural Press, 2004.

Peterson, Christopher. *A Primer in Positive Psychology.* Oxford University Press, 2006.

Pink, Daniel. *Drive: The Surprising Truth about What Motivates Us.* Riverhead, 2009.

Progroff, Ira. *At a Journal Workshop.* Dialogue House Library, 1975.

Rosenberg, Marshall B. *Nonviolent Communication.* PuddleDancer Press, 2005.

Satir, Virginia. *The New People-making.* Science and Behavior Books, 1988.

Schiraldi, Glen R., Patrick Fanning, and Matthew McKay. *The Self-Esteem Workbook.* New Harbinger, 2001.

Seligman, Martin. *Learned Optimism.* Alfred A. Knopf, 1991.

—— *Authentic Happiness.* Atria Books, 2003.

Shiota, Michelle N., and James W Kalat. *Emotion.* Cengage Learning, 2012.

Sousa, David A. *How the Brain Learns.* Corwin Press, 2011.

Steiner, Claude M. *Scripts People Live.* Grove Press, 1994.

Stone, Hal, and Sidra Stone. *Embracing Your Inner Critic.* HarperCollins, 1993.

Tobias, Sheila. *Overcoming Math Anxiety.* W. W. Norton & Co., 1995.

Ward, Francine. *Esteemable Acts: 10 Actions for Building Real Self-Esteem.* Broadway Books, 2003.

Wehrenberg, Margaret. *The 10 Best-Ever Anxiety Management Techniques.* WW Norton 2008.

Index

NOTE: *Book titles are shown in italics; figures are indicated by an "f" following the page numbers.*